LAWYERS AND REGULATION
The Politics of the Administrative Process

This book is a close study of lawyers who practice occupational safety and health law in the United States, using detailed interview and survey data to explore the roles that lawyers have as representatives of companies, unions, and OSHA (the Occupational Safety and Health Administration). Placed in the context of evolving understandings of regulatory politics as a problem of public–private interaction and negotiation, the book argues that lawyers adapt to multiple roles in what prove to be highly complex settings. The core chapters examine stages of the administrative process where various groups attempt to shape the immediate outcomes and the development of OSHA law. These stages include administrative rulemaking, post-rulemaking litigation of government standards, regulatory enforcement, and compliance counseling by lawyers.

PATRICK SCHMIDT received his B.A. from the University of Minnesota (1993) and a Ph.D. from Johns Hopkins University (1999). Prior to taking up his current post as Assistant Professor of Political Science at Southern Methodist University, he was the John Adams Research Fellow at the Centre for Socio-Legal Studies and a research fellow of Nuffield College, Oxford. He has published widely and is co-editor, with Simon Halliday, of *Human Rights Brought Home: Socio-Legal Studies of Human Rights in the National Context* (2004).

CAMBRIDGE STUDIES IN LAW AND SOCIETY

Cambridge Studies in Law and Society aims to publish the best scholarly work on legal discourse and practice in its social and institutional contexts, combining theoretical insights and empirical research.

The fields that it covers are: studies of law in action; the sociology of law; the anthropology of law; cultural studies of law, including the role of legal discourses in social formations; law and economics; law and politics; and studies of governance. The books consider all forms of legal discourse across societies, rather than being limited to lawyers' discourses alone.

The series editors come from a range of disciplines: academic law; socio-legal studies; sociology; and anthropology. All have been actively involved in teaching and writing about law in context.

Series Editors

Chris Arup *Victoria University, Melbourne*

Martin Chanock *La Trobe University, Melbourne*

Pat O'Malley *Carleton University, Ottawa*

Sally Engle Merry *Wellesley College, Massachusetts*

Susan Silbey *Massachusetts Institute of Technology*

Books in the Series

The Politics of Truth and Reconciliation in South Africa
Legitimizing the Post-Apartheid State
Richard A. Wilson
0 521 80219 9 hardback
0 521 00194 3 paperback

Modernism and the Grounds of Law
Peter Fitzpatrick
0 521 80222 9 hardback
0 521 00253 2 paperback

Social Citizenship and Workfare in the United States and
Western Europe
The Paradox of Inclusion
Joel F. Handler
0 521 83370 1 hardback
0 521 54153 0 paperback

Law, Anthropology and the Constitution of the Social
Making Persons and Things
Edited by Alain Pottage and Martha Mundy
0 521 83178 4 hardback
0 521 53945 5 paperback

Judicial Review and Bureaucratic Impact
International and Interdisciplinary Perspectives
Edited by Marc Hertagh and Simon Halliday
0 521 83918 1 hardback
0 521 54786 5 paperback

Immigrants at the Margins
Law, Race, and Exclusion in Southern Europe
Kitty Calavita
0 521 84663 3 hardback
0 521 60912 7 paperback

Lawyers and Regulation
The Politics of the Administrative Process
Patrick Schmidt
0 521 84465 7 hardback

Law and Globalization
from Below
Toward a Cosmopolitan Legality
Edited by Boaventura de Sousa Santos
and Cesar A. Rodriguez-Garavito
0 521 84540 8 hardback
0 521 60735 3 paperback

LAWYERS AND REGULATION

The Politics of the Administrative Process

Patrick Schmidt

CAMBRIDGE UNIVERSITY PRESS
Cambridge, New York, Melbourne, Madrid, Cape Town, Singapore, São Paulo

Cambridge University Press
The Edinburgh Building, Cambridge CB2 2RU, UK

Published in the United States of America by Cambridge University Press, New York

www.cambridge.org
Information on this title: www.cambridge.org/9780521844659

First published 2005

Printed in the United Kingdom at the University Press, Cambridge

A *catalogue record for this book is available from the British Library*

ISBN 0 521 84465 7 hardback

For my father and grandfather

CONTENTS

FIGURES AND TABLES

FIGURES

TABLES

CASES

ACKNOWLEDGMENTS

Many people deserve my thanks for their contributions, large and small, to this book. Woody Howard and Joel Grossman were meticulous and inspiring in the early stages of this project, and no young scholar could hope to find a better pair of mentors. Despite his protests to the contrary, very little of this book or my career would have been possible without David Yalof's direction, professional and otherwise. The support of many institutions and the people in them deserves mention: the Department of Political Science at Johns Hopkins University; the Centre for Socio-Legal Studies and Nuffield College at the University of Oxford; and the Department of Political Science at Southern Methodist University have all provided comfortable homes, supportive environments, and generous support for my work. Finola O'Sullivan, Jane O'Regan, Brenda Burke, and Diane Ilott at Cambridge University Press were supportive and tireless through the whole process. The anonymous reviewers and series editors offered excellent direction. I have long ago lost track of the names of librarians here, there, and everywhere who went the extra step. Numerous colleagues and friends have also given direct support to some aspect of this project. With my apologies to those inadvertently left off, I would like to recognize: Pamela Winston, Margie Brassil, Doug Dow, Doreen McBarnet, Simon Halliday, Denis Galligan, Philip Lewis, Alec Stone Sweet, Liz Fisher, Paul Martin, Bronwen Morgan, Joe Kobylka, and Dennis Simon. Others have provided indirect support, which has been no less meaningful and always deeply appreciated. I am confident that Eric Doherty has provided direct support at some point in the past, but if he didn't he certainly leads the class in this latter category.

The lawyers and other organizational representatives whose anonymous voices are heard in this book graciously welcomed me into their offices. Time is money, and thankfully I have yet to see a single bill for the many hours of time – collectively valued in the tens of thousands of dollars – that was given to this research.

Words can acknowledge but never sufficiently capture my family's contribution. When deadlines required it, my sister, Liz Jennings, eagerly and expertly helped with the final editing details, for which I am most grateful. My in-laws, Gerry and Tim Moore, have often provided a computer in their laundry room that has been a productive sanctuary. I have never doubted the love and support at all levels from my parents and grandparents, and that has lifted me higher than I could ever hope to go on my own. My children, Ailsa and Aidan, provide the hope that drives each day. Most of all, Lea Anne has supported me unfailingly while bearing the brunt of everything that goes along with being married to an academic. In the rest of our lives together I don't think I can hope to repay, except in love, the debt I have already accumulated.

Portions of this book have appeared in other forms:

"Pursuing Regulatory Relief: Strategic Participation and Litigation in U.S. OSHA Rulemaking" by Patrick Schmidt first appeared in print in *Business and Politics* vol 4 pp. 71–89 (Taylor & Francis, 2002) http://www.tandf.co.uk/journals and remains available in an Online Version with the Berkeley Electronic Press: Vol. 4: No. 1, Article 3 http://www.bepress.com/bap/vol4/iss1/art3.

Patrick Schmidt (2004), "Law in the Age of Governance: Regulation, Networks and Lawyers", in Jacint Jordana and David Levi-Faur (eds), *The Politics of Regulation*, Chapter 12 (Cheltenham, UK and Northampton, MA, USA: Edward Elgar) pp 296–319.

ABBREVIATIONS

ABA	American Bar Association
ACC	American Chemistry Council
ACGIH	American Council of Government Industrial Hygienists
AISI	American Iron and Steel Institute
ALJ	Administrative Law Judge
ANPR	Advance Notice of Proposed Rulemaking
APA	Administrative Procedure Act
API	American Petroleum Institute
CMA	Chemical Manufacturers Association (now American Chemistry Council)
DOL	Department of Labor
EEI	Edison Electric Institute
EPA	Environmental Protection Agency
ETS	Emergency Temporary Standard
FCC	Federal Communications Commission
FY	Fiscal Year
IBEW	International Brotherhood of Electrical Workers
GAO	Government Accountability Office (formerly General Accounting Office)
LIA	Lead Industries Association
MSHA	Mine Safety and Health Administration
NAM	National Association of Manufacturers
NAPA	National Asphalt Pavement Association
NESC	National Electrical Safety Code
NIOSH	National Institute for Occupational Safety and Health

NLRB	National Labor Relations Board
NPRM	Notice of Proposed Rulemaking
OCAW	Oil, Chemical, and Atomic Workers
OMB	Office of Management and Budget
OSHA	Occupational Safety and Health Administration
OSHRC	Occupational Safety and Health Review Commission
PEL	Permissible Exposure Limit
PRMA	Paint Remover Manufacturers Association
SOL	Solicitor of Labor
UAW	United Auto Workers

CHAPTER ONE

INTRODUCTION

The late Clark Clifford, advisor to US Presidents and legendary Washington attorney, was famed for warning new clients interested in legal representation before the executive branch and its agencies that he had no "influence."[1] Clifford claimed only to possess the expertise of someone intimately familiar with the workings of the US government, which allowed him to instruct clients on how best to place their views and needs before administrative agencies and executive branch departments. Clifford's caveat has struck many as implausible, even ridiculous, because he clearly offered more than sound legal argumentation: a wealth of "insider" contacts with government officials at all levels, and a reputation that preceded him.

Whatever the real source of his influence – perhaps *sui generis* – Clifford's legacy still clouds our understanding of how lawyers conduct the practice of law before administrative agencies. Indeed, both academics and journalists in search of Clifford's contemporary equivalents seem to hold the notion that if regulatory lawyers are not the equivalent of lobbyists "moving and shaking" the government on behalf of corporate interests, then they are merely technicians of the law without an appreciable impact on administrative politics. The simplicity of these visions is understandable, not least because if the advocacy made by lawyers is not presented with the color and force of a lobbyist, then it is made in arcane legalisms typically understood and appreciated only by lawyers.

Regulatory systems are pervasive in modern society. They are tools with which political systems have found mechanisms, both of

1

convenience and of necessity, for the propagation and implementation of rules. Like the portrait of regulatory lawyers, the contemporary administrative state rests on foundations in tension, between ideals of a free-ranging policy process and a process encumbered by mechanisms of accountability. The most distinguishing feature of regulatory systems is the necessity of discretion – political choice – infused throughout the administrative state.[2] The expansion of bureaucratic processes, perhaps the most profound alteration to the political landscape in the twentieth century, has generated awareness of both the importance and potential problems of discretion. While administrative policymaking often supplements or even supplants legislative decisionmaking, a democratic "deficit" results from weaker mechanisms of accountability in practice. As faith in the expertise of administrators waned in the twentieth century, the emphasis on processes sometimes stood in as one solution to this deficit. In the United States, in particular, the drive to proceduralize the administrative state only generated new concerns about the effects of legalization and judicialization in a system with interest representation at its heart.

Because of the particular foundations, evolution, and culture in the American context, lawyers are basic ingredients in the contemporary regulatory soup as representatives of private interests. Given concerns about the influence of private power on public administration, a general accounting of how bureaucracy translates legislative goals into concrete results simply cannot ignore what lawyers provide as intermediaries. Still, despite substantial attention to the process of governance from both lawyer and nonlawyer commentators, very little systematic attention has been paid to the behavior of lawyers in regulatory settings. The unexamined questions at the juncture between lawyers and regulation are many and basic: What do attorneys do for their clients? How do attorneys perceive their role in administrative settings and how do these perceptions affect their dialogues with clients? In what ways do the activities of lawyers shape – and how are they shaped by – the agencies they encounter? Perhaps most fundamentally, how do the contributions of lawyers *qua* lawyers, with everything that implies for the role of law, construct the politics of the administrative process?

These questions lie at the intersection of two key themes featured in debates about contemporary administrative governance: how regulatory agencies bargain and dispute with private interests over the creation and application of general rules; and, more centrally, the roles representatives of interests, specifically lawyers, play in these processes.

Enormous variation across and within national systems of social and economic regulation fractures our understanding of interest representation, but from this kaleidoscope emerges a pattern of concern regarding the influence and power of private interests. Individuals who represent public and private interests are positioned to shape the distribution of wealth and welfare, and through their actions, to give rise to wider structures of political advantage. Of course, the position of lawyers in America may be unrivaled and uniquely placed in popular discourse.[3] Elsewhere, various professional groups or non-professional representatives may dominate regulatory politics. Nevertheless, at the heart of this book are questions about how a state journeys from legislative mandates to applications of law in practice, with a fundamental tension, every step of the way, between choices of interest and values, on the one hand, and the desire for process on the other.

This study brings together concern for the administrative process and the role of lawyers by focusing on the roles, strategies, and attitudes of attorneys practicing before the US Occupational Safety and Health Administration (OSHA). Established in 1970 and charged with improving and maintaining the safety and health of workplaces in the United States, OSHA's history contains all the hopes, controversies, successes, and failures one could ever wish on a regulatory bureaucracy. As a leading example of a "social regulatory" agency created in a wave during the 1960s and 1970s, its organization contains the two distinct processes – administrative rulemaking and enforcement – that are often considered separately but less commonly are considered together. Though different agencies, even different processes within an agency, might be seen as unique occasions for legal work, the shared endeavor across the OSHA policy process applies beyond the US as well: how should the state, both produced by and interacting with the private sphere, transform abstract policy goals into specific commands and incentives? This is not to limit administration to a "top-down" process. Rather, in the gap between the text of a statute and the behavior of an individual regulated entity, every step of the regulatory process can become a site for interpretation and contestation of what the law means. Selection and design of administrative processes shapes resulting politics and policy, but viewed from a distance, rulemaking and enforcement unite in the common goal of putting flesh on skeletal policy and giving life to law, though they remain important guideposts to where lawyers may become involved. This frame of reference begins to highlight the complex setting for a regulatory bar, defined simply as those lawyers whose work brings them into contact with a regulatory agency and its body of law. After recognizing a group of attorneys who practice occupational safety and health law, are identified as "OSHA practitioners," and collectively form the "OSHA bar," the goal is to lodge an understanding of their practices into wider accounts of public–private interaction in the administrative system.

The tasks of this chapter are, first, to discuss the main themes woven through this book and, second, to provide a brief account of occupational safety and health regulation in the United States as background to the chapters that follow. Alternative perspectives on regulatory lawyers demand our initial attention, but in order to understand their work, I suggest a general understanding of how public and private interests interact. My larger goal in examining network approaches is two-fold: first, to orient the discussion of legal work around the complexities in broader regulatory environments, now a ubiquitous part of political life; and second, with a social science toolbox for analyzing contemporary relationships, to consider the importance of law and "legal" interaction in political activities typically described in "purely" political and social terms.

THE SETTING FOR REGULATORY LAWYERS

Looking at the complex mass of acronym-laden organizations and processes that make up administrative governance, one needs a set of simplifying ideas to give it order. How can one begin to describe in general terms the organizational complexity, multiple loyalties, and diverse constituencies of administrative agencies? Through many attempts at generalization, the notion of "networks" has become a fixture. The catchword resonates with the entangled relationships and labyrinthine processes that, like a sausage-maker, press interests, ideas, and values into law. If nothing else, "the term 'network' merely denotes, in a suggestive manner, the fact that policy making involves a large number and wide variety of public and private actors from the different levels and functional areas of government and society."[4] Like actors on a stage, participants in regulatory affairs relate to each other in almost choreographed style – patterns that we can begin to describe from the repeated actions of the players.

The most important implication of describing regulation as a network is that the administrative agency is not the director or producer of the play, but an actor on the same stage, not necessarily the star of the show. In approaching regulatory agencies today, we cannot assume they sit as central, unchallengeable authorities over private interests, although neither must we assume that they operate in a free market.[5] An agency of the state, such as OSHA, receives delegated authority and power to exercise over individuals and organizations in the private sector, but it comes with explicit and implicit limits, some of which are in the hands of private actors. Three consequences flow from and fill out the understanding of regulatory relationships as networks as they frame the setting for lawyers' work: interdependence, enduring relations, and strategic action.

A basic feature of policy processes is the interdependence of government and private actors in pursuit of their respective goals. Simply, no single individual, group, or organization "gets its way" repeatedly without enlisting the explicit or tacit support of others. This stricture includes government organizations, which are no more "central" to understanding public policy than are private interests. Legislative delegation and decentralization produces administrative bodies with prescribed authority. Public bodies struggle to balance effective governance with their need to retain legitimacy,[6] and so seek cooperation and political support from private actors, particularly to the extent that constituencies (such as regulated entities or the interested public) could otherwise threaten agency authority with appeals to legislatures, courts, or other higher authority. Staff members in government bureaucracies also need other resources that private interests can provide, including information and substantive expertise. Similarly, private actors pursuing goals in the public sphere will encounter gaps in information, capital, personnel, or political power which they must overcome through collective action. Mutual need begets resource exchanges, making cooperation between parties a common occurrence.

Interdependence both encourages and takes place against a backdrop of more-or-less enduring relationships between government bodies and private organizations. Relationships, in turn, set the stage for decisionmaking in networks, particularly in routine affairs. Critics of American politics, in particular, have long argued that "iron triangles" or "subgovernments" develop around administrative agencies, which restrict the access of outside groups to key stages of decisionmaking.[7] Explicit or tight controls on membership are not necessary; narrow and complex issues before many regulatory agencies discourage occasional involvement in administrative processes by individuals and generalist interest groups, leaving a limited set of recurring participants. As individual and institutional relationships develop among these parties, they gain advantages of expertise and access, which in turn solidifies the collective advantage of those inside the circle. The slippery quality of individual interactions does not diminish the significance of enduring relationships among the leading public and private participants, which shape the incentives for participants, contribute to subcultures and norms, and alter the dynamics of lawmaking.

Interdependence and continuing relations combine to produce a third significant feature of regulatory policymaking that is particularly important for the study of lawyers: the prominence of strategic interaction. Strategies and competition flow inexorably from the recognition that political actors have diverging and conflicting interests in the direction of public policies. Governments share with private parties the need to devise strategies for networked political environments.[8] Of course, we would expect any individual to act within formal and informal rules, assess possible courses of action, and use results of those actions to inform future strategies. What is vital is that we recognize regulatory interactions as more than the simple consequence of political ambitions, but also as a constitutive part of political structures, doubly so in that lawyers work within legal structures. "Winning" means achieving desirable outcomes, but also setting the stage for the future. Government strategies for "winning" inspire careful design of political processes and attempts to influence numerous aspects of networks, including membership, terms of exchange, access, or coordination.[9] In so doing, agencies set the context for strategic decisions made by private parties, whose own repeated participation fosters development and evolution of informal rules.[10] Plenty of evidence already points to the factors influencing how such rules and processes evolve, including the size of a regulatory policy area, disparities of resources between parties, goals of the parties, perceptions and beliefs, and cultural and ideological commitments.[11] The fact that most interest groups and agencies themselves are complex organizations makes full explanations very challenging indeed.[12]

The underlying appeal of these concepts partly explains why equivalents are found in multiple disciplines, including organizational sciences, policy studies, political science, and sociology. As applied to the world of regulation, the fundamental concepts associated with networks of public and private interests have spawned many labels attempting to capture different aspects of the phenomenon – among them, "issue networks,"[13] "principled issue networks,"[14] and "professional networks."[15] One deficiency of empirical research in this vein has been the failure to treat "the law" as little more than a background variable when examining regulation as a political and social phenomenon. Administrative politics, especially in the United States – and increasingly outside of it, as discussed later – rarely occurs far from the influence of the law and legal concepts. That is, the basic steps of the regulatory process, such as setting an agenda, deciding the form and content of public participation, making substantive decisions about outcomes, and negotiating policy outcomes, are framed as they are because parties attend to wider legal debates or know that courts may intrude on the "political" decisionmaking among interested parties. Vitally, one cannot underplay the degree to which the law is open to debate and creativity. The process of finding and resolving gaps in the law in both rulemaking and enforcement involves recreating the regulatory process for the future, with the law as the medium.

Taking legal interactions seriously, then, adds another dimension to the richness of regulatory politics. Empirical research about regulatory politics and research about lawyers share a common interest in linking the behavior of public and private actors to wider structures of power in seemingly hierarchical governmental systems. The enduring qualities of regulatory politics aid the effort to generalize about legal work in a context that lawyers themselves often claim lacks routine and evades generalization. For the former, the conceptual framework described in this section may aid the effort to generalize about legal work in a context that lawyers themselves often claim lacks routine and evades generalization, while accounts of lawyers and legal work force social scientists to confront how law and legal norms affect behavior. Ultimately, notions of law and legal interpretation can become a focal point for attempts to bridge the gap between the micro-level interactions of interests and the middle-range attempts to understand how the administrative state "works." In order to probe further into the overlap of lawyers and regulatory politics, the next section begins by dissecting past approaches to understanding the role of lawyers before the administrative state.

LAWYERS IN THE MACHINERY OF LAW

Universal conclusions about regulatory systems are few, but one might be: that legal mandates for regulation never work entirely as planned or expected. Between the intentions of the law's creators – whether envisioned legislatively, judicially, or through some other hand of government – and the targets of the law, translations change its meaning. Law in the twenty-first century no longer appears as a monolithic presence, but as a tool that is created and used by individual actors in a larger process. Given the inevitability of discretion, those involved in the *practice* of law reinterpret, redefine, recreate, and reconstitute the meaning of law in its particulars.[16] Underlying description and explanation is the orientation of social critics, journalists, and scholars, who imbue their dissections from one side of a cliché: whether the glass is half full or half empty. That is, an available perspective explaining how authoritative law applies in particular contexts in turn has generated hypotheses about the role of lawyers. If regulations are born of the aspiration to the public good, then lawyers are a dangerous political force. If regulatory policy and law is fraught with risks, then lawyers help shepherd the law to efficient outcomes.[17] Consider each of the two outlooks.

Making the law work/lawyers as grease

As the prospect of bright-line distinctions between politics and administration grew dim in President Roosevelt's New Deal, administrators of the 1930s confronted key issues concerning the constitutionality of delegation to executive agencies. The politics of delegation generates continuing cross-national discussion owing to the recognition that bureaucratic decisions are authoritative rules of general applicability with the character of legislative enactments, despite being promulgated by unelected regulatory bodies.[18] For many, especially in national traditions that view delegation as unproblematic exercises in expertise under legislative sovereignty, the only remarkable thing is that this debate persists today when delegated authority should be regarded as a necessary evil. The generalities of formal law, by their nature, require the discretion of human actors in order to make sense in different factual circumstances.[19] The possibility of a neutral application of laws is now commonly regarded as a legitimizing myth, and *prima facie* impossible. Further, some argue, the complexity of modern society prevents intelligent legislative discussion of narrow issues. If we accept that laws will address complex social and economic relationships, we must recognize that any government (short of a totalitarian regime) must adapt its regulations to accommodate diverse conditions. Agencies and regulated companies negotiate the application of general norms to particular conflicts.

In his classic work, *The Washington Lawyer*, Charles Horsky portrayed lawyers as the most likely candidates for the role of facilitator, particularly in administrative politics.[20] Congress delegates discretion to administrative agencies precisely because of the complexity of issues mired in scientific, technical, social, and economic details. The quality of information available to agency staff members limits decisionmaking in administrative agencies, so the practical experience of attorneys "can do much to improve the formal rules, increase the utility and availability of informal procedures, and clarify the ethical problems."[21] As in traditional legal settings, lawyers are essential to the construction of agency rules developed through formal procedures, because the quality of decisionmaking depends on the vigorous advocacy of parties to bring all issues to light. By representing clients in nonadversarial administrative proceedings, too, lawyers are the *sine qua non* of the governmental process, for "government is not automotive."[22] Lawyers' expertise in structuring information to a useful form is an integral part of the process through which general rules become private action; without it, agencies would grind to a halt, Horsky thought.

The Washington lawyer, Horsky continued, is essential to the implementation of laws as received by clients. The complexity of government regulations prevents regulated parties from understanding their meaning and keeping current with changes. The presence of the attorney in the process makes compliance possible; businesses and individuals cannot comply with rules they cannot understand. Lawyers communicate the many *informal* elements that government officials intended, but could not encapsulate, in the rules. Lawyers are such an integral part of transforming general rules into private action, Horsky thought, that "without this assistance . . . the government simply could not operate."[23] Horsky did not shy away from lawyers' role as advocates, but saw lawyers as complementing the operation of law by influencing government, declaring that the lawyer's function "broadly, is that of principal interpreter between government and private person, explaining to each the needs, desires and demands of the other. His corollary function is that of seeking to adjust the conflicts that inevitably arise."[24] Lawyers do not create disputes, in this view, even if they advise clients to seek resolution through adversarial processes, because the disputes were latent within the regulator–regulated relationship. Like graphite, lawyers are at worst an inert quantity, and at best a lubricant in the process of accommodating interests.

9

Horsky's analysis of Washington lawyering received acclaim from legal professionals, even as the social atmosphere changed.[25] Perhaps he struck a resonant chord because the fundamentals of federal agency practice seemed to resemble fundamental "practical lawyering" skills. A former commissioner of the Federal Communications Commission (FCC) commented that the regulatory lawyer "learns the rules, customs and personal idiosyncrasies of the officials in his special field, as the county seat lawyer learns his way around the local courthouse."[26] This claim connects the regulatory lawyer to Herbert Kritzer's empirical findings that lawyers can serve as brokers of interests within informal networks, not only as vigorous advocates as suggested by their professional model.[27] Similarly, a study of Silicon Valley attorneys found legal counsel to be important facilitators for the flow of venture capital to high-technology start-up companies, a role which included helping to shape national regulation around the needs of clients.[28] No attorney filled the broker image as well as Clark Clifford, whose career as a Washington attorney ended in the BCCI banking scandal of the early 1990s, because his reputation, credibility, and persuasive skills enabled him to bargain with government officials at all levels.[29] Whether or not attorneys self-consciously approach the task as Clifford did, Horsky and others regard these power brokers as necessary parts of healthy administrative, political, and judicial systems.

Substantive expertise complements procedural expertise in influencing administrative discretion, because discretion in an activist state cannot be controlled solely through judicial mechanisms. Attorneys must engage agencies on the agencies' turf via informal mechanisms that place a premium on substance, *ceteris paribus*. Such lawyers play a part in a new, important calling – "mediating between a technocratic, activist state and individuals' claims of right."[30] Lawyers in the US are matched functionally in other countries by elites who construct areas of bureaucratic policy through expertise.

In sum, from one perspective, the gap between law on the books and law in action results from popular disappointment about the translation of goals into concrete action. Lawyers, it has been argued, assist the process of translation through their efforts as advocates, consultants, brokers, and negotiators on behalf of interests to whom the laws apply. By bringing the state closer to their clients and the clients' interests closer to the government, they provide an essential service.

Frustrating democratic aspirations/lawyers as friction

While the legal profession may gravitate toward theories of benign intermediation, critics have been quick to argue that the "abuses of the few" appear more systematically and substantially than lawyers admit. Since scholars began noting the failings of a "pluralist model," they have analyzed how the relative strength of parties raises potential impediments to realization of democratic decisionmaking, especially in the context of regulation, where accounts developed to explain how privileged interests co-opt administrative agencies.[31] Criticism still heard today – viewing the glass as half empty – assumes that agencies *should* have made other decisions, and *would have* done so, but for the intervention of the defenders of capital.[32]

Critics see lawyers' roles in the administrative process not as benign intermediaries between the regulators and the regulated, but as friction in the transmission of law. Regulated interests depend on representatives, such as lawyers and lobbyists, to communicate group preferences to decisionmakers. A surge of investigative journalism since the late 1960s decried the unseen power of "superlawyers," whose services to clients depend more on relationships with agency decisionmakers than on substantive persuasion in an open forum.[33] Scholars joined in chorus with historical analyses that connected expansion of federal regulation with rising influence of lawyers as interest representatives.[34] Experienced critics like Joseph Califano, Jr. concede one point to Horsky: "Washington lawyers" play substantial roles in regulatory politics, operating "in a very real sense . . . at the interface between public and private interest[s]" and actively participating in the exercise of government power.[35]

The place of attorneys has remained suspect through increasingly sophisticated treatments of regulatory politics and interest mobilization. A recurring theme in many critiques is that lawyers fight administrative battles, in Harold Laski's words, as "the essential mercenaries of the propertied class."[36] Reform efforts since the 1970s have sought to reduce improper lawyerly influence by regulating the "revolving door" between public service and private practice, and by instituting rules governing *ex parte* communications. Concern about the informal influence of lawyers has been joined by concern with the impact of lawyers' adversarial methods. "Prolonged hostilities and warlike aggressiveness," the hallmarks of the new mode of regulatory lawyering, allegedly benefit intermediaries at the expense of the public interest.[37] A movement toward less adversarial processes and more negotiated rulemaking blossomed in the 1980s on the assumption that increased consensus-building would lead to more efficient standard-setting, greater compliance with regulations, and decreased lawyer involvement. Criticizing lawyers for both formal and informal influences may seem contradictory, but such influences form two sides of the same coin. Both criticisms reflect a discomfort with procedural expertise as a mechanism of accountability frustrating policymaking virtues, driven by lawyers who either have privileged access or, failing that, "view the administrative process as a checklist to be reviewed . . . to see if there is some way the agency can be tripped up and blocked for failing to follow all the procedures required."[38]

Critiques of lawyers' roles in regulation can be very powerfully stated. Doreen McBarnet has focused attention on the role of legal creativity in sabotaging regulatory control. Her analysis of British taxation law demonstrates how the interests of capital circumvent rule-based regulation by employing attorneys to probe and expose gaps in legal language. The legal community avoids moral responsibility by appearing to punish ethical transgressors in the bar, but lawyers systematically help clients avoid the spirit and letter of the law. "[A]voidance is not just the prerogative of a few marginal 'tame' members of the legal profession," McBarnet concluded. "It is a normal, routine part of the legal profession's role."[39] Her conclusion echoes Theodore Roosevelt's indictment in a 1905 speech at Harvard, in which the President attacked influential and wealthy lawyers in major cities who "make it their special task to work out bold and ingenious schemes by which their very wealthy clients, individual or corporate, can evade the laws" which regulate in the public interest.[40] Lawyers identify closely with the ideologies of their clients, the argument goes, and because of increased specialization in legal careers, lawyers' primary opportunities may be as "hired guns" for private interests.

In sum, this alternative story of regulatory implementation identifies lawyers as one cause of the variance between legislative aspirations and the meaning of law in action. Contrary to the story told by Horsky, the legal community cannot claim a role as independent contributors to the successful operation of law. To view lawyers simply as legal "grease" that lubricates the application of general rules to particular problems is to overlook that lawyers are coopted by the elite interests they represent. Whatever their methods, lawyers undermine the objectives of regulation.

Lawyers and the complexity of regulatory politics

The assertion that any body of writing, even on a subject prone to sharp viewpoints, suffers from a polar split at either descriptive or normative levels often signals a strawman argument. Some scholars have noted the dichotomous assumptions present in research on lawyers, however. Austin Sarat and William Felstiner, most strikingly, approached the long-standing debate about attorney–client relationships and professional autonomy in the context of divorce lawyers, challenged the dialectic of power and control, and criticized the tendency of scholars to view lawyers as either *dominators* or *dominated* professionals.[41] The power of attorneys, they observed, is negotiated in specific contexts, practiced in routines of social interaction, and recreated in each new interaction. Lawyers may be tactical agents of client interests, paternalistic principals determining clients' interests, opportunists using clients' cases toward other agendas, and so on, but these postures vary dramatically with context and circumstance.[42] Sarat and Felstiner began construction of a subtler model of attorney power from the inside, with all the individual and structural dimensions affecting attorney–client interactions. The work of Maureen Cain has reconceptualized the external contributions of lawyers, because while she begins with the suggestion that lawyers are dependent on their clients in some meaningful way, the significance of lawyering flows from attorneys' position as translators of client views.[43] The creativity brought to bear by attorneys gives meaning to attorneys' practices, since they manipulate logic and language in order to create forms that serve client needs. Yet, the abbreviated understandings of lawyers exposed remain common in the diverse practice areas under the "regulatory law" umbrella.

Bridging the gap between antagonistic claims about lawyers involves accepting their utility, however partial. Though we may now reject an idealized conception of lawyer-as-mediator, Horsky's empirical claim, that lawyers consciously and unconsciously can aid the implementation of public laws, has lacked frontal challenge. Classic socio-legal research in a functionalist tradition points to the multiplicity of roles for lawyers, even within specific fields, where evidence can be found of lawyers assuming the positions of gatekeepers, therapists, brokers, informal mediators, legal technicians, and litigators.[44] Complexity in the empirical portrait of lawyering was hardly unique two decades ago, though this book will reinforce those findings, with repetition still necessary for a profession perpetually rediscovering itself in the midst of seemingly ubiquitous crises and reforms. A full cast of legal roles will be manifest in legal arenas built on adversarial foundations, in which litigation is posed against "structural constraints on practice, social needs, and difficulties with adversariness as a solution for all our problems."[45]

The ambition of building a model of legal practice – one that recognizes the values and interests of individual attorneys as well as the social and economic structures surrounding individual interaction – remains unfulfilled, despite Macaulay's call for a "wider focus" on the indirectly legal "interactions between attorneys, clients, opponents, and legal officials."[46] The most provocative research to date has examined trial court communities, court systems that typically involve a relatively narrow set of recurring participants within an ordered legal structure. These have evolved from accounts of courtroom "workgroups" to incorporate explanations of local legal cultures, power structures, interdependencies, personal relationships, and external communities.[47] Trial courts hold an understandable appeal for scholars interested in applying broadly organizational models to legal interactions: they are ubiquitous, their work usually is easily comprehended, quantifiable data is plentiful, and comparisons between courts are productive.

Administrative bureaucracies present a higher order of complexity in which to find lawyers because the "process" unites policymaking and implementation under one statutory scheme. Regulatory agencies are rarely single court organizations, but rather composite systems with distinct tasks. In occupational safety and health, the focus of this book, both administrative rulemaking and enforcement have complicated internal structures, substantive intricacies, and interwoven power structures. Dozens and sometimes hundreds of interested parties participate in agency rulemaking efforts, which are subject to significant external forces from the legislative, executive, and judicial branches. Further, scientific uncertainty and technical complexity hangs like an albatross around the neck of regulatory policymaking and enforcement. Health and safety issues, like other subjects of administrative regulation, rise above traffic violations and misdemeanor criminal cases. And, unlike much routine criminal and civil litigation, regulation usually involves corporate decisionmakers, themselves complex bureaucracies. Regulatory enforcement proceedings share many similarities with "classic" courts, but institutional differences can be vital. Further, the "court systems" for many agencies spread nationwide and embrace peculiar combinations of regular and infrequent litigants. The tangled web of pressures when translating statutory aspirations to specific situations justifies close empirical research into administrative settings, and ultimately research will need to compare policy domains, time, and national systems if we are to match the level of understanding brought to trial court communities.

Even further, restatement of lawyers' roles at the micro-analytic level provides the groundwork for a more general account of lawyering in public/private networks. The opportunity provided by the reconceptualization of legal practice as constitutive of the legal order, is to bring individual interactions into an aggregate perspective on the effect of lawyering in structuring administrative politics, partly as a result of their conscious strategies of law-creation by clients, and partly by their translation of interests into legal forms. In this book I argue that in enduring, networked regulatory systems the iterations of attorney–client representation become systems where legal representation constructs, reproduces, and innovates wider legal structures. At one level, law is a resource for regulatory struggles and the roles of lawyers may adapt to the setting; at another level, the meaning of "the law" in practice reflects the meanings brought into regulatory spheres through the practices of interested parties and their representatives.

The empirical foundation on which to advance such a project is severely underdeveloped. Relatively few scholarly efforts have tied lawyers to regulatory policymaking, despite the recognition that political networks nourish multiple types of intermediaries, such as coordinators, gatekeepers, and liaisons, who fill the brokering function basic to all social and political communities.[48] Most notable was the project to analyze the structure of interest representation in Washington begun in the early 1980s by John Heinz, Edward Laumann, Robert Nelson, and Robert Salisbury (hereafter, Heinz, et al.).[49] Heinz, et al. interviewed organizations, representatives, and government officials in four policy domains, including labor law. The study by Heinz, et al. is notable for two reasons that warrant attention here. First, they found that networks of interest representation surrounding American regulatory agencies have "hollow cores" without central brokers able to exchange information, form coalitions, and direct the development of policy. Instead, they argued, interest groups and representatives maintain relatively close relationships with others sharing their own interests and ideology. The regulatory networks they found seemed to encourage antagonisms between opponents by keeping coalitions relatively separated, a structure which found its sharpest expression in labor policy.

Labor and management interests sit on opposite sides of a social and political "gulf," across which very few build relationships and contacts. If there ever were generalist brokers in the mold of Clark Clifford, they are very rare or nonexistent today, they argued.

Second, Heinz, et al. reported a surprisingly low occurrence of lawyers among the most "notable" representatives in each policy area, finding lawyers concentrated in specialized settings requiring either particular credentials (such as court appearances) or knowledge of substantive regulations and processes. Contrary to journalistic mythology, lawyers often find their decisionmaking role minimized even within client organizations, limited to episodic needs for specialized expertise. This finding by Heinz, et al. reflects their research design, in which they targeted sweeping areas of policy as the political arenas for organizational representatives. To study labor policy, for example, they reviewed developments across issues of collective bargaining, collective action, union governance, wages, working conditions, health and safety, pensions, and employee insurance. Nonlawyers may dominate discussions and debate over the broad contours of regulatory policy, but sub-sectors of policy areas hold enormous potential for interest representation and negotiation over substantive issues. Indeed, the assumption behind their inquiry seems apparent by their use of the word "policy" when describing their aim. Though a law/politics distinction must be treated gingerly, what approach would one adopt when asking who had shaped a body of "law"? A first reaction when asking this of labor law must be that the field in fact contains many related zones of activity – OSHA law being but one – that have distinct structures, hierarchies, and legal cultures. Differences at this level alter incentives for individual parties, with rebounding effects on other network actors. So, comparative study of policy arenas asks too much. Ultimately we need to know the microdynamics of lawyering in its distinctive legal setting. Aside from the activities of a few dozen "notables," what do the many thousands of Washington lawyers operating in policy subspecialties *do*? The question also is worth asking in light of the concession by Heinz, et al. that they do not examine the "qualitative significance" of lawyers' work in regulatory areas.[50]

Even though Heinz, et al. stopped short of such questions, their work nevertheless raises the potential for integrating legal representation into an understanding of regulatory politics. Supported by an impressive, almost overwhelming, amount of data,[51] they uncovered with considerable precision many links between interest groups, government agencies, and organizational representatives. It appeared as a system of interaction and disputation over the direction and content of government regulation, with pervasive and unyielding uncertainty. Individual organizations and representatives lack control over the direction of policy, perhaps inevitably in the pluralist system of American politics, so policy outcomes flow from a complex set of interactions among numerous actors. The interdependencies, continuing relationships, and strategic maneuvering at the heart of this perspective should lead us into further inquiry at this overlap with the government agencies, lawyers, and clients.

Of course, there are understandable methodological difficulties in attempting research in this area. Scholars may never directly observe attorney–client relationships and other elite interactions. In my investigation of OSHA rulemaking, interviews brought me to both sides of the lawyer–client dynamic (e.g., union officials and their attorneys, trade association officials and their outside counsel), but systematic study of client perceptions in OSHA enforcement was beyond this book's scope (see appendix 1 for an account of research methods). Where I address lawyer–client relationships in OSHA enforcement, I must speak of the perspectives of attorneys, corroborated where possible by the observations of union advocates and government officials.

In sum, legal representation before regulatory agencies deserves scrutiny, but we can recognize from the start that the inquiry will encounter a remarkable array of influences on regulators, regulated entities, and intermediaries. All actors in regulatory networks have interests in how legislative decrees translate to law in action, and all parties possess resources and liabilities that establish strategic positions. Lawyers are among those in a position to help translate general principles into specific commands through interaction and negotiations between government and clients.[52] In these conditions, OSHA practitioners *use* the law in particular cases, analyzing facts and developing tactics by drawing on the law, yet at the same time, they articulate possible interpretations of the law that attempt to build law in the image of their clients. The administrative process is the location for complex political interaction.

ADVERSARIES IN FOCUS: OCCUPATIONAL SAFETY AND HEALTH AND A CENTURY OF CONFLICT

Selecting any case for study necessarily filters our perspective on regulatory lawyering, and the problem may be particularly severe when

17

studying independent commissions and executive-branch agencies of the US government, whose organizational world-views are enigmatically dependent on their idiosyncratic origins, evolution, and experiences. Regulatory bodies differ across many variables, not least of which are the nature of the problems they regulate and their degree of institutional independence. Thus, when selecting an area for focus, it is important to note its usefulness and limitations.

A crucial variable marking OSHA out from others is the scope of its mandate to set and enforce rules for regulated industries. At one end of a spectrum, in a self-regulatory regime, private interests would regulate themselves voluntarily by adopting and complying with standards. Either rulemaking or enforcement can be taken up by the state – or the state can wield these as a threat to force corporate action – while at the other end of such a spectrum, the government can engage in "direct regulation" of firms with administrative control of rulemaking and enforcement.[53] Of course, the model may be imprecise in that a single administrative agency can regulate some industries or issues directly, while partially regulating others.

For all the potential complexity in administrative forms, OSHA furnishes an exemplar of a direct regulatory agency. The Occupational Safety and Health Act of 1970 was part of a wave of new social regulation that focused on the side-effects of modern economies, a wave which included agencies devoted to the protection of consumer product safety, highway traffic safety, and the environment. Although Congress provided OSHA with organizationally separate research and adjudicatory arms – the National Institute for Occupational Safety and Health (NIOSH) and the Occupational Safety and Health Review Commission (OSHRC) – OSHA received the powerful mandates of a direct regulatory agency: authority to develop and promulgate highly protective health and safety standards in the workplace and to enforce these standards with civil and criminal penalties. OSHA's authorizing legislation included provisions such as consultations with employers, employee training, and joint management–labor advisory committees; but the heart of OSHA's efforts has been the creation of new health and safety standards and their enforcement in workplace inspections. Despite changing political tides over three decades, OSHA remains devoted to its mission of protecting workers largely through the same mechanisms of rule creation and field enforcement.

A century of labor–management struggles and wholly inadequate stopgap measures preceded OSHA's creation and undoubtedly gave rise to its contemporary single-mindedness. Before 1970, a trio of approaches aimed at reducing injuries and compensating workers for lost wages: legal liability, workers' compensation schemes, and collective bargaining. To the extent that these systems imposed costs on employers when workers were injured or killed, each system created incentives for employers to improve workplace conditions. Workplace illnesses and injuries continue today, of course, because they necessarily accompany employment. Workplace risks can be eliminated *entirely* only by eliminating workplaces; marginal reductions of risk marginally increase costs.[54] OSHA's direct regulatory mandate derived from the acknowledgment that only higher costs would convince employers to reduce injuries and illnesses further. Thus, OSHA's *raison d'être* involves acting as a force on behalf of safety and health for workers against employers' claims of costs.

Wherever labor and management have engaged one another on workplace safety and health, courts have played key roles in the resolution of disputes. Employers' liability suits, workers' compensation cases, and collective bargaining – all of which still exist alongside OSHA regulation – have provided opportunities for labor and management representatives to serve as local players in a wider struggle. The force of their lawyering has sometimes tipped the balance. Common law principles developed during the mid-nineteenth century favored employers who defended themselves against employees or families seeking damages for their workplace accidents. If injured employees (many of whom were non-English-speaking immigrants) were aware of their legal rights, could afford to hire a competent attorney, and could attract key witnesses despite fear of employer retaliation, powerful legal defenses such as the assumption of risk and the fellow-servant rule protected employers.[55] The judiciary's defense of corporate interests was so effective that over 85 percent of work-related casualties received no recompense.[56]

Nevertheless, employers began to fear increasingly sophisticated plaintiffs' attorneys, growing awareness of industrial health, and juries sympathetic to injured workers. Employers' preference for certainty, allied with pro-labor political action, drove the establishment of workers' compensation schemes, which were adopted in forty-two states between 1910 and 1920, and in every state by 1948. Under compulsory workers' compensation, first passed in Germany in 1884 and in Britain in 1897, injured employees receive compensation for the costs of medical expenses, rehabilitation, and lost wages according to a pre-set payment schedule and irrespective of fault; in turn, employees are excluded from seeking damages in court, except for intentional harm. Workers' compensation served the interests of equity, in that all injured employees received some form of compensation, though payment schedules are notoriously undervalued. In 1966, maximum benefit levels in forty-two states did not even meet the poverty line.[57] Employers may have been the greatest beneficiaries, freed from the fear of frequent liability suits and their attendant legal costs.

Workers' compensation did not provide new incentives for employers to improve workplace conditions, yet the programs assuaged union activism on safety and health for several decades. The specific provisions of union-negotiated collective bargaining agreements were the leading source for preventive safety and health measures before 1970, and this reliance exposed the weakness of nongovernmental regulation. Health and safety issues were not a mandatory aspect of the New Deal-era collective bargaining system until 1967, before which employers regularly claimed that health and safety issues were management's prerogative. Even then, bargaining left a patchwork quilt of protection, and nonunion workers remained outside the fold altogether. Collective bargaining, workers' compensation at the state level, and individual lawsuits left conflicts in isolation, frustrating the labor movement's ability to pool its resources toward a unified strategy. By contrast, the new wave of social regulatory agencies in the 1970s would concentrate policies with diffuse benefits in the hands of a single organization, giving broader "public" interests a single pressure point from which to appeal for protection.

A significant increase in industrial accidents during the 1960s, highlighted by nationally publicized tragedies such as the death of seventy-eight miners in a 1968 West Virginia explosion, awoke legislators from their slumber. The scientific evidence that drew increasing attention to environmental problems associated with petrochemical processing, coal mining, and radioactive materials not only justified creation of the Environmental Protection Agency (EPA) in 1970, but also worker protection. Pre-1970 safety and health programs in the states provided precedents for direct federal intervention. The state programs, generally regarded as "weak, understaffed, and poorly coordinated and organized,"[58] aimed mostly at leveling the playing field for workers by undercutting judicial protection from liability.[59] The Occupational Safety and Health Act of 1970 (the "OSH Act") needed to be more than a federalization of safety and health enforcement, and indeed it was. Breaking with the New Deal and the economic regulatory agencies of the previous generation, OSHA marked a new "regime" of regulatory philosophy.[60] Instead of regulating a single industry (e.g., communications, securities, or aviation), OSHA, EPA, and the Consumer Product Safety Commission were given ambitious mandates of protecting the public from social problems whose sources lay across industry lines.[61] Importantly, proponents of the new regime believed that industry would be less likely to "capture" agencies whose work stretched economy-wide. The new agencies, presumably committed to expert decisionmaking, would be better able to resist the mutually supportive relationships that had subverted administrative agencies in earlier eras. By like token, the compliance costs of new social regulations almost ensured that the new politics would be more adversarial.

Given its origins and underpinnings, OSHA's early history was marked by an unbroken chain of conflicts between the highly partisan advocates of labor unions and business interests. The legislative history of the OSH Act evinces firm resistance by business to a safety and health agency, while the labor union coalition pressing for its adoption acquiesced in a number of important compromises to secure the Act's passage. The result, as discussed in later chapters, was a fragmented bureaucracy for rulemaking and enforcement. Charged with assuring "so far as possible every working man and woman . . . safe and healthful working conditions," OSHA immediately undertook the two duties of standards-creation and enforcement against a backdrop of an uncertain economy and a Republican administration. By the start of the Carter administration, a political backlash was well underway. Critics targeted OSHA's adversarial and legalistic enforcement of "nitpicking" standards as an unconstructive approach that burdened businesses without advancing health and safety.[62] Since the core issue remained the trade-off between employer costs and employee safety, political compromises in the agency's creation did not diminish the passion of management and union interests. Throughout its first decade, rulemaking typically resulted in litigation challenging the standards – often from unions and industry simultaneously – and inspections met challenges from employers at remarkably high rates.

The resistance to social regulation found its ultimate expression in the Reagan administration's deregulatory platform. With the aid of a Republican Senate during its first two years, the Reagan administration significantly cut OSHA's budget and staff. Thorne Auchter, a politically active owner of a Florida construction company, replaced Eula

Bingham, an environmental health scientist who had headed OSHA during the Carter administration. The Auchter administration shifted agency policy to increased use of cost–benefit analysis in standard-setting and "cooperative" enforcement approaches that amounted to a significant weakening of enforcement activity. Labor unions fought back in courts and Congress, ultimately reversing the two-year downward trend in agency funding. Resistance also occurred in the field. The existing platoon of safety and health compliance officers strongly identified with a core interpretation of the agency's mission: inducing employers into preventive safety and health practices by providing a credible threat of sanctions. Top-down reforms could neither transform safety and health enforcers into safety and health advisors nor vanquish street-level skepticism of employers' motivations.

Auchter resigned in 1984 as congressional battles loomed. Business interests never again had such a sympathetic ear within the agency, and the Reagan administration sought only to contain OSHA's growth rather than reduce its accumulated body of regulations. In fact, the first Bush administration raised the ire of business interests by working with Congress to resurrect OSHA's aggressiveness in enforcement. OSHA policy has persevered ever since through a stasis of "conflict as usual," in which calls for substantive reform or more "cooperative" enforcement (such as followed the 1994 congressional elections) are met by a mobilization of unions' political strength. Significant battles since then, such as a fight over the regulation of workplace ergonomics, have led to defeats for unions, but the framework remains intact. The mutual commitment of labor unions and management to OSHA issues and the multiple points of access to decisionmaking have provided OSHA with a near-constant regulatory philosophy through three decades, even if nuances of adversarial and cooperative attitudes have occasionally taken hold.

The continuity and clarity of OSHA's mission makes OSHA an inviting subject for study. As a side effect of labor unions' staunch defense of OSHA, the lack of extreme changes to the agency's statute, organization, or philosophy frees scholars to examine other variables more readily. Scholars, recognizing OSHA's utility as an "ideal type" of a direct regulatory agency, have built a critical mass of literature examining the effectiveness of enforcement approaches.[63] Other research grounds our understanding of safety and health policies from a comparative perspective.[64] Workplace safety and health attracts study also because of the tensions inherent in regulations based on complex scientific data that deal with extremely tangible social ills – traumatic injuries, fatal accidents, illnesses, toxic poisonings, and cancers – enforced by a visible "street-level" inspectorate. By law, OSHA must retain large volumes of data regarding its rulemaking and enforcement activities, a condition that has encouraged scholars to put theories of regulatory behavior to the test. These scholarly efforts, in turn, provide a backdrop for more focused research into the behavior of regulatory lawyers.

Beyond serving as a model of a direct regulatory agency, analyses of OSHA's component parts shed light on other types of regulatory agencies as well. Since OSHA's approach lies near an "ideal type" in the American regulatory experience, it provides a frame of reference when examining less clear-cut regulatory processes. Further, given its history, there would be little surprise in finding lawyers involved in litigation before OSHA as servants of clients. Evidence of other roles, such as those proposed by Charles Horsky, should give us pause to reconsider the standard models of legal representation before administrative agencies, and their likely relationship to different settings for regulatory politics.

BEYOND AMERICAN SHORES

OSHA is a suggestive case study for understanding the qualitative significance of lawyers to American regulatory bureaucracies. Every administrative agency may be said to be unique in some reasonably relevant way on account of the varieties of institutional form and the nature of the policy area, but the unique features of the American system compound the problem and beg the question of the significance of the data reported in this book to the study of regulation, law, and politics beyond American shores. Of the most obvious differences, one might highlight the unprecedented level of litigation, legal form, and lawyers as a mechanism of control that is without peer in the world and present in the American administrative process.[65]

At one level, the themes already set out by this chapter emerge out of academic discourses that are comparative or transnational in nature. Viewed comparatively, the prominence of lawyers in regulatory interactions should be abstracted one step with the recognition that these are interest representatives in policy networks. At both an individual and a systemic level evidence from a US context can be revealing. The relationship of public and private actors occurs through individual-level representatives, elevating in importance empirical questions about how those who exercise public authority are influenced by representatives of private interests. Though the whole set of conditions in the US is unique, as is that of any other national system, any research highlighting discrete variables can contribute to the underdeveloped research exploring individual interactions in contemporary bureaucracies. The themes in the aggregate understanding of regulatory politics, namely strategic interactions and presence of rules (formal and informal), by themselves are found in the study of policymaking and policy implementation across North America, Europe, Australia, and still elsewhere. While American regulation may be more "legalized," law is not absent from other systems. When one examines law not only through its formal definition but also how parties understand what they regard as the rules governing behavior, it becomes possible to consider how these structures operate within the entangled politics of administrative spheres.

Lawyers in the United States use a specialized vocabulary and style of presentation, but a striking impression from interviews is the degree to which they take seriously their role as communicators of substantive policy arguments. Although this book, particularly chapter 3, explores how and when legal strategies can make procedural concerns overwhelm deliberation of substance, lawyers inhabit a space in which language and argumentation matters.[66] Beyond pure power-based models of policymaking, this examination of the work of lawyers aims at a more universal concern about how the articulation of interests as argumentation interacts with institutional settings. At junctures in this study the emphasis is clearly on how parties marshal evidence within the prevailing structure of legal logic in order to maximize control over decisionmaking outcomes. The specific mechanisms of control or key actors may be highly idiosyncratic, but the mode of control is not. Recent work regarding regulation in Australian bureaucracies, for example, points to the dominance of forms of economic rationality, injected into the administrative process as internal "regulatory review."[67] This logic requires translation, elevates the importance of particular actors and their expertise over others, and serves to support market-oriented interests over other claimants. It is a form of "non-judicial legality," the economic equivalent of a system that valorizes the Rule of Law. Though with OSHA the evidence of what interests benefit is very mixed – see the different results enjoyed by interest groups in the rulemaking discussed in chapter 4 – regulatory lawyering justifies a similar approach of close empirical study, especially regarding the strategic battles in the day-to-day politics of the administrative state. These are contemporary competitions which look to higher order logics (whether of law, economics, or yet others) as tools that structure the process.

Beyond these themes and the theory-building that other data in this book suggests, changes in the regulatory regimes at the national and international levels are raising questions about the structure, control, and the emerging style of regulatory politics. The world is in a state of flux, in which it may not be particularly useful to conceive of the American way of regulation as a permanent "other" that stands only as a foil for the rest of the world. As one observer framed the contemporary concern for regulation as a mode of governance, "something transformed government across the advanced capitalist world" over the past thirty years that makes a discussion of US, European, and other regulatory systems possible, even if differences remain.[68] The crisis in "command and control" that OSHA experienced in the last two decades, driving it to discussions of more efficient, consensual, or cooperative alternatives, was experienced in other countries. In the UK, for example, deregulation and privatization undermined old forms of accountability and opened up new concerns about democratic foundations.[69] Germany, like the UK, has moved in some policy sectors from corporatism, meaning that agencies have "stepped from the arms of business to the arms of lawyers and economists."[70] Regulation has risen as a mode of European governance, and with it the problem of creating legitimacy and accountability for a system that is substantially undemocratic.[71]

Lacking the history of open contestation between public and private interests that has long dominated the US, other countries find themselves contemplating the possible directions in which to go. One hope to escape the adversarial conflict produced by multi-party rivalry over regulation is that regulation might remain grounded in a tradition of decisionmaking through expertise. Indeed, lawyers join scientists, economists, and others among the "knowledge-based elites" who populate administrative governance and strongly influence the functional operation of delegated bureaucracies.[72] With this, the hope of remaining free from a creeping American style of regulation may break down in the growing sense, perhaps uneven across policy areas, that these notions of expertise are insufficiently democratic, making necessary some degree of politicization and its attendant problems.[73] Another possibility for limiting the rise of American-style regulatory politics is that adversarial legalism proves to be a condition of institutional forces, such as the ability of legislatures (through political party control) to manage regulatory outcomes so that legitimacy is maintained without recourse to legal interaction. Though change is slow and uncertain, some changes at the domestic level, including political fragmentation, support an argument that the legalism of American regulation is diffusing into the European experience, and perhaps elsewhere.[74] Whatever its sources, evidence of increasing legalism can be found in policymaking, to be sure, but also prosecution.[75]

Forces of globalization are working profound changes on the state, sometimes because the state must be reorganized for global competition, and at other times because globalizing norms reinsert themselves within domestic legal systems.[76] The rise of regional governance, especially in Europe, gives opportunity for the creation of new schemes of governance. Although nearly all European countries would hold themselves out as distinctive from the US (i.e., more cooperative, less legalistic, more confident of state power), a system created today – free of the path dependence, national culture, and inertia that keeps domestic systems as they are – has the potential to adopt norms more akin to American-style governance, especially since it involves a federal system with a concomitantly larger gap in trust. As Martin Shapiro has observed, the appeal of notions such as transparency and openness is strong in the current ethos. While administrative law and judicial oversight may have been anathema to domestic constituencies of corporatist regimes, this was in part because those constituencies did not worry about access to decisionmakers. The Europeanization of regulation has created uncertainty for those interests who now seek access to new decisionmaking bodies populated by non-nationals.[77] Whatever the national styles in Europe, a "European policy style" continues to evolve, not always in the same terms as domestic styles.[78] Some proposals do aim toward greater respect for procedural values, though these tend to be directed at "soft law" and best-practices regimes that leave uncertain whether compliance will be compelled by external forces, such as litigation.[79]

Among the evolutionary developments, perhaps the most important has been judicial review as a mechanism for maintaining procedural values in administration. Though judicial deference to legislatures historically has been strong, concepts that invite judicial review of administrative lawmaking give a window for an independent judiciary to expand its scope of control. Having been encouraged to act as guardians of political values, it is reasonable to question what effective limits operate on an independent judiciary with broad discretion. Chapters 3 and 4 of this book describe the sustenance that judicial oversight of regulatory policymaking gives to lawyers and legal strategizing. Such oversight has found its parallel in creeping European litigation over principles such as the need for agencies to give statements of reasons and exercise a "duty of care" when developing rules. So noteworthy are the trends at all levels that one author has laid a roadmap, saying that "administrative lawyers who specialize in resolving [questions about transparency and public access] at the domestic level can now turn their attention to transgovernmental regulatory activity."[80] Beyond Europe, there are signs of change in the high deference traditionally given by many national courts to administrative bodies, though in some cases these developments do not yet add up to a transformation of the national styles.[81] Still, much has already happened to encourage litigation as a key force in administrative politics, and although European judges continue to recoil at the thought of going as far as the US,[82] a line has been crossed that makes the key issue to understand the ways that litigation and judicial review affect bureaucratic decisionmaking.[83] "In the eyes of many Europeans," Shapiro writes, "the trick is to go a little way but not too far down the American path."[84] As this is a lively, contemporary debate for regulators and judges, there may be no more appropriate time to examine, through empirical evidence, the meaning and operation of "the American path" in practice.

ORGANIZATION OF CHAPTERS

The following chapters portray lawyering at different stages of the regulatory process, wherein are found the full range of situations: intense disputes and accommodation, corporate intransigence, and proactive compliance. The fidelity of lawyers to clients, it appears, does not demand unbending opposition to regulations; sometimes, just the opposite. In chapter 2, I begin an examination of OSHA lawyers by describing the broad contours, demographics, cleavages, and identities of the "OSHA bar." Chapters 3 and 4 examine the opportunities and travails of lawyering in OSHA rulemaking. I first turn to the administrative procedures themselves – a forum not monopolized by lawyers – and then turn to litigation challenging administrative rules. Though these stages of rulemaking involve different sets of incentives and problems, administrative and judicial aspects of rulemaking should be considered complementary parts of a unified process. An extended case study of OSHA's "Lockout/Tagout" rulemaking and numerous other examples move us toward an appreciation of the strategic possibilities in regulatory law.

Chapter 5 shifts from OSHA rulemaking to OSHA enforcement. This involves different networks of parties and sets of incentives and roles for attorneys. After describing in detail the major players in the enforcement system, I discuss the issues faced by attorneys and their clients when OSHA conducts an investigation and prosecutes violations, as well as the strategic choices faced by parties. In chapter 6, I examine the most private aspect of legal work, the compliance counseling conducted by OSHA lawyers outside the scope of active investigations. Beyond the government's view, how lawyers assist clients in the task of complying with government regulations goes to the very core of the public/private interactions. How lawyers respond to the challenge is the central question of this chapter. Chapter 7, in conclusion, summarizes the range of lawyer roles found in the study and presents in further detail the connection between the empirical model of lawyering and the network perspective on regulation. As a step toward a wider model of the law in complex networks, I present a typology of the forces and influences on OSHA lawyering.

As a method of organizing this research, rulemaking, rulemaking litigation, enforcement, and compliance counseling can be viewed as separate arenas for legal representation. Nevertheless, these convenient distinctions should not obscure the conception of administrative regulation as a single process that transforms general principles into specific commands. In the entirety of the process, the forms of practice, from rulemaking to counseling, are just sites where lawyers develop law in the trenches through their more immediate strategies of representation. In complex networks for regulatory law, the roles of lawyers depend on far more.

CHAPTER TWO

THE CONTOURS OF A REGULATORY BAR

Communities of lawyers rarely are homogeneous populations, especially when they stretch across entire nations. Complimentary popular myths about the solo practitioner and the elite, large-firm attorney only hint at the multifaceted nature of the legal profession. For legal scholars and sociologists, cleavages within the bar have provided gateways to understanding the relationship of lawyers to the legal system, mainstream politics, and society. The most common strategy of commentators has been to identify a set of legal "elites" within the bar or society in order to explore diverse issues, including the collective inaction of lawyers, collective impact, intra-bar disputes, the homogenization of legal concepts, and lawyers' relationship to political legitimacy.[1] However defined, descriptions of legal elites generally emphasize the importance of social background in elevating a subset of the bar to positions of leadership and control over the profession's collective voice. The success of this approach in empirical research calls for recognition of the social status of lawyers whenever attempting to assess their role in wider political and legal systems.

This chapter provides an overview of the OSHA bar, both the divisions within the bar and those that distinguish this regulatory practice from other segments of the legal profession. Most attempts to understand lawyers have focused on geography; an account of a "regulatory bar" has few precedents to suggest the perspective of attorneys in this field. Since much of what is reported in subsequent chapters is bounded by the guarantee of anonymity to research subjects, the data in this chapter are essential in giving context to otherwise disembodied interview data. The first section explores the cleavages within the bar that suggest its core and peripheries. Since lawyers' work, experiences, and perspectives depend on their standing in the bar and their communities, these distinctions frame descriptions of their activities in later chapters. The second section examines OSHA practitioners as a group. When OSHA lawyers are compared to lawyers in other contexts, to all lawyers in the country and to the national population, this regulatory bar's standing comes into sharper relief. In short, management attorneys active in OSHA matters are among the *nouveau riche* of the legal profession: commonly partners in large firms and with above-average social backgrounds, but overall not members of the corporate "elite."

THE ORGANIZATION OF THE OSHA BAR

In many ways, the experience of meeting a random member of the OSHA bar should conform closely to the "average" or "typical." The downtown office tower you visit will likely be well appointed, though not as lavish as the offices of the most famous law firms of New York, Washington, or London. If you have been able to catch a corporate OSHA lawyer on a day when he – overwhelmingly it will be a white, middle-aged "he" – is not traveling to visit client facilities, you will walk through a maze of corridors, offices, and secretaries' stations to a partner's office that is tamely decorated, only sometimes featuring anything marking out the attorney as a practitioner of occupational safety and health law. Perhaps a hard hat (a gift from a grateful client) adorns a coat-stand, but whether an attorney is a leading OSHA specialist or an infrequent participant in OSHA matters, there are few outward indicators of the attorney's specialty, save perhaps the number of OSHA-related books on the shelf behind the desk. If your random selection happened to be one of the six to eight "core" lawyers who represent labor unions, it is about a fifty–fifty chance that that lawyer is a woman; your visit may take you to a small to medium-sized "union" firm, or equally likely outside a firm environment to a public interest group or academia.

Both corporate and union interests hire lawyers as representatives in OSHA matters.[2] Every realm of administrative policy attracts groups with competing interests, but lines rarely are drawn as clearly as in labor policy. The interests of the parties explain only one level of the categorical opposition. The union and "management" bars serve one camp exclusively because, as one union attorney declared, "this is fighting typically from two almost diametrically opposed views about normative goals – what's right, what's fair, what's reasonable, and what's just." Some union lawyers have organized into pro-union law firms, and union representatives easily point out their opposites, the reputedly "union-buster" firms. Conceptually, union and management attorneys form two halves of the same bar, but similarities end there. Management attorneys outnumber union attorneys to such a degree that, except where noted, in lawyers' parlance "the OSHA bar" is synonymous with the management bar.

Unlike many areas of law, OSHA practice is a very narrow subspecialization. By the year 2000, it was estimated that the United States had over 1 million lawyers, one for every 267 people. The vast majority of the approximately 500 attorneys listed in the Martindale-Hubbell Law Directory under the category "Occupational Safety and Health" represent management interests.[3] Even the more diverse ABA Occupational Safety and Health Law Committee reflects management's numerical dominance. The Committee claims 327 members: 73.4 percent represent management interests, 6.7 percent serve unions, and 19.9 percent are listed in other categories.[4] Committees within the ABA's Section of Labor and Employment Law share the imbalance, but some are much larger: for example, there are 1,592 members of the Equal Employment Opportunity committee and 1,340 members of the Employee Rights and Responsibility committee. Beyond labor law, over 1,000 attorneys identify themselves in Martindale-Hubbell as practicing "corporate" law in the District of Columbia alone.

While the number of OSHA attorneys has grown in the past decade, the political vicissitudes surrounding OSHA's efforts have restricted the bar's size. The size of the bar correlates with the economics of OSHA compliance and enforcement, which turn on the government's policies and activities in the field. The "purely" legal threat of OSHA enforcement may compel the use of an attorney, but companies may first seek the assistance of in-house counsel, or, if the process allows, may attempt to resolve the matter informally before lawyers become necessary. Company in-house attorneys, generalists by nature, rarely have enough OSHA work to justify acquiring further expertise in OSHA law. Compliance work would seem to bring more attorneys into the OSHA bar's fold, though OSHA regulations compete with other external pressures on a company's agenda. Compliance with regulations involves two decisions: how aggressively the company will comply (if at all), and whether attorneys will be used to assist those efforts. Attorneys

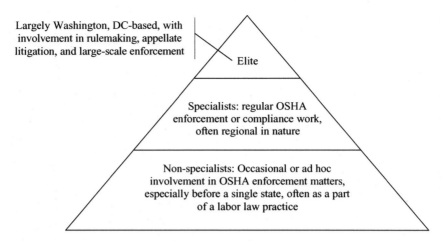

Largely Washington, DC-based, with involvement in rulemaking, appellate litigation, and large-scale enforcement

Elite

Specialists: regular OSHA enforcement or compliance work, often regional in nature

Non-specialists: Occasional or ad hoc involvement in OSHA enforcement matters, especially before a single state, often as a part of a labor law practice

Figure 2.1: The pyramidal organization of the OSHA bar

compete with nonattorney staff, safety and health consultants, and in-house counsel for the business of monitoring compliance; companies have responded to waves of regulation by bringing expertise in-house, including through nonlawyer compliance experts.[5] In some periods of aggressive OSHA enforcement – when the higher expected costs of non-compliance can justify their higher fees – attorneys may be better able to construct a market for legal expertise. The size of a regulatory bar can be subject to change over time, depending on the play of factors in the decision calculus of regulated firms.

Concentration is a related feature of a regulatory bar. Many attorneys can be considered "members" of the OSHA bar by virtue of occasional activity in the field; the core of the bar remains those who regard themselves as OSHA specialists, with a still further elite among those who engage in rulemaking and the largest enforcement litigation (see figure 2.1). The idea of a regulatory bar implies specialization, but a palpable distinction exists between peripheral practitioners and specialists. The distinction hinges on attitude and intent. Some attorneys do not actively seek out OSHA cases, though as long-time labor law counsel for a stable of clients, they regularly handle safety and health issues as they arise. Other attorneys mention a continuing interest in OSHA law, despite their practices having changed focus over time. Specialization, in part, depends on the size and complexity of the body of law at issue. In practice areas where greater weight is placed on specialized knowledge or experience, attorneys can command higher premiums for their

TABLE 2.1: Percentage of surveyed
attorneys' practices devoted to OSHA work

Amount of work	Attorneys surveyed (%)
0 to 25%	81.1
26 to 50%	11.4
51 to 75%	3.1
75 to 100%	4.4

Source: 1998 Survey of OSHA Bar (N = 228).

services and enjoy higher status among peers and clients. The boundaries of the bar in such areas are more fluid than areas with steep learning
curves or barriers to entry.

Political winds also prevent attorneys from specializing solely in
OSHA work. Table 2.1, data drawn from a survey of the OSHA bar (see
appendices), reports the proportion of OSHA work in OSHA attorneys'
practices. Very few attorneys sustain purely (or even largely) OSHA
practices. Indeed, only two of 228 attorneys surveyed dedicate 100 percent of their time to OSHA work, with an average rate of 18.1 percent.
OSHA work occupies more than half the practices of a mere seventeen
(7.5 percent) of the attorneys surveyed. The large number of attorneys
with less than 25 percent OSHA practices includes 71.1 percent of self-
identified OSHA specialists in the survey.

Though the scientific issues of safety and health can be complex,
OSHA law is relatively approachable. Attorneys can ply the field as
specialists without being completely immersed in it – indeed, industrial hygiene as a field, supplemented by other nonlawyer safety and
health consultants, bears witness to the ease with which individuals
with a grounding in the legal or applied practice of health and safety
can offer services in this field. The plain antagonism of some interviewees to health and safety consultants, reflected in the belief that some
consultants essentially "practice law without a license," emphasizes the
interest of attorneys in protecting the value of their specialization.
Nevertheless, it bears noting that "OSHA specialists" claimed to dedicate 25.1 percent of their time to OSHA work, against just 4.6 percent
for nonspecialists.

OSHA attorneys recognize an important cleavage between the
"rulemaking" and "enforcement" bars. Representation in enforcement
matters, the bread and butter of the OSHA bar, does not prepare

practitioners for rulemaking. Very early in OSHA's history, some union and management attorneys began specializing in OSHA's standard-setting and related litigation. The subject of chapters 3 and 4, these stages in the process offer lawyers opportunities for interest advocacy. The relatively low number of rules that OSHA produces, however – approximately eighty over three decades – limits the size of the rulemaking bar. In the survey of management attorneys, only 12.3 percent reported dedicating *any* percentage of their OSHA time to rulemaking.[6] Among these attorneys, rulemaking work consumed 21 percent of their OSHA work; OSHA work, in turn, accounted for 44 percent of their practices, well above the mean for all attorneys in the study.[7]

On the union side, two Washington law firms are noted for their experience in OSHA rulemaking litigation, complemented by a small number of independent practitioners. The Health Research Group of Ralph Nader's Public Citizen also has represented union interests in OSHA issues. In all, union interests draw on about a half-dozen active practitioners for rulemaking. The dividends for these attorneys are long-term relationships with specific unions, while trade associations have tended to be fickle in using outside counsel. One union-side attorney, interviewed in an office only slightly larger than a walk-in closet, suggested that the specialization by union attorneys made it more likely for them to be called upon for all OSHA-related activities, including rare legislative work, "partly because there are very few people on our side of the issue who are really knowledgeable about it. I mean, the people who do union-side standards litigation could all fit in this room. Easily."

Among attorneys reporting time worked on national OSHA rulemaking, half work out of Washington area law offices, and Washington-based practitioners devote a larger percentage of their OSHA practice (31 percent) to rulemaking. Department of Labor interviewees estimated that upwards of 90 percent of the attorneys they see in judicial review litigation are based in Washington, although employers' suits in appellate circuit courts deemed favorable may involve a regional firm as well. Because of a recent trend for industry filings in the Fifth Circuit, firms in New Orleans have handled administrative details for litigation directed from Washington.

What are the advantages of being located in DC? Some are obvious, such as proximity to the headquarters or Washington offices of nearly all national trade associations and unions. Many major corporations also station their government-relations activity there. More than being "where the action is," it is where the client is. Many interviewees perceived that relationships with clients require greater attention than with government agencies. The activity of rulemaking participation comes in waves and troughs. Both present challenges to attorneys: working with the client when awash in activity, and staying in the client's mind when the river runs dry. Participants in rulemaking also regard proximity to the OSHA national office as an unqualified advantage. Typical was one attorney's metaphor: "[W]e have the luxury of knowing essentially whenever they take a breath, whenever they're about to inhale, what's going on while the air's inside, and when they're about to exhale." Proximity produces information, bit by bit.

The management rulemaking bar draws from a variety of specializations. According to attorneys reporting time spent on OSHA rulemaking, 43 percent specialized in labor law, 36 percent in environmental law, and 29 percent in administrative law. Labor law specialists are less prevalent than in the OSHA bar as a whole (see table 2.2). In addition to the management–labor conflict, the scientific and economic underpinning of health and safety standards rewards an expertise in environmental law, creating a synergy between EPA and OSHA work. This expertise allows attorneys to speak to the integrated problems faced by clients who produce or use toxic substances. Corporate environmental managers must confront the impact of a particular chemical; but because government agencies have split the jurisdiction, two types of assistance are required. As one attorney put it, "OSHA is inside the fence-line for health [and] the EPA is outside the fence-line for health." For rulemaking, at least, some experts can cross that line. Administrative law specialists similarly claim applicable skills for OSHA rulemaking, only it is procedural rather than substantive. The administrative law governing the rulemaking of all federal regulatory agencies allows attorneys not conversant in occupational safety and health policy to handle some appellate court litigation. As a practical matter, some administrative law specialists over time have developed a reputation for substantive expertise. Interest groups have hired certain lawyers in the belief that they would not have to pay "start-up costs" for them to develop knowledge about an industry, a body of law, or a body of science.

Many Washington attorneys at the top of the policymaking pyramid also rank as the elite attorneys of the "enforcement bar," though one private practitioner brought to mind "a bunch of terrific OSHA lawyers around the country [as] the people I think of as my competitors." Regional hubs and cities with industrial bases, including Atlanta,

TABLE 2.2: Areas of specialization, all respondents

Specialization	%
OSHA	66.4
Labor law (any) – checked at least one of the following subcategories:	59.7
Labor law – Employment discrimination	53.2
Labor law – General	45.5
Labor law – Labor relations	38.1
Labor law – Other	22.1
Litigation – General	18.2
Environmental law	16.9
Construction law	13.9
Workers' compensation	12.1
Administrative law	11.3
Mine safety (MSHA)	10.4
Commercial litigation	7.8
Insurance defense	7.4
Corporate law	4.8
Appellate practice	4.3
Toxic tort	3.5
Personal injury plaintiff	3.0
Criminal defense	2.6
Government contracts	2.6
Probate	2.6
None/General practitioner	2.6
Other	7.0

Source: 1998 Survey of OSHA Bar (N = 231, multiple responses permitted).
Note: Nine categories (e.g., tax law, admiralty and maritime, bankruptcy) had fewer than six respondents each.

Chicago, and Cleveland, have firms with well-established OSHA practices. OSHA litigation reflects regional variations in industry type. For example, OSHA's Region VI, which includes Texas, enforces many of the rules written for the petrochemical industry. Regional firms gain familiarity with substantive issues and the region's enforcement authorities. Washington attorneys still handle a significant number of the largest cases, even if their claim to expertise is less strident than in rulemaking. Lawyers who straddle rulemaking and enforcement practices commented that a DC base has fewer benefits and more costs (such as increased travel time) for enforcement practices. Numerous

TABLE 2.3: Distribution of attorneys' time within
their OSHA practices

Type of OSHA work	Mean %
OSHA enforcement defense	61.4
Counseling clients regarding OSHA issues	33.4
OSHA rulemaking	2.6
OSHA policy issues	1.4
Other	1.2

Source: 1998 Survey of OSHA Bar (N = 229).

attorneys conceded that, collectively and individually, DC attorneys
have encouraged clients to *believe* that a Washington firm offers unique
advantages. One attorney claimed a psychological advantage from feel-
ing able to take a taxi to the Labor Department at a moment's notice.
His location may indeed increase his likelihood of using OSHA as
a resource. Willingness to initiate contacts with OSHA may derive
more from familiarity than proximity, however, and the high number of
Washington attorneys with public sector experience prevents us from
easily disentangling the two.

Beneath the elite and specialist attorneys in the enforcement pyramid sits a wide base of attorneys who have little interaction with OSHA
rulemaking, and whose primary involvement begins when client companies are faced with compliance questions or active OSHA investigations. Most self-identified OSHA lawyers – the "enforcement bar" –
represent employers when, in the words of one attorney, "the law at
10,000 feet" has struck earth in the form of enforcement citations
and penalties for OSHA standards violations. Among all attorneys,
enforcement work dominated the bar's focus – providing over 61 percent of attorneys' estimated OSHA time. The closely related business
of counseling clients outside the scope of enforcement matters provided another third of attorneys' work (see table 2.3).[8] Rulemaking
and policy issues are small, though important, facets of OSHA practices
generally.

The presence of an elite among a small enforcement bar should not
surprise even casual observers of the legal profession. Attitudes reflected
differing professional status. One attorney, well regarded in the field, was
openly hostile to "typical" OSHA attorneys, i.e. litigation specialists or
general labor lawyers who are only irregularly asked to handle an OSHA

case. Arguing that effective advocates in any field find the most efficient path to the resolution of disputes because of intellectual and interpersonal familiarity with the subject, he opined that "the typical lawyer who litigates an OSHA case does not know very much about OSHA – and they make it difficult for everyone else. They will litigate cases that shouldn't be litigated, jamming up the works for everybody, they antagonize compliance officers who are just trying to do their job, and they antagonize the judges [with] . . . defenses that are just patently unmeritorious." Given the broad implications of social regulation – yet the high costs of attempting to alter the law as it is made – one must expect that more foot soldiers are fighting battles over regulation in enforcement skirmishes than there are elite warriors fighting full-fledged rulemaking and appeals-court battles.

Indeed, most surveyed attorneys reported contact with regional OSHA officials and administrative law judges in their OSHA practices, with much lower levels of work before courts of appeals or the national office in Washington. Over 80 percent of all respondents (82.3 percent) and 90 percent of declared OSHA specialists (90.8 percent) had engaged with federal OSHA's regional field staff in the previous five years (table 2.4). Less than a third of attorneys (31.9 percent) had occasion to work with OSHA's national office staff, although specialists were more likely to do so. Specialists also were significantly more likely to represent clients across multiple regions, and before formal adjudicators and appeals boards, such as federal administrative law judges, the Occupational Safety and Health Review Commission, and state OSHA review boards. Appellate litigation appears to be one area in which nonspecialists appear on close to equal footing with specialists, possibly due to the use of generalist appellate litigators when cases reach that stage. Overall, however, OSHA lawyers are least likely to be found before a federal appeals court.

Specialization in the OSHA bar as a whole, more notably, reflects how the gladiators choose different weapons for skirmishes than for battles. Enforcement attorneys overwhelmingly specialize in general labor law or one of its subspecialties, like employment discrimination or collective bargaining (see table 2.2). Despite a general trend toward legal specialization in the past few decades, attorneys who practice only OSHA law are rare and few can foresee further specialization. The economic reality is simple. OSHA enforcement infrequently touches the typical employer. While employers decry the thousands, or possibly millions, of dollars required to comply with OSHA regulations, as

TABLE 2.4: Fora engaged in by OSHA attorneys in past five years

	All respondents (N = 226)	OSHA specialists (N = 151)	Nonspecialists (N = 75)	Significance between groups (χ^2)
OSHRC ALJs	61.9	70.2	45.3	13.14**
Federal: multiple regions	46.0	60.3	17.3	37.18**
OSH Review Commission	41.2	52.3	18.7	23.43**
Federal: one region	36.3	30.5	48.0	6.67**
National office	31.9	37.1	21.3	5.73*
State OSHA review board	28.8	38.4	9.3	20.68**
State: one state	28.3	29.8	25.3	0.49
State: multiple	27.0	35.8	9.3	17.76**
Federal courts of appeal	23.5	25.2	20.0	0.75

Source: 1998 Survey of OSHA Bar.
Note: * p < .05; ** p < .01; df = 3.

chapter 5 makes clear, those who violate those regulations face relatively low penalties, making many companies bet that hiring a lawyer is not cost-effective.[9]

Occupational safety and health issues join a broad range of labor law questions that nearly every employer must address, including numerous "hot button" topics like sexual harassment and civil rights. If an OSHA inspector is at the door, companies are more likely to know and contact a labor attorney than an environmental lawyer. Further, as discussed later, general labor issues are often entangled with OSHA enforcement issues, particularly in unionized workplaces. Attorneys familiar with the dynamics of labor relations are more sensitized to the potential complications in OSHA litigation. Lawyers with backgrounds in environmental issues still appear, but less frequently than in rulemaking practice. When attorneys describe their "run of the mill" cases, they mostly include violations of safety standards – such as the risk of falling, or the dangers of machinery without guard protection – which require much less substantive expertise to investigate and defend than health standards based on the exposure of employees to chemical hazards. Skill as a labor litigator takes precedence over experience with the science of toxic chemical exposure. Significant minorities of OSHA attorneys specialize in construction law, workers' compensation, and mine safety, all of which overlap OSHA issues in some workplaces and circumstances.

The base of the representation pyramid is the wide assortment of both lawyers and nonlawyers who represent employers in OSHA investigations and litigation. As described in more detail in later chapters, employers have many opportunities to settle disputes with OSHA before reaching an adversarial setting; and some companies may not hire counsel, even after litigation is underway. Cases published in one OSHA reporter show that nearly 20 percent of companies before administrative law judges or the next level of appeal were represented by a nonlawyer officer, owner of the company, or in-house counsel.[10] We would expect an even higher percentage of nonlawyer disputants in cases that never advance to litigation. As with identifying those who "lump it" in dispute resolution, it is very difficult to identify those who do *not* turn to counsel, especially when the processes involve informal negotiations and "one-shot" players. What can be known of the dynamics of representation must be learned from the behavior and beliefs of the attorneys repeatedly involved in OSHA disputes.

THE OSHA BAR: DEMOGRAPHICS AND CHARACTERISTICS

The "management OSHA bar" – referred to by some practitioners as the "corporate OSHA bar" – bears many of the traits common to corporate attorneys. The mythical "typical" OSHA lawyer would be a middle-aged, white, male partner of a large law firm, located in a major urban center in a populous Midwestern state. He practices labor law and handles OSHA law as one part of that practice. Like any straw man, this caricature ultimately must be disaggregated in favor of a more nuanced description of averages, tendencies, and medians.

Location and size of practices

OSHA practice, almost necessarily following workplaces, reflects the concentration of legal practice in urban centers, in turn reflecting styles of lawyering. As cities grow into centers of commerce and business, they acquire a legal community skilled at negotiating the hazards of contracts, complex litigation, antitrust statutes, and tax law that punctuate their environment.[11] Lawyers in those communities specialize, and have organized into "full-service" firms. Where business goes, so go lawyers, geographically as well as substantively. In recent decades, nearly all of the nation's top 100 law firms have established multiple branch offices in leading cities as they compete for clients in a national and global economy.[12] Large firm – hence, large city – practice sits on a high rung of the social and economic ladder, in contrast to the higher proportion of solo practitioners and small firms found in small towns and rural areas, who have greater involvement with the legal concerns of individuals (such as divorce and criminal defense) and a lower ranking in social status and salaries.

Administrative law and politics unavoidably generate much activity in the nation's capital, the locus of myriad federal policymaking bodies, tribunals, and review boards. The New Deal explosion in social and economic policy transformed Washington from a "sleepy Southern town" to the seat of power for vast bureaucracies. Lawyers accompanied this transformation, giving the city the highest proportion of lawyers in the country, with one for every fifteen people, well ahead of second-place New York's 1:195 ratio.[13] Since the administrative regulation of business – founded on the federal government's authority over interstate commerce – extends throughout the fifty states, the term "Washington lawyer" encompasses more than simply those attorneys who live in Washington itself. Even to Charles Horsky in 1952, the term included all attorneys whose "legal practice is largely caused by the direct impact of the federal government on the interests of their clients," whether they practiced in "Dallas or Seattle, Detroit or Savannah."[14] OSHA lawyers, then, have one foot in Washington and one foot in their respective communities.[15]

OSHA's historic emphasis on industrial safety and health brings much of its enforcement activity to major urban centers and concomitantly to the medium and large firms most likely to employ large-firm lawyers. The entire database of attorneys developed for this study's survey research, though flawed in some respects (see chapter 1), allows a geographic breakdown of OSHA law practices by providing addresses for 783 lawyers who have expressed past interest or recent activity in OSHA law.

The distribution of OSHA lawyers, reported in table 2.5, roughly follows the general population: Ohio, New York, Illinois, Pennsylvania, California, and Texas all fall within the top ten states. Compared to the distribution of all private practitioners in the nation,[16] OSHA lawyers are overrepresented in Ohio and Washington, DC. Over three-quarters (77.1 percent) of Ohio's OSHA-connected lawyers

TABLE 2.5: Leading geographic concentrations for OSHA-related lawyers

	OSHA bar (%)	National bar (%)	Difference (%)
Ohio	10.6	3.6	7.0
Washington, DC	9.6	3.3	6.3
New York	6.8	11.7	−4.9
Illinois	6.0	5.6	0.4
Pennsylvania	5.9	4.5	1.4
California	5.6	13.8	−8.2
Texas	4.7	6.1	−1.4
Colorado	3.2	1.7	1.5
Georgia	3.1	2.3	0.8
Missouri	3.1	1.9	1.2
New Jersey	2.7	4.8	−2.1
Michigan	2.7	1.9	0.8
Louisiana	2.3	1.8	0.5
Wisconsin	2.3	1.3	1.0
Maryland	2.2	1.8	0.4

Sources: Address Database for 1998 Survey (N = 783); Curren and Carson, *The Lawyer Statistical Report* (1994).

practice in one of the state's three major cities – Cleveland, Cincinnati, Columbus – and the remainder practice in notable industrial locations such as Toledo, Dayton, and Akron.[17] OSHA lawyers are underrepresented in New York and California, where complex financial and service economies diversify the state bars. The regional hubs of Denver, Atlanta, and St. Louis concentrate higher-than-predicted proportions of OSHA lawyers.

Larger cities allow for greater specialization and larger law firms. Regulated companies benefit from and sustain the legal expertise of regulatory lawyers.

The relationship between OSHA specialists and large law firms, enumerated in table 2.6, suggests that even nationally dispersed regulatory bars follow in spades the general trend toward a more elite tier of lawyers. Nearly half of OSHA specialists work in firms of over 100 attorneys. Just 2 percent are solo practitioners. Non-OSHA specialists in the sample – many of whom are specialists in related areas, such as labor law – also tend to work in law firms, though more often in firms with twenty attorneys or fewer. Larger firms can retain a dedicated

TABLE 2.6: Firm sizes and specialization

	OSHA specialists (N = 152) (%)	Non-OSHA specialists (N = 77) (%)	All respondents (N = 232) (%)	National bar (%)
Solo practitioner	2.0	11.6	5.2	44.7
Small firm (2 to 20 attorneys)	22.4	44.2	29.7	29.7
Medium firm (21 to 99)	29.6	26.0	28.9	13.0
Large firm (100+)	46.0	18.2	36.2	12.6
specialist versus nonspecialist significance: $\chi^2 = 28.4, p < .001, df = 3$				

Sources: 1998 Survey of OSHA Bar; data for national bar from Curren and Carson, *The Lawyer Statistical Report* (1994).

OSHA attorney; smaller firms more often rely on labor law or litigation generalists to cover their clients' OSHA needs. Small firm attorneys are an important part of management's response to government regulation, but they are more likely to approach OSHA law as nonspecialists.

Social background: age
On a professional level, age tends to translate into experience and expertise. While younger or associate attorneys were not explicitly excluded from the survey, the nature of the research and the sources used to generate names ensured an "older" response group. Attorneys belonging to the ABA practice area committees, or claiming narrow practice areas in their Martindale-Hubbell biographies, typically have practiced for at least five years. Thus the OSHA bar's age distribution naturally reflects an upward bias in attorney age. Overall, the average age of an OSHA attorney (46 years old) was five years over the mean for all lawyers in the United States (41 years old), and well above the average age in the general public (34.6 years old). A majority of the respondents (55.7 percent) were between ages 45 and 64. Attorneys under age 35 constituted fewer than 12 percent of the sample (versus 25.9 percent of attorneys in the profession as a whole), and attorneys aged 35 to 44 (31.3 percent) were also slightly below the national bar's average (35.5 percent). Yet the very low percentage of OSHA attorneys over the age of 65 (1.3 percent) suggests another characteristic of

the OSHA bar – it has "grown up with" the agency. Attorneys typically select practice areas early in their careers, sometimes after a stint with the government. As of 1998, the OSH Act itself was twenty-eight years old, and few OSHA attorneys had reached retirement age. A survey of an older policy system should find a larger percentage of attorneys over age 65 who maintain their practices into later life.

Social background: sex and race

The high social status of the legal profession – maintained despite criticisms of lawyers – has been accompanied by a history of formal and informal barriers to women and minorities. The collective interest of lawyers in limiting the number of attorneys (in order to limit competition) has allowed the bar to filter its composition and erect its exclusivity at the expense of certain groups.[18] A comparison of the OSHA bar also explicates the nature of a regulatory bar relative to other parts of the legal community. In this case, the OSHA bar is more male and more white than the national bar.

In the last three decades, women have experienced a dramatic turnabout of fortunes. Between 1967 and 1983, the proportion of women enrolled in ABA-approved law schools increased by 1,650 percent, from 4.5 to 37.7 percent of all students.[19] Women's entry into private law practice and partnership in law firms has not matched their entry into law schools, however. When women choose private practice they are more likely to choose between the extremes of very large firms or solo practices; men still reach partnership at higher rates than women.[20] Women's advancement in the legal profession relative to men has slowed qualitatively and quantitatively, perhaps a natural *ritardando* following a revolutionary movement, though perhaps also signaling that a glass ceiling remains.[21]

Minorities, too, have joined the bar in unprecedented numbers and have risen to the highest ranks of the profession, yet they are still significantly underrepresented. Glass ceilings affect minorities even more so than women: minorities constituted only 3 percent of partners in the country's 250 largest law firms.[22] Overall, the relative success of women entering the bar points to the importance of class. As structural and attitudinal barriers to their entry fell, a large pool of middle and upper class women were able to capitalize on their strong educational backgrounds and pursue the law as a career. Minorities, deprived of similar educational and financial backgrounds, have been unable to enter law school in similar proportions.[23]

The OSHA bar falls below average for participation of women and minorities. Women accounted for 15.2 percent of survey respondents, and minorities a mere 2.2 percent – substantially less than their segments of all lawyers in the country (29.5 percent and 7.5 percent respectively). More surprisingly, the sample of 227 responses included no African-American or Asian-American attorneys (see table 2.7).[24] Many factors contribute to these data. Specializations must be developed over time, so a portrait of a specialist bar "freezes in" the demographics of an earlier generation of law students.[25] Heinz and Laumann's 1975 survey of the Chicago bar (including analyses of general corporate, large corporate, and regulatory practices) revealed that the backgrounds of corporate regulatory lawyers rise above the mean, even though they fall short of the upper tier.[26]

Further, the bar's concentration in the Midwest likely depresses the proportion of minorities. Another possible explanation is that the substance of OSHA work – involving on-site inspection of construction companies or petroleum refineries – proves unattractive for female attorneys building a practice. In the least, the current, more diverse generation of lawyers does not appear to be fighting to replace the senior generation of OSHA practitioners.

Social background: religion

Lawyers, on the whole, are not representative of the US population in terms of their religious affiliation, yet religious affiliation has declined in importance. In their re-examination of the Chicago bar twenty years after their path-breaking study, John Heinz and Edward Laumann found that ethno-religious identities had less effect on the organization of legal work, in part because elite employers were forced to draw from a broader pool of lawyers as the overall demand for legal services increased.[27] When surveyed for this research, a notable proportion (5.7 percent) did not answer the religious affiliation question, many questioning its relevance in the margin. Whether or not religious affiliation currently influences the organization of legal work, its past significance demands continued scrutiny.

The OSHA bar's pattern of religious affiliation, reported in table 2.7, broadly follows the national bar's deviation from the national population, with just a hint of a Midwestern bias. Unfortunately, no recent data exist regarding the religious affiliations of the national bar. Auerbach's 1975 survey of law school students stands in as a cautious approximation of today's bar, though his study did not report the

TABLE 2.7: Demographics – OSHA bar and comparison groups[28]

	OSHA bar (%)	US bar (%)	US population (%)	Rural Missouri bar (%)	Supreme Court bar (%)
Age	(N = 230)				
Median	46.0	41	34.6	n.a	42
Mean	45.3	n.a.	n.a.	43	n.a.
Sex	(N = 231)				
Male	84.8	70.5	48.9	99	92.7
Female	15.2	29.5	51.1	1	7.3
Race	(N = 227)				
African American	0	3.4	12.6	0	1
American Indian	0.4	0.2	0.9	0	n.a.
Asian, Pacific Is.	0	1.4	3.7	0	n.a.
Caucasian	97.8	92.5	72.1[29]	100	98
Hispanic	0.9	2.5	10.7	0	<1
Other	0.9	–	–	0	n.a.
Religion	(N = 218)				
Jewish	11.9	12	2	0	23
Protestant	37.2	53	56	83	34
Roman Catholic	35.3	29	26	14	24
Other	3.2	6	7	1	4
None	12.4	–	9	2	15

Sources: 1998 Survey of OSHA Bar; US Bureau of the Census, *Statistical Abstracts of the United States* (1997); American Bar Association, *Miles to Go: Progress of Minorities in the Legal Profession* (1998); Auerbach, "Legal Education and Its Discontents" (1984); Landon, *Country Lawyers* (1990); and McGuire, *The Supreme Court Bar* (1993).

percentage claiming no affiliation. The average OSHA survey respondent graduated from law school in 1979, legitimating a comparison. In this survey, Catholics account for 35.3 percent of the sample, compared to 29 percent in the national bar and 26 percent in the general population. Jewish attorneys represent 11.9 percent of the OSHA bar, mirroring the national bar. The OSHA bar also reflects the bar's changing demographics. OSHA practitioners who graduated after 1979 included more Catholics (46.9 percent, compared to 26.8 percent of pre-1980 graduates) and fewer Jews (7.1 percent compared to 17.0 percent among pre-1980 graduates). As in Kevin McGuire's study of the Supreme Court bar – certainly an "elite" bar – and Heinz and Laumann's survey of Chicago regulatory lawyers, this study found a double-digit percentage of lawyers claiming no religious affiliation, which represents only a slight margin over the general population. Underrepresentation of Protestant lawyers balances the bar's overrepresentation of Jewish and Catholic practitioners. Overall, the OSHA bar follows the pattern set by other portions of the bar, all of which differ from the general population.

Social background: political party affiliation
Building on evidence that OSHA attorneys are older, more male, more white, and better educated than the citizenry and bar at large, evidence of political party affiliation helps us to interpolate the bar's position between "elites" and the "average" population. Research in other contexts has demonstrated the relevance of political perspectives when studying lawyers. The high proportion of Democrats in Heinz and Laumann's studies of the Chicago bar (even among corporate attorneys) was understandable in light of the Democratic dominance of Chicago politics. When Democratic dominance waned, they found that political identities had less influence on the organization of the bar.[30] Kevin McGuire suggested very plausibly that liberal dominance in the Supreme Court bar resulted in a preference among liberal interest groups for Supreme Court litigation as a law reform strategy.[31] Liberal dominance in the OSHA bar would be considerably more difficult to explain. Representation in OSHA disputes carries a political charge not felt by lawyers in other contexts; clients may be predisposed to a firm anti-OSHA stance. Attorneys who are ideologically distant from their clients may create tensions in their attorney–client relationship or be forced to compensate for the conflict created by their role as zealous advocate.

A moderate conservative bias among respondents mirrors the politics of lawyers in general. Democrats account for just over a third (35.3 percent) of OSHA practitioners, while Republicans claim a plurality (41.6 percent) of the bar's members.

Compared to the national distribution (see table 2.8), OSHA lawyers appear to be more partisan – only 23.1 percent describe themselves as "independent," compared to 33 percent generally – and more

TABLE 2.8: Political party affiliation of OSHA practitioners

Party	OSHA bar (%)	National population (%)
Democrat	35.3	37
Republican	41.6	31
Independent	23.1	33

Sources: 1998 Survey of OSHA Bar (N = 221); Stanley and Niemi, *Vital Statistics on American Politics, 1997–98.*

Republican.[32] Unfortunately, no recent comparative data exist for the national bar. One poll taken during the early 1980s found that Republicans outstripped Democrats, 54 percent to 37 percent.[33] While these figures are dated, over the past fifteen years the Republican party has enjoyed a sustained rise in support at the expense of the Democratic party, so a sharp shift to the left by lawyers in that period seems unlikely. The OSHA bar joins social elites generally by tending to support conservative politics, but they do not do so overwhelmingly. Many lawyers, indeed, may not be fundamentally opposed to the regulators' mission. These data suggest a diversity of dispositions toward public policies, and, as later chapters describe, these sentiments can play an important part in how attorneys perceive their role.

Socialization to the law: law school
The legal education of attorneys serves as a proximate predictor of career routes and status in the legal profession, for more than mere self-selection. Law firms, and by extension their clients, select lawyers based on their law school; some students at less-prestigious schools may be unable to interview with elite law firms despite excellent academic records. Law schools also differ in their approach to legal education. Top law schools' more academic approach to legal education may contribute to a fundamentally different professional orientation than the more applied and "how to" approach offered at less-prestigious institutions.[34] Legal education itself changes students and weans certain types of students from the profession.[35]

OSHA lawyers were asked to identify what law school they attended. Of the 170 law schools accredited by the ABA at the time of this research, the 231 survey respondents named 110 (64.7 percent), suggesting a diffuse pattern of education. Table 2.9, reporting the leading law schools of attorneys surveyed, presents a curious pastiche of

TABLE 2.9: Leading law schools of OSHA practitioners

Law School	N	%
Georgetown University (DC)	11	4.8
University of Virginia	8	3.5
Case Western Reserve (OH)	7	3.0
Harvard University (MA)	7	3.0
George Washington University (DC)	6	2.6
University of Michigan	6	2.6
Ohio State University	6	2.6
Albany Law School of Union University	5	2.2
University of Dayton	5	2.2
University of Toledo	5	2.2
Capitol University Law School (OH)	4	1.7
Southern Methodist University (TX)	4	1.7
Syracuse University (NY)	4	1.7
Tulane University (LA)	4	1.7

Source: 1998 Survey of OSHA Bar (N = 231).

institutions. Georgetown University, with the largest enrollment of any law school in the nation, supplies the most OSHA practitioners, many of whom practice in Washington alongside graduates of George Washington University and the University of Virginia.

Other "prestigious" law schools included Harvard University and the University of Michigan, but five of the fourteen most frequently mentioned law schools are located in industrial Ohio. The two New York law schools mentioned are Albany Law School and Syracuse University rather than the highly regarded Columbia University and New York University law schools. These data suggest a bar whose members are tied to their respective communities. Unable to draw solely from the most-prestigious "national" institutions, the OSHA bar developed students from well-regarded regional law schools. Management OSHA lawyers tend to spring from their communities via above-average law schools.

A closer examination of the OSHA practitioners' legal educations bears out this interpretation. In order to analyze the educational backgrounds of OSHA attorneys more systematically, I followed the method adopted by Kevin McGuire in his study of the Supreme Court bar.[36] All law schools were grouped into one of five ordinal categories corresponding to their rankings in a national survey of academic programs.[37]

TABLE 2.10: Law school ranking of OSHA practitioners

Law school ranking	OSHA bar (%)	National bar (%)	Supreme Court bar (%)
Distinguished	22.7	15.0	32.4
Strong	21.0	14.6	18.5
Good	19.2	19.7	18.5
Average	20.1	23.0	13.9
Below average	17.0	27.8	16.7

Sources: 1998 Survey of OSHA Bar (N = 229); *The OfficialGuide to US Law Schools 1998–99* for national bar; and McGuire, *The Supreme Court Bar* (1993).

Attorneys' backgrounds were sorted into these categories. The rankings, which give substantial weight to resources and faculty, ultimately stand in for the "softer" assets that all recognize accompany a diploma: prestige and reputation. The current enrollments of all law schools were also sorted, and those proportions are used to approximate the categories' proportions in the national bar. These data, plus McGuire's findings, provide a fruitful comparison for the OSHA bar (table 2.10). The proportion of OSHA practitioners from "distinguished law schools" (22.7 percent) lies at a midpoint between the national bar and the elite Supreme Court bar. OSHA attorneys, on average, are educated at more prestigious schools than the national bar, though a sizable proportion (39.3 percent) attended "average" and "good" schools, only slightly below the proportion in the national bar (42.7 percent). At the bottom of the spectrum, significantly fewer OSHA attorneys attended below average law schools (17.0 percent) than in the national bar (27.8 percent), but in a proportion similar to McGuire's study (16.7 percent).

Combined, these two studies indicate that a measure of an "elite" bar is not the absence of attorneys from less-prestigious schools, but rather, the extent to which it can attract attorneys from the most prominent schools. By that measure, the OSHA bar is above average, though not exceptional.

Socialization to OSHA law: career experiences
Law school may instill the most "intuitive" understanding of professionalism and roles, but careers shape attorneys' understanding of applied ethics, public policy, and the business of lawyering. Though private

TABLE 2.11: Government experience of OSHA practitioners

Public sector experience	%
None	56.0
Federal or state OSHA/DOL/OSHRC lawyer position	9.5
OSHA, federal or state (nonlawyer position)	0.9
Non-OSHA-related federal government position	16.8
Non-OSHA-related, nonfederal, other position	12.5
Clerkships (all levels)	7.3

Source: 1998 Survey of OSHA Bar (N = 232, multiple responses allowed).

practice employs the most attorneys, attorneys can choose many paths before arriving there, and many later leave private practice for employment in private companies or outside the law entirely. One common route for law school graduates, government employment, provides more specialized experience in a particular area of law and a chance to "earn one's stripes" before moving into private practice. After a few years' experience as a government attorney, young attorneys can pursue higher salaries by switching from the prosecution to the defense. Though some critics contend that the one-way "revolving door" provides law firms with free apprenticeships and insider connections, its popularity extends into all legal systems, from the most prestigious federal agencies and departments, such as the Department of Justice and the Internal Revenue Service, to state and municipal governments.

OSHA enforcement personnel are typically not lawyers, but rather health and safety professionals, and those credentials are rare among law school graduates. Unlike some regulatory bodies in which lawyers perform much of the direct enforcement work, most of OSHA's field-work occurs without government lawyer involvement. As a result, few practicing OSHA lawyers – under 1 percent – reported career experience with OSHA (see table 2.11). More attorneys (9.5 percent) had legal experience with the Department of Labor's Office of the Solicitor (which handles OSHA's litigation before administrative law judges), the Occupational Safety and Health Review Commission (OSHRC), or a state-level OSHA litigation team.

The most common career source of government experience was in other federal positions (16.8 percent), particularly the National Labor Relations Board (NLRB), but many others (12.5 percent) found

experience in nonfederal positions, most commonly as state-level prosecutors. Judicial clerkships are uncommon among OSHA practitioners;
instead, over half proceed directly from law school to private practice.
Without the benefit of similar data for other regulatory bars, the full significance of these data eludes us, but considering the distribution of law
schools among OSHA attorneys, it appears that graduates from strong
regional schools are more easily wooed by in-state law firms than by
the call of public service. The relative size and prestige of the agency
may aid the decision. Since few attorneys dedicate their practices to
OSHA work, experience on the government side would not pay dividends through most careers.

As discussed earlier, attorneys often develop "specialist" status over
a number of years and tend to be older than the average practitioner.
Advancing age brings professional advancement as well. Survey respondents had been in private practice an average of 16.3 years and the
vast majority of those in law firms (81.7 percent) had earned the status of "partner," with 14.6 percent as associates (3.7 percent being "of
counsel"). In the national bar, the figures for partners and associates
were 61.6 percent and 34.4 percent, respectively. The survey method
was not designed to exclude associate attorneys, but certainly it had
that effect, as it would in any attempt to identify a group of specialists.
Partners are best positioned to assess the economics of the firms' OSHA
practices. Experience builds expertise, whether the experience is with
the government or while in private practice.

CONCLUSION

A regulatory bar is built by the needs of corporate clients. The management OSHA bar, organized pyramidally, provides a select few specialists in rulemaking for centralized policymaking in the nation's capital,
and a wider base of attorneys to defend companies in OSHA enforcement and compliance matters. Like their corporate clients, regulatory
attorneys share some of the financial rewards of corporate lawyers and
larger law firms. On account of its pyramidal organization, the OSHA
bar draws from social and demographic backgrounds that often reflect
their communities more than a social elite. In legal education, particularly, the OSHA bar reflects a dual character – a core elite and an
extensive army of footsoldiers.

The structure of a regulatory bar has important reverberations for
policymaking and enforcement. Chapters 3 and 4 turn to a close

network of lawyers and interest groups who have played a major role in making OSHA rulemaking what it is today. Then, if lawyers are to serve as mediators for enforcement disputes – consciously or inadvertently – the frequency of attorney–agency and attorney–client relations is expected to play a part. If regulated firms hire attorneys without extensive OSHA practice, the quality of information they receive may suffer. The strategic choices of attorneys may differ depending on their familiarity with agency strategies, their substantive knowledge of health and safety standards, and the trust given to them by their clients. Though comparative study of other regulatory bars is needed, the background of the OSHA bar illuminates what these attorneys do.

CHAPTER THREE

ADMINISTRATIVE RULEMAKING

In its thirty years, the Occupational Safety and Health Administration has endured a notorious reputation for having complicated, lengthy, and litigious rulemaking. Other social regulatory agencies share some of the symptoms, but OSHA's troubles are pervasive: of the health standards promulgated since 1972, all but a handful have been met with lawsuits challenging the agency's decisions. Safety standards have fared better, but approximately half still have faced court review. Rulemaking is long, laborious, and sharply contested, and even then, some have argued, the rules are less than ideal. What or who is to blame? Among the suspects are: highly contentious labor–management relations, appellate courts, the structure of administrative law, American litigiousness, the OSH Act, and the uncertain science of health and safety. Others blame the lawyers.

What is the significance of lawyers to rulemaking? The answer is shrouded in the mythology of the Washington lawyer, who walks through the revolving door of government agencies to capture the ear of former colleagues. Attorneys have not monopolized OSHA rulemaking, at least not numerically. Quite the contrary, health and safety rules often develop for many years without attorneys present as advocates for interested parties. Although Washington political folklore points a finger of suspicion at regulatory lawyers, some research finds a surprisingly low number of lawyers in policy networks. The modern attorney, however prominent in courtroom advocacy, no longer serves as a "generalist" problem-solver and rarely ventures into other fora.[1] Among legal scholars, obituaries written for the slow death of administrative rulemaking commonly (and perhaps unsurprisingly) make judges, not lawyers, the grim reapers. Courts, it is argued, saddled agencies with increasing burdens of "hard look" review and the close oversight of complicated substantive matters beyond the traditional capacity of courts. Lawyers in such accounts have merely cameo roles as simple litigators.

The common story is not so much incorrect as incomplete, because it ignores the wider processes through which courts exert control over regulatory agencies. While regulatory lawyers do indeed go to court, the place to begin to understand the legal dynamics surrounding OSHA rulemaking is the "informal" rulemaking processes themselves. Litigation, and more importantly, legal discourse, does not begin with oral arguments before appellate courts. Before looking at litigation, the subject of the next chapter, this chapter looks beneath the long shadow cast over the administrative process by litigation. Before an agency publishes a rule – and before any party has formally initiated litigation – lawyers have deeply influenced the process. The language and incentives that attorneys have imparted to OSHA rulemaking point to the interdependence and common ambitions of parties within the field, all of whom are locked together in a system from which no party can easily escape. Since this chapter and the next both concern this state of affairs, an important starting point must be to understand the legal setting in which OSHA's regulatory politics takes place.

OSHA RULEMAKING IN OVERVIEW

The authors of the Occupational Safety and Health Act of 1970 crafted a major change in the protections afforded to American workers, and the scale of the transformation was appreciated by the bill's opponents. Unlike the palliative workers' compensation system, the OSH Act created a comprehensive preventive scheme. It imposed two burdens upon employers. The first, known as the "general duty" clause, requires each employer covered by the Act to "furnish to each of his employees employment and a place of employment which are free from recognized hazards that are causing or are likely to cause death or serious physical harm to his employees." The second is to "comply with occupational safety and health standards promulgated under this Act."

The Administrative Procedure Act of 1946 (APA), the guiding framework for American regulatory agencies, envisions two processes for agency rulemaking: formal and informal. Formal rulemaking follows adjudication as a model and has all the trappings of a court, including a judge and cross-examination of witnesses. The burden of proof falls on the agency, and reviewing courts pass on whether the agency has provided "substantial evidence" to justify its findings. Informal rulemaking under the APA, on the other hand, assumes a legislature as its model and was designed to make rulemaking more efficient. An agency need only provide the opportunity for written submissions on proposed rules in "notice and comment," though it may allow oral presentations. Once a decision is made, courts can set it aside only if the agency was "arbitrary and capricious," an apparently far less burdensome legal hurdle. A third leading process for agency action, negotiated rulemaking, was codified into the APA in 1990. As explored later, "Reg Neg" (as it is sometimes called) evolved out of the failings of both formal and informal rulemaking to produce optimal rules in an efficient way. As the name implies, Reg Neg involves adding a period of multiparty negotiations to notice-and-comment rulemaking in the hope of identifying workable regulatory solutions outside the constraints of the traditional forms of rulemaking.

Not all OSHA rulemaking must meet APA requirements. Congress placed OSHA in the Department of Labor and empowered it to promulgate three types of standards. First, for the first two years of the agency's history, OSHA was required to adopt en masse any national consensus standard or established Federal standard, unless the standards would not improve employee safety or health. The rules were already familiar to industry, created by private standard-setting bodies with employer representation, and at any rate Congress expected that these plainly inadequate standards would be only interim regulations.[2] Second, OSHA may issue an "emergency temporary standard" (ETS) free from the APA when a "grave danger" to employees compels quick action. After an ETS has been issued, OSHA must begin work on a permanent standard through normal rulemaking procedures, to be completed within six months.

The procedures for establishing permanent standards, the third and most important type, are outlined by Section 6(b) of the Act. With information submitted by any interested party, including "a representative of any organization of employers or employees," the Secretary can establish an advisory committee to provide recommendations for a standard. In practice, most rulemakings advance to a Notice of Proposed Rulemaking (NPRM) without advisory committee input, having been developed by a team of standards-writers within the agency. The primary expertise on rulemaking teams comes from the program offices, the Directorates of Health, Safety, and Construction. Team members from the Policy Office and the Office of the Solicitor of Labor (Solicitor's Office) contribute economic and legal information. Some rulemaking efforts have included an Advance Notice of Proposed Rulemaking (ANPR) or a Request for Information, published in the *Federal Register*, asking for comments and submissions about a developing issue. In almost all cases, OSHA informally solicits feedback from interested parties before the NPRM is published. Once a rule has been proposed in an NPRM, the Act then provides for steps typical of "notice and comment" rulemaking, including the opportunity to submit written data and comments.

The statute adds a ripple to notice-and-comment rulemaking by providing that anyone filing written objections may request a public hearing. This placed OSHA rulemaking a step beyond the APA's framework, which had left hearings completely to the discretion of the agency. The origins of the clause lie in the Conference Committee's compromise between a Senate bill with "formal" rulemaking and a House bill with "informal" rulemaking.[3] The hearing stage, discussed in detail later, firmly marks OSHA rulemaking as an example of so-called "hybrid" rulemaking. Presentations and cross-examinations are transcribed and become part of the rulemaking record. As the system has evolved, questions now fly in all directions: OSHA to participants, participants to OSHA, and participants to each other. An administrative law judge (ALJ) presides at hearings as a "traffic cop," but does not render decisions on the merits.

After accepting a first wave of written comments and possibly holding hearings, OSHA often leaves the record open for submissions and briefs to discuss new issues that may have arisen in the course of the public phase of the rulemaking. After the record is closed and certified by the ALJ, the rulemaking team crafts the final rule. Communications with interested parties, as well as the Office of Management and Budget, continue during this period.[4] When a final rule is published, the formal regulatory text is supplemented by a "preamble" providing a history of the development of the rule, a discussion of the major issues raised in the record, an analysis of the risks or hazards being targeted, an exposition of the technical and economic feasibility, and a section-by-section justification of the rule. Upon promulgation of the final rule, any person "adversely affected" by the rule may file suit in the United States Court of Appeals challenging the standard, but must do so within sixty days. OSHA's legal representation is provided, again, by attorneys in the OSHA section of the Solicitor's Office, organizationally separated from OSHA in the Department of Labor.

Quasi-judicial, multi-party hearings are one result of the compromise struck during the passage of the OSH Act. A second result – a more stringent standard of judicial review – helped thrust OSHA into the era of "hybrid" rulemaking. The statute provides that "the determinations of the Secretary shall be conclusive if supported by substantial evidence in the record considered as a whole."[5] For new standards to survive challenge, OSHA must endure judicial scrutiny about their underlying evidence and analysis. Other clauses in the Act raise legal hurdles for the promulgation of standards. OSHA must set any standard concerning "toxic materials or harmful physical agents" so that it "most adequately assures, to the extent feasible, on the basis of the best available evidence, that no employee will suffer material impairment of health or functional capacity . . ."[6] Having introduced the question of what constitutes the "best available evidence," the Act specified research, demonstrations and experiments in particular, as well as "the latest available scientific data in the field" and other considerations. These interlaced statutory requirements not only open the possibility of more rigorous judicial review, but also impose crosscutting priorities that provide both industry and unions with issues to pursue on review. On the one hand, employers may challenge a rule if OSHA does not demonstrate why a new rule "better effectuates the purposes of this Act" than existing national consensus standards or, if it *is* better, why it is feasible. On the other hand, OSHA may not establish just any feasible standard – it must set the most protective feasible standard.

In an area where questions of science and policy frequently face legal scrutiny, lawyers undoubtedly will play at least some role. Litigation is necessary to define the statutory requirements and to measure an agency's performance against them. Legal thinking penetrates further, however. DeTocqueville's observation that there is scarcely a political question that does not resolve itself into a judicial one has special meaning in OSHA rulemaking. Given the statutory framework, there is scarcely a scientific question that cannot become a judicial question. Participants in OSHA rulemaking, whether attorneys or not, are very conscious of the legal legacy bestowed on the agency.

LAWYERS AND THEIR CLIENTS

With the years of legal mythology about the ability of Washington attorneys to achieve the impossible, *deus ex machina*, as background, attorneys tell a less dramatic story. Numerous attorneys used metaphors to describe OSHA regulations. One attorney described OSHA as an asteroid heading to Earth. An early warning system might enable the inhabitants of Earth to nudge the asteroid off its course, saving the planet. If discovered too late, an extraordinary effort will be required to destroy the meteor. Another attorney likened OSHA to a ship crossing the Atlantic. Change the course by just a degree or two when it first leaves England, and you will land at a far different point down the American coast. The metaphors of altering a moving object speak to three related facets of a lawyer–client relationship: who hires lawyers, when are lawyers hired, and what are the clients' goals? Drawing on their experience with a meteoric agency such as OSHA, most attorneys answer the questions of "when" and "what" with certainty. Effective legal representation begins before the parties are on the courthouse steps. A client's goal is accomplished more easily if participation comes earlier rather than later. Further, the client's goal must be narrow – one does not need to destroy a meteor, just deflect it; the client will be safe as the rock plunges on through space. "Sophisticated" clients, it is claimed, understand these axioms from the start; others must be made aware of them. Of the millions of American businesses potentially affected by OSHA regulations, some will never contact lawyers at all.

Who uses lawyers?

OSHA rulemakings attract a diversity of participants: trade associations, unions, union locals, companies, government bodies, academics, professionals, and unaffiliated individuals. The level and type of participation varies also, depending on the rule at issue and the stage of the process. Every rule lays a footprint. Some chemicals such as methylene chloride, the target of a January 1997 rule, are manufactured by only a few corporations for use in a wide variety of workplace settings. Other "generic" standards apply very broadly, such as a 1994 proposal to regulate indoor air quality including secondhand tobacco smoke, and more recently, OSHA's attempt to regulate workplace ergonomics – the watchword of modern offices everywhere. OSHA also promulgates rules for certain industry classes, including construction and shipyards.

59

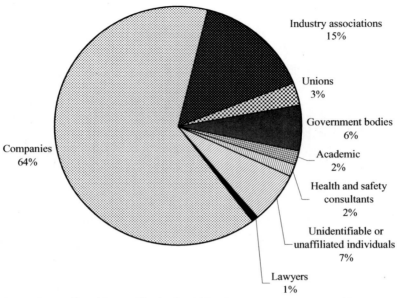

Source: Data collected from OSHA Docket Office, Department of Labour, Washington DC

Figure 3.1: Source of comment letters for twenty-five rules completed 1990–7

Whatever the footprint, individual companies are the targets of regulations. At the grassroots, they must make initial decisions about whether
to participate in rulemaking, and secondarily, whether to participate
individually, through a trade association, or both.

Business interests, specifically individual companies, provide an overwhelming majority of the comments submitted to most rulemakings.
No simpler evidence is required than to peruse the letters submitted to
OSHA, which reside in the agency's Washington, DC, docket office.
In the twenty-five rulemakings completed over a seven-year period,
January 1990 to February 1997, NPRMs, requests for comments, and
reopened records attracted an average of 121.7 comments.[7] Figure 3.1
shows the distribution of commenters in response to OSHA proposals and notices. Companies and industry trade associations account
for nearly 80 percent of all comment letters submitted to OSHA.
Labor unions provide only 3 percent of the total, outpaced by government bodies (6 percent) such as NIOSH, other federal regulatory
agencies, government departments, and state-level agencies. A swell
of letters from construction workers for OSHA's 1996 scaffolding standard boosted the relatively high percentage of "unaffiliated individuals"

(7 percent), though the ambiguities of the data source boosted this figure as well.

The numeric dominance of business interests over union commenters should not be a surprise, except perhaps for the degree of the disparity. A single union may represent workers from hundreds or thousands of individual companies, so we would expect an imbalance in the ratio.[8] Further, unions have seen their membership drop sharply in the second half of the twentieth century, stifling local and national unions' ability to participate. As discussed later, unions sometimes turn to one union to "take the lead" in a rulemaking, replacing quantity with quality. The advantages of business in resources does not ensure dominance on the merits, in OSHA rulemaking or elsewhere.[9] The pattern of comment letters nevertheless suggests the potential base of interested clients for regulatory lawyers.

Converting potential clients to actual clients is a separate matter. The OSHA docket records list lawyers or law firms as the sole author in just 1 percent of all comment letters. Only rarely do attorneys contribute *as attorneys* or by writing "on behalf of" their client. Even after noting when letters to OSHA are signed by corporate in-house counsel or law-trained executives (designated by "Esq." after their names), the proportion reflecting attorney involvement increases to 3.4 percent of all letters, with the largest sub-group being trade associations' outside counsel, reflected in 1.1 percent of all comments. These data miss some attorney involvement. The files of comment letters reveal the common practice of a cover letter from an organization's president or higher officials to the attached substantive comments or evidence, masking for the docket index the actual authorship of the letters. Some attorney interviewees added that the rulemaking letters they wrote always "went out on" their clients' letterhead. Still, these data caution us against overstating the rate of attorney involvement in comment-letter writing. Of the many companies that seek legal assistance for compliance advice or representation in enforcement cases, few turn to their lawyers for rulemakings. Economics drive this decision. As one interviewee said simply, "Most of my clients are not particularly interested in spending money on me or anybody like me to go through the process . . ." In most companies, a person with technical responsibility for safety and health assumes the responsibility for monitoring OSHA regulatory developments. Depending on the initiative of that individual and interest of upper management, that person then bears the responsibility for reviewing the proposed rule and fashioning a response. Few

TABLE 3.1: Advocacy of company rulemaking participation: companies interested in providing written comments to a rulemaking should participate through a trade association and should not participate individually . . .

Response	%
Strongly disagree	12.2
Disagree	40.1
Agree	40.8
Strongly agree	6.8

Source: 1998 Survey of OSHA Bar (N = 147).

companies hire outside counsel for this task, though one attorney suggested that their clients' comments would have a greater impact if they turned to them more often. "[O]ur advice to these people is by all means participate," said one attorney. "If you want to participate successfully, here's what you have to do, and if you really want to do a good job at it come and see us." The potential market is there: although individual companies are the numerically greatest contributor to rulemaking dockets, these letters may come from just a fraction of the total number of companies affected by proposed health and safety regulations.

One reason for the low frequency of attorneys in the rulemaking dockets may be that legal counsel actually *suppresses* rulemaking participation. Some management attorneys advise clients to avoid participation in rulemakings entirely. Asked by survey whether companies interested in providing written comments should participate through a trade association and refrain from individual participation, nearly half (47.6 percent) of OSHA practitioners agreed (see table 3.1).

Industry input to a rulemaking is essential; each individual company's input is not. A company's comments will likely be a pinprick to the meteor. Worse, from an enforcement attorney's perspective, the comments could be damaging in another forum. One attorney, formerly a high-ranking Labor Department official, was asked how often clients ask him to participate in rulemakings.

> To file comments for them? Seldom. To advise them on the positions they take in terms of criticizing issues? Frequently. I typically advise my clients that they are foolhardy individually to file comments. Why make statements about practices within their company, or issues that contain

ADMINISTRATIVE RULEMAKING

negative statements that can be used later on to impeach their position? I mean, there's no upside at all on that.

Also, a company might face repercussions in the court of public opinion. A comment letter may seem innocuous, but a letter stating a firm position might be cast as an attempt to influence the agency unduly. Management attorneys counsel clients about the public relations aspect of public participation. One lawyer tells his clients that,

> [A]ny kind of a filing in a rulemaking proceeding is a potential for a positive result and a potential for disaster, because you have to assume that it can be picked up by somebody on the Hill [or] be picked up by reporters and put in the press. So when you file something you want to make sure you're presenting it in a way that you're going to feel comfortable with being reflected on the front page of the *Washington Post*.

Participation is exposure. Numerous attorneys suggested that many companies fear being targeted if they stake out too vigorous a position. When pressed further, no interviewees could suggest a case where a company had been targeted in an enforcement action due to a public stand taken against the agency. Unionized companies are more concerned that a needlessly aggressive stance could poison labor relations, and, at least anecdotally, one attorney suggested that such concerns were not irrational.

Whether from the lawyer's advice, or more likely, internal calculations of costs and benefits, many companies that participate in rulemakings do so through trade associations.[10] Membership allows some companies to outsource their political participation, take advantage of associations as repeat players in regulatory politics, and receive political cover, even when the activities of the association are directed by just a few lead members.[11] Equally important from the attorney's perspective, the statutory requirements for OSHA rulemaking create analytical advantages for acting through a group, particularly when addressing the feasibility of a rule. OSHA analysts attempt to demonstrate technological and economic feasibility through various means, commonly including an assessment of the rule's impact on a "typical" or mid-range company. If an "above-average" company in an industry provides evidence to OSHA, the standard may be set too stringently for other firms. Companies choosing a trade association, and a trade association choosing a lawyer, have agreed to a filter for the information that flows into a rulemaking record. One attorney expressed that the main fear is that an "above-average" company will participate individually, only without the advice of counsel.

> I just dread it when I hear any client is going down there to talk to them, because you know perfectly well what it is they're going to say that's supposed to be "helpful". But that can be said by the industry group without anybody saying it alone, and the fear is that they're going to go in and say something they shouldn't say that will be used against everybody.

By hiring counsel to assist their well-practiced committee structures or internal staff, trade associations have the ability to screen comments and testimony.

Trade associations are organizationally diverse, and the reasons for hiring outside counsel reflect that diversity, with two factors particularly important. First, assistance may be necessary due to organizational constraints. Trade associations vary in size and sophistication. The largest support "in-house" legal staffs of up to twenty attorneys. Others rely on much smaller staffs or none at all.[12] Although larger trade associations may seem better positioned to handle OSHA work internally, that is rarely the case. Some of the largest trade associations in terms of resources, such as the National Association of Manufacturers (NAM), the American Petroleum Institute (API), and the American Chemistry Council (ACC) are also the most broadly engaged, on issues from international trade to social regulation. Even a large legal staff by trade association standards may not have expertise in particular areas of law, especially ones as narrow as OSHA.

Even in-house counsel experienced in dealing with OSHA may be handling an EPA or congressional matter simultaneously. Full-scale participation in a rulemaking, while infrequent, is a substantial undertaking. One trade association attorney described the "scream factor" implicit when deciding whether to use outside counsel: an initial assessment of how serious the issue is to association members, weighed against how much time they have to respond. Delegation to outside counsel has obvious advantages. Said one management attorney, "[trade associations] like letting the lawyers worry . . . They oversee everything, and if they don't like it you hear about it real fast, but they're expecting you to do the job of putting it all together."

Second, the issues themselves drive the choice of outside counsel. Although trade associations sometimes have established relationships with particular firms or attorneys, rulemakings offer cues about what type of problems to anticipate and what type of expertise, such as litigation, might be needed in response. Expertise certainly has its price. Discussion with one trade association attorney suggested that the primary tension was between expertise and the attorney's reputation for value.

> Q: Have you used the same attorneys?
> A: It has been very flexible. We use a range of firms.
> Q: Based on their substantive expertise?
> A: You might guess that, but it's been more human than that. Sometimes there is an arcane issue with a learning curve, so that if you've got somebody who has already been through it, you'll hire them. But sometimes you want a fresh perspective, too, and more often it is just that you know them, you know how they work, and you've worked well with them in the past.

Pressed to explain the importance of "knowing them," this attorney noted that a leading concern is organizational maintenance: "Their billing practices are very important. Everybody is just so strapped for dollars that you get to know the ones that are good at estimating how much it's going to take for a particular job."

The activities of attorneys in rulemakings depend on the goals of the clients, but follow the tendency among rulemaking participants to provide comment letters without appearing in the hearings. Among all attorneys surveyed, 26.3 percent had participated in some aspect of rulemaking, although the figure was 36.0 percent of self-identified OSHA specialists. Table 3.2 reports the specific services performed by the subset of attorneys with past rulemaking activity. These specialists most often report being called on simply to advise clients about the rulemaking process. Over 60 percent also assisted in writing comments, and 40 percent prepared hearing testimony. A large number had reviewed clients' comment letters, again pointing to attorneys' "hidden" participation. Less common was direct participation in hearings. Behind the simple percentages reported in table 3.2 is a skewed distribution in which there is an elite core among this already rarified form of OSHA practice. Fifteen attorneys (25.0 percent) reported doing seven or more of the ten items; thirty-five (58.3 percent) claimed four or fewer. Moreover, a clear distinction lay between the office-bound activities of advising and preparing comment letters, and the four activities – cross-examination at hearings, stakeholder meeting attendance, and pre- and post-promulgation meetings with OSHA – that bring lawyers into face-to-face contact with the agency. Just twelve attorneys (20.0 percent)

TABLE 3.2: Forms of attorney participation in OSHA rulemaking

Service	%
Advised client on process and strategy	86.7
Assisted client in deciding what position to take	76.7
Wrote comment letter	61.7
Reviewed comment letter written by client	45.0
Met with OSHA informally prior to rule proposal	45.0
Prepared client's hearing testimony	40.0
Met with OSHA after final rule was promulgated	33.3
Attended stakeholders' meetings	26.7
Observed hearing but did not participate	18.3
Cross-examined witnesses at hearing	16.7

Source: 1998 Survey of OSHA Bar (N = 60, multiple responses permitted).

had done three or all of those four, while twenty-six (43.3 percent) had done none of them. More commonly, among office-bound work, a substantial majority (76.7 percent) reported having assisted clients with decisions about what position to take. These data suggest two conclusions: that attorneys often find themselves poised as gatekeepers, shaping when and how clients will participate in rulemakings; and that a smaller subset of attorneys are called in, perhaps because, owing to the urgency of the situation, clients trust attorneys' perceived substantive expertise in addition to the lawyers' procedural skills.

Financially, the decision to hire outside counsel is difficult for trade associations and exceptional for individual corporations. Unions participating in OSHA rulemakings, by comparison, have a relatively easy decision. Generally speaking, unions have been unable to afford outside counsel until a rule has been promulgated and a challenge is being considered.[13] The important wrinkle in union lawyers' involvement is that historically many of the most significant rulemaking efforts by OSHA have been forced into activity by union suits that claim that OSHA inactivity violates its statutory mandate to protect workers. So, union lawyers sometimes have an early role assisting in the agenda-setting process. Once a rulemaking is underway, however, finances strictly affect union participation. Union officials interviewed mentioned cases where they had to raise money from locals to hire attorneys for suits, and where individual unions virtually "dropped out" of judicial review litigation for lack of funds. Unions have developed in-house resources to participate in OSHA rulemakings, so much so that a union official said unconditionally: "Myself and my staff here, to the extent that we get involved in rulemaking, we develop all the testimony, we do all the cross-examinations at the hearings, [and] we don't rely on attorneys for that at all." Unions turned to in-house counsel to assist their safety and health experts for some of the major rulemakings of the 1970s, including efforts to regulate lead, coke ovens, and arsenic, because unresolved legal issues about the nature of the OSH Act itself were under active discussion in the hearings. With those issues now resolved, in-house counsel are called on less frequently.

Still, the organizational factors that force trade associations to hire outside counsel also drive unions. One union director uses union firm attorneys to draft comment letters when "swamped" with other work. If the issue is not important enough to justify this expense, there is a measure of comfort in the relationship with other unions. If resources are thin, union health and safety directors are generally comfortable "signing on" to the work done by another union, such as the AFL-CIO. Extensive coordination among unions has helped to stretch resources. The directors of safety and health for the unions meet every two months at the AFL-CIO in a "Staff Subcommittee on Occupational Safety and Health." When a rulemaking is about to begin, they discuss who will "take the lead" (in one official's words). Sometimes the decision is natural, based on which union is most affected by the rule. If a rule has a wide-ranging impact, coordination prevents wasteful duplication of efforts.

For both lawyers and nonlawyers on the union side, the difference in rulemaking representation is clear. One labor attorney summed up the formulaic struggle: "the unions will have their safety and health people in – who are very good – and industry will have their safety and health people, *plus their lawyers*."

When are lawyers hired?

A regulatory arena like OSHA exposes the limitations of trade associations, especially the largest ones, which usually make decisions by committee. Typically, full-time trade association staffers and representatives of member companies comprise the standing committee on safety and health, and ad hoc committees may provide supplemental support on major or exceptional issues. Company representatives often have technical backgrounds in safety and health (e.g., industrial hygiene) as well. Although it is difficult to generalize, company representatives are among the most likely parties to view OSHA as a foreign and feared entity, depending on factors such as the company's size, whether or not they are heavily unionized, and their type of industry. This committee model of industry response to OSHA is susceptible to some problems. For one thing, trade association committees are generally reactive, further entrenching the management's critical perspective. Time, geography, and expense prevent company representatives from meeting more often. When they do meet, it is easier for committees to analyze proposed rules rather than to develop initiatives on other issues. For another, the technical strengths of company representatives are sometimes matched by political naiveté. These conditions shape the decision as to when attorneys are hired and the role attorneys may play in helping clients to define their goals.

Trade associations can minimize the risk of reactivity by retaining an attorney, active in OSHA matters, to monitor for developing issues. If the trade association lacks internal staff to keep abreast of developments in OSHA law, a lawyer on retainer may provide an early-warning system for the regulatory meteor. The conditions are ripe for attorneys to market their services to existing or past clients. "We don't wait for clients to call," one lawyer said.

> In many cases we monitor what the agency is doing and if we think there's a client that has an interest we notify the client. There are clients who have told us they're interested in an issue and we should look out for it. When that happens and we see that there's something developing, or we think that there's something developing, we'll contact the agency and give them some views on the issue, with the idea that we can educate them and inform them so that they're better positioned to make a clear decision . . .

Serving as monitor for a trade association requires an ongoing relationship. This may not be the norm for the majority of interest groups.[14] Given the relatively few rules that OSHA generates, an attorney in this area can monitor quite assiduously and still contact the interest group infrequently, skewing the apparent extent of that activity.

Even when OSHA is not actively developing new rules, attorneys' long-standing relationships with trade associations cement a two-way flow of representation, helping to educate clients about the agency when not educating the agency about client interests. Regulatory attorneys commonly keep trade associations abreast of OSHA developments by giving speeches at annual or semi-annual gatherings of industry executives or safety and health representatives. In their speeches,

attorneys address both rulemaking and enforcement concerns for companies eager to learn what issues are on OSHA's enforcement agenda.
Regular appearances before company representatives – some attorneys
speak frankly about this – can be the keystone of a lawyer's marketing efforts. While helping a trade association to inform and mobilize
its membership, that practitioner's expertise may be on the minds of
company officials if OSHA compliance officers appear at their door.

Absent an ongoing relationship, advocates are hired with a specific
rulemaking in mind. All attorneys in private practice were asked how
far an issue usually has developed when it comes across their desk.
Invariably, they replied that there is no "typical" rulemaking, yet their
answers reveal the range. With exasperation, attorneys emphasized that
the sometimes wayward decision to seek legal counsel means their
involvement begins

> anywhere along the spectrum, from beginning to end. A client could call
> us two days before the comment period closes on a rulemaking and say
> "please review these comments," or "I was planning on writing comments
> but I ran out of time, could you put something together real quick?",
> [another client] notifies us way in advance, "we'd like you to draft a com-
> ment or draft testimony for the hearing, draft post-hearing comments,
> and be prepared to file a petition for review in the Court of Appeals if
> we can't prevail on the things that we think are important." The whole
> range.

The "whole range," typical of attorneys' responses, is more limited
than meets the eye. The range is very narrow and is centered around
the development of comments – relatively late in the game. Following this pattern was another attorney's comment: "If it's going to be
any good," participation should begin with the ANPR, when issues are
being shaped, but "certainly at a bare minimum . . . at the proposal stage,
to help assist in drafting comments." The extreme is to be called after
OSHA has promulgated a rule, or worse (but not unheard of), after the
deadline for filing a challenge to the rule has passed.

The extreme is rare, of course, because an OSHA rule does not appear
suddenly, and rarely stealthily. OSHA rules begin under a variety of
circumstances, some as a result of union petitions or litigation, others when a scientific consensus has developed around the need for a
standard. While a rule is being contemplated within the agency, frequently OSHA will gather informal input from leading interest groups.
OSHA staff have been known to leak early drafts of rules to parties to

gauge reactions. More recently, OSHA has held "stakeholder" meetings, informal conferences between OSHA staff and parties identified as having a major stake in the outcome of the rule.[15]

OSHA officials and staff can recall attorneys accompanying groups in developmental meetings – not always, it was claimed, with a positive impact on group dynamics. Still, the vast majority of pre-rulemaking meetings do not involve attorneys. The preference of lawyers is to begin their involvement with the development of the comments. To my surprise, one attorney even eschewed early meetings when working on health standards. When he hears about a rule, he commented,

> We have an opportunity to go down in the early stages and talk to OSHA, although I think what happens in the early stages is rarely very influential. It's what happens later on that molds things.
> Q: It isn't the early stages?
> A: Well, when it comes to medical issues, OSHA has a mindset. It has its own medical people and they see things differently from outside consultants. That's one of the two principle issues. The other one is economic feasibility, and when you're down and talking and they haven't even decided what it is they're going to propose, you can't really talk much about that. But you can begin to get a feel for where it's headed and begin to start going out and getting your own army of consultants.

For health standards in particular, involving attempts by OSHA to set permissible exposure limits for toxic substances, early warning is not useful until and unless it provides a fixed reading on OSHA's meteor.

Unless management attorneys have maintained a relationship with clients for rulemakings, such as with a trade association, they are usually called in when OSHA has moved from the formative stages of rulemaking to a specific proposal. Then, attorneys prefer to become involved before their clients define their objectives, for the comment letter in response to a proposal is the first presentation to the rulemaking docket, and the docket casts a long shadow.

What do clients want?
A classic tension for the legal profession is between the lawyer's obligation to provide vigorous advocacy on behalf of a client and the lawyer's own sense of the public interest, particularly when the lawyer disagrees with the position being advocated or the strategy urged by the client.[16]

Among the forces bearing on the lawyer are the economics of working for a law firm and the strength of the client relationship. For most attorneys in the OSHA bar, private practice means working in a law firm, and the pressure to generate billable time and new clients is – even to one of the most senior attorneys – "relentless." Attorneys must worry about client satisfaction and client retention as well.

The tension for the legal profession lies in the struggle between making clients happy while still securing autonomy and independence in defining and carrying out its work.[17] Shared values between attorneys and clients may minimize the potential for disagreement about goals. All attorneys were asked, "what attracted you to this line of work?" Union attorneys frequently highlighted a conscious choice to "do good" when deciding to forgo the more lucrative salaries of industry representation.[18] The distinct line between labor and industry representation filters the range of clients and positions the attorney will represent, thereby preventing some ethical disagreements with client goals.

Attorneys may achieve independence by paying another price. The work of Heinz, Laumann, Nelson, and Salisbury found that among all interest group representatives, outside counsel and consultants were the most likely to have refused a potential client or work assignment. Their research suggests that greater flexibility is available only because lawyers specialized in litigation are removed from broader discussions of policy.[19] When OSHA attorneys are hired by a trade association to assist in the preparation of written comments, it may simply be reviewing, not writing, the submission. Discretion in minor tasks seems a Pyrrhic victory in the battle for professional autonomy.

A sense of independence can be found in areas other than choosing clients or work assignments. Certain characteristics of OSHA rulemaking buttress professional claims to "expert" status. Different types of expertise, analytical and experiential, are intertwined in attorneys' description of client relationships. Analytical skills include the ability to synthesize conflicting evidence into a general claim as well as to write letters and testimony which most clearly establish the essential points. Experiential skill is knowledge, based on past cases, of what OSHA is likely to find persuasive and what will stand up to judicial review. These two types of expertise are manifested in tempering and narrowing the client's position, a typical position for attorneys.

Past OSHA rulemakings reveal that motivations can depend on the history of the developing rule, and as is known about corporate approaches to regulation generally, companies are not always opposed to regulation.[20] For example, the "Hazard Communication" rule, requiring that employers provide employees certain information about chemicals in the workplace, originally was promulgated in 1983 under the Reagan administration when chemical companies supported national regulation in order to preempt "right to know" laws adopted by various states.[21] Regulations can level the playing field in other ways. One management attorney described how companies that have been proactive in adopting safety and health programs will support new rules, simply because "they would like to see their competitors who may not be doing as much, have to do that much and spend that money also."

While varying motivations may animate individual corporate behavior, the more typical stance of business has been strong opposition to many regulations. When meeting with their attorneys, clients' anti-regulation response is almost visceral, even though some rules may ultimately result in savings by reducing workers' compensation costs and other legal liabilities. One interviewee reported that company clients react with particular vigor to safety standards that establish specific procedures. They view these hazards, such as falling from a high place or dangerous machinery, as best handled by the "people on the floor." "What you have to do," a lawyer explained, is to

> have people stop focusing on the fact that they don't want the federal government intervening in their workplace and recognize that it's difficult to write a standard that is applicable across a broad variety of workplaces, and that if it's going to be any good, just saying "I don't want to do this," or "screw that," isn't going to do it. You've got to come back with something that makes sense.

The instinctive responses of individual companies come into play in trade association discussions as well, because the ultimate position of the trade association is shaped through discussions with member company representatives. As one in-house counsel for a trade association suggested,

> You might be sitting there with the committee on a particular issue, and there may be a committee member from Podunk who is upset at the government. You have to say, "you may think it's unconstitutional, but . . ." Lawyers can make it work either way. Lawyers can either toughen up the organization's stance or they can mediate the response and make it more subtle, shape it up and put in the stronger arguments.

If a trade association is dominated by a few larger members, the position of the attorney grows stronger or weaker depending on his relationship with those companies. As one management attorney noted, "when the big members say 'let's do something about it,' [the trade associations] jump and get their act together and begin to look at it from a potential litigation perspective."

Tempering a position means, as with steel, making it stronger. Tempering involves moving the client away from an anti-OSHA conviction in order to craft a position that will result in the best possible position for the company or industry. Clients who insist that lawyers make particular arguments may put vigorous advocacy in tension with effective advocacy. An attorney may still make the more extreme argument, but the lawyer has to inform the client of reality. A management lawyer put the obligation this way:

> It's very rare that you can get a rule set aside. It has happened, but I can't in conscience tell a client, "no problem, I can stop it." If you want me to try, I'll try, but is that the guaranteed outcome? No. Now what's your next objective? Your next objective is to get a rule that makes some sense . . . The objective in most rulemaking is "get a sensible outcome" . . . and make the agency fully appreciate what the impact will be of what they're doing, which is not easy because they don't want to do it most of the time.

Just as the vigorous advocate may need to make losing arguments, so the effective advocate will also tailor the arguments to achieve a result the client "can live with." Skillful attorneys in the OSHA rulemaking process must adjust positions to where the strongest legal arguments lie. Simply put, fundamental policy arguments about the value of OSHA in general, or the need for a new rule in particular, will seldom be successful with OSHA once a rulemaking is underway.

Attention turns – while the rulemaking proceeds – to the possible impact of litigation on the rule. This means not just what the courts might do, but also what OSHA does in anticipation of what the courts might do. Analytical expertise involves assessing the evidence to anticipate what can be sustained as a matter of policy by meeting the "substantial evidence" standard set for OSHA's own hybrid level of judicial review. Even more, the attorney provides experiential knowledge of how the interest group's position can force OSHA to consider or back away from a position, based on what the agency and courts have said about rulemaking records in the past. With clients, OSHA, and the courts as players, the "game" in crafting a client's position (such as in a post-hearing brief) centers around a tempered, narrowed goal. One lawyer described reaching it as follows:

> Well, you lay out as much as you can a case for the proposition that whatever OSHA has proposed is not only wrong but won't withstand court review. And you never quite say it that way, but you have it in mind when you're writing it. And the agency got beat in the *Benzene* case, but on an extremely narrow ground, and otherwise I'd say that they've had their way on health issues. Courts are extremely reluctant to overturn it. So the issue that's always intrigued our clients is, is there a way you can use the feasibility provisions of the statute to insure that while you may have what you consider to be an overly stringent health standard, it doesn't burden you with excessive engineering control requirements? That's the game.

The game necessarily includes organized labor. As industry pushes against regulations, labor pushes for regulations. Through petitions and lawsuits to initiate rulemakings, unions advance the statutory imperative of the most protective standards feasible. Union goals often must be narrowed, too, by describing legal constraints to union officials. One labor attorney suggested the problem was with clients in general, but certainly with unions in OSHA rulemaking.

> If you ask your clients what they want, it's always Christmastime. And it's human nature. If you ask somebody what they want [and] give them a glass of milk, they want a cookie. I think there's an education part that lawyers have to pursue quite assiduously in explaining to clients what's possible as opposed to what they want, and that can be difficult. That can be difficult. For one thing, clients always want standards in place much more quickly than you can get the agency to do it. For another, clients want components to standards that may be very difficult to get from a reviewing court, like medical removal protection or some kind of engineering control.

The union image of the agency is remarkably similar to that of management – OSHA is not easily budged. The source of OSHA's immovability is not a hierarchical system of public agency versus subordinate parties, but rather a conviction shared by many interested parties on both sides of the union–management divide that OSHA is, first, a bureaucracy with all the trappings that implies for the mentality of bureaucrats, and second, closely aligned with their respective "opponents" across the divide. Indeed, a striking feature of this research taken as a whole was the accusation from both union and management representatives that OSHA regularly bends to the interests of the other. OSHA may be linked to all parties in the public/private network, but it is not perceived as being equally distant from them. The nuance for union attorneys is that OSHA's course tends toward the stationary position, and, once there, inertia keeps it there. Despite desires to force OSHA into activity, union lawyers are realistic about the political and administrative limits on the agency. Recognizing the need to remind clients of this fact, one attorney relied on the strength of the attorney–client relationship. "I feel it's very easy with virtually every one of our clients to say 'look, I know why you're saying this is the way OSHA is doing it, but they're legally within their rights and it makes sense. Forget it.'" Long-term relationships and trust allow attorneys to be candid when the clients – health and safety specialists – view OSHA's actions as the triumph of politics over science. Many of the unions most active in OSHA issues, including the AFL-CIO, the United Steelworkers, and the United Auto Workers, have maintained relatively stable associations with particular union attorneys and firms.

Have the union attorneys sacrificed involvement in more fundamental policy questions, forsaking the freedom to be candid about (narrower) legal questions? All interviewees were asked, "where are you most and least influential?" One union attorney inadvertently revealed the vagueness of the line between law and policy when noting the distinct, almost superior attitude of union committee members: "They make the policy and the lawyers help them implement it. We're not the policymakers. *We* didn't come up through the ranks." But the political reality that lawyers bring to clients can trim the loftiest goals. Indeed, the quoted attorney added seconds later that lawyers are most influential in determining what OSHA wants to hear and is willing to hear, and working within that framework. In short, lawyers steer the regulators as well as the regulated toward a version of "reality."[22]

Although their clients are less inclined to involve them in the step-by-step process of rulemaking, union lawyers are called on to make important decisions about what the agency and the courts might do. It might appear, then, that the basis of the lawyer's autonomy in representing clients in the OSHA rulemaking process is that both labor and management clients must anticipate the effect of court review. According to the industry attorney's ideology of expertise, building a record for court review requires the analytical abilities of legal counsel. The OSHA bar thereby has escaped the boundaries created by specialization and opened up an area for legal expertise: agency rulemaking.

LAWYERS AND HYBRID RULEMAKING

When an OSHA effort has become a proposed rule, to a significant degree the die has been cast.[23] A rule of some form can be avoided in only the most remarkable circumstances, and much of the proposed rule will be promulgated without revision. The most interested constituencies already have provided input about the rule, either through low-level discussions between their (mostly) nonlawyer representatives and agency staff or through more formalized mechanisms for stakeholder participation. The "notice and comment plus" or hybrid rulemaking that follows has many dimensions, one of which is symbolic. In accepting comment letters, a government agency shows its openness to citizen input. Any hearings will further open up the rule's authors to probing. By accepting post-hearing briefs and evidence, the quasi-legislative "discussion" continues with no stone left unturned. In the minds of some interviewees, the presence of attorneys shatters this pristine image of the deliberative process. Though some industry lawyers have developed substantive expertise through their years of participation, collectively they are criticized as procedural mavens, using procedural expertise cynically and ironically to derail discussion.

Beyond symbolism, research explaining OSHA's failings has blamed in part the judicial process.[24] One cannot necessarily connect the ills of the legal system to the behavior of lawyers, yet criticism of attorney participation in rulemaking suggests that the symbolic and practical critiques may be linked. Indeed, the construction of rulemaking as a legal process alters the incentives of participants. Before the meteor has struck, lawyers help to establish the framework of alternatives.

Patrolling the record: rulemaking as preparation for litigation
OSHA law has had over a quarter-century to develop. Two landmark cases, the *Benzene* and *Cotton Dust* decisions, combined with a number of other early decisions, settled important questions of statutory interpretation.[25] These included the meaning of "significant risk," "feasibility," and the relationship of cost–benefit analysis to standards promulgation. Also settled are fundamental questions of constitutional law, such as whether the discretion afforded to OSHA by Congress violates the nondelegation doctrine.[26] Thus, the law constrains the

discretion of reviewing courts. Similarly limited in the policy issues, the courts' role is to determine whether, based on the record, OSHA acted reasonably in its decision, with a central question being the sufficiency of the evidence presented. This narrower, statutory hurdle of "substantial evidence" still presents considerable discretion, because what evidence a "reasonable mind might accept as adequate" lies between the "preponderance of the evidence" and the "arbitrary and capricious" standard of the Administrative Procedure Act.[27]

To win on review, a party needs to show that OSHA disregarded important evidence, mishandled the evidence it relied on, or lacked evidence to justify its assumptions. As the rulemaking develops, participants are conscious of the range of possibilities supported by the record. A lawyer naturally seeks to advance a party's affirmative case for the "ideal" version of a rule, but when a lawyer contemplates the possibility of subsequent litigation, management attorneys view their role as also being able to: (1) anticipate the questions courts will ask, given the legal framework and the structure of the substantive issue; (2) introduce evidence that challenges alternative rule formulations; (3) reduce the credibility of the evidence and testimony for those alternative positions; and, ultimately, (4) increase the possibility that OSHA will appear to have acted in error if a non-ideal rule is adopted. One management attorney explained his approach:

> [Y]ou're trying to build an evidentiary fence around the record so that it leaves the government with very few options. It's not simple to do, because ultimately the judicial test for review is substantial evidence test, which means if it's 50/50 they can do what they want and you're not going to be successful in challenging it. So the task is to patrol the record by challenging submissions by the government and by others which seem to be at odds with your clients' interests, trying not only in terms of developing pre- and post-hearing comments to respond, but at the hearing trying to engage people in examination for the purpose of trying to discredit what they are saying.

A lawyer participating in a rulemaking could simply concede that OSHA's decision will be adverse to the clients' interests and, like an attorney at a jury trial, will prepare to use the court as a check – one that may be more favorably disposed to client interests.

Patrolling the record is both a substantive and a procedural activity, lodged between a legislative and an adjudicatory process. As the DC Circuit emphasized when reviewing the agency's cotton dust standard, the courts "ensure that the regulations resulted from a process of reasoned decisionmaking."[28] For example, the Third Circuit twice set aside portions of standards when the Notice of Proposed Rulemaking did not advise the public of all issues under consideration.[29] Lawyers advance their clients' interests when close scrutiny reveals an agency's errors. Because of OSHA's increased experience, such procedural objections may be unavailable. Substantive issues become leading arguments when participants' contributions to the rulemaking record cast OSHA's decision into doubt. Thus, lawyers may actively create issues of feasibility and significant risk, not merely scrutinize for procedural errors.

A management attorney patrolling the record frames the problem in the following way. Suppose a union is pushing OSHA for a very low PEL for a particular chemical, e.g., no more than 1 part per million (ppm) in the air, while OSHA proposed 3 ppm and industry groups want 5 ppm. It is of no use merely to show affirmatively that 5 ppm would be beneficial. OSHA's more protective proposal will stand so long as it is feasible and addresses a significant harm. Industry representatives need to make the negative case that OSHA would not be reasonable in concluding that 3 ppm was necessary or feasible. Even if OSHA's 3 ppm becomes the final rule, however, union participants may sue for a more protective standard. Thus, the management attorney must lay the evidentiary groundwork to ensure that a court could not conclude that OSHA was unreasonable when rejecting the union's suggestion of 1 ppm. This "textbook" case reveals the complexity of the strategic decision involved. Industry participants might rationally fight a union proposal by supporting the agency's proposal, such as by advancing evidence supporting the agency's position. If industry wants to fight both proposals, attorneys must craft the more complex argument that, assuming *arguendo* OSHA's proposal passes scrutiny, the union proposal could not pass.

There are many ways for attorneys to define success. Attention and participation by a wide array of private interests itself has an effect on the agency. The anticipated responses of regulatory agencies can amplify the effect of external forces.[30] Some practitioners find success in the decisions OSHA makes before the record reaches a reviewing court. By making the record point strongly toward a particular conclusion, the agency may have no recourse except to conclude in that way, even when agency decisionmakers are not persuaded as a matter of substance. The desire to avoid litigation generates the goal of establishing a credible threat to the agency, made possible by acquiring skill in both rulemaking and litigation. As one management attorney put it:

> Our approach is to focus on making sure that the information in the record is sufficient that you cannot legally make a decision which goes against us, and if you do, we're going to have a very easy time of it because it's going to be clear to that appellate judge under the terms of the statute.

This interviewee concluded somewhat boastfully: "I think at this point we have built a reputation with the agency that they ignore our comments at their peril."

There are other possibilities shy of reversal by a reviewing court. As a wrinkle in the process, when a court has found the agency's justification of a rule inadequate as it concerns an industry sub-group, the rule as a whole generally survives review. Reviewing courts tend either to uphold an agency's action or remand a portion of the rule to the agency for further explanation and justification.[31] From industry's perspective, that may simply gain enough time to prepare for the costs of compliance and to adjust operations. Alternatively, if the record could support either side on a particular point of science or law, OSHA (or its attorneys) might be reluctant to risk a judicially imposed result. Without necessarily being persuasive in the first instance, industry can position itself for a favorable settlement after the rulemaking. The "technical corrections" issued by OSHA and published in the *Federal Register*, as well as compliance directives provided to inspectors, may be sufficient to deflect the impact of the rule.

Successfully patrolling the record can be difficult, as it depends on a multitude of factors, including the level of judicial deference given by individual judges and, of course, whether the facts can ultimately support OSHA's action. Also, industry lawyers have competition. Union officials describe the historic success of unions in OSHA litigation as a product of the same ability to create the records necessary to undermine industry proposals, justify OSHA's proposals, or win more stringent measures. When asked where the "action" occurs within the rulemaking process, one nonlawyer union official pointed to the opportunity for public participation. "Although the foundation, the approach gets set with the proposal, without a doubt," he observed,

> the other reality is that by coming in and laying down evidence around an issue it actually can effectuate the outcome both administratively and particularly legally, and I think if you go back and you look at the

various challenges to rules that have taken place, one of the reasons why the unions have been so successful is based upon the record evidence: showing that there are people at risk, that there are feasible methods of control, and that the agency ignored them or made the wrong determination.

Those less cynical about OSHA's responsiveness seek an administrative outcome. As one union-side attorney said hopefully, "I start out with the view that everybody is subject to salvation, including OSHA people." Yet both management and union representatives anticipate and plan for litigation.

Whether anticipating an administrative or a legal resolution, one must present a strong argument to OSHA. The first stage of rulemaking involves building the record in response to an NPRM. The initial salvo is the comment letter, followed possibly by rulemaking hearings. The capstone is the post-hearing brief, which has a somewhat different character. The following two sections consider the strategies involved in written and oral contributions to rulemaking records.

Written submissions
Submissions in writing are the most common method of participation in rulemaking. While not viewed by interest groups as the most effective method, these organizations employ written comments "very frequently" or "always" over 75 percent of the time, surpassing informal contacts or coalition building as a strategy.[32] The overwhelming majority of comment letters are between one and three pages in length. The content of comment letters can be diverse. In an NPRM, OSHA often asks a series of questions that some letter-writers address sequentially. Small businesses and individuals are less likely to respond in that fashion, often directing a one-page letter to the rule as a whole or a particularly worrying provision. More sophisticated letter-writers include comments on provisions with which they agree – described by one trade association in-house counsel as "atta-boy" letters – as proof of the agency's reasonableness on a topic. Some letters are very extensive, numbering dozens of pages and including appendices of scientific literature, independent studies, or documents describing industry efforts in the field.[33] The level of reasoning supplied in the comments similarly varies widely from the assertive "this is too stringent" or "this is not stringent enough" to robust discussions of a clause.

In 1994, the agency's proposed standard regulating indoor air hazards – including secondhand smoke – drew an estimated 100,000 comments, mostly from smokers mailing pre-printed postcards. A trade association or union can encourage member companies and local unions to send letters, sometimes based on a "suggested" letter sent by the national office. For attorneys, volume has its place. The sheer number of comments can support challenges to the rule by more clearly signaling to the judge what the key issues are. As one trade association attorney said, "If it's just one letter, the judge might say 'I can see why OSHA overlooked their points on this,' but if there are fifty letters, they can't say that."[34] The technical validity of the comments aside, courts' responsiveness to multiple comments reflects their interest in the representativeness of administrative systems.[35]

The number of comments may backstop one's arguments, but numerical superiority does not drive most participants. The target audience, if not the courts, is the agency's standards-development team. While the political issues may be addressed by OSHA administrators, the scientists, engineers, and staff experts on health and safety issues are most likely to respond favorably to technical presentations. No one imagines that civil servants are apolitical, of course. In the logic of standard-setting, however, professional decisionmakers may respond to one incisive comment from a technically trained contributor, versus volumes of letters from advocates. Cigarette smoke may be a serious air contaminant, 100,000 angry smokers notwithstanding.

Less clear is what impact the source of a comment letter should have on expert judgments. Every comment received is given a record to ensure that it is reviewed when agency staff produce the final rule. Individual work habits of agency personnel vary. One OSHA standard-writer cuts up copies of comment letters and organizes the pieces topically, essentially making every comment anonymous. Another standard-writer interviewed feels that the identity is important to assess bias in the comment. Whether or not individual identities remain known, interviewed standard-writers in OSHA asserted that comments written by attorneys are easily separated from comments written by technical specialists.

Under pressure from courts, litigants and its own lawyers, OSHA gives comments considerable scrutiny. Even if participants cannot be dissuaded from challenging the final rule, the agency strengthens its bargaining position by very thoroughly addressing important comments.

From the agency's earliest days, OSHA administrators recognized the need for attorney involvement in the standard-setting process. A highly protective standard does not improve the lives of workers if courts delay its implementation pending a further statement of reasons. Once they recognized how frequently rules were being challenged, OSHA staff tried to become better attuned to the legal requirements of promulgating standards. They adopted a team approach to the creation of standards and included the Solicitor's Office in the early development of rules – even when legal counsel was not urgently required – so the staff would become more sensitive to legal issues and the attorneys would "derive a basic understanding of the health and technical considerations involved."[36] OSHA's status as a "mission" agency required attorneys who were educated in, and devoted to, the issues.[37]

The Solicitor's Office attorneys patrol the record from the inside, trying to ensure that all major issues on the record have been addressed, and reinforcing the legal focus driven by external forces. Agency lawyers are particularly aware of the authors of comment letters. One government attorney commented:

> I wouldn't say it affects the way you deal with it in a decisional sense. I think OSHA at that point is going to make the decision it's going to make. It does affect the pressure . . . to make certain that we know that "this is somebody who always appeals." That if AISI [the American Iron and Steel Institute] is saying something – that's an easy one, they challenge almost everything – let's be sure if they want something, and we're doing something that's exactly the opposite, that we have a good explanation and good support . . . whereas with some other groups there wouldn't be as intensive scrutiny.

One observable manifestation of those pressures is the preamble to the regulatory text published in the *Federal Register*, the daily publication disseminating rules, proposals, notices, and other documents relating to regulatory agencies and the executive branch.[38] OSHA's arguments to the court must be defensible on the official record, so when comments to a rulemaking are extensive and sophisticated, the preamble's analysis concomitantly expands. OSHA obviously desires to keep preambles short, since 100 pages in the *Federal Register* is the equivalent of a 320-page book. Early in its history, very brief preambles – as few as two pages for the asbestos standard – accompanied standards until courts cited the inadequate "statement of reasons" when vacating and remanding two standards.[39] During OSHA's first three years (1972 through

1974), *Federal Register* documents for final rules averaged a scant 6.9 pages, increasing to 18.75 in the next three years. Since those early years, OSHA's final rules ballooned and have not declined.[40] From 1990 through 2002, the average *Federal Register* document ran to 92.7 pages. Figure 3.2 displays the median and mean number of pages per final rule, grouped in moving five-year increments.

Why did rule preambles grow so markedly? The early years have the most clear-cut answer. As noted by Benjamin Mintz, the Deputy Solicitor for OSHA from the agency's founding until 1982, the agency was reacting to early court decisions setting aside rules.[41] A tone was set that was reinforced by subsequent behavior of all parties involved. It did not help OSHA's cause that the 1970s were characterized by declining deference toward administrative agencies by appellate courts.[42] Other factors contributed also to some of the variation in later years, including the scope and complexity of rules as well as the growing sophistication of participants in providing more information that deserved comment. Page-lengths declined slightly during the Reagan administration, in part because the rule proposals of that era were less offensive to business interests and fewer efforts were necessary in order to protect rules from industry lawsuits. Even so, preambles far exceeded in length those of the early and mid-1970s. Final rule documents show no signs of returning to the early levels, suggesting a fairly steady defensive posture against the legal strategies of constituents.

Preparing a final rule for publication is an extensive project. If all comment letters made the same argument, the discussion might be relatively brief, but if opponents' aim is to delay promulgation, an arms race of ideas ensues. One skill claimed by attorneys is the ability to focus on specifics and make distinctions between particulars. By breaking down industry groups further and further, pointing out variations among work practices and working environments, the apparent rationality of an across-the-board standard, procedure, or PEL is called into question. Consequently the agency must go to further lengths to justify its action, whether or not the distinction captures a real difference.

In 1991, OSHA published a proposed standard regulating methylene chloride after denying an earlier petition by the United Auto Workers (UAW) for an ETS. Methylene chloride, widely used as a paint stripper, is produced by just a few manufacturers. The consumers of methylene chloride, including thousands of small businesses, were unlikely to participate in rulemaking, not only because of their size and lack

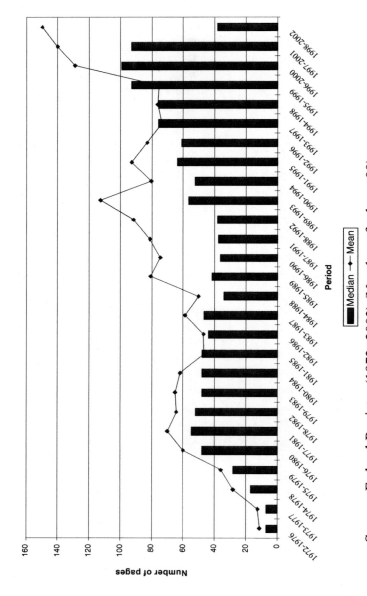

Source: Federal Register (1972–2002) (Number of rules = 99)

Figure 3.2: Length of OSHA final rule documents in the *Federal Register*, moving five-year medians and means, 1972–2002

of resources, but also because substitutes for methylene-chloride-based paint strippers were available. The potential mass movement to alternative products threatened manufacturers of methylene chloride.

In March 1994, OSHA published a Supplementary Request for comments on a specific study that had appeared.[43] Of the thirty-seven comments received, twenty-three were from the Paint Remover Manufacturers Association, an organization which lists only a post office box address in Vincennes, Indiana. The PRMA claimed twenty-one industry committees, representing various *user* groups of methylene chloride, such as the Church Pew Committee, the Archeological and Museum Committee, the Antique Restoration Committee, and the Aircraft Refurbishing Committee.[44] Each letter sent to the docket was just one page and well-crafted. The first paragraph was nearly identical in all of the letters, except that the name of the industry sub-sector was changed. Drawing attention to what appears to be flagrant agency unresponsiveness, the letters began:

> I have reviewed the request for information published by the Department of Labor, in the *Federal Register*, March 11, 1994 concerning the occupational exposure to methylene chloride. The document covers only the exposure in the furniture stripping and flexible foam manufacturing industries [e.g.]. During the testimony before the OSHA panel at the September 17, 1992 public hearings, information was submitted proving that OSHA had failed to include or ignored the effect of this regulation on the cabinet shop industry [e.g.] This is an industry that relies on the use of methylene chloride paint removers that are used to remove paints and finishes from kitchen cabinets. It appears that neither OSHA's Preliminary Regulatory Impact Analysis nor Mr. Green's re-examination has recognized this industry and the effect that this regulation will have.[45]

The second paragraphs outlined in four to twelve sentences how methylene chloride is used in those industry sectors, and asserted for each that the proposed standard was "impossible to attain." The last paragraphs, again identical except for the name of the committee, paired a demand with a taunt: "The Cabinet Shop Committee requests that OSHA perform an analysis of the impact of this regulation on the cabinet shop industry. This was pointed out at the public hearings but it appears that OSHA has taken no action on this matter." The manufacturers of methylene-chloride-based paint stripper spoke for its consumers, pressing OSHA into a feasibility analysis and justification for each industry sector.

Though OSHA finally was able to promulgate the rule in January 1997, a government attorney on the receiving end of the docket perceived the group of letters as an orchestrated strategy and chastised those responsible for it:

> Industry had letters get sent in from all kinds of people, and they said something like "I strip paint on church pews and that's a unique situation because it has to be done indoors with high ceilings," or "I refinish frames for artwork, and that's a situation unlike any others," or whatever. And all of that takes time because OSHA has to deal with each comment. I don't know if industry appreciates how much time and resources it takes for the staff to produce a response to each of these letters so they can avoid challenges.

The authorship of the letters supports this attorney's suspicion that the letters' claims were more strategic than impassioned. A combined eight individuals, writing as chairs of committees, claimed authorship for the twenty-three letters. David L. White, president of the PRMA, authored five of the letters, while the President and General Manager of Besway Systems, Inc. "chaired" seven of the committees. The PRMA's collection of letters was a highly refined method of using OSHA's anticipated defensiveness as a tool in an offensive strategy.

Of course, industry's efforts to disaggregate the analysis may prove that a proposed standard cannot be applied across-the-board, just as a national speed limit of 30 miles per hour would be overly stringent even if entirely appropriate on some roads. Reduced to absurdity, a preamble could discuss the rule's impact on every employer in the United States and still fail judicial scrutiny if the evidence for each application weighs against it.[46] The logical suggestion for the design of policy systems is one with a long pedigree: begin enforcement without a rule, establishing all rules *ex post facto* through agency adjudication. In OSHA's hybrid rulemaking, the generality of legislative judgments must confront the particularity of judicial determinations, here pressed by the PRMA's judicially motivated strategy. A wave of legal scholarship has questioned whether "hard look" scrutiny has outstripped the capacity of administrative agencies as decisionmakers and has proposed a variety of alternatives, including increased informal rulemaking and greater judicial deference to agency decisions.[47]

If agency success depended solely on responding with adequate evidence to each interest's concern, OSHA would face only the twin limits of scientific uncertainty and staff resources. Ironically, OSHA's efforts to anticipate and avoid challenges to rules may aid the efforts of other potential challengers. Longer preambles to rules make contradictory language more likely, or in the least, increase the chance that the agency's action will appear to be arbitrary. Labor attorneys were asked whether union strategies were similar to reported industry strategies. One union attorney noted that:

> Not only do you patrol the record but you patrol even more assiduously the agency's own statements. I mean, the best way to hook an agency is to hoist them on their own petard, and typically in these rulemakings . . . the preambles are laden with things that cast doubt on the rationality of the rule . . . In many of the cases I litigate where the agency has gone, in our view, not far enough to protect workers' safety and health, there is generally sufficient concern elsewhere in the record about how far the agency needs to go, so that you can construct an argument based on that.

OSHA responds to a record laden with scientific uncertainty. The evidence marshaled and entered into the record rarely provides a clear answer as to when a worker is at risk, much less how far it is feasible to control the risk. A body of scientific evidence may include contradictory studies. At its best, science may point in a particular direction or to a range of plausible answers. Amid pervasive uncertainty, decisions must be quasi-legislative in nature. The quasi-judicial burden of accounting for all the evidence requires the agency to lay bare the subjectivity inherent in scientific decisionmaking.[48] OSHA has no easy route out of this dilemma. Parties have a right to raise issues and OSHA must respond. It is extremely difficult to resolve issues to the satisfaction of both labor and management, and even more difficult to explain the resolution satisfactorily. The simple political result – a compromise – usually cannot be justified by the scientific case made by either side.

Evidence will not speak for itself in the *Federal Register*. OSHA will make it speak. Before the docket closes (but after any hearings), a common strategy for active participants is to submit a post-hearing brief. The brief is typically much more extensive than the initial written comments, sometimes totaling hundreds of pages, since it builds on the entire record that has been developed. Parties submit post-hearing briefs with a number of goals in mind. First, participants provide additional evidence that OSHA requested, or that responds to arguments made by other participants. Second, many participants view the brief as a symbolic gesture that reflects the significance of the rule to a constituency, in a last effort to show that one's "chips are on the table" (in the words of one attorney). Union representatives also noted the symbolic weight it has for workers who were brought to testify – they get to see their role in the larger argument made by the union.

The most important use for post-hearing briefs is as a summary and analysis of the docket as a whole. One union official, echoing the skepticism of others, noted: "I'd like to say the goal is to convince OSHA to do the right thing, but if we haven't convinced them before we write the brief, then we're not likely to convince them in the brief." Rather, if OSHA is predisposed to a particular conclusion, the brief has already laid out the evidence, ready for inclusion in the preamble. For attorneys, the brief also outlines a case for what "substantial evidence" requires. The submission caps the effort to patrol the record and demonstrates to the agency how strong a position will be in court if a lawsuit becomes necessary. A brief unlikely to persuade nevertheless may still provoke further caution and preparation by OSHA.

With their written comments rulemaking participants attempt to limit OSHA's range of discretion. One management attorney, who viewed written submissions in "notice and comment" rulemaking as limited compared to hearings, explained why:

> It's hard to get the agency on the record. The agency determines what the record is. They can take your comment, rephrase it, and in effect answer a different question. And they frequently do that. So [in hearings] you can accomplish a lot of things. I mean, you can actually break people down, break experts down just like you can at a trial. Break them down and beat them up and raise serious questions about the credibility of the evidence the agency may be relying on.

Historic rivals like labor and management tend to fear that the other has the ear of the decisionmaker. If OSHA acts as a legislature then political influence may triumph over the merits. The more court-like the rulemaking process can become, some believe, the greater the likelihood that the evidence (and not politics) will reign, or at least constrain the decisionmaker.

Rulemaking hearings
In concept, OSHA hearings are relatively simple. Though the OSH Act provides for hearings at the request of an interested party, OSHA routinely anticipates such requests and announces hearings with the publication of the proposed rule. Based on requests in initial comment letters, hearings may be scheduled at locations around the country in addition to those in Washington. At the hearings, OSHA presents a panel of experts to discuss the basis, intent, and meaning of the proposed rule. Other parties may present their own panels by notifying OSHA in advance. Participants are requested to provide an advance copy of their testimony for distribution to other participants, though in practice testimony is often not available to others until the day of the hearing. Written testimony carries the same evidentiary weight as oral presentation. Participants then voluntarily make themselves available for cross-examination. An important, generally accepted norm is that only parties who have made presentations are entitled to ask questions of other participants.[49] An administrative law judge oversees the proceedings, and a transcript is taken.

When clients hire attorneys to assist with rulemakings, attorneys frequently assist in the drafting of hearing testimony. Both trade associations and unions are able to provide technical input, but attorneys of both stripes reported that they are responsible for organizing it into a meaningful presentation. Unlike trials, where parties may present testimony for weeks, the time of rulemaking participants is sharply limited, and complex issues must be narrowed to a brief synopsis. The leading consideration for one management attorney is simply knowing the audience: "What does the agency really want to hear? You've got sixteen minutes. What is the best use of your time?" In the group process of preparing for hearings, the lawyer may have the specific role, in the words of one union attorney, of taking the client's technical and political input and "organizing the material in a way that we think will be effective for the particular structure we're feeding into."

At one level, hearings simply provide a sense of participation and an opportunity to be heard. Though oral and written testimony weighs equally before OSHA, one union official prefers witness testimony because "it psychologically weighs more to our workers if we're there and present it." Interest groups frequently bring workers or plant managers – people on the front lines – to provide practical input on a rule. Testimony by injured or sick workers, or by the widows and co-workers of deceased employees, can be emotionally powerful.

"Practical" testimony also makes points not easily expressed in a comment letter and underlines the most important points from the written submissions. Unions in particular have made extensive use of panels of workers, a technique one leading union adopted for rulemaking in the late 1970s, following success with panels in collective bargaining disputes. A union member's contention that a co-worker would still be alive had the proposed rule been in place provides affirmative evidence for the general claim that the rule would prevent needless deaths. As a form of expertise, such testimony may not be broad-based, but it is difficult to contest. Cumulatively, personal narratives can stiffen the agency's backbone on feasibility issues. Industry can benefit from practical testimony as well, casting doubt on the agency's expertise and forcing the agency to prove feasibility in particular cases, not just the aggregate. Many participants think the agency's technical staff will be more receptive to technical testimony. As one trade association attorney emphasized,

> One of the most persuasive things we ever did was bring a bunch of technical guys to an OSHA meeting. These were guys from out in the field and they were in their red flannel, we were in our blue suits; it was kind of funny. But these guys said "you mean we would have to do 'blank'? That's crazy," and it really made an impression on OSHA.

Because OSHA and courts operate at 10,000 feet rather than at ground level, industry representatives commonly point to the significant effect of practical experience on specific points, whether they are pursuing administrative or judicial resolutions.

When testimony or evidence builds a positive case for a claim, cross-examination follows by those attempting to distinguish or diminish it. Since patrolling the record involves making negative arguments (i.e., "3 ppm is unreasonable") as much as making affirmative ones ("5 ppm would be reasonable"), attorneys particularly emphasize their role in the cross-examination of witnesses. The written format for initial comments allows participants to state boldly, or to overstate, their case; cross-examination may discredit an opponent's case or expose its weaknesses.[50] OSHA's experts themselves are leading targets. Their responses to cross-examination may reveal their own biases or unreasonableness. What is the evidence they relied on? What helped them resolve uncertainty? How do they defend weaknesses in their evidence?

Some limits are in force during cross-examination. Time is limited, though the ALJ may grant extensions. Rather than probing all issues in a written submission, one must emphasize the key weaknesses – go for the jugular, so to speak. The voluntary nature of participation in hearings works against that pressure. One management attorney described seeking a delicate balance in cross-examination:

> If there's any lawyer's art involved in this particular process, this is it, because at an OSHA rulemaking hearing one is not technically required to submit to cross-examination. You're allowed to make a statement, read it if you want to, make an extemporaneous statement, say "thank you very much" and go home, if that's what you want to do. Most people, however, are willing to accept questions, and the lawyer's art in that environment is to engage people – enough so you can examine them.

In the adversarial model, the goal is to challenge and minimize the opponents' testimony and evidence, not to engage in a discussion. The attorney quoted above acknowledges that the full force of trial techniques must be restrained, because rulemaking participants are not bound to cross-examination as in a trial.

If the examination mode triumphs over the discussion mode, moreover, the questions may be more important than the answers – where the mere question says all that needs to be said. When practitioners describe their objectives in questioning, they emphasize asking questions that point out errors. If attorneys have had advance opportunity to research upcoming witnesses, their questions will attempt to cast doubt on the record, not proof. One management attorney's experience illustrated the approach. In an OSHA rulemaking, he recounted,

> OSHA and the unions had called several witnesses who sought different types of controls in industry. Some of those witnesses were very well qualified, and some of them were not, and to say, "isn't it true that you're relying on outdated data there?" or that "your analysis was rejected by a peer review magazine?", these are questions designed to point out weaknesses . . . It's those kinds of questions so that the limitation or weaknesses of that testimony, if there are any, are very clear to the OSHA panel.

The classic warning for trial lawyers is never to ask a question without knowing the witness's answer. The same caveat applies in hybrid rulemaking, where the advocate's perceived expertise comes to the fore. Skillfully phrased questions draw attention to particular facts and imply a wider conclusion. One management attorney even refuses clients who press to ask a question at hearings. When asked why, the lawyer replied:

> Well, the trouble is, people who don't do any cross-examination think that the witness, when asked a certain question, is going to collapse. And these witnesses by and large are not fools. And you ask them the wrong questions – and the layman is more likely to do that than the lawyer – then the record's filled up with more goop that can hurt you . . . If they think they have a good technical question, they can always feed it to the lawyer and let him ask it.

Underlying this attorney's fear is that a technical expert may not appreciate that patrolling the record requires an expertise too. This "expertise" can be learned through experience, of course, without acquiring a law degree. One union official – well regarded by management attorneys as an effective hearing participant – warns new union participants not to expect an industry CEO to collapse and repent, because "it ain't Perry Mason."

The side-by-side participation of management lawyers, union lawyers, and nonlawyers generates comparisons of style and skill. A frequently heard criticism is that industry attorneys pursue lines of questioning with excessive vigor.[51] One union attorney pointed to the "wind up," a question meant to impress the client because it begins with a long introduction to the dramatic conclusion: "isn't that right, sir?!" Another union attorney criticized the questions of management attorneys with an adversarial tone. "I see management go up there trying to trip up witnesses," the interviewee said. "They'll go in and [say] 'reconcile this statement for me with that statement,' [and] put the person on the spot. It's not really supposed to be that kind of proceeding."

Conclusions of what questions are appropriate presume a view of what hybrid rulemaking should be, as do suggestions from some interviewees that attorneys themselves are inappropriate to the process because they lack substantive expertise. A lawyer who examines an unskilled, though experienced, laborer may be ignorant of the production process, but must still attempt to undermine the worker's testimony. Complained one union official:

> I think that some of the most unfortunate things I've seen in the public hearings are attempts by lawyers to go after people, "so you're not an engineer, you're not a scientist," [to a person] who is coming as a worker to lay out their experience and add to the rulemaking effort and participate

in their government, and some jerk, an arrogant attorney, is trying to make a person look like they have no credibility.[52]

This union official echoed complaints that attorneys have well-developed "game plans" pursued with each cross-examination. The game plan establishes what an attorney wants to "get" from each witness rather than working to develop the issues.

Union and management attorneys share an image of rulemaking in a way that justifies their involvement. A union attorney, coming to the same conclusion, even suggested that the underlying problem of both union and trade association participation is the nonlawyers' failure to narrow their expectations realistically. He commented:

> I think lawyers are just more skilled at asking harder, more sharply honed questions than nonlawyers. I also think that, because the whole point of the question and answer colloquy for the lawyer is to put in a safe place record information that you'll use for judicial review, there tends to be a more deliberate sense of why. See, in most of these hearings, you're not trying to persuade OSHA. You know what OSHA is going to do. You have a pretty good sense of what OSHA is going to do. You're trying to build the record so you can persuade that what OSHA did was wrong.
>
> Q: Then why do so many nonlawyers ask questions?
> A: I don't know. I think it's because they hold out that belief that this may well influence OSHA's decision. The fact of the matter is that, once OSHA puts out an NPRM, it's like a big, big ocean liner. Steering it is very hard. Imagine an ocean liner with no rudder. The only way you can steer it is by jumping up and down on one side, and that's not going to make a big difference. And yes, those questions may be like jumping up and down, but they're not going to get the agency to change course more.

While union and management lawyers share many of these views, the visions of lawyers and technical experts can be very different. In separate interviews with a management lawyer and a nonlawyer union official, the two interviewees ironically named each other as worthy of praise. Both had in mind an image of the "true nature" of rule-making that they felt their opponents had reached. The union official praised the attorney (and a few select other management lawyers) for developing substantive expertise through years of experience in OSHA rulemaking. Yet, this official credited the substantive knowledge of management attorneys to necessity because "it is not legal issues

93

that are under debate. It's substantive issues that are under discussion. So having a more substantive background in safety and health is more important than having a legal background." The management attorney pointed to "a certain kind of training" that makes lawyers stand out in the process. Noting the exceptions, he praised this union official's "gift" for doing this: "[He]'s not a lawyer, but [he]'s really very, very good."

What does it mean to be skillful in OSHA rulemaking? The relevant question must be: what is the goal of participation? For attorneys, the goal is patrolling the record, a conscious focus on how the record will be developed for judicial review. Some nonlawyers do share that goal, while some seek to persuade a legislative-like OSHA. Differences in goals trace back to the uncertain balance of quasi-legislative and quasi-judicial functions of the agency. Those who see a judicial model in OSHA rulemaking emphasize the skill of attorneys in asking questions. The legislative model emphasizes the skill of nonlawyers in discussing the issues. In the hybrid, these visions are in competition.

CONCLUSION

According to some scholarship, lawyers appear as marginal players on the grand stage of Washington politics. Perhaps this is so. The observation that lawyers are not central figures in labor policy does not deny, however, the significance that lawyering and legal strategies can have in a policy domain. The cumulative effect of past judicial review, learned participant strategies, and anticipated agency defenses has made OSHA rulemaking a frequent posterchild for the "failure" of delegated policymaking. In the development of OSHA regulations, union and management lawyers, and even some nonlawyers, prepare the issues for the agency with a legal framework firmly in mind as they prime potential disputes for the court. The judicial process may be fundamental to the decline of American rulemaking, but the process by which that happens requires individual actions within the wider framework. It requires interest groups, companies, and unions who are alert to the process, anticipate litigation, and prepare early for it. Without these links, or if the incentives were at all different, the process and the decisions of OSHA may very well be different.

As this chapter has suggested, the behavior of interests in the administrative process is grounded in their mindset, which is in part set by the influence of attorneys as advisers.[53] The assumptions of counsel permeate their methods and styles of participation. Foremost is the assumption of unresponsiveness by OSHA decisionmakers held by both management and union attorneys. The "sophisticated" participant, these lawyers counsel, must assume that efforts to affect rulemaking rarely will succeed with agency decisionmakers. That cynicism engenders the appreciation by attorneys that rulemaking participation is the initial stage of a judicial record. Clients' arguments to OSHA must be narrowed and tailored to reflect the legal realities that lawyers perceive.

The political and social context, to be sure, structures decisions made by lawyers and their clients. In OSHA rulemaking, the historic conflict between labor and management reinforces the view of attorneys that an external check must be brought to bear on the agency. Wherever scientific uncertainty can be found, at least two parties will probably arrive to defend the assumptions and conclusions most agreeable to their interests. In chapter 4, I shall examine the continuing impact of these struggles in the decision to file suit. OSHA's statutory framework, largely unchanged since 1970, provides argumentative space in which to challenge agency determinations. With the science of safety and health sandwiched between what is "feasible" and "most protective," the lawyers for employers and employees have another opportunity to assert the advantages of legal expertise in administrative policymaking.

CHAPTER FOUR

RULEMAKING LITIGATION

The gaps left by broad delegations from Congress leave enormous scope for discretion.[1] In the balance of quasi-legislative and quasi-judicial elements in OSHA's "hybrid" rulemaking lies the project of creating rules with legislative effect while serving essential procedural values. Broad public participation, hearings, and the statutory roots of rule-making suggest that agency decisionmaking mimics legislative practice, but judicial oversight of administrative agencies opens up additional avenues for private parties to challenge government action, forcing more formal rulemaking procedures and legal constraints on agency decisionmaking.[2]

Framing the practices explored in chapter 3, serious and sustained opposition, often extending into legal conflict, has plagued the Occupational Safety and Health Administration, along with the other social regulatory agencies created in the late 1960s and early 1970s.[3] Much scholarship in recent years has confronted the side-effects of the contemporary administrative process, as well as the apparent disconnection between the theory of administrative policymaking and its practice. Beyond those criticizing contemporary American administration from points within the prevailing paradigm, others have sought to push the administrative process in new directions. Most significant has been an array of approaches that seek less adversarial processes, particularly by encouraging discussion, collaboration, deliberation, and consensus-building.[4] A regulator that spends as much time preparing for, and involved in, litigation as OSHA would seem to be a strong candidate for alternative designs.

As viewed by lawyers, formal administrative processes may not be the most significant stage of regulatory policymaking. After months or years of research, deliberation, and informal consultation, the concrete has already hardened around many agency rules. By the time for written submissions and public hearings, it would seem that interest groups have already had ample opportunity to make their views known, making the formal process a tool for litigation but not independently valuable. By the same token, litigation may be perceived as the select way to move the agency's mountain.

What kind of system has emerged in practice? Given the prominence of the legal/procedural dimensions, what significance do lawyers assume in this process, and what roles do they play? In order to provide a better understanding of the administrative landscape under fire, this chapter extends the micro-level examination of regulatory interactions into litigation, the phase when OSHA rules are challenged before courts by private interests. In doing so, it highlights the complex and path-dependent nature of regulatory participation and litigation. Drawing on an extended case study of OSHA's Lockout/Tagout rulemaking, this chapter further develops an account of how the structure and substance of legal interactions shape the agency's policy. In its own right, lockout/tagout involves significant questions of public interest, if only for the human and financial costs at stake, though it is also cited as an exemplar of rulemaking gone wrong.[5] Also emerging here is a greater sense of how lawyers' participation in rulemaking and the substance of the parties' contributions to the rulemaking process shape parties' strategies for the post-rulemaking period and their eventual policy and legal outcomes.

STRATEGIC SUITS AND SETTLEMENTS

Unlike some regulatory statutes, which require parties to participate in rulemaking procedures and exhaust administrative remedies before challenging an agency decision in court,[6] the Occupational Safety and Health Act allows any person who "may be adversely affected" to challenge standards. Rarely have parties been denied standing.[7] The statute directs petitioners to file in the federal circuit court of appeals wherein "such person resides or has his principal place of business," at any time "prior to the sixtieth day after such standard is promulgated."[8] Some federal appellate courts have read this to require that procedural challenges be made "pre-enforcement," before parties know how

TABLE 4.1: Leading objectives in OSHA rulemaking suits

Objective	%
To overturn the rule	47.6
To shape how the rule would be interpreted	21.4
To win concessions from OSHA in settlement	11.9
To compel reconsideration by OSHA on remand	9.5
To postpone the rule's implementation	4.8
To defend the rule from another suit	4.8

Source: 1998 Survey of OSHA Bar (N = 42).

the rules will be interpreted and litigated in the field. Overall, interested parties have a wide berth to challenge OSHA standards in the courts, reflecting the now well-established themes in social regulatory systems of broad public participation and external oversight of agency decisionmaking.[9]

Protecting clients' interests: internal motivations for suits
In litigating rulemaking, the prospect of total victory is low. Except in the most extraordinary circumstances, constitutional and statutory arguments that the agency *cannot* regulate a subject are generally less likely to win than arguments that OSHA *did not* justify its regulation. Judicial emphasis on procedural integrity makes the more likely goal a remand to the agency and a temporary set-aside; the courts may stay the effective date of a regulation while the standard is under reconsideration. The resolution of fundamental questions in the agency's first two decades has since allowed for greater certainty in the range of possible outcomes and a decision calculus based on technical assessments of the facts. One management attorney hastened in an interview to suggest these considerations to clients, cautioning that "the client may not like the outcome of a rulemaking, but you might say 'the agency has got a slam-dunk record here. Your chance of prevailing is very, very slim. So do you want to bother spending the money on it?'" Conversely, when parties go ahead with a suit, they see a window of opportunity to overturn some portion of the rule.

Among attorneys with experience in rulemaking litigation, a plurality reported that "overturning the rule" was the most common objective of their latest suit (see table 4.1). Other attorneys were less sanguine about what can be accomplished. With a combined 42.8 percent seeking concessions through settlement, reconsideration on remand, or a favorable interpretation, attorneys and clients commonly seek evolutionary, not revolutionary, change.

Both union and management clients also consider organizational factors when contemplating a suit. The three types of litigants which dominate OSHA rulemaking suits – companies, trade associations, and unions – are mired in intra-organizational impulses among general counsel, technical specialists, outside counsel, the broader membership, and the leadership. Unions must determine the significance of a proposed rule to their membership, typically weighing factors that are not easily quantified against very limited budgets, especially when contemplating use of outside counsel. Some unions use committees to assess the policy implications and make a recommendation; union safety and health staff thus take the lead, with the active interest of union general counsel and the union leadership. Litigation decisions in companies similarly flow from the staff, who are responsible for monitoring and assessing the impact of new regulatory initiatives, to legal counsel and corporate executives making the final determinations. Trade associations also may rely on staff members to monitor for regulatory initiatives, but the matter must receive consideration from a committee of member company representatives. The costs and risks of litigation force a review, and in-house and outside counsel may be involved in the decision. One attorney, a former high-ranking official in the Labor Department, was asked what the goals of litigation were, given challengers' low odds of success. Panic and simple cost–benefit analysis supplant the strength of the legal argument, he replied, because

> when the individual members, or some subset of influential members, say "hey, this thing is awful, this is going to kill us, it's going to cost us billions, we need to fight this thing," associations are especially reactive, especially when the big members say "let's do something about it." . . . And of course, most companies want to hide behind their association and not be "attackers" of the rule.
> Q: One would suspect that the attorney, their role would be to tell them that their chances aren't . . .
> A: [interrupting] Yeah. Your original point was that [suits] aren't usually very successful. That's true . . . but there have been enough successes, maybe on narrow issues, but enough successes, and maybe the success is only you litigate for three years and you get a remand to the agency and they take another year. I mean, time is money, so you've bought time.

The high costs of litigation can be offset by the aggregate benefit flow-ing to members of a trade association. Indeed, as Jerry Mashaw wrote, "almost no better engine for promoting litigation rather than compli-ance can be imagined than a scheme that permits immediate review while avoiding all compliance and penalty costs."[10] A trade association also provides anonymity to an entire class of companies that would be lost were the challenge raised in an enforcement proceeding. Trading health and safety measures for profits generates poor public relations, a cost that legal counsel bear in their role as public advocates of the cause.

Parties cannot always foresee the impact of new rules. When it is time to apply a new rule in the field, OSHA inspectors receive offi-cial interpretations and instructions from the national office. The first applications of a new rule receive attention in the industry press and companies may develop an understanding of what a rule means for their operations. Pre-enforcement challenges to rules put interested par-ties in an awkward position of limited information. Attorneys position their clients for the worst-case scenario and so begin to think creatively about possible constructions. One management attorney's strategy is to take the first step toward litigation, even if only to collect more information. He said his advice "to any client of a large size that's going to be affected, even if it's a trade association, honestly, is just about file a petition for review in every proceeding. The problem is," he explained,

> you've only got sixty days to file a petition. Otherwise you're reduced to challenging the standard in an enforcement proceeding, which is defi-nitely more difficult and is limited to the enforcement proceeding . . . If you have some issues in mind, in my mind, you file a petition for review, which gives you a ticket to participate. Then you've got time to think about it, saying – "are these things important enough?" or "what's the agency going to do?" and "how is this thing going to be interpreted by them?" – because [the standards] are so ambiguous that you don't know how the rule is going to be interpreted.

Attorneys are partially responsible for encouraging clients to take the first step toward litigation. Corporate clients, already fearful of uncer-tainty in the regulatory environment, may not need much goading. Attorneys perceive an obligation to offer the most foreboding possibil-ities to their clients so that companies and trade associations preserve a legal means of redress, even if the alleged harm later dissipates.

Ironically, regulated firms may have developed a heightened need for "attorney-conjurers" by their own desire for "performance" standards. In their call for regulatory reform, vast sectors of business have praised standards that set objective targets but allow individual firms to determine the means of compliance most appropriate in their particular operations. "Specification" standards, many contend, ignore more cost-effective means of compliance.[11] Vague performance standards, often preferred by industry, result in short-term uncertainties about OSHA's definition of compliance. Critics, including some management attorneys, noted that enforcement of the 1992 Process Safety Management rule (establishing standards for chemical company handling of chemical processes) created disagreements between compliance officers and company officials over the level of detail required in the "clear procedures" required by the standard. Having witnessed past instances where performance standards gave way to burdensome, ad hoc requirements in the field, management attorneys warn clients when new rules present a Pandora's box, such as to "inspect the workplace as often as necessary" or "give employees appropriate information and training."[12]

Lawsuits, then, flow from diverse incentives. Suits may be the course of action for parties who *undoubtedly* object to specific provisions and desire a change in the rule, or they can be motivated by *uncertainties* abounding in rules not yet engaged in specific factual circumstances. In the former, lawyers accelerate the competing interests toward a final conflict before a decisionmaker. In the latter, lawyers protect clients' interests by allowing them a chance to make more educated assessments of issues. Deciding to litigate involves factors far more nuanced than a cost–benefit equation involving the strength of the case, anticipated costs, and anticipated benefits.

Protecting clients' interests: anticipating settlement

Cases often dissolve before the parties present them to judges for decision. Cary Coglianese, in his analysis of EPA rulemaking litigation, found that 47 percent of the 322 suits between 1979 and 1990 were voluntarily dismissed by the parties before hearing.[13] Of the major rules promulgated and subsequently challenged under the Clean Air Act and the Resource Conservation and Recovery Act, less than 17 percent received judicial review. While comparable data are unavailable for OSHA rulemaking litigation, the cases discussed in this chapter exemplify that broad pattern.[14] The vast majority of civil and criminal cases

101

never reach trial, with settlement being a leading result and a reality of litigation in general.[15] So it is with OSHA.

What forces drive settlement? Judicial review generates uncertainty for both government and private litigants. Courts lack the technical and scientific expertise to make accurate judgments of reasonability, meaning that "anything can happen" when the parties allow the issues to reach the bench.[16] Full briefing and hearing before an appeals court may cost $200,000 or more. In situations involving litigation to resolve *uncertainties* in a standard, filing suit merely protects the interests of clients beyond the sixty-day limitation while direct negotiations continue over the meat of the matter. Litigation may be put on hold while the parties actively work on the standard; often they do not even contemplate adjudication. Going to court is the shotgun that stays in the closet. For example, the Hazard Communication standard, requiring employers to notify employees of hazards in the workplace, suggests how intricate the issues can be as agency staff develop guidelines for enforcement staff in the field. One interviewee noted that OSHA inspectors have "a 120-page field instruction on how to interpret a ten-page standard, [so] basically what happens is the compliance instruction becomes an initial rulemaking."

Cases involve more than vagueness. Both management and union interests file suits to provoke settlement on substantive issues when they "cannot live with" a promulgated rule. Susan Olson's study of the disability rights movement found that suits seeking equal access to transportation emphasized the significance of suits as an effective component of larger strategies, particularly if the parties will compromise their principles to reach a settlement they can live with.[17] No longer is this an "outsider" strategy. Leading interest groups select litigation to create similar opportunities. One Department of Labor attorney, sensing this pressure, attributed the strategy to counsel. Pointing more to "management lawyers, but I'd say union lawyers are not exempt from this," she chastised lawyers who "too frequently see the challenge as simply an extension of the rulemaking." Their object, she said, was to get "things they couldn't get through the rulemaking, [believing] that once they challenge the case they can then function at a different level and try to apply a different kind of political pressure." Judicial review suits are rooted in pragmatism, with settlement a means to an end.

The uncertainty of litigation hits the agency even harder than private litigants. Years of work can be thrown back to the drawing board by a remand, discouraging and demoralizing staff members. Simply, the additional work involved in preparing for court exerts pressure on OSHA and the Solicitor's Office, and exposes the differences between OSHA regulators and the Solicitor's Office. Throughout development of a rule, advice from the Solicitor's Office helps the technical and scientific staff frame their conclusions in legally defensible terms. When handling post-promulgation suits, the Solicitor's organizational and professional independence complicates the dynamics of settlement negotiations. A government agency cannot "fire" its lawyers, unlike attorney–client relationships in the private sector. The Solicitor's independence goes one step further. Bypassing the Assistant Secretary for OSHA, the Solicitor reports directly to the Secretary of Labor. The Solicitor gives advice to advance the interests of the Department of Labor and the President, rather than the interests of individual program agencies headed by Assistant Secretaries. The Assistant Secretary and the Deputy Solicitor of Labor for OSHA typically resolve disagreements themselves on matters of policy. Interviews suggest that staff in both units commonly recognize that if the Solicitor and the Secretary of Labor must become involved personally, the Assistant Secretary likely will lose the dispute.

Political ramifications flow from legal advice. Attorneys who tell the client "why you can't" may be perceived as using legal reasoning to shelter different political goals. Attorneys self-constrained to "how-you-can" advice also may create problems with the client.[18] During the 1980s, many health and safety professionals in the agency were deeply suspicious of the Republican political leadership. OSHA's attorneys, committed to the agency's mission, limited their advice to political appointees, simply explaining the legal opportunities to delay or avoid new regulations. The attorneys valued working relationships with OSHA's staff, even as they assisted political appointees. One government attorney described the tension as follows:

> We just dealt with [agency leadership] because they were our client and we had to deal with them . . . And [because] we *could* occasionally say "OK, if you don't want to do that, there's a way not to do that," I think that a lot of the people in the program directorates became real suspicious of the Solicitor's Office, too. They saw us as not having ethical standards, moral backbone, not being ideologically pure enough. And we're not. We're lawyers.

Differences in the roles of lawyers and scientists are compounded by the workload incentives faced by government attorneys. The government has no choice over the number of suits filed against it, while budgets and staff levels remain relatively steady.

The frequency of litigation and the difficulty of the cases are in part the responsibility of OSHA itself. Government counsel speak to the difficulties of litigating cases containing obvious flaws in OSHA's analysis. One attorney pointed to a recent case where the agency had failed to respond to a comment letter that had submitted data from tests contradicting OSHA's own studies. The interest group had not attended hearings and the comment letter had been largely unnoticed. The Solicitors "were able to do what in candor was post-hoc rationalization," this attorney said, "but we were able to get away with it. I mean, we had looked at [the tests] and criticized them, but it wasn't anything that OSHA had done on the record." Frustrations from past litigation inspire calls for greater involvement in future rulemakings.

Government attorneys on standard-setting teams attempting to prevent litigation are responsible for testing the agency's final conclusions against the rulemaking record. An OSHA official, who described recent attorney–client relationships as relatively healthy, observed that "the lawyers don't want to overrule us on our characterization of the evidence – they just want us to characterize it." Others may not take the probing so charitably, especially when deficiencies in the record prevent the staff from doing what they regard as "the right thing to do." Staff in the safety and health program directorates develop a sense of ownership over projects that can span a decade; the attorneys step in at a relatively late stage. Compounded by lack of control over the Solicitor's Office, OSHA's collective frustration at its lawyers is not irrational. The Solicitor's Office has been described as a bottleneck in the standard-setting process.[19]

Agency personnel lose another degree of control when a rule is challenged. The possibility of losing a standard in litigation creates a strong incentive to settle; but settlement means compromise, such as granting a delay in enforcement while industry adapts to the new rule, or allowing alternative forms of "compliance" than what was intended. OSHA staff members are known to allege that attorneys will accept significant revisions in order to avoid litigation. On the other hand, lawyers are positioned to appreciate the risks of litigation. Health and safety standards cannot live in a vacuum. One government counsel implicitly suggested that antagonisms arise from different professional perspectives.

Q: How is OSHA litigation different from any other type of litigation?
A: You have to deal with OSHA.
Q: Everybody has a client.
A: Everybody has a client. Mine's more dysfunctional than the rest. OSHA has a lot of sort-of permanent staff, the civil servants, and there are a lot of people who have very strong beliefs about what should be done. They have a very strong sense of ownership of their projects. I think for the most part that's really good, but occasionally it makes them a bit unwilling to understand that there are outsiders here.

Though Solicitor's Office attorneys work closely with OSHA to articulate the agency's position in settlement discussions, the lawyers' professional judgments constrain more scientifically "principled" decisionmaking. The attorney in the preceding quote added, "there are plenty of times when I've gone in and said 'I understand what you wanted, but you didn't do it right, and you know, we're going to have to do something.'"

Disagreements, even antagonisms, are hardly unique to OSHA. Department of Justice lawyers similarly experience role conflict between responsibility to the federal judiciary and aggressive advocacy of the agency interests they represent in appellate litigation.[20] Though independence must be balanced with efficiency, government counsel help ensure that bureaucratic decisionmakers are accountable to external demands – and successful in federal court.[21] For private attorneys, intragovernmental conflicts create multiple points of access. The difference in perspective was apparent to one management lawyer, because "if you go down to the office of health standards, you're going to hear about health. And [if] you go to the Solicitor's Office, the attention there is 'yeah, we want to do the best thing we can do on health, but we don't want to get overturned.'"

The simple, bilateral model of rulemaking suits focuses on the government, with suits naming OSHA, the Secretary of Labor, or the Assistant Secretary of Labor for OSHA as respondent. Because of frequent settlements, however, parties in rulemaking suits are acutely aware of the behavior of other parties. If litigants have challenged independent parts of the rule, OSHA often updates each about ongoing negotiations with other parties. "But it's not unusual," one management attorney noted, "to have OSHA work out a resolution with someone and then inform the others about what's happened, and the others be a little ticked off with the way it was resolved." Industry settlements with

OSHA can directly affect the interests of workers, and vice versa. Inter-viewees emphasized the degree to which judicial review litigation is a multi-party (not a bilateral) affair. The client may not *want* anything from the government, interviewees emphasized, other than to avoid harms caused by an adversary's settlement. "Some people have filed petitions for review as a protective matter," one management attorney revealed,

> not only because they want to negotiate with the agency, but maybe instead because they thought the other side was going to file suit and they thought that this would give them a little more leverage as well: they're better off having direct party status than intervenor status . . . There are all kinds of reasons people file suit even though in their heart of hearts they don't want to go forward with a full briefing and argument.

Because lawyers need to protect their options *and* protect against damage done by opponents, the enduring union–management conflict makes the initial decision to sue much easier. "If you don't [file suit]," said one management lawyer, "you're at the mercy, not only of what the rule might be, but the fact that the worst case you can look at is [that] the AFL-CIO files a petition and OSHA enters into a settlement agreement with them." The apparently universal belief that the oppo-nent holds key cards with the government in the settlement process amplifies the incentive already created by the jurisdictional window. There is room to speculate, at least in OSHA's situation, that even without a jurisdictional time-limit, labor and management would still move toward litigation, if only to raise the stakes on the agency's extra-rulemaking discussions with the other, threatening that if the agency concedes too much, full-fledged litigation will follow.

The lawyers' obligation to anticipate and defend clients from the worst-case scenario makes even favorably written rules worrisome. Suc-cess in the administrative phase by one side of the labor–management divide may provoke a volley from the other side, compelling OSHA to undo its earlier conclusions. But success makes a rule difficult to chal-lenge. Attorneys first must identify the basis for a suit. One union attor-ney had worked on a major rulemaking where the promulgated standard was favorable to labor's interests. The rule was "pretty comprehensive," this attorney recalled, and

> frankly, we had a hard time finding stuff to be critical of, but we made a tactical decision that we wanted to be involved in the litigation that we knew was coming. So we found five or six issues that if we had a

wish list we would have wished that they could be better, and we filed a petition for review based on that. But I have to say, frankly, that it was never anything much. It wasn't life and death stuff . . . We were primarily interested in being in the litigation to defend what was there already.

Legal requirements for filing (e.g., standing) must be fulfilled and parties must closely consider the basis of their appeal. Another union attorney suggested, however, that her clients had "never really stretched to come up with an issue" that would serve as a ticket to the proceedings. Absent an immediate, fundamental objection, clients must also be convinced that involvement in litigation is necessary, a difficult task for organizations that react more quickly to bad news than good news. Corporate complacency with regard to OSHA regulations can have serious consequences for the final result of a rulemaking effort. Labor unions are more accustomed to defending legislative and administrative gains from employer backlashes.

Thus, settlements and attorneys' *awareness* of settlement complicates the structure of incentives in rulemaking litigation. Filing suit offers direct benefits to parties, including further opportunities for discussion with OSHA, increased leverage toward settled resolutions, and opportunities to bring discussions from OSHA to the Solicitor's Office. The settlement process itself becomes an arena for positioning and renegotiation of substantive issues. Alert to other parties' use of settlement, parties desiring a stake in the post-promulgation proceedings must consider their own suit, almost irrespective of whether they have been wronged by OSHA's action.

Protecting clients' interests: anticipating the courtroom

Industry and union interests in a given rulemaking do not necessarily conflict; they may be ambivalent about the adversary's leading issues. But by introducing new sets of interests, multiple parties filing suit to challenge agency rulemaking push the disputes toward judicial resolutions. An expert agency, in principle, is positioned to make the best decisions possible based on the evidentiary record, not by identifying the compromise position. Indeed, in many regulatory situations – particularly in matters between labor unions and corporate employers – the quest for acceptable compromises seems quixotic. Administrative rulemaking allows the agencies to adopt conclusions by *fiat*; settlements require affirmations from the parties to a suit. Reduced to absurdity, if all rulemaking participants entered into post-promulgation litigation, the situation would be exactly the one the Administrative Procedure Act sought to prevent: all parties seeking a politically acceptable compromise. Any party not satisfied with the compromise could opt to pursue the matter in court. "Polycentric" problems, especially common in social regulatory agencies, tend to increase the transaction costs of reaching negotiated agreements, the legal uncertainty for all parties, and thus the incidence of litigation.[22] Evidence bears out this observation. In Coglianese's study of EPA litigation, when environmental and industry groups were in conflict, 62 percent of the cases were adjudicated; when they were not in conflict, only 30 percent of cases were adjudicated. Conflict correlates with the number of parties; adjudicated cases on average had twice as many litigants as cases that were dismissed by the parties.[23]

Attorney behavior also illustrates the connection between multi-party filings and anticipated adjudication. When filing petitions for review following highly contested rulemakings, attorneys go to great lengths to position themselves for court review. To attorneys, the choice of circuits as venues for suits justifies extraordinary means to achieve adversarial advantage, since different circuits bring different bodies of precedent and political ideology. Federal courts of appeal advance lines of precedent that may conflict with other circuits until the Supreme Court resolves disagreements between them. Different circuits, thus, can offer substantially more favorable grounds for appeals.[24] The formal requirements to file are little barrier: most trade associations have members headquartered in each circuit, and most major corporations have diversified locations. Unions, too, have affected employees and local unions in nearly every state. Therefore, lawyers for all parties can attempt to minimize the uncertainties of litigation by selecting the most favorable circuit in which to file the suit.

Federal law before 1988 required the agency to file the rulemaking record in the circuit that received the first petition filed.[25] Early battles between unions and industry associations raised a threshold question: when does a rule become a rule? Following a venue fight over its emergency temporary standard for benzene, OSHA declared that a rule has been promulgated once "officially filed in the Office of the *Federal Register*." The game was afoot. Litigation in the late 1970s repeatedly saw industry and union groups racing with increasing sophistication to file in their preferred circuits as soon as possible after the filing. They applied increasing pressure on the system. On November 13, 1978, representatives for both the United Steelworkers of America and the Lead

Industries Association (LIA) were at the Office of the *Federal Register*. Both groups had open telephone lines to representatives stationed elsewhere – the Steelworkers to a telephone near the clerk's office for the Third Circuit, and the LIA to a telephone near the clerk's office for the Fifth. After OSHA's filing, both petitions were filed at 8:45 a.m. Counsel for the LIA filed an affidavit comparing their timing methods to that of the Steelworkers and arguing that the LIA had filed earlier by "some ten seconds or more."[26] At a loss to adjudicate the dispute, the Third Circuit declared that "unlike race tracks . . . courts are not equipped with photoelectric timers, and we decline the invitation to speculate which nose would show as first in a photo finish."[27] The court transferred the suits to the DC Circuit, where neither party had filed, but where neither party could claim to be burdened by the venue.

Reacting to the "unseemly" behavior of lawyers in such races, the Administrative Conference of the United States proposed eliminating some incentives for venue races, much of which was signed into law in 1988. The revised law allows ten days for parties to file petitions, after which a lottery is held between the circuits to select which venue will hear the case.[28] The lottery removes the most physical aspect of forum-shopping, but not the continuing interest in venue selection. Where incentives exist, creative and competitive lawyering will follow, as witnessed in the long-simmering problem of asbestos litigation. After a long effort and continuing litigation, OSHA filed a revised standard for asbestos exposure in 1994. Five roofing contractors, six flooring companies, and two industry trade associations each filed in the Fifth Circuit. Two unions filed defensively in the DC Circuit. The Judicial Panel on Multidistrict Legislation's lottery sent the dispute to the Fifth Circuit. The lottery consists of circuits, not the number of petitions. So what advantage did industry groups win with so many petitions from companies? The union groups' motion to transfer the appeal to the DC Circuit opened them to counter-claims by industry groups that this forum would prejudice the interests of local companies involved in the suit. One union attorney thought this claim was disingenuous, since she "only dealt with two attorneys the whole time representing all those people. We all knew what the deal was." Still, having learned a lesson from this encounter and appreciating her adversary's skill, this attorney chuckled, "it was a very smart tactic which I hadn't considered. I mean, we could have had all of our [affiliated unions] file petitions instead of just going in and filing as [one organization]." The outcome

deepens the lesson: the Fifth Circuit, vacating the shipyard and construction asbestos standard as it applied to asphalt roof coatings and
sealants, found that OSHA had not provided substantial evidence for
the harm claimed.[29]

Battles over venue highlight the bargaining power and uncertainties
generated by court action amid ongoing regulatory disputes, which may
either provoke or frustrate negotiated settlement of disputes. Strategies
also change over time, dependent on the moves of others. For many
years, union attorneys had regarded their clients' choice as the easiest
to make. One labor attorney, reflecting on the long pattern of union
rulemaking litigation, noted that in the 1970s the unions assumed that

> the greater threats to the rules were coming from management, and the
> unions would file suit, to some extent to get it into a favorable forum, and
> then advocate for more, thinking that posturing OSHA in the middle
> made the agency look more rational, and that would help in the long
> term to defeat industry criticisms. By and large, in the early cases, I don't
> think that the unions anticipated that their suits would result in stronger
> standards. They were there to set the case up.

Litigating unions sought to occupy the extreme position in order to
deflect judicial criticism of the agency. The model was particularly
appropriate when OSHA promulgated highly protective standards that
drew immediate opposition from business. Since 1981, the unions'
position has been less certain. With OSHA under less-strident leadership, union litigation appeared increasingly "offensive" relative to
industry.

The change in ideological position has complicated the advice union
lawyers give to their clients, though the lesson was first learned dramatically. In an effort to overcome the deficiencies of the rulemaking process, in 1988 OSHA embarked on a "generic" rulemaking to
update 428 permissible exposure limits from their 1971 levels. With
the recommendations of the American Council of Government Industrial Hygienists (ACGIH) as a baseline, OSHA lowered the PELs for
212 substances, set new PELs for 164 previously unregulated substances,
and left 52 PELs unchanged for which the ACGIH had proposed revisions. Twenty-eight companies and trade associations, plus the AFL-
CIO, filed suit in various circuits, which the lottery brought together to
the Eleventh Circuit. Industry groups argued that the massive scope of
the PELs project prevented the formation of an adequate record. Labor

unions argued that the process yielded standards inadequate to prevent "material health impairment."

The rulemaking short-circuited discussion, but most of the revised PELs were uncontroversial. Industry generally supported many of the new standards, which did not impose new costs on 80 percent of the regulated companies.[30] Only one substance, perchloroethylene ("perc"), was contested by both sides, and it took center stage both in the hearings and in the court's opinion. Industry petitioners argued that OSHA lacked substantial evidence to establish either a substantial cancer risk from perc or the feasibility of limiting perc to the new level. The unions countered that the new PEL, albeit half the previous level, would still permit a significant cancer risk – a fact conceded by OSHA. The agency did not show that the lower limit was infeasible. Throwing up its hands, the court concluded, "from the record and the final rule as presented, it is impossible for this court to determine which claim is correct."[31] Without undertaking a similar examination for the other 427 substances in the rulemaking, the court vacated the entire standard – all 428 PELs – and remanded the matter to the agency. The court held that the agency must provide an adequate statement of reasons for each substance. One Department of Labor interviewee admitted that OSHA's treatment of perc was a "fault in the rulemaking," but its status as the only substance challenged by both management and labor suggests it was an atypical example. Science and major parties supported the agency's standards for many substances, but OSHA ran headlong into judges who offered little deference to the agency's expertise.

Bargaining power changes because the administrative environment and strategic resources are dynamic. The old litigation strategy of unions backfired in an altered political and legal environment. The calculations of labor attorneys have changed in the aftermath. "You're trying to say that the agency is acting arbitrarily and irrationally," said one union attorney, "and it can end up convincing the court . . . that they were acting irrationally every which way from Sunday." Before the PELs case and the lockout/tagout case (examined in the next section), labor attorneys "probably would have concluded there's nothing to lose by the union filing suit and everything to be gained, the worst we can do is support OSHA," another union lawyer said, "[but] in my current dealings with clients I'm not so quick to rush into court and sue them over the whole standards."

The most common images of lawyering involve adversarial posturing in litigation. Legal expertise seemingly propels attorneys and their

111

clients into court to win vindication, justice, or profit. In the particular climate of OSHA politics, parties enter rulemaking litigation defensively as well as offensively, seeking bargaining positions and legal leverage. The choices are complex. Attorneys construct the costs and benefits of adjudication, but woe unto those who expect past events to fully predict future ones. Uncertainty remains one of the great levelers of administrative regulation. The expertise of OSHA practitioners involves skills that are experiential, never complete, and reluctantly learned. Legal expertise, then, is not the ability to win. Rather, litigation expertise is understanding how the process allows attorneys to put clients in the best possible position under the ever-changing circumstances bounded by law, other parties, and clients themselves. In practice, interest representation in rulemaking litigation takes place in complex circumstances.

THE LOCKOUT/TAGOUT RULEMAKING

For much of its history, OSHA struggled to write regulations requiring preventive measures for workers at risk from the ubiquitous machinery and equipment, from saws and cranes to pipelines and electrical generators, that can injure and kill if it unexpectedly "reenergizes" or "releases," such as during servicing and maintenance. "Lockout/Tagout" – the common name for "The Control of Hazardous Energy Sources" rulemaking – refers to the two main forms of preventive measures. "Lockouts" are locking devices applied to a system preventing it from moving or releasing. "Tagouts" are prominent warning devices signaling that a system must not be reenergized at that time. By the nature of the problem, lockout/tagout issues appear frequently across diverse settings in nearly all industries, and by OSHA's estimates resulted in over 150 fatalities annually.[32]

Following activity in the private sector since the early 1970s and some coverage in an earlier set of standards, movement toward an OSHA lockout/tagout rule began when the United Auto Workers (UAW) petitioned the agency for urgent action in 1979. The agency refused "emergency" action, and work then stagnated under the Reagan administration. OSHA finally published its "Notice of Proposed Rulemaking" in April 1988. Table 4.2 outlines the two decades of activity (and inactivity) encompassed by this case.

Since the new standard was intended for "general industry," the agency proposed a comprehensive, uniform, yet generic guide for

TABLE 4.2: Chronology of major events in OSHA's lockout/tagout rulemaking

Stage of the Process	Date
UAW petitions for an emergency temporary standard	May 17, 1979
OSHA announces intention to create new rule	June 17, 1980
OSHA publishes proposed rule	April 29, 1988
Rulemaking hearings, Washington, DC	September 22–23, 1988
Rulemaking hearings, Houston, Texas	October 12–13, 1988
OSHA publishes final rule	September 1, 1989
OSHA releases "compliance directive" for the rule	September 11, 1990
Court asks OSHA to defend certain choices	July 12, 1991
OSHA replies to the court remand	March 30, 1993
Court dismisses remaining suits	October 21, 1994
OSHA holds public meeting for review of the rule	June 30, 1997
OSHA publishes conclusions from review	June 20, 2000

lockout/tagout practices without "definitive criteria" about how to control energy in specific operations or equipment.[33] OSHA instead hoped that employees would select appropriate methods of control once provided with objectives, minimum procedures, and training. Wherever employee activities involve potentially dangerous machinery or energy, the proposed standard required employers to "develop, document, and implement" procedures to control the energy. To ensure the procedures' implementation, employers were required to inspect "at least annually," to train all "affected employees," and to retrain employees when necessary. Adding potential paperwork, the proposal included a "certification" requirement that employers document employee training.

The key issue lay in OSHA's decision against setting criteria for choosing between locks and tags – a choice between locks that make switches and levers inoperable when, say, someone is repairing an industrial saw, versus warning labels over such switches. A combination of locks *and* tags obviously provides the greatest, if somewhat redundant, protection for employees. The proposed rule required only that "appropriate and effective lockout *and/or* tagout devices shall be affixed to each energy isolating device,"[34] because in practice the choice depends on many factors, including the machinery involved and the level of employee training. OSHA expressed a clear preference for locks but

113

allowed the use of tags when locks would be "unnecessarily restrictive and burdensome" and when effective measures have been developed to supplement tags. In the special circumstance known as "group lockout," where an entire crew must be protected from a hazard, responsibility lay with an authorized employee to place a single lock or tag and ensure the safety of the crew. Where group protection is needed, placing a single person in charge of the lock means convenience for the foreman; the more complex – and secure – alternative would be for each worker to place a personal lock on each switch. To the extent that one can describe business interest groups as a monolithic entity, they were pleased with the flexibility of this regulation, so much so that some may have been complacent as the UAW prepared to launch a vigorous campaign to win an across-the-board preference for locks over tags and individual locks in group lockout situations.

Variations in scope and application fine-tuned the generic regulation to an estimated 39 million employees in 1.6 million workplaces. Some industries and situations received exemptions from the general industry standard, reflecting in varying degrees both actual distinctiveness and the ability to persuade the government of their uniqueness.[35] The rule proposed in 1988 reflected over a decade of dialogue. The process of defending, winning, and fighting small clauses and words in federal regulations reflects how political resources can be multiplied or squandered through legal interaction. The experiences of three industry trade associations – the Edison Electric Institute, the American Petroleum Institute, and the National Association of Manufacturers – illuminate the complexity of micro-level administrative strategies.

The Edison Electric Institute: keeping the agency at bay

Ongoing struggles   The interest of the Edison Electric Institute (EEI) in the lockout/tagout rulemaking was just one step in an ongoing battle over the status of electric utilities. Historically, electric utilities – companies engaged in the generation, transmission, and distribution of electricity – were covered by a set of industry standards, the National Electrical Safety Code (NESC), while electrical hazards in other areas were covered by the National Electric Code. OSHA recognized this distinction in its safety standards and developed separate codes, but over the years threatened to blur the two.[36] The EEI's interest in protecting their categorical exemption from general industry standards had led to litigation following a separate 1986 rulemaking concerning electrical standards in construction.[37] The most serious concern to the EEI arising from that rule was a change in that area to allow non-utility generators of electricity (such as oil refineries powering generators when burning off excess gas) to share their exemption. By the implicit logic, the industry worried, facilities of electric company compounds not *used for* electrical generation might be covered by general industry standards. Arguably, an employee fixing the lighting in the plant manager's office would be governed by the general industry standards, but when the same employee began repairing the wiring on a generator, the NESC procedures would apply. Lockout/tagout was ground zero in this debate, since utilities' separate status allowed the industry to avoid stricter lockout standards suggested for general industry.

In fact, the court hearing the EEI's 1986 lawsuit ultimately dismissed the challenge because it could not find that the agency had affected the utilities' exemption in any way. Even though this earlier rule's provision for lockout/tagout in construction clauses consisted only of reordering paragraphs from earlier regulations, the EEI had argued that OSHA had reinterpreted the old language to require the use of locks by utilities. OSHA denied changing its interpretation of the rule and offered as evidence a letter from then-Assistant Secretary John Pendergrass to the EEI's counsel admitting that "there may be unique elements of utility power generation facilities that would make the application of locks . . . impracticable."[38] The court concluded that the language of the provision and "the agency's position in this litigation confirm that the meaning of that provision has not changed and that positive lockout is not always required."[39] While the court apparently imparted a defeat on the EEI by dismissing the suit on a technicality, the EEI had gained a court's written opinion confirming the industry's unique qualities, a position the industry would only need to preserve in the coming lockout/tagout rulemaking.

Active participation in rulemaking   Since the 1988 lockout/tagout rule proposal reiterated the utility exemption, the EEI's "principal comment . . . [was] to congratulate OSHA" on recognizing the uniqueness of electrical utility workplaces and work practices.[40] In its brief comment letter, submitted by its long-time outside counsel, the industry association again criticized tying the applicable standards to whether an installation is *used for* electrical generation. The group tempered its hostility to general industry standards with willingness to be regulated separately. "The question," according to the EEI, was "not whether electric utilities are going to be regulated; clearly, they are, and expect to be." The question was, rather, whether OSHA would regulate all hazards – electrical, mechanical, or others – in one standard exclusively for the electric utilities. Antagonism to generic regulation put the EEI in the position of accepting government regulation. Indeed, in the mid-1980s management and a leading union, the International Brotherhood of Electrical Workers (IBEW), developed standard practices of electrical safety. These negotiated proposals ultimately became the basis of a "vertical" standard for electrical generation proposed in 1989.

Though its interest was very narrow, the EEI's lawyer was the most active (and nearly the only) industry participant at the first two days of hearings, September 22 and 23, 1988, in Washington, DC. In cross-examination, both he and OSHA's witnesses recognized that the interrogatory might affect future litigation, rulemaking, and enforcement. In one revealing episode, OSHA's expert on electrical safety suggested that the general industry lockout/tagout standard would apply to machine shops operated by electric utilities. Asked to provide more examples and define the scope of the new standard, he hesitated. "I don't know if it's appropriate at this time to take various nonelectrical energy media and speculate or cite examples," he said. "It would be necessary to look at the facility. I suspect that utilities are different from one another sufficiently that there would be special cases in each. And to speculate, I think would just be merely speculating."[41] Even if a rule will ultimately rely on nuanced distinctions when applied in specific cases, OSHA must articulate and defend the rule's general criteria for the rule to withstand legal hurdles. The reluctance or inability of agency officials to elaborate about their rule does not mean that they could not do so in court, only that at this time they must guard their flanks, given the potential for litigation.

The EEI's own presentation at the hearings emphasized the distinctiveness of the utilities from general industry. A safety expert at a member company testified that in electric utility companies, "respect for tags is akin to an orthodox religion" which is "taught to the employees, [and] reinforced by training, supervision, discipline and operating practice."[42] The EEI also testified to the "exorbitant" costs of lockouts in their industry. The evidence suggested a strategic rhetoric of "utilities exceptionalism" that did not undercut the interest of labor unions in stricter regulation for less conscientious industries. As the hearings continued, the EEI's representative repeatedly cross-examined union witnesses who claimed that lockouts were necessary. His questions did not prove that tagouts were preferred over locks in all cases, only that union evidence often did not address electric utilities in particular. Cumulatively, these exchanges added to the impediments that OSHA could expect when applying general rules to EEI-member companies.

Outcome: qualified victory   To the EEI's satisfaction, the final lockout/tagout standard left unchanged the industry exclusions. Equipment and machinery "for the purpose" of power generation, transmission, and distribution would be covered by a separate standard. Though this left intact the confusing patchwork of regulations already governing different types of equipment within power plants, the existing problem of regulatory overlap posed less threat to utility companies than mandatory lockout. The vertical "electric power generation, transmission, and distribution" standard, proposed in January 1989 and based on the joint EEI/IBEW draft, was promulgated five years later in January 1994.[43] The EEI's counsel thus achieved an administrative victory by maintaining an exemption from the general industry rulemaking and allowing the industry to present its case for tagouts outside the complex politics of the wider labor–management struggles. In the very least, with industry self-regulation bolstering its claim that government regulation was unnecessary or counterproductive, the attorney helped delay by a few years the arrival of mandatory lockout in the electric utility industry.[44]

The questions, presentations, and exchanges with OSHA officials in the hearing transcript would have signaled clearly to any court the factual frailty in the position OSHA might have preferred. Even though the UAW dominated the record with evidence supporting locks over tags (described in the next section), general evidence could not match the EEI's specific evidence about the apparent uniqueness of its industry. OSHA had no room to maneuver.

The American Petroleum Institute: desperation diplomacy

Present but not accounted for: complacent participation   The most polished efforts by industry groups in the lockout/tagout rulemaking sought narrow adjustments for particular industries. The American Petroleum Institute concentrated on complex systems and "piping networks." In a six-page letter, the API generally approved of OSHA's attempt to create a performance standard for the deenergization and control of machinery.[45] Process systems and piping networks, the group argued, are fundamentally different. The hazards are potentially reactive substances under pressure or high temperatures, rather than moving parts. In separate letters, petroleum companies such as Texaco, Amoco, Marathon

117

Oil, and Pennzoil reiterated their claim that the agency was attempting to "force-fit" the industry into the rule. The API instead invited OSHA to mandate "work authorization procedures" already common in the industry.

The API and Dow Chemical Company offered one witness each at two further days of OSHA hearings held in Houston on October 12 and 13, 1988. By contrast, large unions – including the UAW and the AFL-CIO – presented twenty-one there. Union witnesses included long-time employees of major chemical, petroleum, and manufacturing companies, including safety and health experts. Their testimony that employers used locks regularly undermined the idea that locks were commonly infeasible in piping networks. Their experience with "group lockout" devices questioned the supposed "complexity" of process networks and piping systems. With each story of co-workers' tragic deaths, a default policy of lockout over tagout became more compelling. To read the transcripts from these four days of hearings, one might feel that tags had scarcely a friend in the world.

The advantage for unions was numeric but also technical: the information presented by industry representatives did not support the generalized argument they wished to make. Dow Chemical, for example, asked OSHA to recognize that their advanced system of tags and training was highly effective in preventing injuries. This company's experience appeared persuasive, but it stood alone. The API's representative, when pressed to name companies that used tags effectively, could name only Dow. He further conceded that other companies chose locks voluntarily. Negated by unions' stories of poorly managed tag systems, Dow's success did not support tags as a matter of policy, and thus left OSHA confident in their evidentiary case for locks. Management representatives, interviewed for this research, confided that their presentations lacked sophistication. One management attorney attributed this failure to a lack of coordination between legal and technical experts. "The lawyers weren't paying enough attention to the technical issues and missed the fact that there was this substantive issue that needed documentation in the record," the lawyer said. At the same time, "there weren't enough lawyers advising the health and safety people about the right way to put information in order to achieve their objective."[46] Rulemaking neither begins nor ends with the hearings, but these were a turning point which taught these representatives a lesson: legal argumentation and technological presentations are resources that must be cultivated if they are to be used effectively later in the process.

Negotiating in the shadow of litigation   In post-hearing briefs submitted to OSHA, the API tried to distance itself from the barrage of union evidence. While the group diplomatically avoided criticizing the UAW's evidence as it applied to the auto industry, the API proposed detailed changes to the proposal allowing "work authorization" procedures and tagouts for process systems and piping networks.[47] The petroleum industry seemed willing to concede the effectiveness of locks in other industries, as long as it could defend a fallback position of a limited exclusion. The Chemical Manufacturers Association articulated such a fallback in post-hearing comments to the agency that admitted a "general preference" for lockout and tagout while using the experience of a few prominent companies to justify "tags alone" in some circumstances.[48] The evidence supporting this brief was again thin, parasitically drawing on the testimony of Dow Chemical and selected union commentators.

In group lockout situations, the final rule retained a choice of "lockout or tagout," but now instead of a sole "authorized" employee responsible for the operations lock or device, "each authorized employee shall affix a personal lockout or tagout device to the group lockout device."[49] It is a clear indicator of how fully labor unions had built their case for their preferred policy of "one person, one lock, one key". Also, while the evidence offered by petroleum and chemical companies distinguished the devices in piping networks and process systems ("bolted blank flanges" and "slip blinds") from locks in general industry, OSHA still concluded without fear of contradiction that the procedures used in "work authorization systems" were encompassed by the principles of the general industry regulation. While rejecting industry's claim that the general industry regulation would be a "force-fit," the agency recognized that modifications or "tailoring" of the rule might be necessary, and so seemingly invited further discussions.

Because management lacked a well-developed record on which to mount an overwhelming challenge, a sense of panic struck some industry attorneys as they approached the sixty-day deadline. Without a lawsuit pending, interest groups have little leverage with which to bring OSHA into negotiations for any kind of informal relief. One industry attorney in the suits described the parties' tense moments:

> We dropped the ball on this rulemaking. We didn't build the record for our position, and when the rule came out we found we couldn't comply with the changes that were introduced. There is a sixty-day filing

119

deadline, and it went thirty days before we realized that we would have to challenge the rule. I know it's politically incorrect to say, but we were all running around like a Chinese fire drill.

The API's evidence on the record was weak but it cleared the minimum hurdle for a plausible lawsuit, and oddly, the evidence becomes stronger when viewed from a court's perspective. When a legal brief with arguments presented to a court includes twenty pages discussing evidence, the court does not know – without delving into the record itself – whether the brief is based on twenty or two thousand pages of testimony. An agency looking at it from the court's perspective may conclude that a minimally plausible lawsuit is a realistic threat.

OSHA, industry groups, and labor unions began joint discussions toward settling their multiple lawsuits, but the number of parties at the table made the meetings professional but contentious. The strength of the record allowed the UAW to establish an aggressive position for the principle of "one person, one lock, one key," even as OSHA signaled its willingness to compromise with industry on some issues. The API, conscious of its weaker evidentiary position, eagerly sought a settlement that would ease the group lockout requirements. One lock would be acceptable, but personal locks in group situations, characterized by an industry representative as "locks on top of locks," seemed overwhelming in complex processes. A team of 25 workers, each applying a personal lock to 100 valves being shut off, would have to apply 2,500 locks in a petroleum refinery before beginning work.

Outcome: tolerable compromise The API had reached the position one would predict for many parties to rulemaking: the ability to file suit and create uncertainty in the eyes of the agency, but without a case strong enough to force concessions in the final text of the rule in light of union positions. The API and OSHA found a compromise in the form of instructions and technical information placed into an appendix of the agency's compliance guidelines to investigators. Drafted by the agency after input from industry representatives, the nonmandatory guidelines described acceptable methods of group lockout/tagout – now including specific acceptance of tagout procedures in "complex" situations. The agency also made clear in a *Federal Register* "correction" that "work permits *or comparable means*" could substitute for group lockout when employees serviced complex operations.[50] Unlike the rule-bound result won by the EEI, the API appendix lacked legal authority. But it fulfilled the API's immediate desire for a national policy while it gave

OSHA the flexibility to change its policy at a later date without initiating new rulemaking.

The other parties challenging OSHA did not settle, and perhaps the only winners in the subsequent litigation (discussed in the next section) were the API and Dow Chemical, who participated as intervenors to preserve their settlement from union challenges. Their briefs repackaged the rulemaking testimony for consumption by the court and defended the post-promulgation revisions as "reasonable" and "supported by the record." The legal briefs themselves communicated to OSHA as well as the court that their position was not without some merit. The judges could not have known that the intervenors virtually exhausted the meager stock of evidence in the record. Yet the sparse evidence, unpersuasive at the first hurdle, was now entirely sufficient to establish legal plausibility, and it allowed a continuing process of negotiation.

The National Association of Manufacturers: late arrivals to the dance

Litigation without participation The National Association of Manufacturers (NAM) had been interested and involved in lockout/tagout issues for decades, including earlier efforts by OSHA to collect the views that led ultimately to a sympathetic rule. With key member companies interested in the issue, and a record of close attention to OSHA activities, there were no apparent reasons why that should change. Yet, perhaps reflecting complacency with a satisfactory rule proposal, the NAM did not submit its views in the comment period following publication of OSHA's proposed rule and did not contribute to the September 1988 hearings. Like the API, the NAM entered litigation after publication of the final version, and new compliance instructions would have satisfied the NAM's members, but promising discussions stumbled in part over OSHA's power to revise such guidelines in the future without input from the trade association. As the parties headed to court, the NAM grasped for new footholds. The manufacturers' threadbare rulemaking participation – even relative to other industry groups – guaranteed an uphill battle.

Forced to look beyond the rulemaking record for a hook on which to hang its challenge, the association grasped the argument that provisions of the OSH Act authorizing the creation of safety standards unconstitutionally delegated legislative power to the agency. While the NAM would have preferred an informal settlement with the agency that would have eased compliance, taking the broader question to court was appealing as well, allowing it to express its ideological commitment to the view that government had grown beyond its constitutional limits. One interviewee asserted that litigation represented "an opportunity for us to make it clear to OSHA that the requirements did apply to them, [and] so we took advantage of it." The group felt it had, according to one representative, some "very important" and "fundamental" goals it could advance through a judicial forum. Nevertheless, the resort to constitutional argumentation tinged the suit with a hint of desperation. Necessity is the mother of legal creativity.

The litigation turned on two clauses in the OSH Act. A decade earlier, the Supreme Court had held that Congress had effectively limited the power delegated to OSHA to set "health" standards (covering exposure to dangerous chemicals like formaldehyde) by requiring in Section 6(b)(5) of the Act that worker protection only extend "to the extent feasible."[51] But Congress provided little guidance for setting "safety" standards – such as Lockout/Tagout – except to define "occupational safety and health standards" in Section 3(8) as rules that are "reasonably necessary or appropriate to provide safe or healthful employment and places of employment." Even if this clause provided the constitutionally required check on the agency's discretion, the NAM argued, OSHA abused its discretion in this rulemaking.[52] The NAM argued for an interpretation of the statute that would require cost–benefit analyses for safety standards. Thus, the NAM's counsel set out to alter the legal landscape for administrative rulemaking.

Two unions, the UAW and the Oil, Chemical, and Atomic Workers (OCAW), responded with equally creative constructions of the OSH Act, arguing that hazardous energy was a "harmful physical agent" under the statute. Thus, the rule should be governed by the standard for health standards – "to the extent feasible" – so long as the costs incurred did not "threaten the competitive stability of an industry." The unions also challenged the "improper procedures" that led to revisions for "minor" servicing and "complex" group lockout.[53] Since unions were more satisfied with the final rule, they assumed a defensive position and sought only narrow revisions to it. Their primary goal was to justify the rule OSHA had adopted.

Defending itself from both attacks, OSHA asserted the presence of limits on its delegated authority and rejected the unions' call for additional protections in the rule. In its brief to the court, the agency claimed that "health" standards must concern risks to health that are "subtle" and "insidious" like carcinogens.[54] The agency sought safe ground in the nebulous definition of "occupational safety and health standards" in Section 3(8). In light of the Supreme Court's landmark *Benzene* decision, "reasonably necessary or appropriate" placed a ceiling on OSHA's discretion by requiring that a rule substantially reduce a significant risk without being technologically or economically infeasible.[55] The agency asserted, in response to union claims, that its approach to group lockout was "realistic and practical."

Outcome: delay and legal defeat   In its July 1991 decision, the DC Circuit rejected the "dictionary game" played by unions in order to place Lockout/Tagout under the same standard as health standards. The court held that Section 3(8) could govern the creation of safety standards, as the agency had hoped, but repudiated OSHA's interpretation of it. OSHA had acknowledged that its rules must be feasible, a concession which may have been sufficient had it been used solely as a defense against the NAM's attack. Yet, by also refusing to adopt a more stringent rule even if (as labor claimed) additional protections were feasible, the agency had asserted discretion to adopt any policy between taking "the industry to the verge of economic ruin" and doing "nothing at all. All positions in between are evidently equally valid."[56] Labor's attempt to position OSHA in the "reasonable" middle exposed the fact that the agency's authority had a ceiling but no floor.

Section 3(8) *could* limit the agency's decisionmaking, the court continued, if interpreted to include some form of cost–benefit analysis.[57] The NAM failed in its bid to reshape OSHA's statutory obligations, however, because cost–benefit analysis was only a *permissible* interpretation, and other interpretations might also prevent OSHA from claiming unlimited, unconstitutional discretion. The court remanded the rule to OSHA for further consideration.[58]

The rulemaking dance labored slowly and quietly to an uneventful resolution. The court refused to make the remanded rule void but ordered bimonthly reports from the agency. A year later – and three years after the publication of the final rule – the appellate court lamented "it is certainly hard to detect any affirmative evidence of Department compliance with our mandate," and found the Department's behavior "not inconsistent with complete recalcitrance."[59] In March 1993, OSHA released its "careful examination" of the statutory criteria and humbly protested that it "certainly did not intend to claim . . . unfettered authority in the lockout/tagout rulemaking."[60] The agency, quietly defending its turf, outlined six factors that limit

123

discretion and denied the need for formal cost–benefit analysis. The court relented. In October 1994, the court rejected much of OSHA's reasoning as mere restatement but conceded that the Act adequately limits discretion by requiring a "high degree of worker protection" from rules.[61] The panel refused to decide whether the Act requires cost–benefit analysis since the costs and benefits in this case were "reasonably related." After settling the fundamental issues, the court accepted OSHA's defense of the substantive issues, including the preference for lockout. Four years of litigation thus ended without a substantial change to the lockout/tagout rule.

Litigation on constitutional principles confirms expectations about the interplay of rulemaking participation and subsequent litigation. Without its substantive views on the rulemaking record, the NAM was unable to affect the final rule, and in fact, the lack of industry participation allowed labor unions to sway the final rule. The lack of participation, or the failure to develop a plausible case, threatens to place an interest group outside the sphere of negotiated solutions. The question cannot be whether the NAM was in error in pursuing the constitutional argument. Rather, its error was in not allowing itself the choice at that stage by participating substantially in the rulemaking record, which might have changed the incentives for OSHA before the agency published its rule, or opened up opportunities for continued informal negotiation with the government.

Lessons learned

On June 30, 1997, the US Occupational Safety and Health Association called a perfunctory hearing to review the impact of Lockout/Tagout.[62] The ragged Department of Labor hearing room in Washington, DC filled with a diverse collection of business lobbyists, lawyers, and labor union representatives, who chatted comfortably across partisan lines before watching organizations from their ranks offer statements and witnesses to a panel of agency officials. Few, if any, of the representatives expected momentous change to result from this hearing, which OSHA was conducting as required by Executive Order 12866 and the Regulatory Flexibility Act. As if to match expectations, the review published on June 20, 2000 concluded that no change should be made to the rule.[63] The attendance at the 1997 meeting by a full complement of opposing business and labor groups would not be noteworthy but for the shared history among interest groups affected by OSHA's Lockout/Tagout rule. In the broad analysis, the ability of labor unions to alter the course put forward by OSHA reinforces the lesson that the obvious resource advantages of business interests do not always translate into policy success.[64] More specifically, the gathering of lobbyists and lawyers laid bare the understood cause of the surprising policy shift: uneven levels of participation by labor and management interests in the formal stages of the rulemaking process. Those industry groups, burned once, could not ignore this regulatory review hearing, however minor. Given the inevitable clashes between the public sphere and corporate interests, the choice for firms "is not whether to participate . . . but how and when to participate."[65]

The organizational lapse that prevented more effective rulemaking participation by the petroleum and chemical industries is easily appreciated. Why the NAM, after decades of recorded interest in lockout/tagout issues, did not become significantly involved in the administrative rulemaking is more difficult to understand. Nevertheless, contrasted with the experiences of the API and the EEI, it evidences the effect that overlapping spheres of administrative and legal decisionmaking have on the interactions between public and private parties in regulatory policymaking. The introduction of evidence and arguments into the administrative process serves a dual purpose: persuading the agency on the merits, if at all possible, and building anticipated legal cases from existing structures of statutory obligations and judicial precedent, with the goal of changing the agency's incentives. Allowing this are legal structures that are themselves malleable and transformable.

Private interests accumulate the "resources" that allow influence in public decisionmaking over the short and long terms. The EEI's pursuit of lockout/tagout issues stretched across multiple rulemakings and it already had evidentiary resources stockpiled when the general industry proceedings began. The positions of interest groups are highly fluid, because rather than a store of political and experiential capital – which the NAM has in spades – the legal currency of the system follows different processes. In the discrete encounters that are individual rulemakings, repeat players have advantages but must utilize them in order to claim them.[66] Not all windows can be opened once the process has shut them. Political power is reconstituted through the formal, fact-driven process in which interest representatives engage OSHA and one another.

Although political scientists have recognized the importance of legal culture to the informal relations that develop in policy networks,[67] scholars have been slow to connect the legal strategies of interest groups with the institutional setting of policymaking.[68] Setting aside the normative concerns some scholars raise about the resources of time, money, and expertise necessary to credibly threaten litigation and enter post-rulemaking negotiations,[69] bargaining power flows from the creation of regulatory positions that are persuasive within the manipulable logic of the law as understood by courts. The industry representatives who flocked to meet with OSHA for the uneventful hearing in June 1997 had come to appreciate that relief from regulation would be found where scientific merits and political interests also could be translated into legal possibilities. Moreover, the bridge between the individual behaviors and legal frameworks can be traveled in both directions, as frameworks shape behavior and behaviors create frameworks.

LAWYERS AND THE SEARCH FOR CONSENSUAL RULEMAKING

Appellate litigation during the agency's first decade frequently involved landmark issues for the development of OSHA and administrative law. Because attorneys knew that early decisions would shape future OSHA rulemaking – and because of fundamental substantive disagreements – the agency, labor, and management reached few compromises once battle lines were drawn. "Missionary" zeal commonly drives regulatory agencies in their early years, creating a game of regulatory "chicken" where no side benefits by being the first to compromise. The natural progression toward narrower, more technical issues decreases the risks associated with negotiated resolution of suits. In settling the API's lock-out/tagout suit, for example, the agency satisfied the industry's immediate needs with a compliance directive, yet eluded the group's call for a formal "settlement agreement," which would have placed the court's imprimatur on the revision and limited the agency's flexibility. Interests, not ideologies, were at stake in the "complex group lockout" exception.

The evolution of OSHA law in the 1980s coincided with an intellectual and political movement toward negotiated rulemaking. Challenging the APA's commitment to "agency expertise," Philip J. Harter led the call for consensus-building processes to short-circuit the notice-and-comment format.[70] In a typical "Reg Neg" an agency organizes a committee of interested parties and gives them wide latitude to develop a rule proposal. The agency participates in the proceedings, but the moment belongs to the private parties, who address each other directly in an attempt to find mutual agreement. After the agency has introduced the topic under discussion, the parties may draw on any bargaining chips. Two parties normally at odds may bargain with otherwise unrelated issues. The groups' compromise proposal then becomes the agency's formal proposal, and "regular" notice-and-comment rulemaking ensues. Since major parties have already accepted the rule, the rulemaking should be smooth, quick, and with fewer surprises, though the parties retain rights to seek judicial review. Proponents of negotiated rulemaking believed that consensus-building keeps agency policy out of the hands of lawyers and courts.[71]

The EPA experience with Reg Neg since 1983 has done the most to clarify the limitations of negotiation.[72] Since the public creates the proposal, the question of who participates is even more important than in conventional rulemaking: normatively, so that the rule reflects the consensus of a pluralist society, and instrumentally, because failure to include parties with genuine stakes in the outcome increases the likelihood of court challenges. Yet, too many parties make negotiation and collective action more difficult. The Department of Labor recommends that the number of distinct interests "must be no higher than can be adequately represented on a committee of 25 or fewer members at the table, provided that this includes all the key interests."[73] Agencies have learned another lesson: not all issues are amenable to negotiated rulemaking. Broad policy questions, particularly those involving core values, are least suited to negotiation. "How to" decisions, such as the rules for exemptions from regulations, or the choice of technologies when the acceptability requirements have been set, increase the prospects for resolution.[74] The combined requirements of size and substance may be too difficult to meet. Between 1983 and 1996, only thirty-five final rules – a mere 0.07 percent of all rules by federal agencies – were promulgated through negotiated rulemaking.[75]

OSHA has struggled to apply Reg Neg. OSHA's first attempt in 1983 and 1984 on a benzene standard stalled short of a draft standard, so OSHA completed the rule through conventional rulemaking – 1,526 days after the Reg Neg effort was announced. OSHA credited this first attempt with having narrowed the issues, and the rule was not challenged in court. The agency may have learned more from litigation than from negotiation, however, since the previous attempts at a benzene regulation had already spawned years of litigation. The agency's second attempt at Reg Neg began in 1985 for the carcinogen methylenedianiline (MDA), and though a final rule based on the negotiated recommendations was not issued until 1992, the rule was not challenged in court. OSHA's third negotiated rulemaking, for the steel erection industry, began in May 1994 with Philip Harter as facilitator. In July 1997, the committee presented a consensus proposal to OSHA, an NPRM was published in August 1998, and the final rule was published during the closing days of the Clinton administration in January 2001.[76]

OSHA might take comfort in the growing evidence from other agencies that negotiated rulemaking cannot speed up rulemaking or prevent suits challenging final rules.[77] Despite expressing continued interest in negotiated rulemaking,[78] OSHA has targeted very few rulemakings for Reg Neg. Many potential issues have been unsuitable because the acceptable exposure levels for workers, and corresponding fundamental value questions, have been in dispute. But OSHA's difficulties – probably more serious than those of other agencies – have been compounded by internal delay and opposition to the recommendations of Reg Neg committees.[79]

By some accounts, the agency is frozen into a regulatory framework that focuses on answering scientific questions rather than practical, technical questions amenable to compromise. Consider OSHA's approval of a joint agreement to reduce asphalt fumes in highway paving. OSHA had proposed a PEL for asphalt fumes in the failed "air contaminants" PEL project, and mounting evidence pointed to the fumes' carcinogenicity. Yet, the scientific research provided few clear answers, particularly regarding whether the moderate exposure of road construction workers significantly increased their risk of cancer. The situation was classic. One interviewee active in the issue anticipated "a huge battle" if OSHA ever went forward with a rulemaking. "People were just going to be beating each other bloody over the interpretation of the research and the data," he said, "and it would be one Ph.D. on one side versus one Ph.D. on another side." When the National Institute for Occupational Safety and Health (NIOSH) and the Department of Transportation drafted a research conclusion labeling asphalt fumes a carcinogen, the fear of third-party tort liability motivated industry groups and their attorneys to join organized labor in joint negotiations with NIOSH.[80] With a long-time union attorney acting as an intermediary and consultant, the National Asphalt Pavement Association (NAPA), the Laborers' International Union of North America, the Laborers' Health and Safety Fund, the International Union of Operating Engineers, and the country's six manufacturers of highway-class asphalt pavement equipment negotiated an agreement to install engineering controls on new road pavers. Under the agreement, signed January 9, 1997, new highway pavers must include ventilation systems to capture at least 80 percent of the asphalt fumes, effectively lowering worker exposure to safe levels, even allowing for the uncertainty of present medical research. The agreement was completed in approximately eighteen months.

Why was this negotiated agreement so quickly (if not easily) accomplished? Most important, the parties narrowed the dispute by agreeing to disagree about the scientific evidence, and focus instead on existing technology as a means of abatement.[81] All six manufacturers agreed to the standards, keeping the competitive playing field equal; and the agreement excluded smaller, nonhighway pavers while setting aside the question of retrofitting existing highway pavers. In short, consensus was built around narrow, practical questions rather than the difficult science of health risks. The parties subsequently overcame resistance within OSHA to win the agency's endorsement for the agreement. OSHA officials, nearly frozen in belief that the science underlying a PEL must be resolved before moving forward, avoided making perfect the enemy of the good once they were persuaded that scientific research could continue and future regulatory options would remain open.

OSHA's reluctant nod toward consensus-building includes the use of "stakeholder" meetings prior to proposing rules to solicit input from interested parties. Stakeholder "dialogue" occurs in both informal meetings with individual interests and facilitated meetings with diverse groups, which the agency uses to share concept papers and working drafts of proposed standards. Most major rulemaking efforts since the mid-1990s have included outreach to stakeholders. Both union and management interviewees were hopeful but sanguine about such efforts, noting that stakeholder meetings symbolically repackage the efforts OSHA has *always* made to solicit feedback. The lockout/tagout rulemaking demonstrates that participants have extensive opportunities to offer their opinions to the agency, sometimes years before a rule proposal. "The agency would be foolish to go out with a proposal that only people inside the agency have ever seen," a high-ranking OSHA official said, "so we've always vetted various options around quietly. Now we're doing it a little more publicly, I guess. That's probably the way it has changed."

Without a change in the agency's responsiveness to public input, stakeholders will be disappointed by their early intervention. OSHA personnel keep an unofficial list of issues raised at stakeholder meetings but do not take a transcript. One management attorney found that after a stakeholder meeting, written comments to the docket were still more important, because

> the agency didn't quite listen the way they should have. So we filed these comments and the director of safety standards, who was at a [trade association] meeting, lately said "well, we really do think that [the trade association] did us a favor by filing these comments, because I've been trying to look at some of these issues. After we got these comments we didn't have any choice, now we've got to look into it." . . . I'd rather put it on the record that we've raised it and let them see if they can really respond to it.

OSHA and industry remain adversaries. Only the formal weight of a written comment can compel agency action. Indeed, the lawyers' imperative to protect client interests makes litigation likely, despite OSHA's expanded public participation. The best their clients can hope for, one management attorney opined, would be that "the stakeholder process would flesh out some of this stuff so that [OSHA staff] don't make dumb mistakes. Are the rules still going to be challenged? Absolutely. Eventually somebody's ox gets gored and somebody will . . . challenge these regulations." Interests and ideologies run deep.

"Consensus has never been a realistic or achievable goal for OSHA," one union attorney interviewee argued.

> Seeking it out essentially gives people who are opponents of regulation a potential veto . . . Once it gets into the stakeholder process and it is in this big forum for seeking consensus, it's harder for the agency to move forward without having some consensus. That gives the opponents of regulation the opportunity to veto something that would regulate themselves, which is always going to be in their economic interest to do so.

The mutual frustrations of labor and management about negotiated rulemaking echo Cary Coglianese's conclusion: added regulatory procedures are "not really even like a *house* of cards, but rather like the addition of an extra *room* to a house with an unsteady foundation."[82]

Rulemaking litigation encourages negotiation in ways that other processes cannot: the parties are limited to those who have both the significant interest and resources for litigation, judicial decisions create uncertainties for all parties, and court deadlines encourage parties to make hard decisions. Litigation also provides ripe disputes about how to apply the rule, rather than nebulous discussions about policy. "It's kind of nice" to negotiate after a rule has been published, one trade association attorney noted,

> because you've got the enforcement people, and the lawyers, and the people that actually developed the rule all working together, whereas at previous stages of the rulemaking process that typically doesn't happen. Typically they don't bring in the enforcement people during the development stage, at least not in a major way, to analyze the rule and to try to figure out how they would implement the rule and enforce it.

Litigation extends the rulemaking and transforms policy questions into concrete disputes. Whether or not settlements should be faulted as deviations from administrative procedure, their arrival must be appreciated as a concession to pragmatism and an evolutionary step for the OSHA policy network.[83]

Settling suits with the agency is the most common form of settlement. More extraordinary are the select rulemakings in which private resolution supplanted public settlement. Rather than reaching settlements in their suits against the agency, the lawyers for labor and business negotiated language that would satisfy both sides, and then asked OSHA to make those revisions to the rule. The first case of extra-agency negotiation occurred in OSHA's long battle to regulate formaldehyde. In the 1980s, labor unions petitioned OSHA for a lower formaldehyde PEL, and then won a court order to compel action from the Reagan administration.[84] After an extensive rulemaking involving 1,400 exhibits and 30,000 pages of hearing transcripts, OSHA promulgated a standard in December 1987, lowering the formaldehyde PEL to 1 ppm and requiring employers to provide both personal protective equipment (e.g., gloves) and medical surveillance for employees exhibiting formaldehyde-related symptoms. When a "substantial segment" of industry complained of the expense and paperwork burden also imposed by the rule, the OMB sympathetically "disapproved" the "hazard communication" provisions.[85]

Four unions, Public Citizen, the Formaldehyde Institute, and a company filed suit. The unions argued that the PEL should be set as low as 0.5 ppm and they challenged OSHA's failure to include "medical removal protection" for employees, which would temporarily maintain employees' salary, benefits, and seniority when they are removed from work due to excessive formaldehyde exposure. In June 1989, the DC Circuit agreed in part with the unions, describing parts of OSHA's reasoning as "impenetrable" and "feeble." The court remanded two issues for reconsideration: OSHA's failure to include medical removal protection and the decision to set the PEL at 1 ppm.[86]

The remand put OSHA between a rock and a hard place. The interpretations of the scientific data put forth by unions were plausible, so OSHA could not defend its rule with the level of scientific certainty demanded of it. But neither could OSHA simply alter the rule to reflect the unions' scientific evidence. The OMB had deleted numerous requirements for emergency safety requirements, exposure monitoring, and medical surveillance from the 1987 rule – changes which, OSHA officials protested, made the rule less protective for workers.[87] The continuing oversight of this powerful executive watchdog, encouraged by industry's outcries, limited OSHA's discretion as effectively as the courts (spurred by unions) had compelled OSHA to action. In its quandary, OSHA delayed responding to the remand, and the courts refused to set a specific deadline.

Industry and labor, animated in large part by uncertainty over what OSHA would do on remand, began negotiating independently. Though clients must approve such developments, the attorneys had opened the lines of communication during the litigation, building a professional trust through intermittent consultations about procedural issues. Contrasting the fundamental antagonisms of labor and management with the professionalism of intermediaries, one participant in the negotiations concluded that "you end up having cordial, respectful relations with your adversaries, even though your clients may really just want to beat one another's brains out." Having winnowed the parties to the litigants, outside counsel for the UAW and the Formaldehyde Institute led a series of meetings over the course of several months. The negotiations were described as at once "contentious," "tough," and "at times not constructive," and yet generally "positive," "fair," and "never truly rancorous." The process "wasn't just like we snapped our fingers and it was resolved," said another attorney in the negotiations, but "it was not a very difficult agreement to reach."

One factor contributing to settlement was the indifference of some parties to their opponents' chief objective. The UAW, though certainly concerned with consumer product safety, was willing to accept revisions to "cancer warning" labels feared by manufacturers in exchange for greater worker protection. The manufacturers, who produce formaldehyde in "closed" systems with low employee exposure, were less concerned about a reduction in the PEL and an increase in medical benefits for overexposed workers, which would have a greater impact on formaldehyde users. By reducing participation in the post-promulgation horse-trading, the legal process had helped to focus the priorities of negotiators. Neither consumers nor formaldehyde users lacked advocates, moreover, due to the active participation of Public Citizen and the National Particleboard Association. The result was a compromise, not a consensus, which was preferred to an uncertain future with OSHA, the OMB, and the court. The parties split the difference between the proposed PELs, arriving at 0.75 ppm. They loosened the hazard communication requirements, and added medical removal protection and training for workers. "Everyone was somewhat grumpy," one union participant recalled, and "since both sides were equally grumpy, we figured that we had come to some kind of reasonable resolution of our differences." Having protected their clients' immediate interests, they could jointly walk away from litigation.

Independent negotiators cannot guarantee the acceptance of their recommendations, since OSHA subjects such proposals to careful review. Labor and management linked their fortunes together in a series of agreements: both sides would lobby for its acceptance, and if part of the proposal failed, the whole proposal failed. They further agreed to a détente in the upcoming notice-and-comment process, according to one attorney, so that "neither of us would load the record up with things to cover our asses in case [OSHA] didn't do this." The proposed revisions were presented to OSHA at an all-party meeting in June 1990, attended by twenty-one people, including eight counsel.[88] On the record, OSHA responded with the caveat that it could not "make any commitments."[89] Off the record, agency staff exhibited a range of emotions. Agency officials initially appeared "somewhat mystified by the whole thing . . . somewhat miffed by the scope of the proposal, and surprised that the two sides could get together," one management attorney recalled. OSHA approached the proposal with a careful eye, but did not look a gift-horse in the mouth.

Reaching a compromise did not end the lawyers' job. To pass muster in the judicial process, OSHA must be able to defend the rule by the administrative record already developed. Three days after the full OSHA meeting, attorneys for the UAW, the Formaldehyde Institute, and OSHA discussed strategy for implementing the joint proposal.[90] They agreed that under the court's remand order, OSHA was authorized to amend the rule "should OSHA after review and consideration, conclude that the amendments are warranted."[91] The scientific foundation for the rule was still uncertain, but the parties persuaded OSHA that the evidence on the record could justify the new version.

The science mattered to the OMB. The executive oversight office initially rejected the proposed revisions and returned the rule to the agency for reconsideration, accompanied by a critical letter stating its objections. The overseers were befuddled as to how the agency could lower the PEL and introduce medical removal protection – "regulatory actions . . . not mandated by the court" – while still being unable to justify the previous, less-stringent version criticized by the court.[92] Agency officers, offering no new justifications, conceded that "OSHA cannot further explain the cancer risks, as the Court said it should, and why it decided that no significant risk of cancer remains at 1 ppm."[93] The OMB's strident response again delineated OSHA's faulty analysis and noted the agency's inadequate reply to the OMB's previous inquiry. Despite OSHA's failings, this second letter ended surprisingly: "because you have assured me that the proposed amendments are necessary to respond to the remand issues . . . I am concluding review of this proposed standard."[94] The OMB's sudden reversal was not simply a change of heart. Industry attorneys had intervened and persuaded the OMB that management now supported the regulation. Advocates thus deactivated what they had so successfully energized before. OSHA acted swiftly to propose the modified rule, shorten the comment period, and dispense with hearings. Most of the thirty-five written comments were brief and supportive.[95] The rule became final in May 1992 and was not challenged further in court. The process has been repeated in at least one subsequent instance. In 1998, the UAW and the Hologenated Solvents Industry Alliance resolved their suits challenging OSHA's methylene chloride standard through a similar process of post-promulgation negotiation. The factors driving negotiated settlements depend overwhelmingly on the particular parties and issues at the table. Still, litigation – perceived by some as a total collapse of civility – seems oddly capable of inspiring compromise and settlement.

CONCLUSION

One might be forgiven for drawing out of the experiences of OSHA lawyers a certain chaos-as-usual quality in the administrative process. Particular encounters between OSHA and private parties can be described readily enough by looking to any number of forces, such as economic incentives, professional ideologies, legal constraints, organizational imperatives, and brute clashes of personality. Practitioners and academics alike can build some generalizations about the litigation and negotiation in OSHA's regulatory process in practice. For interest groups like the American Petroleum Institute, the Edison Electric Institute, and the National Association of Manufacturers, in particular, the vicissitudes of administrative politics teach lessons to be taken into repeat encounters. Even so, the number of parties, the complexities of science, and the changing politics of courts and agencies make each rulemaking a new occasion with the potential for new lessons. Included among the variables is the law itself, which both sets the context for interest group participation and provides a tool to develop for the future. Rulemaking and subsequent litigation is the art of the possible, with the "possible" being redefined at each step. The environment set by institutions and broader economic forces plays a significant role in such a legalized environment, but, just as much, the very fact-driven and path-dependent process makes representation an exercise in situation-management and strategy.

While the OSHA bar may not be the most influential group in the administrative process, the bar does, then, guide all parties through complex interactions toward both immediate and durable results. Lawyers share in a sphere of politics that attempts to transform general policy into more tailored rules, and they supply participants with understandings, approaches, and positions that filter into regulations. For critics who seek a way for American social regulatory agencies to escape their current pathologies, the interactions guided by lawyers have led in one particularly significant direction: settlement. Lawyers craft facts and law through notice-and-comment rulemaking in order to position their clients for negotiated outcomes, and in the shadow of courts resolution can be brought to seemingly interminable labor–management conflicts. The effect may be to turn on its head the search for consensus that has been pursued through the APA and Reg Neg: compromise can be had, but in doing so rulemaking settlement escapes those frameworks both as to the values they represent and the representation of interests the established mechanisms ensure. Both borrowing and ignoring veins of quasi-legislative/quasi-judicial rulemaking, lawyers assist the creation of a process that short-circuits procedural guarantees and encourages tailored substantive results.

The roles of lawyers are as complex as the system. On the one hand, the adversarial dimensions, no better exemplified than by races to the courthouse, come to the fore in rulemaking litigation. Bargaining and settlement through litigation enhance the contributions of lawyers as they construct, deconstruct, undermine, and build up the "facts" relevant to litigation. On the other hand, the final and remarkable disposition of the formaldehyde rulemaking displays how advocates can consciously temper the contentiousness long typical of OSHA health regulation. The tools of administrative law give lawyers opportunities to frustrate the goals of other parties, like friction in the cogs of the process, or to grease those cogs by crafting a legally and politically defensible solution. The OSHA bar is one group in the crowded space of regulatory politics, and its contribution often occurs in the background, but lawyers can manage uncertainty and transform conflicts as torchbearers for interests they represent.

CHAPTER FIVE

ENFORCEMENT

Enforcing OSHA standards can seem a world away from the cauldron of administrative rulemaking. Policies that began as general goals in congressional mandates face particular problems in workplaces, and as conflict becomes fixed on a private firm, the process shifts from the quasi-legislative to the explicitly prosecutorial. Yet, since policymakers cannot imagine all the discrete cases that a statute and its rules must address, the resolution of OSHA enforcement disputes is united with rulemaking in one passage: both phases involve the creation of law, not "merely" its administration or implementation. Public officials inherently hold some scope for discretion as individual cases are brought within wider frameworks of governance. With each case, as with each new rule, the law advances or retreats interstitially.

Regulatory enforcement by the state and, as discussed in chapter 6, corporate decisions about compliance, are as complex as any problems in the administrative state. For more than two decades, scholars from around the world – particularly Common Law countries – have devoted enormous effort to understanding and improving the impact of regulation in practice. The result has been the recognition that simple models of public–private interaction are difficult to sustain. Law cannot be said to be authoritative in any pure sense, yet neither is compliance with the law simply a matter of opportunistic cost–benefit analysis by corporate actors. The connection between the aspiration of regulation and law "in action" in the field is moderated by a stunning array of variables, including organizations, individuals, social norms, the institutions of governance, and others.[1] Among these, perceptions and

understandings provide a context in which law is understood and negotiated to meanings in practice, in turn creating the context for future
action.[2]

Thus, we must attend to how parties to enforcement come to understand what the law requires, what their options may be, and how they
should evaluate those options. As Keith Hawkins has demonstrated in
a study of occupational health and safety regulation in the UK, prosecutors bring cases against defendants depending on shifting forces that
include, but are not limited to, the legal merits of a prosecution.[3] The
black box of corporate decisionmaking is ripe for similar investigation in the recognition that many layers influence the ways in which
all parties talk about and contest the meaning of regulations.[4] Parties
to OSHA enforcement do not make decisions in isolation, but often
engage in conversation with others, including lawyers. Lawyers and
corporate clients, like prosecutors, are individuals working within a
complex public–private setting, one in which the law claims authority.
Treating OSHA enforcement as but one stage in creation of law, this
chapter examines the position of lawyers as defense counsel for regulated companies and the complexity of decisions that shape OSHA law
in action. After discussing the major participants and the process of
OSHA enforcement contests, I weave a stage-by-stage analysis of the
enforcement process.

DIVIDED GROUND: PARTICIPANTS AND PROCESS

Organizational flow-charts have limited use in understanding regulatory
enforcement. Public enforcers and private firms are locked interdepen-
dently in a situation where all actors can impose costs on and reward
other actors.[5] Power is both real and perceived. Advantages of knowledge, access, economic resources, and legitimacy increase the capacity
of parties to alter authority relationships and influence decisionmakers.[6]
Successful policy implementation therefore requires some level of cooperation among all actors rather than unswerving reliance on legal
sanctions imposed from above. The ultimate product of negotiations,
interactions, and compromises among interested parties constructs the
formal boundaries and informal meanings of "the law" in practice.[7] For
lawyers, the fractured governmental organization encountered in workplace safety and health enforcement creates points of entry and opportunities to get the outcome clients desire.

The Occupational Safety and Health Administration
OSHA follows the Department of Labor's division of the nation into ten regions with subordinate area offices. The national office coordinates efforts through compliance directives detailing how new standards should be applied, written answers to resolve the meaning of standards, and review of major enforcement actions. Little more than 1,100 safety and health inspectors, or "compliance officers," in the field are responsible for inspections in twenty-nine states, a total which one management attorney interviewee conceded is "nothing."[8]

Inspections follow a simple format. OSHA may enter any workplace to inspect the site and equipment, and may question privately any employer, owner, or employee. The Supreme Court has held that an administrative warrant is required when requested by an employer, except for imminent dangers to life and health.[9] After an opening conference with the employer, inspectors may focus on a specific hazard, or perform a "walkaround" and complete "wall-to-wall" inspection of the facility, observing employees at work and taking pictures, air samples, and noise measurements. Inspections can range in length from hours to months. Compliance officers discuss the results of the inspection with the employer at a closing conference and then submit recommendations to the area director, who formally issues the citation and specifies what steps are required to abate the hazard. When violations are found, the statute requires the issuance of citations, except for *de minimis* violations and variances granted from standards.

Mandatory first-instance citations prevent the agency from performing on-site consultations, which leads to criticism that compliance officers are "traffic cops" who focus on citations and penalties, rather than health and safety experts who strive to prevent injuries and illnesses. OSHA suffered ridicule in its first few years, when it adopted en masse hundreds of previously voluntary industry "consensus" standards without comprehending the perils of converting suggestive guidelines into mandatory prescriptions. Compliance officers in the field dutifully cited many minor violations, including companies' failure to provide split toilet seats and coat hooks.[10] OSHA's lack of discretion over much of its enforcement agenda compounds the resource limits of fewer than 1,200 inspectors for 7.1 million worksites. By law, "imminent dangers" are its first priority, followed by investigation of accidents resulting in any fatalities or the hospitalization of more than two employees. Only after responding to its third priority – employee complaints – can

OSHA focus on "programmed inspections," aimed at specific high-hazard industries, substances, or workplaces.[11]

When a citation is issued to a company, the area director determines the penalties by assessing the gravity, or characterization, of the violation, discounted by the employer's size, compliance history, and good faith. OSHA can characterize citations as "willful" when an employer makes no reasonable effort to correct a known violation; "repeated" when an inspection reveals a violation cited in an earlier inspection; "serious" if the violation carries a substantial probability of death or serious physical harm; "other-than-serious" if the violation affects job safety and health without threatening life or limb; and "failure to abate," carrying a *per diem* fine for earlier violations left uncorrected.

OSHA may prescribe up to $70,000 for each willful or repeat violation, and up to $7,000 for each serious or other-than-serious violation. OSHA has little discretion over issuing citations for observed violations, but nearly limitless discretion over penalties – discounts may total up to 95 percent of the gravity-based amount. An employer may request informal discussions with the area director, and the parties often reach a settlement. OSHA proposes the maximum penalties in only 2.1 percent of all violations with penalties, and imposes the maximum (after settlements) in less than 1 percent of the violations.[12] Unless a settlement is reached, a company must file a "notice of contest" within fifteen days to challenge the characterization of citations, penalties, or required means of abatement. Settlement discussions past this point typically move from the area director's hands to the Department of Labor's regional office, where the solicitors take command.

The Solicitor's Office of the Department of Labor

As with rulemaking, OSHA does not choose its attorneys for enforcement matters. The OSH Act gives that role to the Solicitor of Labor, though at the discretion of the Attorney General.[13] Authority in turn has been delegated to a Deputy Solicitor of Labor for OSHA. The Solicitor's Office for OSHA consists of approximately fifty attorneys divided into five primary work groups: standards, appellate litigation, regional litigation, egregious cases, and general legal advice.[14] The regional litigation and egregious groups oversee enforcement cases from the national office. Regional Solicitors of Labor, who counsel OSHA in the regions, are also responsible for other Labor Department litigation, such as wage and hour enforcement.

Area directors call on the Solicitor's Office for assistance with administrative warrants and subpoenas, and for developing evidentiary records when cases involve major issues. In the majority of cases, government attorneys are unaware of specific enforcement matters until an employer contests a citation. Lawyers then begin to prepare OSHA's position for litigation before an administrative law judge of the Occupational Safety and Health Review Commission (OSHRC), the sole forum for challenges to federal OSHA citations. The regional solicitor has the authority to settle the case at any time before going to court. Briefs and possible oral arguments for appeals to the three-member Review Commission are handled by the national Solicitor's Office.

Disagreements have animated the OSHA–Solicitor's Office relationship from the start and remain common lore. OSHA and its attorneys have been at odds institutionally and individually, substantively and personally. Compliance officers often disagree with the terms of settlement or level of priority given to a case by the regional attorneys, and can be disappointed when a long investigation results in compromised sanctions. Solicitors answer by criticizing undertrained or overzealous compliance officers for bringing cases that fail to meet the higher burden of proof demanded by courts. In private sector civil litigation, clients may drive a lawsuit forward even when lawyers advise against it. In public sector prosecution, regulators may not have that control. Frustrations develop: one agency official said, when

> we want particular cases litigated because our compliance officers feel like this guy is really a horrible employer, and we're going to throw the book at him; and the attorney says, "well, I'm working on a MSHA [Mine Safety and Health Administration] case," or "I'm doing something else and I really don't have the resources. I'm going to have to settle this case." Our people feel sold down the river by the fact that they can't get the attorney to litigate the case . . . The attorney is probably giving good advice, but then the agency feels "do I have to take this advice or not?"

This official conceded that the Solicitor's Office serves as an internal check on overly zealous compliance officers and area directors. Some labor interviewees, strong critics of the Solicitor's Office, regard those checks as, in one person's words, "the most conservative force in the agency" that at times have undermined aggressive enforcement.

The more nuanced criticism is that regulators and solicitors construct different understandings of the agency's mission. Area directors and compliance officers echo those criticisms. "A missionary-minded

141

agency like OSHA," an official candidly noted, "believes that the solicitor ought to be as mission-minded as the agency is." Continuing, he said,

> To vacate a citation, or in some manner back away from the enforcement position which OSHA's field people have taken, is somehow a betrayal of the mission. Settlements are looked upon in some way as backing off . . . The solicitors do consult with the agency, but the tension often finds itself coming out into the open and there's some bad feelings.

A former compliance officer criticized the "deal and appeal" system maintained by solicitors, who obtain large fines in settlements by granting employers more time for abatement.[15] Safety-minded compliance officers view penalties more as a means rather than an end, but attorneys may not understand abatement issues as easily as penalties and characterizations. In some regions, disagreements over the terms of settlement have culminated in so-called "treaties" between solicitors and administrators. The two also have met in conference retreats to coordinate enforcement strategies and settlement policies and to encourage consultation among them.[16] Ultimately, loyalty to the client mission gives way to other pressures, legal and political.[17] Resource shortages for solicitors, the most commonly cited problem, may bottleneck OSHA's work even more than the agency's own resource constraints. In many cases, attorneys lack funds for travel, depositions, and expert witnesses, forcing trial attorneys into calculated risks about what evidence will be necessary to sustain the citations before the ALJs. Government attorneys interviewed say that in some cases they can "wing it," particularly if the cited employer has not retained counsel, but often settlement proves the better part of valor.

The Occupational Safety and Health Review Commission

The expansion of regulatory agencies has provoked concern that the combination of policymaking, enforcement, and adjudication functions within the same organization erodes due process by creating strong incentives for biased decisionmaking. Indeed, one aim of the Administrative Procedure Act of 1948 was to safeguard the independence of judicial fact-finding.[18] The OSH Act of 1970 stepped further toward the complete separation of functions, forging a compromise between Democratic proposals to place all administrative functions in the Department of Labor, and industry proposals to create three separate bodies for rulemaking, enforcement, and adjudication. Breaking the stalemate, the independent OSHRC consists of three members serving six-year terms after presidential appointment and Senate confirmation.[19] In the parlance of practitioners, the Review Commission also refers to the cadre of Administrative Law Judges (ALJs) who hear initial trials.

After an employer challenges a citation, hearings before ALJs are held as close to the worksite as possible, and the "trial" follows formal rules of evidence. Depending on the circumstances, an employer may choose an "E-Z Trial" proceeding, designed to encourage *pro se* defendants, reduce paper work, and minimize legal expenses.[20] Dissatisfied parties may petition for discretionary review with the Review Commission, which may make findings of both fact and law, based on the trial record below.[21] Its joint status as an expert and legal body – unlike typical appellate bodies, which review only questions of law – helps to explain why the OSH Act does not require that Commissioners have legal training.[22]

One expects consistency between the enforcement decisions and policy positions of "classical" regulatory bodies in the United States, such as the Securities and Exchange Commission and the Federal Communications Commission, where the panel reviewing enforcement actions also has general policymaking duties. Because OSHRC Commissioners hold discretionary jurisdiction independent of OSHA policymaking, they have been prone to charges of judicial activism when overturning enforcement actions. The accuracy of the charge may be contested, but many industry lawyers, while benefiting from OSHRC activism, see the criticism as uncontestable. "The Review Commission," in the words of a management attorney, "is by and large a backwater agency that has attracted backwater appointments," known more for their political views than judicial craftsmanship. Another attorney, very familiar with the Commission, candidly admitted that both Democratic and Republican appointees have been "outrageously political and biased – regardless of who is in charge, whether it's industry or labor. They haven't been truly judicial folks." A third attorney even claimed that "the Review Commission is not a court. The idea of a court is that it has consistency and fairness . . . Consistency means that they follow *stare decisis*. Fairness means that you feel as though it's a neutral arbiter."

Ideological conflict between OSHA and the Review Commission raises the stakes of independent review. For two decades, circuit courts split over what deference was owed to OSHA, a debate settled by the

Supreme Court in favor of the rule that the Commission should defer to OSHA's interpretations of ambiguous standards, so long as those interpretations are reasonable.[23] One might conclude that Congress did not intend the Commission to frustrate policy objectives vested in OSHA.[24] Institutional arrangements such as the separation of functions are a common check that Congress builds into authorizing statutes, however, so the vagueness inherent in "ambiguous" and "reasonable" gives the Review Commission a role to play in creating the meaning of OSHA law.[25]

Employees and labor unions

Since 1970, labor unions have attempted to defend the agency from industry assaults, and their successes in Congress have been noteworthy even at times when political trends were against them.[26] Unions have had less of a role in enforcement, however.

As a supplement to OSHA's limited inspections, the OSH Act empowers employees to make anonymous complaints to OSHA regarding specific hazards, with protection against discrimination when doing so.[27] An authorized employee representative may join the employer and compliance officer during the inspection and may attend both the opening and closing conferences. The role for employees sharply narrows as disputes progress from investigation to prosecution. After a citation is issued, employees may challenge only the period of time allowed for the hazard to be corrected, not the method or adequacy of abatement. When an employer contests the citation, employees or a union may elect party status to participate in discovery and present witnesses. In practice, workers may address any issues that the employer has raised, though courts of appeals have split on this question.

Because the majority of citations are settled informally or shortly after the employer has contested citations, the role for unions in the settlement process potentially carries higher stakes. If employees elect party status, their role during settlement discussions depends largely on the Department of Labor's willingness to involve them. Employees must be informed of settlement negotiations and given an opportunity for "meaningful participation," but what that means is largely at the Labor Department's discretion.[28] Some labor interviewees noted regional variations in the Solicitor's Office's openness toward unions, such as the struggle to "break into" cases in Texas and Louisiana. After settlement, employees retain only the right to object to the period of abatement provided in settlement.[29]

Even broad legal protections are meaningless if employees do not choose to participate. In the wake of the OSH Act, major unions multiplied the resources committed to workplace health and safety, and overall awareness followed suit.[30] OSHA enforcement generates a "two-tiered" system of health and safety regulation, with more protection for workers in unionized workplaces.[31] The long-term decline in union strength and the trend toward a nonunionized workforce, however, has made union participation in enforcement disputes the exception rather than the rule. Leading national industrial unions encourage union locals to elect party status, but typically limit themselves to serving as a resource for local representatives. A 1984 GAO study of fifty-six cases found that unions participated in only eight (14 percent) after they had been invited to informal conferences.[32] Hence, employees are placed to have only a mixed impact on the OSHA enforcement.

Congress

Scholars have given much attention to the issue of congressional control of bureaucratic discretion, and it is clear that bureaucratic outcomes follow to some degree the preferences of elected legislative or executive branch officials, thus preserving a hierarchy of control and accountability.[33] Some companies under threat from OSHA believe that Congress can affect the outcomes in specific enforcement actions as well. Interviewees reported regular congressional interest when constituent letters complain of heavy-handed enforcement or perceived injustices at the hands of OSHA compliance officers. The full measure of this activity escapes enumeration, but available archival documents suggest the character of these communications. A February 1981 letter to Indiana Republican Congressman Elwood Hillis from Tony Herman, owner of Herman Tool & Machine Company in Matthews, Indiana, asked for "any influence you can exercise on my behalf" regarding a $240 citation he had received. Representative Hillis's office asked the agency to report on the disposition of the case and the cost of conducting such inspections. OSHA reported that the case had been settled after reducing the "serious" citation to "other-than-serious" and vacating the $240 penalty, but the agency politely informed Representative Hillis that OSHA's costs in this inspection could not be ascertained without a great deal of further cost.[34] Available archival records reveal that employers have sought help through Congressmen, Senators, and the President; in cases large and small, and at least once while the matter was before a court of appeals.[35]

Criticism of the agency helps to drive broader control of regulation, such as through appropriations riders specifying how OSHA may *not* spend money (for example, prohibiting enforcement of regulations against small farms), and the more general Small Business Regulatory Enforcement Fairness Act (SBREFA) of 1996, which encouraged agencies to ease the regulatory burden on small businesses. If nothing else, both the House and Senate labor committees can use oversight hearings to put pressure on OSHA regarding its enforcement agenda and policies. Aside from general oversight hearings, the Assistant Secretary of Labor has been called to account for major workplace disasters. In hearings about disasters, often held near the accident site, the committee typically wants to know why the disaster happened or why OSHA responded as it did.[36] Whether OSHA "should have prevented it" or "let the employer off the hook," the political heat the agency takes inevitably affects its orientation to future activities in the field, where it interacts with companies and lawyers.

CLIENTS UNDER INVESTIGATION

Despite OSHA's reputation as a highly legalistic enforcer, lawyers are not ubiquitous in OSHA cases. Out of thousands of annual inspections, some disputants simply "lump" their dispute and pay the fines; others negotiate citations or penalties without the assistance of counsel. Still other employers contest citations *pro se*. How do employers use legal services, and with what impact? Though scholars have recognized the significance of regulatory enforcement, precious little data has aimed at an understanding of how lawyers operate in these systems.

The "footprint" of enforcement policies plays a large role in setting demand for legal representation, with two important dimensions being: the type of industry and the size of the employer in terms of the number of employees (see table 5.1).[37] As high as 60 percent of the total inspections occur in companies with between one and nineteen employees, an effect of the agency's emphasis on construction companies, but manufacturing firms receive a higher percentage of overall penalties.[38] Other industries, including the service sector and agriculture, account for less than 20 percent of all inspections, citations, and penalties.

Many factors limit the demand for lawyers in regulatory enforcement. Most lawyers assert that the decision condenses into a question of risk versus cost, and a clear dynamic of their relationships with clients sets potential penalties against the cost of retaining counsel. As discussed

TABLE 5.1: Total OSHA inspections, citations, and penalties by type of firm and number of employees, FY 1997, versus OSHA bar's clientele

	Inspections (%)	Citations (%)	Penalties (%)	Lawyers' clients (%)[39]
Type of firm				
Manufacturing	30.4	44.9	42.7	51.8
Construction	51.5	35.3	41.6	33.5
Maritime & Other	18.1	19.9	15.7	14.7
Total	100.0	100.1	100.0	100.0
Size of firm				
Small (1–99 employees)	84.7	80.9	65.0	29.7
Medium (100–249)	8.4	10.6	13.7	25.3
Large (250+)	6.9	8.5	21.3	45.1
Total	100.0	100.0	100.0	100.1

Sources: 1998 Survey of OSHA Bar (N = 229) (for client characteristics); OSHA internally generated statistical reports, FY 1997, acquired by Freedom of Information Act request (for enforcement data).

later, there is much more at stake and lawyers seek to reframe the cost–benefit decision so as to count other risks. The situation may be a catch-22. Without the advice of counsel, some companies may be unaware of the risks they face; companies experienced in regulatory matters know to employ a more complex equation when hiring counsel. Still, attitudinal or organizational barriers to decisionmaking – or simply inexperience – imply a version of "bounded rationality" by firms.

Repeat regulatory encounters are not limited to large firms, but firms often are unable to respond by hiring attorneys, a fact reflected in the wide disparity of survey respondents' clientele reported in the last column of table 5.1. Large firms receive over 20 percent of OSHA penalties from less than 7 percent of the inspections, and these companies in turn provide 45.1 percent of the bar's clientele. Medium and large companies (firms with more than 100 employees) comprise 70.4 percent of the clients from only 15.3 percent of all inspections, and 35 percent of the penalties. Given the economics of law firm practice, we can expect that large firm clients compose an even larger segment of the OSHA bar's revenues. The clientele of the bar more closely follows OSHA's pattern across industry types, with only a slight bias to manufacturing, where

TABLE 5.2: Average initial penalties assessed in
attorneys' cases

Penalties	OSHA Attorneys (%)
Less than $5,000	9.0
Between $5,000 and $10,000	19.8
Between $10,000 and $50,000	46.2
Between $50,000 and $100,000	17.5
Between $100,000 and $500,000	5.7
Over $500,000	1.9

Source: 1998 Survey of OSHA Bar (N = 212).

larger firms are found. Attorneys do not flock to particular industrial
segments, but to clients with larger penalties and larger pocketbooks
to fight them. Table 5.2, reporting the average initial penalties seen by
surveyed attorneys in their OSHA cases, demonstrates the attraction.
One-quarter of the attorneys surveyed handle cases with average initial
penalties of more than $50,000, and nearly three-quarters handle cases
with penalties in excess of $10,000.

By comparison, in fiscal year 1997, the average penalty per inspection
in companies with less than 100 employees was $2,899; between 100
and 249 employees, $6,200; and more than 250 employees, $11,688.[40]
Across all categories, penalties from 110,270 citations yielded nearly
$88 million, at an average of $3,781 per inspection. Only 9.0 percent
of attorneys (and 4.1 percent of self-identified OSHA "specialists")
reported average penalties under $5,000.

Business responses to regulatory encounters are inherently reactive.
Companies require clear and convincing evidence of a problem and
assurance that risks are higher than known costs before resorting to
counsel. All interviewees were asked, "typically how far has a case
progressed when it first comes across your desk?" From a wide range
of possibilities, a clear pattern emerged. Legal representation typically
begins either near the start of investigations or when clients decide to
contest citations.[41] Survey respondents also were asked "over the past
five years, approximately, at what stage in the process have you first
become involved in your cases?" The data confirm the pattern observed
through interviews (see table 5.3). In practice, the distinction of entering the process *before* or *during* an inspection can be simply whether the

TABLE 5.3: Stage of attorneys' entry into OSHA cases

Stage of Process	Average %
Before OSHA began the inspection	15.5
While inspection was in progress	22.5
After inspection, but before notice of contest	46.3
After employer has contested the citation(s)	14.3
Other	1.2

Source: 1998 Survey of OSHA Bar (N = 219).

attorneys beat OSHA to an accident scene. A combined 38 percent of attorneys entering during the inspection stages mark it out as an important gateway for advocacy, exceeded only slightly by clients' decisions to challenge OSHA's administrative findings (46 percent).

The decision is not purely economic and rational. The threshold of uncertainty and panic can strike with the awareness that a line – perhaps moral, certainly "legal" – has been crossed. In the words of one interviewee, "it's more a 'hell, we're in trouble, what do we do next?' response."

Subject to an investigation: the call to counsel
The beginning of an investigation can offer a number of cues to a company. Because investigations triggered by injuries and fatalities are seldom routine in the lives of companies, they trigger "crisis management" responses. Accident cases are not particularly common for OSHA either, with investigations following accidents accounting for less than 5 percent of inspections.[42] But OSHA executes its charge with a singular concern that resides deep in the agency's psyche.[43] OSHA compliance officers can arrive on the scene within hours, sometimes with the media already there. Past experiences with congressional inquiries require that prosecution proceed carefully, yet the gravity of the harm gives OSHA a sense of political cover. Its officials anticipate little justifiable criticism when they aggressively prosecute corporate bosses who (in the agency's accounting) *maim* and *kill* workers. Some management attorneys criticize a saying of OSHA officials in accident cases – "there's blood on the floor" – as emblematic of the agency's presumption of fault. If an employee has been injured or killed, *de facto* the employer *must* have done something wrong and must pay.[44] In accident

cases, one attorney suggested, "OSHA does not act like a regulator; OSHA acts like an avenger." Blame is easily fixed. Prosecution is, in addition to law enforcement, an expression of the agency's construction of norms and values.[45]

A confluence of factors in accident investigations makes involvement of lawyers likely. The sheer emotional upheaval in fatality cases tends to cloud the judgment of company officials and workers alike. Clients will exhibit a variety of responses. One attorney, experienced in major accident cases, found that his first step, as a person emotionally removed from the situation, is simply "to get the client to pause."

> It's a very confusing period of time, and there's all sorts of responses triggered at that level: emergency responses, sympathy responses, trying to cooperate with the government kinds of responses, and trying to assess their liabilities, all at the same time. Hopefully, it's something they don't experience very often, so the first time we're contacted [we] try to get the key players to isolate themselves from all that at the moment . . .

Missteps or hasty words by employers can provide harmful evidence to both OSHA and plaintiffs in secondary, wrongful death litigation. Concern with "collateral effects" of OSHA investigations drives many actions during the early stages. One attorney reported that by the time he arrived at the scene of a major accident, the families of the deceased and their lawyers had already formed a plaintiffs' lawyers' committee.

OSHA citations can directly affect secondary litigation. The OSH Act does not create a cause of action against employers, but courts in most jurisdictions allow OSHA citations to be admitted as evidence of negligence. In at least two states, violation of OSHA safety regulations is negligence *per se*. Indeed, a "willful" citation, by definition, means that the employer had advanced knowledge of a condition that seriously risked an injury or fatality. Because the potential impact of plaintiffs' litigation far exceeds the potential penalty, lawyers investigate possible exculpatory evidence, such as employee mistakes or employers' *bona fide* efforts. Alternatively, some attorneys reported, alerting clients to the risks of secondary litigation and other potential liabilities can condition them to accepting later strategies, such as conceding a large fine in exchange for a favorable citation characterization or avoiding criminal prosecution. Lawyers work early to construct clients' preferences.

Beyond accident cases, the appearance of compliance officers "at the door," especially a large team, raises red flags for company officials. An obvious role for lawyers is to engage classically "legal" questions. If compliance officers "push the envelope" too far, counsel can help limit the inquiry and resulting citations. Experience with the agency's guidelines helps. One prominent management attorney described the jostling this way:

> I got a call yesterday. I've got a client down in Alabama that's in the middle of a big OSHA inspection that said "we need help," and I couldn't come down but I got one of my guys there today. We'll handle the issues that come up during the investigation, and usually that's issues like "what's the scope going to be?" They're there on a complaint. Can they just look at the complaint, or can they go over this part [of the site]? Can they look at these records? Those kinds of things come up. And OSHA has got guidelines on how to do it, but individual compliance officers will push the envelope, and unless an employer has got somebody who knows the way the game is played, they'll get away with it.

Similarly, a client may need advice on whether to bar an OSHA compliance officer from entering the premises without a warrant. While OSHA typically has little difficulty getting warrants, delaying an inspection for a few hours can give a company time, in the words of an interviewee, to "clean house" and get "up to code." Warrants or not, it is clear that some companies have deliberately delayed inspectors or simply cleared accident scenes before inspectors could arrive.[46]

Attorneys who construct their role in purely legal terms cannot justify the expense of continuous, on-site involvement during inspections. The day-to-day work of assisting OSHA inspectors with the rudiments of the workplace and corporate practices can be handled by a plant manager or safety and health expert, with substantially lower costs for the client. Lawyers may retain substantial input in decisions, but this is done remotely as advisors rather than as advocates to OSHA. One former Labor Department official, now in private practice, suggested that this practice is almost a necessity for the most prominent members of the bar. During the investigation phase, he said,

> it's typically nonlawyers on my clients' side that are dealing with the nonlawyer compliance officer . . . I may be advising, and often do advise my clients about positions to take during the course of the inspection, but . . . as a practical matter, given the hourly rate that I charge and the hourly rate of [several leading OSHA attorneys] . . . it's just not cost effective for our clients.

Sophisticated issues about the investigation must be negotiated at a later stage with area directors, regional administrators, or regional solicitors. Lawyers with diversified law practices, in particular, may narrowly construe their expertise and limit involvement to traditionally legal questions.

Other attorneys, especially specialists, believe their "nonlegal" expertise in safety and health issues justifies early, continuous involvement in inspections. The structure of regulatory enforcement in OSHA leaves ample room for attorneys to frame their practices around substantive arguments. Regulations embody language in tension, such as OSHA's statutory obligation to protect workers to the *maximum level feasible*. Static language applies to dynamic workplaces, in which the forced elimination of one hazard might create a bigger one elsewhere. The assessment of risks requires a blend of procedural and substantive acumen. With experience, attorneys may claim the ability to discuss workplace risks with inspectors or, alternatively, they can recognize the potential for argument and hire specialists to assist them. About half of surveyed OSHA attorneys (51.9 percent) "frequently" or "always" attend the on-site investigation and walkaround, and a similar percentage (46.7 percent) frequently or always perform full audits of worksites after an accident, presumably preparing for a subsequent defense. Relatively few attorneys (14.1 percent and 11.7 percent, respectively) *never* respond with these strategies.[47]

"Expertise" is also built around political and legal settings. To one lawyer, open communication with compliance officers is essential. "OSHA is a bureaucracy like any bureaucracy," he said. "Once something is written it has a life of its own. A lot of citations are misunderstandings. Sure, there will be some that are correct, but it's surprising to see how many citations are the results of misunderstandings." Another management attorney spoke highly of a compliance officer in a recent case who pointedly listed to the attorney his "concerns" during an investigation. Welcoming the invitation, the attorney treated each concern as a potential citation, brought in independent experts, and prepared a presentation for the compliance officers.

> We had a total of 221 concerns. We ended up with 38 of them actually being citations, and we eliminated the remainder. In the end, as to what existed when we finally settled everything out, it was two. So we got from 221 down to two. That's what can be done when you're active during the inspection. A lot of clients don't get us involved during the inspection because they see it as a high expenditure of funds, and sometimes it is. I think your money is probably better spent there than later, but that's OK, it's their choice. It's sort of like a "pay me now, pay me later" sort of thing.

Lawyers can "defeat" citations before they are issued if they invest time and resources in preparing for substantive issues. Constructing for clients an image of the bureaucratic nature of prosecution, made worse by information disparities, helps grow the market for lawyers. Even attorneys with smaller practices sometimes service multiple clients in particular sectors, such as newspaper printing or petroleum refining, while inspectors typically have broad but shallow experience across diverse industries. Compliance officers are trained in inspection procedures and OSHA standards, but they often have to learn on-the-job how airplanes are manufactured or fertilizers are produced. As a result, said one management attorney, "we know where they're going, and we can tell them even before they start why they're going to end up not being able to establish what they want."

Attorneys sell clients the ability to sell knowledge to OSHA, leveraging the gap between law and practice. Some advocates describe their contribution as "education," helping compliance officers observe and evaluate workplace hazards from all angles. The roles of educator and advocate coexist.[48] Few observers fear that employers can co-opt compliance officers. The regulators' emotional distance from the regulated companies prevents that. The more serious concern is that undertrained inspectors accede to management's evaluation of problems. A benign understanding of the educator's role involves *translating* the clients' interests into the bureaucratic terminology. "I can't tell you how often it arises that they [inspectors and clients] talk past each other," one attorney complained. For example,

> the inspector will say, "I'd like to see the maintenance records," and so the company says, "here they are," and the inspector will say, "well, where's X" and the company will say, "what do you mean?" because the company included those in their capital budget and they don't think of them as maintenance . . .
>
> It's not that the company hasn't done this particular function, it's just that it's kept under another heading in their computer. So you're there translating for them, because you as the lawyer understand what you're there looking for, you're able to say to the client, "I know you did maintenance on this refinery this year, where are the records of that?" and they'll say, "oh, yes, capital budget," and they'll be able to produce that.

The attorney-as-educator must be sold to clients who are more familiar with the image of advocate and litigator. While pressing the notion of a cost–benefit even the most prominent members of the bar must compete for clients with general labor lawyers or litigators, whose fees are much lower. Legal fees are a particularly uncomfortable topic within attorney–client relationships. "We tend to be more expensive than their local people," one attorney said of his firm,

> and when they hear our rates – which I try not to talk about – they sometimes get a little scared. I say I try not to talk about rates, because when we talk to the clients I try to get them to focus on what their case is going to cost long-term. What's the bottom line going to be? . . . They may charge you two-thirds of what we'll charge you, but we'll get it done in half the time. Long-term you save money with us. That's the kind of thing we deal with.

In most cases, representation begins after OSHA has completed its investigation and issued a citation. Nothing makes cost–benefits clear to clients like learning the proposed penalties. Despite their strong preference for pre-citation involvement, most attorneys expect cases will cross their desks after OSHA has "made its point" to the company.

Gradations of "sophistication" are pervasive in how attorneys describe clients. When comparing their clients, attorneys often use the word "sophisticated." Sophisticated clients – usually considered good clients – seek help from attorneys at the earliest possible stage. Sophistication is a relative, not absolute, concept; attorneys for Fortune 500 companies and small businesses alike use the word. The most sophisticated large companies seldom wait for an inspection to comply; they ask for compliance assistance. Sophisticated smaller companies, by comparison, bring lawyers in for a portion of the inspection or the closing conference – later, but early enough to make a difference. As others have noted, "management matters."[49] Ability to recognize risks in regulatory enforcement – even when experiencing it for the first time – marks sophisticated managers.

One lawyer for smaller companies identified decisionmaking hierarchies as a barrier to sophistication. Lower level officials must recognize the risks in a situation *and* overcome corporate inertia. Smaller companies, he said,

> don't necessarily see OSHA that often. We always use that as a rationale for saying why we should be there, because you're not really used to dealing with these guys. But many companies tend to look at this as just "it's another dealing with the government, we can handle it, and if there's a problem, we'll call you." So we tend to get into the cases . . . after something bad has happened.

Q: Legally, or . . .?

A: Legally, right. And that tends to be right after they've had the inspector leave, or they've just received the citations. Now, we've had safety directors for some of these smaller companies tell us: "listen, we'd love to have you there, but from my standpoint I need to have something bad happen before I can call you in. There has to be something that I can say to my boss that he can say to *his* boss about why you have to be there, because otherwise they don't understand it." So there's a level of education there, too, in terms of why it's important to be there early.

The least sophisticated clients, observed another attorney, "think they're not getting into anything" when the inspector knocks. Then, lawyers only begin involvement after citations have been written and the opportunity to "educate" OSHA has passed.

Employers must contest citations within fifteen days to keep legal options open, but the notice of contest moves the dispute from OSHA to agency solicitors, raising the question of whether litigation should even be contemplated. The decision to litigate "is always the clients' call – it's his money," one attorney interviewee maintained. Still, earlier involvement allows counsel time to learn more about the client's case and the client time to reflect. Large employers know whether to litigate "without us having to tell them," this attorney continued, "[but] if he's a small or medium-sized employer, he'll definitely need counseling as to whether it's worthwhile to litigate." Entering later invites hasty assessments of risks and options. Equally serious, attorneys lose the opportunity to build relationships with clients, which hinders client trust. As will be discussed later in this chapter, since attorneys' advice about entering or avoiding litigation may run contrary to clients' instincts, building trust is necessary to overcome questions of loyalty.

In sum, costs and benefits set the baseline in determining when attorneys are used in enforcement, but information, expectations, and conceptions of lawyers' role may contribute to those decisions. In practice, the most common result may be that repeat-player companies take advantage of the services of repeat-player attorneys.

Know thy enemy: expectations and reputations

Because all parties enter enforcement actions with limited information, "soft" knowledge – instincts, impressions, and reputations – plays a vital role. Reputations are slippery: difficult to measure, dependent on whose eyes perceive them, and subject to change at every action and inaction.

Reputations nevertheless exert an influence on the process that makes them real. Reputations work in countless combinations: lawyers and clients may have reputations with OSHA, the Solicitor's Office, and each other; clients also have reputations with unions and the public. In their particular contexts, reputations may be a positive strategic resource or a negative complicating factor, but in the least they provide information. The further an agency's resources are stretched, resulting in fewer interactions with regulated companies, the more likely an agency will depend on intermediaries and reputations for information. In a game of reputations, perception creates some of the reality of regulatory encounters.

OSHA's reputation precedes it, so attorneys often encounter ill-tempered responses from clients regarding the government. Most companies interact with OSHA enforcement irregularly. Even in larger companies, individual factories or offices may avoid inspection for years if there are no injuries or complaints. Managers and corporate officials thus typically lack personal familiarity with compliance officers and area directors in their region. Contrary to the aphorism, lack of familiarity can breed contempt. Inspectors seem to be most hated in their absence. Employers who worked with the OSHA "reinvented" from its 1970s and 1980s approach say that the agency's historic abuses no longer infiltrate the process: a follow-up survey of companies inspected in 1993 found that two-thirds believed OSHA had a positive impact on safety and health, and three-fourths thought OSHA inspectors conducted the inspections professionally.[50]

All lawyers interviewed were asked the question: "when you begin a new case, typically what are your clients' expectations of what you can do for them?" Only one attorney refused to discuss client expectations.[51] Differences between large and small companies reappeared as imperfect shorthand for the difference between "one-shotters" and "repeat players."[52] One-shotters are the least clear about what to expect from the OSHA process itself – except complete victory. Clients, said one attorney, "just want to win. They're not clear on exactly what are the probabilities . . . This is typically true of a medium-sized company that does not have an in-house attorney or an in-house attorney that has regulatory expertise. They really just do not know what they are facing." At the opposing ends, this attorney added, larger clients are "savvy," and small clients are "just completely in the dark." The inexperience of clients, complicated by emotional reactions, creates

156

unrealistic perspectives on how a regulatory case would proceed. "Most clients expect us to make it disappear altogether," said another attorney. "Most clients that I have . . . are emotionally biased against anybody claiming that they're unsafe . . . and . . . come in with the impression or expectation that we'll fight [everything] . . . the citation, the abatement period, and the penalty." Tactically, attorneys may indeed object to everything when filing a notice of contest, but on the home front they begin to prepare clients for negotiations by describing the limitations of their defense.

Regulatory attorneys uniformly acknowledge that clients make the strategic decisions, but they hope to shape clients' thinking. One lawyer, contending that many employers are insufficiently concerned about the future costs of abatement, tries to "generate" concern for the "appropriate" issues, so that the client does not set conflicting priorities during subsequent settlement negotiations. Clients, like OSHA, can get "set in concrete" too early, requiring attorneys to raise or lower clients' sights accordingly. Indeed, one attorney thought, too many companies simply hope to get a characterization changed or a penalty reduced by half; "in OSHA you don't need to hire a lawyer in order to probably achieve that in 90 percent of the cases."

Though clients have the right to make final decisions, lawyers predictably attribute divergent opinions to irrationality. One lawyer described his frustration with clients who, on being cited by OSHA, "just can't stand the idea of it and they fight it. They don't have a real good reason for it and they always lose."

Q: Can you persuade them otherwise?
A: They're very hard to persuade – the very litigious-type client who doesn't really observe the regulations. People say "gee, what a great client because they're always in trouble and they're always paying fees." In point of fact, they're really not great clients, because it takes so much more time and effort to get them to do what they ought to do. You don't have much chance of winning, and if you like to win, it's no fun. And then they don't want to pay you all the money they've charged up because it has taken so long.

Lawyers may have definite ideas about the *ideal* or *proper* response to OSHA, but after raising the issues, advocacy requires servicing clients' desires. One noted attorney, asked whether clients expected a particular type of lawyering from him, answered:

They assume that I'll pursue it the way they tell me to pursue it . . . and that's a question I ask with any client. First of all, what are your objectives? Where do you want to get to? And then, what are your interests along the way, what do we have to be careful of? Yes, you may want to win the case, but at what cost? How much money? At the cost of what relationship? Even if you're in an OSHA citation context . . . if you have organized labor, if you have a union, your ability to talk to those folks, your reputation for being honest and forthright, and for not being a flame-thrower is helpful to any client in that environment. So you take direction from the client – at least I do – in terms of the level of bombast or style.

Lawyers simultaneously adapt to their clients and try to educate them – a process of exchange and negotiation of perspectives.

A key element of this negotiation for lawyers involves becoming sensitive to their client's reputation, so that strategies balance legal and business interests. Even strategies entirely within employers' legal rights may seem unnecessarily aggressive to others. One attorney's client had accidentally released tons of chlorine into the air, causing a public outcry. Later, the attorney filed a brief just before the deadline – typical when working under tight schedules – and "didn't think twice about it." Unfortunately, she noted, "that then appeared on local TV saying I faxed it in just before the close of business, and that sounds dreadful, as though you're trying to sneak in under cover of darkness." Consumer products companies in particular eschew negative publicity, and attorneys have no need to impress on these clients that public relations are at stake. The legal goals of large, established companies can be very narrow in scope. The role of counsel in such situations narrows to that of a surgeon.

Poor labor relations prior to an accident or investigation dramatically complicate the situation, making the public less understanding of the employers' position and bolstering the agency's doggedness. Employer reputations are *data* that reflect an image, however distorted, of the company's efforts on behalf of workers and the public. In a case in Maine under the Clinton administration, an employer's poor public relations encouraged the agency to flex its regulatory muscle. After years of minor run-ins and 1995 violations resulting in penalties totaling just a few thousand dollars, pressure mounted for decisive action against DeCoster Egg Farms of Turner, Maine, the world's largest producer of brown eggs. When Maine's Department of Labor notified OSHA of DeCoster's lack of cooperation and failure to abate serious hazards, the story appeared in the local press, and a group of state legislators toured the facilities. Emboldened by the public attention, OSHA responded with a substantial inspection in January 1996 and levied a $3.6 million fine, citing conditions "as dangerous and oppressive as any sweatshop we have seen."[53] Although DeCoster showed signs of wanting to fight the citations, the media exposure continued. Local papers published graphic photos of raw sewage, contaminated water and dilapidated housing for workers.[54] One Labor Department interviewee noted that it was apparent from the pre-trial maneuvers that the Maine law firm representing DeCoster lacked extensive experience in litigating OSHA cases. Agency officials were aware of consumer demands at grocery stores for new suppliers of eggs. The company's sagging reputation now affected more than its standing with OSHA – it hit the bottom line. DeCoster, attempting to find a new market in Europe for its eggs, agreed to a sweeping settlement in May 1997 that many believe strongly favored the agency.

OSHA exploited information about DeCoster's reputation to strengthen its adversarial position. Overcoming reputations to spur cooperative relationships may be more difficult. According to one attorney, "there's a general view [in the business community] that if you push at an agency, they're going to push back at you" with more stringent follow-up inspections. Attorneys walk a tightrope between zealous protection of clients from current liabilities and employers need to maintain good relations with the government. Whether or not lawyers employ "bombast," the mere appearance of counsel may antagonize the compliance team and area director, and escalate the apparent level of conflict. Much criticism of American regulatory bureaucracies has been aimed at the deep-seated opposition to cooperative approaches.[55] Yet, this classic dilemma, in which both parties flee from cooperation out of fear of worse outcomes, may stem just as much from lawyers' distrust of OSHA as an even-handed regulator.[56] When reputations are involved, strategic decisions are particularly difficult.

Styles of lawyering in regulatory enforcement

Repeated participation in OSHA matters elevates different strategic preferences to generalizable styles of lawyering. In describing their own practices, leading attorneys frequently contrasted their approach to the opposing side of a cooperative/adversarial dichotomy. This dichotomy mirrors American legal discourse concerning the "scorched-earth litigator" and its alternatives. Regardless of their approach, interviewees nearly uniformly framed their choice of style as their own interpretation of professional obligations to provide effective advocacy. Whether these personal styles stem from their considered assessments of professional responsibility or, more fundamentally, from a confluence of personalities, socialization, and experiences, lawyers' approaches contribute to their public reputations. Underlying the attorneys' interest in reputations are the two groups – clients and the government – who act as "consumers" of legal reputations.

If two lawyers approach a similar case in opposite ways – one cooperative and one adversarial – which serves the client's interests better? Attorney assessments of costs and benefits lead some to conclude that if a lawyer gains a reputation for aggressive tactics, OSHA may be "shy" in future encounters. Aggressive responses to OSHA, especially in large or complex cases, immediately affect the case at hand by putting pressure on Labor Department solicitors. Unless money and "client shyness" prevent it, said one leading attorney,

> if we litigate a case according to the way we like to litigate a case, we will come out with guns blazing. OSHA will file its complaint, and we'll file *not just* an answer to the complaint. No. We'll file an answer to the complaint, plus our request for the production of documents, plus a set of interrogatories, plus a request for a discovery conference, plus sometimes we'll press for admissions, plus we'll call the OSHA lawyer and we'll say "we'd like to set up a depositions schedule." In other words, we let them know early on [that] "we know what we're doing" and "you're going to litigate this case because we're going to make you." They don't have the resources to litigate these cases with such intensity, sometimes they don't have the skill, and sometimes they don't have the time.

Though cases can be dispersed nationally, attorneys know one another: 87.8 percent of OSHA specialists and 77.8 percent of all surveyed attorneys agreed that they frequently deal with OSHA officials and solicitors encountered previously.[57] In repeat encounters, identical measures may be unnecessary – or so attorneys hope. One younger-than-average attorney believed he could convert his growing reputation into added value for his clients by reminding compliance officers about past experiences. "It's better to have a reputation of being tough with OSHA," he thought, because

> they are pro-safety and you're defending the employer. You are *already* seen as part tough-guy. What you're doing is tough on *them*. When you depose someone it is humiliating, it is exhausting, it's not pleasant. You

can expect they'll be reluctant the next time. And I'll joke about it with them, like "well, Joe, we're going to be spending a week in depositions on this one," and you can see him sitting there saying, "oh shit."

Another attorney, a former Department of Labor official who echoed the thought, noted the influence of personality:

> A lot of it frankly depends on the regional administrator or the regional director out in the field, if he develops an attitude toward the lawyer or the company. Some of them will say "hey look, I went up against this guy before and I got burned. I'm going to be real careful before I do it again." Some of them will just go after you time and time and time again.

If initial discussions about citations do not proceed well, "adversarial" attorneys (employer resources permitting) can begin the process toward litigation with extensive document requests and depositions. Noting that the OSHA community is "very small," another attorney added that limited resources particularly constrain the Department of Labor and give defense counsels' threats additional credibility. Asked how one can build credibility with OSHA, he boasted "we beat them, basically . . . They know who we are. They know that if they're going to take us on we'll tie up an entire area office. They'll grind to a halt. They know that because we've done it to them." Over three-quarters (76.0 percent) of attorneys reported having made broad discovery requests and extensive depositions of OSHA officials. Most choose such aggressive strategies selectively, however; only 16.3 percent choose the aggressive strategy "frequently" or "always."[58]

Aggressive tactics must be used with discretion. Though some companies require warrants at every inspection, most do not.[59] Once OSHA knows of such policies, they automatically secure warrants before visiting anyway. Employers can challenge warrants strategically, such as when they face the possibility of criminal liability or the need to evaluate liabilities after an accident. Even then companies often choose not to demand warrants, fearing that the approach will show a lack of good faith or will cause the agency to *assume* the presence of violations.

Employer fears may be justified, according to both interviews with former Labor Department officials and research showing that companies which refused entry received almost twice as many alleged violations and total penalties.[60] As reported in table 5.4, the tactical preference of attorneys is irregular. The important cleavage lies between those who *never* advise clients to refuse warrantless searches and those who sometimes, frequently, or always do. Thirty percent would never so

TABLE 5.4: Attorneys' preferences for strategic OSHA inspection decisions: in the course of an OSHA investigation, should an attorney . . .

	Never (%)	Sometimes (%)	Frequently (%)	Always (%)
Advise clients to refuse the warrantless entry of compliance officers? (N = 203)	30.0	59.1	7.4	3.4
Refuse a request for documents unless accompanied by a subpoena? (N = 205)	29.3	63.4	4.9	2.4
Brief clients but limit direct attorney involvement to avoid antagonizing OSHA compliance officers? (N = 195)	31.3	41.5	23.1	4.1

Source: 1998 Survey of OSHA Bar.

advise their clients, while one in ten (10.8 percent) frequently or always do so. Attorneys split in similar proportions over whether to demand a subpoena before allowing inspectors to view company documents.

Attorneys' motivations to challenge OSHA's authority go beyond pragmatic balancing of costs and benefits. One survey respondent from a small Midwestern firm explained his firm's perspective in constitutional terms:

> Our belief that clients should insist on an inspection and search warrant in many cases rests on the fact that our fore fathers [sic] fought for and died for our constitutional rights restricting unreasonable intrusions by the Federal Government on our privacy . . . We feel that businesses owe a duty to our fore fathers and our posterity to keep and enforce these constitutional protections rather than waive them. If everyone were to continuously waive these constitutional protections, and if it were to become fashionable to say that a business should waive these in deference to reliance on the Federal Government to be fair and reasonable, eventually these protections would no longer exist.[61]

Most respondents do not share this view. A substantial majority (59.1 percent) only occasionally advises clients to challenge warrants, which suggests pragmatic decisionmaking. "I feel almost like a traitor doing it, but it's sort of a practical thing," said one former Labor Department attorney, who had advised a major corporation to ask for a warrant when OSHA began a "programmed" inspection on a non-industrial facility that went uninspected for years. The company had no idea what inspectors might find. "You know that when OSHA comes out, they're going to cite *real* things and they're also potentially going to cite a lot of little *crazy* things that don't make any sense," he warned, "and my sense in saying 'let's get a warrant' was: 'let's look over our stuff and make sure there isn't any really goofy stuff' . . . We wanted to do it before OSHA came out." Enforcement defense is a minefield of risks which attorneys attempt to negotiate situation-by-situation.

"Cooperative" attorneys, by comparison, hope to avoid such risks by reaching the disputants early and helping both sides find mutually acceptable terms before litigation motions must be made. The ability of OSHA area directors to discount penalties encourages some advocates to seek early settlements, knowing that clients' total bill (i.e., penalties plus legal fees) will be lower. By staying "out of people's faces" and negotiating agreements, one attorney claimed, his firm "can get most of the results, virtually all of the results, that other law firms can get through a hearing, a very costly hearing." Indeed, some attorneys believe that aggressive tactics justify an equivalent response from the agency. "Quite often companies and their counsel have a hostile approach to an enforcer or a regulator," a former Department of Labor official and prominent management attorney warned, but

> that's really not going to get you anywhere because they couldn't care less what you think. They couldn't care less. They have a job to do and to a certain extent if you're going to be hostile with them, if you're going to be difficult with them, if you're not going to respect their function, then you're going to give them license to go after you even harder.

Cooperative lawyering does not eliminate the scope for advocacy, particularly in developing positions to be taken in negotiations. Nor should the notion of cooperative lawyering imply that "aggressive" lawyers reject opportunities for early settlement. But a succession of interviewed attorneys suggested at least a rhetorical difference between the two styles. Defining the "good lawyer" in OSHA cases, one management attorney cautioned: a lawyer "does not serve his client well by simply demonstrating the differences between the client and OSHA, and how you can beat the hell out of the agency . . . There's plenty of imbecility that comes out of OSHA citations, I can guarantee it," he said, "but you can't hit them over the head with a two-by-four, and you can't call them imbeciles."

An essential facet of cooperative approaches includes concern for building positive client relationships with OSHA, as distinct from avoiding damage to them. The ideal opportunity is before an inspection occurs. This strategy tends to be limited to those companies that expect recurring contact. One prominent management attorney outlined his tactics for opening up communication between OSHA and company personnel when a company has difficulty complying with a particular standard. He brings company officials to the area director's office in a grassroots approach described as follows:

> We'll go into the area office and say "here's Joe, from Company X, and we've got an issue we'd like to talk to you about. We've got a problem with guarding this machine."
>
> Q: Is this blinded?
>
> A: No, it's not usually done that way because we want to paint the image in the mind of the area director that this is a good guy. "They've got a problem and you're supposed to be the expert: help us with the problem."
>
> Q: Is that something over which there is disagreement with your colleagues?
>
> A: I'm sure that there are colleagues who would never go in and identify a client, but we've got a program we're doing for a client right now where we're going in and trying to meet every area director, sit down, and where possible discuss a specific problem unique to that workplace to solicit their assistance . . . OSHA's got a policy that if they go to the plant and see a violation, they have to cite it, but you can talk to them all day in the office and they won't issue a citation.
>
> Q: There must be resistance to that.
>
> A: Oh, yeah. The client is a little suspicious at first. You've got to prove it to them. But OSHA's very responsive to that. They like that. That's the "new OSHA" – it's created some really good experiences. When [a major industrial client] got into trouble, we got every plant manager in the country into meetings, telling them "you're going in to meet your area director and you're going to develop a good relationship with that person." We sent them all on their way.

In this strategy, local relationships with OSHA field officers are primary; the particular compliance problems brought to OSHA are almost an afterthought. The strategy is not altruistic, but seeks to establish a measure of good faith that may enable the company to avoid citations if inspected. A number of OSHA attorneys described having done

TABLE 5.5: Client knowledge of attorneys' styles

	Strongly disagree (%)	Disagree (%)	Agree (%)	Strongly agree (%)
Clients usually know my style or approach to litigation when they hire me. (N = 182)	1.1	19.8	64.3	14.8
My OSHA practice mostly involves "one-shot" clients who then do not require further representation or counsel. (N = 220)	16.4	60.5	19.5	3.6
significance: $\chi^2 = 30.6$, p <.001, df = 9				

Source: 1998 Survey of OSHA Bar.

this, and interviews with union and OSHA officials confirm that some lawyers are known for bringing clients into compliance.

The directness of a cooperative strategy may surprise new clients, yet some attorneys believe that its benefits transcend particular clients and attract future clients. No attorneys admitted having "marketed" this style, yet some believe that their reputation for cooperation draws clients in certain industries. High-ranking OSHA and union officials, in turn, are so familiar with leading defense attorneys, that one union director of safety and health could "almost tell by which attorney they bring in: do they really want to solve the problem or do they just want to litigate? If they bring in [name removed] or [name removed] you know they want to stall, delay, and fight to the last drop of blood, but if they bring in [name removed] they want to actually get on with their life."

Companies tend to select and return to like-minded representatives. Nearly 80 percent of surveyed attorneys agreed that their clients know their style or approach to litigation when they are hired (see table 5.5).

Repeat patronage contributes to client knowledge. Asked to identify the source of their most recent OSHA case, two-thirds of survey respondents (67.1 percent) had previously represented the client in other matters.[62] These data do not necessarily foreclose the possibility that lawyers are "hired guns" who fill niches in the market for legal services but may be poorly positioned to transform client attitudes about

styles of disputing.[63] Attorneys perceive their influence on client decisions when they may just be preaching to the choir. The question that
cannot be resolved through these data is how to disentangle the relative influence of attorneys and clients in setting the tone and style of
disputing. Yet, at a minimum, the interview and survey data do suggest
that compliant firms do use attorneys as reputation-building tools in
regulatory enforcement.

Even cooperative attorneys may encounter difficulty with compliance officers and area directors, who sometimes deal with lawyers cau-
tiously. The "missionary" zeal of the safety and health inspectorate
feeds skepticism of lawyers in general, and prevents cooperative attorneys from leveraging their reputations with some low-level staff. "After
all," said one defense attorney, "they know that you're there primarily
to protect the client. They therefore know that they need to some-
how get around whatever barriers or protection you're trying to set
up." In the language of some interviewees, attorneys must assume that
they wear "black hats" until they earn a "white hat" by slowly building
personal relationships. Given sometimes "awkward" inter-professional
relationships with safety and health experts, lawyers may consider a
third alternative: staying out of the way. One attorney put it this way:
"There are some contexts in which I will just brief the client and say
'OK, this is your script, go and deal with these people'." The very appearance of lawyers at the investigation stage might inhibit an early resolution. Over two-thirds of these attorneys (68.8 percent) reported that,
at least once, they had limited themselves to advising clients privately
to avoid antagonizing compliance officers (see table 5.3).

Relationships in administrative networks involve give and take.
However scientific and technical the issues, personalities matter. Attorneys' attitudes and styles affect perceptions of facts, strategies, and
client relationships. But attorneys cannot afford to let their preferences
become a legal hammer that turns every case into a nail. The development of legal strategies must adapt to the uncertain, high-stake situations in which they operate.

LAWYERS AND SETTLEMENT IN REGULATORY ENFORCEMENT

The first step for attorneys in OSHA investigations involves positioning
clients for a positive resolution by gathering data, constructing defenses,
and beginning relationships with agency compliance officers. Despite

the historical contentiousness of OSHA regulation among companies, OSHA shares the high rate of settlement in common with other court systems. OSHA officials and scholars have often cited a figure of 90 percent in all contested cases. This underestimates the experience of the 1990s, in which over 94 percent of *contested* cases settled.[64] Remembering that employers contest less than a quarter of inspections, numbers alone do not limn a worrisome portrait of conflict. What typically remain unseen are the dynamics leading to settlement in regulatory enforcement. A discussion outlining the factors explicitly at issue when lawyers and clients discuss strategies for OSHA disputes serves as a gateway to a discussion of attorneys' perceptions and roles in enforcement disputing. I then turn to management of cases in the enforcement process, describing where attorneys create and exploit opportunities to find satisfactory resolutions for their clients.

Pressure: leading issues in enforcement disputes
While the issues under discussion vary with the circumstances, lawyers generally mention seven concerns when responding to OSHA enforcement actions: penalties, abatement costs, legal costs and burdens of fighting OSHA, desires to be vindicated or win on the merits, company relationships with the public or unions, possible criminal referrals, and threats of secondary litigation.

Penalties Actual penalties must be distinguished from perceived penalties. Larger absolute penalties may be less significant to large corporations than smaller penalties assigned to medium-sized firms. To avoid congressional criticism that the agency unfairly hurts small businesses – and to retain deterrent effects on large companies – it is in the agency's interest to penalize all employers proportionally. Table 5.1, above, showed that OSHA has at least partial success in this. Larger companies receive 21.3 percent of all penalties from 6.9 percent of all inspections.

Though the statute limits penalties to a maximum of $70,000 per willful violation, in the mid-1980s OSHA devised a penalty multiplier, known as the "Egregious Penalty Policy," to increase penalties sharply in certain situations, usually involving large corporate offenders. Instead of attaching the fine to a particular physical condition, the agency attached the fine to *each employee* exposed to the same condition. If an employer failed to record 100 injuries, instead of collecting these as one $10,000 "recordkeeping" violation, OSHA could now penalize each omission, for a total penalty of $1 million. Similarly, if

50 employees worked near a willful violation that would normally incur a $70,000 fine, OSHA could opt to invoke the multiplier to assess a $3.5 million penalty.[65] Though very few cases ever qualified for the Egregious Penalty Policy, its rise had a salutary effect on the proportionality of OSHA enforcement, though the policy's use has been sharply curtailed by OSHRC.[66]

Abatement costs In rulemaking disputes, companies collectively fight regulations because they add to the "costs of doing business" by increasing capital expenditure on new equipment, facilities, and employee training. The specter of compliance costs recurs in individual enforcement disputes when OSHA cites the conditions that must be abated. One attorney, when asked "what motivates your clients?," rephrased the question:

> Why do people pay us? I'd love to know the answer to that question, because you could argue that a good deal of OSHA litigation is a game not worth a candle . . . If you're a cold-blooded businessman, you'll be most likely to litigate an OSHA case when the abatement requirements are very expensive. In fact, when you were walking in I was working on such a case. The abatement requirements are enormously expensive. The penalty in this case is peanuts and everybody knows it's peanuts. What's driving the litigation – and it's very expensive litigation – is the prospect of enormous abatement costs.

In a "cold-blooded" analysis, compliance costs vie with employees' health and safety. More concerned employers object when they disagree with OSHA's assessment of the problem, believing that the abatement expenditures are unnecessary or misdirected. In the above case, this attorney added, abatement costs were entangled with the client's view that "application of the OSHA standard to his situation is just stupid – which it is."

Indirectly, abatement can hurt an industry's or company's competitiveness. Some "technology forcing" regulations, such as the health standard governing cotton dust exposure, threaten entire industries by requiring such high compliance costs that alternative industries become price-competitive. Rulemaking provides a forum for those industry-wide claims, but case-by-case enforcement also creates uneven competitive effects within industries. One attorney interviewed described a construction industry client that had been cited for hazards associated with a type of widely used spring-form equipment that allows for rapid construction of concrete shafts. The new technology allowed companies to complete construction projects much faster, but OSHA regarded the previous generation of equipment as safer. This company's concern, their attorney reported, was that since they were the "only contractor who had been cited so far, [they] would have to add days or weeks onto their bids," with the result being "they won't get those jobs."

Legal costs and burdens on the company Legal costs occur in the margins, but can tip the balance given the generally low penalties and sometimes inexpensive abatement (such as providing better signs and instructions). Many employers will soon determine that they "just don't want to bother," a practitioner reported, when abatement would cost $5,000 and litigation before an ALJ would cost $10,000. The indirect costs of litigation – decreased employee morale, lost productivity, and stress – cannot always be quantified, but contribute to wariness about the road that lies ahead.

Vindication and winning on the merits Businesspeople are not cold-blooded calculators; emotions play a part in attorney–client discussions. Political principles and opposition to OSHA can account for some adversarial behavior, as does natural defensiveness to accusations of wrongdoing. Interviewed lawyers, while believing that most company officials are well intentioned, nevertheless pointed to clients' belief in their own infallibility. "Unlike some of the other laws that I deal with in the Civil Rights area and so forth, where there certainly are companies that are biased in one direction or another," one experienced attorney commented,

> I don't think anybody on the business side truly ignores a safety problem. It's not necessarily because they love their employees, they just don't want injuries and people being killed on their job sites . . . They really believe citations are unfair, because they've done a lot to provide [for safety] and they spend a lot of money on it . . . That they're *annoyed* when they've been cited is an understatement. I've never had an employer come in and say, "whoa, did I screw up" . . . and I don't think I ever will. Most of them pride themselves on having a good safety program and a good safety record, and *even the ones that don't have a good safety record* still psychologically believe they're doing everything they can in the industry they're in.

Though companies of all sizes can display indignation at enforcement actions, evidence points to the influence of lawyers on these constructions. One management attorney, a former Labor Department official, had witnessed the "sense of outrage" that strengthens the will of company officials and leads them to say: "hey, as a matter of principle, I think I'm getting screwed here" or "I just think this case is a lot of crap and I'm not going to take it anymore." The lawyer observed:

> Those kinds of decisions are essentially made by somebody in the corporate chain who just has the chutzpah to say, "I'm going to pursue this." In most cases that's what it is. In some cases that resolve on the part of some corporate official hinges on the attitude and approach of the private counsel. There are some counsel out there who are inclined to settle these cases and aren't going to encourage the corporate people to fight on, and there are others who *are* going to encourage the corporate people to fight on. They'll give them the legal options and then say "but I think you're getting screwed here."

Some union interviewees criticized attorneys who provoke employer anger at OSHA, implying that lawyers' motives are financial. Management attorneys concede that companies driven to litigation by emotional responses are less likely to consider lawyers' fees as part of their decision calculus, sometimes even ignoring costs altogether.

Public and union relationships   The external relationships of companies can become strained during OSHA enforcement actions. Whether reputations are at stake depends on very specific factors, including the type of industry, the size of the firm, the reason for OSHA's visit, and the company's history of labor relations. In high-publicity cases, one leading practitioner reported, companies may "say 'get us out of this. We don't want this hanging over our head for years. Just get the best deal we can, get the best publicity we can. We're willing to pay a lot of money, just get us out of here.'" External relationships are not static; strategic responses can aggravate or placate labor and the public. OSHA, too, will attempt to exploit such strains wherever possible. When Hudson Foods, Inc. of Noel, Missouri recalled 25 million pounds of potentially tainted ground beef in August 1997, OSHA used the highly publicized incident to draw attention to its own investigation and $332,500 proposed fine, which the company had contested the previous month.[67] In light of the statute's origin, labor relations present special issues for management, some of which are discussed later in this chapter.

Criminal referral   OSHA cases rarely lead to criminal investigations, with never more than 20 referrals to the Department of Justice in any one year, and only 151 in total between 1972 and 2003.[68] In OSHA law, the possibility of criminal referral arises only when employers exhibit clear disregard for employees; mere noncompliance is not enough. Still, criminal inquiries are a powerful deterrent to employer negligence and OSHA proudly heralds rare convictions with news releases. When criminal penalties are an issue, the topic is a very high priority, as one may well imagine.

Secondary litigation The OSH Act did not supersede the rights of employers under preexisting civil litigation remedies and workers' compensation, but the results of OSHA disputes affect their likelihood of success. Attorneys thus try to minimize the "collateral damage" of citations by seeking exculpatory language and "unclassified" citations. "Willful" or "serious" citations support conclusions of employer negligence, while "unclassified" citations have "positive ramifications for subsequent tort litigation."[69] Some attorneys regard classification as the leading issue in accident-generated cases.

To discern the relative importance of these factors in OSHA enforcement, survey respondents were asked to rank client interests "when you have discussed their objectives and strategies in OSHA enforcement matters."[70] The results, reported in table 5.6, reaffirm the importance of context. The table sorts the issues according to the combined percentage of respondents who ranked them in the top three. Attorneys perceived penalties as the leading issue for their clients, given top billing by 39 percent and placed in the top three by nearly 80 percent. Interestingly, client interest in "minimizing total penalties" does not correlate significantly with, or depend on, the *actual* penalties reported by attorneys (see table 5.2).[71] While we cannot infer much from the absence of a relationship, this result distinguishes perceived from actual penalties, a necessary condition for a fully proportional penalty system.[72]

Over half of attorneys thought "modifying the time or costs of abatement" and "winning on the merits (being vindicated)" were among their clients' top three issues. The latter – cited by over 21 percent as the most important concern – reflects principled and adversarial resistance to OSHA investigations. The different sources of OSHA inspections explain the balanced distribution of responses for the next category, "avoiding secondary litigation such as plaintiffs' suits." Programmed inspections, unlike investigations following injuries and fatalities, do not raise the specter of secondary litigation.

This very context-dependent distribution contrasts sharply with the normal distribution of responses for "minimizing legal expenses, burden

171

TABLE 5.6: Important concerns in attorney–client discussions about OSHA enforcement (ranking from 1 = most important to 7 = least important)

	% = 1	% = 2	% = 3	% = 4	% = 5	% = 6	% = 7
Minimizing total penalties	39.0	26.6	14.1	8.5	6.8	4.5	0.6
Modifying the time or costs of abatement	14.7	17.5	20.3	20.3	10.7	11.9	4.5
Winning on the merits (being vindicated)	21.5	17.5	12.4	18.1	13.0	7.9	9.6
Avoiding secondary litigation, such as plaintiffs' suits	9.6	16.4	17.5	11.3	18.1	16.9	10.2
Minimizing legal expenses, burden on company	1.7	14.1	24.9	21.5	19.2	12.4	6.2
Avoiding possible criminal referral	11.9	5.6	6.8	10.7	15.3	14.7	35.0
Preserving relationship with union or public	1.7	2.3	4.0	9.6	16.9	31.6	33.9

Source: 1998 Survey of OSHA Bar (N = 177).

on company." Legal expenses and burdens, while a consistent factor in OSHA enforcement cases, rarely become the primary issue.

Qualitative evidence suggests that clients are very concerned with avoiding possible criminal referral, but the large percentage of attorney rankings in the bottom three (65 percent) reinforces the rarity of that possibility. According to counsel, only "preserving relationships" received less attention in attorney–client discussions. Most OSHA investigations do not receive substantial (if any) public or media scrutiny, and union involvement plays a crucial role in a handful of select cases. Overall, penalties present the most consistent threat to employers, followed by abatement costs. Rational economic management can also give way to employer interests in vindication, however. OSHA advocacy goes beyond cost–benefit analysis. Disputing involves interests but occurs between individuals.

TABLE 5.7: Stage of attorneys' resolution of
OSHA cases

Stage of process	Average %
Reached pre-citation settlement	7.3
Reached settlement with OSHA (after citations were issued)	37.4
Reached settlement with solicitors/counsel	35.8
Resolved by ALJ or initial court decision	11.6
Resolved by full Review Commission or appeals court decision	7.8

Source: 1998 Survey of OSHA Bar (N = 213).

The path to success: points of resolution
Securing satisfactory outcomes for regulated companies requires finding
only one of many decisionmakers in the system who can be persuaded,
coaxed, or pressured. Judicial systems typically offer many incentives
for litigants to overcome their differences before surrendering decisionmaking to a third party. In this respect, the OSHA enforcement process is no different. The organizational bifurcation between OSHA and
the Solicitor's Office, nevertheless, presents two partially independent
stages for employers to plead their case. To reach settlements, attorneys
choose arguments most suited to the forum, and to some degree, attorneys choose the forum based on the available arguments.

Even though the method for selecting the survey sample drew on
the roster of litigators from recent judicial decisions, respondents still
reported that fewer than 20 percent of their cases were resolved by adjudication. As table 5.7 shows, surveyed attorneys distributed settlements
almost equally between the OSHA and Solicitor's Office stages of the
process, apart from pre-citation settlements.[73]

According to the attorneys, what propel settlements typically are the
"facts of the case." "Each case is resolved on its own pressure points,"
said one former Department of Labor official, and "those pressure points
are various carrots and sticks." But many respondents, mingling health
and safety facts with political and legal contexts, offered varied explanations of what forces guide their approach to negotiations.

Importantly, the choice between negotiations with OSHA and the Solicitor's Office negotiations appears to be a conscious effort at forum-shopping. Cooperative-style attorneys get involved early to avoid the costly entanglements of adversarial litigation. Just as he attends inspections to "educate" inspectors, so one management attorney believes that the longer negotiations continue, "the more firmly entrenched in concrete the agency's position becomes . . . and the more difficult it is to find common ground between an employer and OSHA." Yet, another adversarial-style attorney preferred "dealing with the compliance officer because I can probably be more intimidating. By the time we're dealing with OSHA lawyers, it's lawyer to lawyer." Adversarial approaches have advantages in negotiations with OSHA, he added, because the presence of lawyers "tends to make [OSHA officials] more careful. They're not as rambunctious at times."

Early settlement, nonetheless, appears to be more a product of a client's need for quick resolution than of attorney style. The recent rise of pre-citation settlements supports this while also highlighting the potential for enhanced government sanctions to increase incentives for settlement. The Egregious Penalty Policy (also known as Compliance Directive 2.80) was initially viewed as an innovative response to a single case, specifically, blatant noncompliance by Union Carbide following the disaster in Bhopal, India in 1985. OSHA assured Congress, on the basis of "records-inspections," that the company's domestic operations had excellent safety records. But by August 1985, OSHA officials found themselves explaining to Congress (and, specifically, Senator Robert Byrd) why a Union Carbide plant in Institute, West Virginia had leaked toxic chemicals, sending six employees and 135 area residents to the hospital. Congressional skepticism that OSHA's proposed $32,100 fine would motivate Union Carbide matched Labor Secretary Bill Brock's frustration after a closer inspection revealed that Union Carbide had falsified its injury records.[74] A committee of four people (three from OSHA and one from the Solicitor's Office) developed alternatives for increasing the penalty. With approval from the OMB's Office of Information and Regulatory Affairs, OSHA cited Union Carbide for *each instance* of faulty recordkeeping. Combined with other violations, OSHA proposed over $1.3 million in penalties; Union Carbide contested the citations and settled for over $242,000.

Shortly after the Union Carbide case, OSHA increased scrutiny of recordkeeping and discovered a relatively widespread pattern of faulty and falsified recordkeeping. The policy of instance-by-instance penalties, conceived in response to a particular case, became an appropriate tool for directing corporate attention to health and safety issues. Due to the substantial resources each egregious case required, OSHA could pursue only a few dozen cases annually; but since the large fines attracted press coverage and word-of-mouth attention within management circles, just a few cases could accent particular health and safety issues, such as lockout/tagout or ergonomics. OSHA expected – and received – sharp opposition in the Union Carbide case, but very quickly a new pattern emerged when the agency extended the policy innovation to new situations. "Much to our surprise," according to one former Labor Department official,

> the [companies'] lawyers were saying "look, how can we get rid of, how can we settle, these cases?" So we quickly realized that we really had a gold mine here. We can go after these companies for a million dollars and all they want to do is get rid of the case. They'll settle, they'll abate, and give us a fair chunk of money to boot . . . There were a couple of exceptions, but these were all large, major multinational Fortune 200 companies, and they just wanted to get out of these cases.

Like a teacher who sends a misbehaving student to stand in the corner, OSHA hoped to spur good behavior by making painful examples of a few companies.

Pre-citation settlements became the exit strategy from egregious cases. OSHA can indicate its willingness to negotiate an ongoing investigation; but companies and their counsel make the first move, offering to pay a lump-sum penalty and not to contest the citation, in exchange for a lower classification or even exculpatory language. OSHA often will insist on other conditions, such as new safety and health programs beyond what is required by OSHA standards, and "corporatewide" abatement (not just in the facility under investiga-tion). Pre-citation settlements would appear to satisfy all parties, in that OSHA secures wider compliance than it is legally able to impose, and companies reduce damage to their reputations. In fact, somebody's ox is always gored. Pre-citation settlements weaken the prospects of liability suits – one of the three pre-OSHA protections – and they short-circuit union opportunity to elect party status.[75]

To secure pre-citation settlements, employers must be cooperative and committed to safety and health.[76] Fortunately, according to a for-mer Labor Department lawyer, the attorneys most likely to become involved in egregious cases are "repeat-players" who tend to welcome settlements:

> Q: What characterizes the [egregious] cases that won't settle?
> A: Stubbornness and recalcitrance [by the company].
> Q: Ever encouraged by the attorney?
> A: Yes, to some extent, but here I'm going to draw a distinction. There's a national OSHA bar and then there are local OSHA bars. The national OSHA bar for the most part, with some limited exceptions, is very supportive of the process, very supportive of the program, good with their clients, and amenable to settlement. There are local lawyers out there whose motto is "fight to the bitter end and it's cheaper in the long run."

Lawyers in the "national OSHA bar" seem more likely to adopt cooperative strategies.[77] Even unconsciously, attorneys may support the policy for selfish reasons. Many interviewees credited the Egregious Penalty Policy with restoring the viability of OSHA practice after the lean Reagan years. By all accounts, the number of active OSHA practitioners, and membership in the American Bar Association's OSHA section, has grown many times over since 1986. A former Labor Department official involved in the creation of the policy joked: "the OSHA bar ought to have a damn monument to me. Every one of them ought to be sitting there saying, 'thank you,' because before the stakes weren't very high, and now the stakes are a lot higher."

Egregious Penalty Policy cases receive joint OSHA–SOL attention from the start, including formal approval and coordination from the Solicitor's Office in Washington. Egregious cases require substantial investment of resources, so solicitors help protect that investment by assessing the strength of the evidentiary record and maintaining consistent legal theory across cases. In most nonegregious cases, by comparison, regional solicitors enter cases after citations have been challenged, by which point the evidentiary and legal basis largely have been set. Errors inevitably occur. A leading union director of safety and health feels sympathy for solicitors because "they do have resource limitations." "I've seen a lot of citations by OSHA that were just written wrong," he added. "I think that OSHA compliance officers and regional administrators need a lot more education about what kind of citations are going to fly and which kinds won't from the beginning."

When defense attorneys lack a distinct reason for settling early (such as avoiding adverse publicity), the stronger incentives are to negotiate with the solicitors, who have invested less personally in cases. Practicing attorneys perceive that the two-step process generates a sense of autonomy for Labor Department solicitors and a source of "reasonableness" for developing safety and health law. The perceptions and strategies of the following management attorneys are instructive:

> When the [OSH Act] was first passed, the attitude of the agency was one of a policeman, very much so. They took a very hard line. So did the Solicitor's Office in those days. Over the years the [agency] directors have taken less of that, but they still tend in that direction . . . while the Solicitor's Office has gotten much more realistic about what really happens on the job, what happens in the factory, and so forth. I've seen sort of a division between the investigative regional offices, regional directors, and the Solicitor's Office. More often than not, they're not necessarily on the same page.

> With the solicitor, [my approach] is: "we're attorneys, both of us, and I would like you to recognize a certain weakness in some of your arguments here, and if this is going to go to trial, these are going to be some of the problems." And I find that most of the Solicitor's Office lawyers are pretty practical-minded and take a skeptical view of their investigators in the field. In other words, they don't accept what they're told. They're not the crusaders that the investigators are. Fair-minded may be overdoing it, but objective may be a better word. They're not the advocates that an attorney in private practice would be for a client.

> Once the agency becomes entrenched through the issuance of citations, there is another opportunity to resolve a matter and that is before the regional solicitor's office. Once the issue becomes a legal matter, it is once again much easier to resolve. It's almost as if the concrete gets chipped away a bit and you have two foci of authority and power. One is the client – the OSHA client – and the other is the relatively independent regional solicitior's office that has to approach this matter not only from the merits perspective be it "my client violated X standard," but they've got to take a cost–benefit analysis, "do I have the kind of case that I can prosecute with success?" Does it make sense to devote the resources to prosecute this case, and is abatement achieved substantially by virtue of what [the private attorney] is offering on behalf of his clients, as opposed to devoting resources to perhaps litigating? So those considerations begin to impinge on the solicitor's office, whereas they never impinge on the client.

Different perspectives hardly imply that OSHA is *incapable* of a fair result, only that the Solicitor's Office analyzes cases with the

177

interest in prosecutorial success, a different frame of reference but one inherent to prosecutorial decisionmaking.[78] Prosecutors face it every time enforcement officers hand them a case, whenever legislative goals must be translated into practice.

Private attorneys thus see multiple points of access to exploit. One attorney explicitly treats the stages of the enforcement process in sequence, encouraging clients to get what they can from negotiations with OSHA in order to bolster their position in negotiations with the Solicitor's Office. "What we always tell our clients," said a management attorney, is that

> even if we're going in [to OSHA] with something that we don't think is going to go anywhere, it's still a helpful process because if we can get some things knocked down conceptually, that is going to be on the table when we get to the government attorney . . . We always treat that as "OK, we've lowered the bar a bit, now we're going to start from that point. Now we want to move down from there with the government attorney." The government attorneys, at least from my experience, will find out where exactly we were in the negotiations and that sort of becomes 'the worst it's going to get.'

However complex the frames of prosecutorial decisions, the bifurcated system limits the solicitors' view of cases and condenses decisions into more focused, pragmatic exchanges, though still dependent on complex legal and nonlegal factors, including the statutory mandates, the stringency of the reviewing courts, the strength of the evidence provided by the inspectors, as well as the solicitor's understanding of burdens of proof.

Even with close coordination between OSHA staff and solicitors, moving from mission to legal standard can be difficult. In an extraordinary but revealing case, Secretary of Labor Robert Reich committed a serious public relations gaffe in 1994 when he hand-delivered a $7.5 million citation to Bridgestone/Firestone's Dayton Tire plant in Oklahoma City and asked the federal district court in Oklahoma for a temporary injunction to force compliance with OSHA lockout/tagout standards, claiming that the plant posed an "imminent danger" to workers. The company, with counsel, countered that compliance costs would force it to shut down the plant, a threat which made employees fear that they would pay for OSHA action with their jobs. In the ensuing public relations backlash, the Bush-appointed judge rejected the agency's ambitious motion and sent the issues to the Review Commission.[79]

However skilled its lawyering, the agency cannot control judge selection and shrewd opposition. Reich later conceded that OSHA's mission inspired a sense of righteousness in his actions, which blinded him to the possible pitfalls.[80]

Defense counsel appreciate not only the solicitors' prosecutorial examination of the merits, but also the emotional independence from the case. One business attorney recalled his attempts to rehabilitate a client's relationship with OSHA when an "old guard" manager at mid-level saw agency abatement requirements as intrusions on how he "ran his operation" and voiced highly inappropriate comments to the young, pregnant, compliance officer. The attorney thought that the manager was beyond personal rehabilitation and incapable of performing an "act of contrition" to the offended officer. OSHA officials "were very upset with the way they had been treated – probably rightfully so," he observed, "but basically the negotiations had nothing to do with the facts of the case and had everything to do with the emotions of the moment." To by-pass what this lawyer called the "emotional stuff," he took the case to his government counterpart, lawyer to lawyer, and settled the $70,000 proposed penalty for $1,000.

Such stories, though through the eyes of management counsel, emphasize that regulatory enforcement and legal negotiations are built on the actions of individuals in institutions. Management attorneys caution that their prospects of settlement with either OSHA officials or solicitors depend on the particular personalities they encounter. Personalities, like reputations, are mercurial but crucial forces in enforcement processes, shaping perceptions by all parties of what can be achieved, altering strategies, and changing roles. Constrasting with the closeness of industry lawyers and OSHA's solicitors, union participants often feel disadvantaged in enforcement networks. They can file a complaint, join the walkaround, and participate in the closing conference, only to find that in the solicitor's office, as a leading union's director of safety and health complained, "there is no foundation of a relationship or an understanding, and the solicitor is handling [the case] from a more narrow perspective of what's on their plate, how many cases they've got to process, and without any historical context."

Union participation in enforcement actions, though limited to certain issues, necessarily adds complexity to any case. Union positions during the inspection and negotiations are typically at odds with management interests, of course; interviewees concurred with the observation of one union lawyer that union participation "stiffens OSHA's backbone." Available evidence seems to confirm one labor leader's speculation that OSHA officials "think that 'well, if this issue is important enough for a union to show up, then we need to do the right thing,' and so I think we get better settlements."[81] By that token, management attorneys claim strategic potential in encouraging union involvement when unions have healthy relationships with employers. "That's where you can get some big concessions," a large-firm attorney said. "When the union agrees with the employer, OSHA doesn't have an ally and they don't know what to do." His colleagues in the bar split on the issue: 28.2 percent of surveyed attorneys "never" seek the assistance of union representatives, 58.8 percent "sometimes" recommend it and the remaining 13 percent "frequently" or "always" do so.[82] The instrumentalism of management attorneys comports with their skeptical, even cynical beliefs, voiced in numerous interviews, that unions commonly create and exploit OSHA disputes for ulterior reasons, such as aiding organizing drives or gaining bargaining chips in collective bargaining. In reply, union directors of safety and health noted defensively that, if OSHA inspections reveal violations, the motives for complaints are irrelevant. One director revealingly parsed the issue: "it's fair to say that safety and health does get caught up with other issues – it does – and to the extent that employers are treating their workers badly, you have labor relations problems. So it's not surprising that there are OSHA complaints." Across the labor/management divide, it all depends on perspective.

The low number of union lawyers involved in OSHA enforcement makes generalizations difficult. In perhaps a handful of major cases per year, the major national unions may turn to the small cadre of union lawyers for assistance in developing the issues, assisting nonlawyer participants, or briefing cases en route to ALJs or the Review Commission. The few union attorneys who participate in rulemaking litigation know the national Solicitor's Office attorneys, and from time to time they attempt to persuade the national office about the strengths and weaknesses of a case. As lawyers, they may sympathize with the Solicitor's Office's lack of resources and need for discretion; as labor advocates they want "sound" results in individual cases and a sense of direction in enforcement policy. Labor unions may rely on Department of Labor attorneys to advocate for safety and health, but their lawyers perceive a role for themselves as defenders of OSHA's weak flanks. A leading union attorney was comforted by his clients' recognition that

> the ideal thing is to have the union independently represented, so that
> I'm there along with the solicitor with ideas, suggestions, assistance, and
> sometimes a little extra pizzazz to say, "you can do it. Don't be concerned
> that they've got 11 lawyers and 22 paralegals lined up against you. We
> will be able to jointly see our way through this situation."

Given the limited role of unions in OSHA settlements, the impact of
their lawyers is hard to gauge. As one union lawyer soberly cautioned:
"the law is they have to give us a meaningful opportunity to participate,
but they don't have to listen to us."

The uncertainty and costs of bringing cases to trial serve as powerful deadlines, and so settlements dominate enforcement disputing in
OSHA, as they do in many legal systems. As in rulemaking litigation,
the impact of judges may be greatest when influencing the incentives
for negotiation. How does OSHA's "split enforcement" model, dividing
OSHA from the Review Commission, affect enforcement litigation?
From the agency's perspective, its ability to set standards and issue interpretations means that, in most cases, the Review Commission is merely
a procedural footnote. Many interviewees, from all sides of the OSHA
system, consider the Review Commission an important body only as a
potential relief in specific disputes. Management lawyers are those most
likely to profit from an independent reviewer. A former Department of
Labor official, now in private practice, compared his current and past
perceptions of the Commission:

> I spend more time when in private practice thinking about the Review
> Commission and thinking about what the impact might be, because
> that's my avenue for litigating cases up the line, and you have to think
> about what the administrative law judge is like and how this would play
> with the Commission. When I was inside the Department I sort of blew
> the Commission off, because the action – from the Labor Department's
> perspective – is what the Court of Appeals says, and it was basically a
> matter of getting through the Review Commission and getting a case to
> the Court of Appeals to establish some *serious* precedent, whatever the
> issue was.

State OSHA cases have even less precedential value, but adjudication provides another gateway to a satisfactory outcome in specific
disputes.

Even some management attorneys, however, question the Commission's role in the lives of clients, much less wider discussions of safety

181

and health policy. One prominent practitioner recognized the divergent opinions among the bar's elite that were apparent in interviews:

> I don't think the Review Commission does much, frankly, although depending on who you talk to, some think that the Review Commission is the answer to everything in the OSHA world . . . For the most part the tough legal issues are pretty much done. The law is pretty settled and all the defenses are clear. I never tell a client that the relief you seek is going to be at the Commission, because you're talking years down the road. We try to settle cases.

Since litigation reaches an appeals court only after proceeding through both an ALJ and the three-person Review Commission in Washington, attorneys and their clients consider appeals *as policymaking* only in rare cases. The basis on which to appeal may not exist, even if the money does. A management attorney with a diverse portfolio of clients found that "for smaller employers that don't have the wherewithal to take something up to the Court of Appeals, they're often stuck with the Review Commission's, or even the judge's, opinion. So you can say that the Commission is not that relevant . . . but if you can't appeal, or you don't want to, then you're stuck with it." Thus, the primary contribution of the adjudication hierarchy is as an escape-valve for irreconcilable differences; secondarily, it is a stepping-stone to appellate litigation of OSHA law.[83]

Where all else fails, the popular understanding of regulatory lawyering insinuates that power brokers with "friends in high places" can bring political leverage to bear on client agencies. Directly appealing to Congress for relief in enforcement actions may seem a natural response by clients to "heavy-handed" bureaucracy. Survey evidence corroborates archival data, which shows that some companies contact members of Congress when under investigation. Of the 22.6 percent of all respondents who had contacted Congress regarding an OSHA issue on behalf of a client, nineteen – 38.8 percent of the subset (8.4 percent of all attorneys) – had made their contact in "a review of an enforcement action."[84] Though few would deny Congress's considerable statutory and political influence on OSHA, bringing advocacy to Capitol Hill risks doing more harm than good. The Solicitor's Office is certainly mindful of congressional interest in cases, but letters can confirm that they have a strong case. "When we looked at cases," one former Labor Department attorney recalled, our first concern was "is this a legal case and can we make it in front of the courts?" Our secondary consideration was if we're going to be stepping on some Congressman's toes. If you can make [the case] to the courts, you can make it to the Congressman . . . Should a private lawyer bring congressional pressure on his case? The answer to that is absolutely not, because it made us think, "hey, you guys don't have a legal defense so now you're trying to bring political pressure," and that's generally the case, [so] we treated it that way with the Hill.

Congressional pressure may unwittingly tip management's hand to opponents. Additionally, the strategy does not endear attorneys or the client to OSHA. One prominent management practitioner cautioned:

when clients say "how much good will it do to call my Congressman?" I say "forget it. Don't even bother. It won't do you any good, and it will just offend the agency." By the way, I once had a really savvy client who asked me that as a test question. So I said, "don't do it." and he said, "good, you know what you're talking about."

Perhaps administrative decisions in other fields, such as communications, food and drugs, or environmental protection, provide fertile ground for congressional strategies. This field instead revolves around the two-stage process of negotiations and settlements with OSHA and the Solicitor's Office. Where statutory and organizational choices have established procedures, networks and relationships develop like lichens to a rock. The relationships among the parties are personal as well as political, routine as well as unique, and attorneys clearly play a part. In their search for the ideal forum, lawyers exploit gaps in the system, and by bringing together their clients and the government, they facilitate the settlement of enforcement actions.

CONCLUSION

From a point within the practice of OSHA law, cooperative and adversarial strategies can each have a "logic." This logic need not flow from objective, prescient predictions about outcomes, but from perspectives gained from situational, individual, or environmental forces. From OSHA's mission-minded perspective, the mere appearance of lawyers implies an adversarial stance toward the agency's mandate. Attorneys interested in working with OSHA staff must establish credibility and trust by working within OSHA's value system. Attorneys able to operate can dissolve the cooperation–adversarial dichotomy. Indeed, attorneys reasonably assert, cooperation without the ability or will to respond aggressively when appropriate will encourage agency aggressiveness. Nearly all interviewees advocated a strong offensive reserve as a prerequisite for effective negotiations. That point is an important truism: the merits of the case, and the credible threat to prove it in court, matter. A prominent "cooperative" attorney, formerly a high-ranking official in the Labor Department, observed that good advocacy does not alter relationships. OSHA officials and private attorneys "all know each other," he said. "We're just like professional football players. We just put on different jerseys now and then. And they know that if I'm representing a client I'm going to raise whatever issue I can raise."

For reputation to lead to cooperation, both attorneys and employers must reveal an attitudinal commitment to the agency's mission. In social regulatory schemes, the regulators and regulated may not share the same assessments of costs, benefits, definitions, and means of compliance. Even more fundamentally, they may disagree about abstract social priorities. OSHA personnel, in particular, doubt employer concern for employees until it has been proved. Attorneys believe they build credibility for themselves by ensuring that, at a minimum, clients are committed to their workers' health and safety, even as the parties combat the intent, meaning, and application of health and safety standards. OSHA officials *expect* opposition, but willful disregard for safety and health encounters no tolerance. One attorney, held in high regard by Department of Labor officials even though renowned for his "hardball" tactics, maintained that credibility is built with the advice given to employers in the private sphere, not the public world of litigation. He explained the reason:

> Many of the folks at OSHA have a fairly simplistic view of things and they tend to look at the outside world as good guys and bad guys. If you are perceived as an industry advocate, but whose heart is in the right place; you are not out to hurt people; you are understood to be a lawyer who's just as likely to say to a client, "look folks, you can't continue to do it this way," – which happens a great deal, believe me – if you are perceived as a lawyer who's willing to say in appropriate cases to a client, "no, you just can't do that, we'll find a way to make this work but you've got to change the way you're doing this"; you're perceived as someone who's honest, an honest broker if you will . . . that helps.

Whether opponents like or dislike you is important but not crucial, he added. Crucial is whether they'll do business with you.

184

In a contenious world of labor–management, public–private dialogue, facts and law matter, but attorneys just as importantly bridge
gaps of emotion and attitude by helping to construct themselves and
their clients in ways understandable and acceptable to OSHA. A high-
ranking Labor Department official attributed attorneys' styles to differences in personality that do not disturb the working relationships
within the core of the OSHA bar. For some firms "[OSHA] pretty much
gets ready to go to court," he said, "and we know the ones who want to
settle all the time" but

> they have a right to represent their people and how they do it is fine.
> I think when maybe people try some underhanded thing we'd get con-
> cerned with one of them, but by-and-large they're pretty above board.
> Some are very hard-nosed and don't want to settle cases, but by and large
> we work with all of them, we know them all. Some are very difficult to
> deal with, but some of our good friends are very hard-nosed attorneys.

If attorneys balance respect for the staff's function with the role of pre-
senting the client's perspective, a former government official observed,
"everyone can come out with as close to a win–win as possible." By "trying to understand where [the staff] are coming from," he suggested, the
lawyer can "help them achieve their objective and help them achieve
your objective."

Regulatory relationships depend on some measure of respect among
the regulator and the regulated. Lawyers, as diplomats, can inject grease
into the cogs of regulatory justice. Whenever lawyers move clients to
a more cooperative relationship with the government, they put the lie
to the notion that attorneys are only friction in the pursuit of worker
health and safety. Attorneys may prepare for litigation and be the mes-
sengers of contention; but sharing a concern for employee health and
safety can carry an important message on behalf of their clients.

CHAPTER SIX

REGULATORY COUNSELING

For all the conflict, effort, and expense involved in disputes between the government and regulated companies, regulatory enforcement represents one path to the law's goal: compliance. In creating regulatory enforcement schemes, too much attention can be paid to methods of sanctioning law-breakers at the expense of encouraging compliance. Similarly, by focusing on lawyers' roles in fighting enforcement actions, one can overlook lawyers' roles in the nonadversarial process of compliance counseling. This chapter complements previous chapters by describing the roles of lawyers outside the scope of active rulemaking and enforcement matters. Like rulemaking and enforcement, counseling involves bargaining in the shadow of a legal process. Yet, removed from an active dispute or interaction with the regulator, lawyers are on very different turf.

Enforcement policies set the stage for the decisions companies make about how to comply with government regulations, a fact reflected in prior research. Building on decades of research exploring how businesses "capture," transform, and use regulations for their own purposes, scholars have examined the ways in which agencies prevent and punish compliance. Much academic discussion revolves around the relative merits of economic and social sanctions (such as moral "shaming" and criminal penalties) for promoting compliance.[1] Some advocates believe that cooperative regulatory programs generate better results than adversarial, punitive measures.[2] An underlying question for these debates is to understand how companies decide how – even *whether* – to comply. Of course, rational economic analyses, focusing on the costs and benefits of compliance, offer elegant simplifying assumptions and one account. But the roles of professionals in the process broaden the inquiry beyond the rational to include the norms and rationales devised to explain what the law should mean for company decisions. As was shown in chapter 5, regulated companies exhibit varying responses to regulatory enforcement actions, affected also by the social and psychological consequences, including public relations, the need for vindication, and imperfect client knowledge.

As in rulemaking and enforcement, compliance counselors view their clients' interests as the *raison d'être* of legal practice. However, since counseling mostly occurs outside formal governmental processes, it exposes the potential significance of legal ethics and lawyers' roles. What do attorneys perceive as their purpose and goals when advising clients? Some critics fear that counsel can convert their expertise into roadmaps to noncompliance by predicting what clients can "get away with." Alternatively, regulatory lawyers can bring the public interest into attorney–client discussions.

OF PROFESSIONAL NORMS AND LEGAL ETHICS

Since public oversight of corporate compliance with rules is imperfect, the terms of the compliance debate have often boiled down to debates about ethics, both corporate and legal. The most recent "wave" of corporate malfeasance, of which Enron and WorldCom are the poster-children, produced a prodigious amount of discussion among scholars, regulators, and legislators about how to compel behavior that not only is "perfectly legal" but accounts for the public interest.[3] This is not a new innovation, but a theme appearing whenever economic boom turns to bust and a concomitant political crisis. The many formal statements of legal ethics make explicit that attorneys have other duties beyond zealous advocacy for their clients. According to the American Bar Association's "Model Rules of Professional Conduct," lawyers shall be one step removed from their clients' interests and may even bring alternative interests to bear on their clients' decisionmaking. Rule 2.1 recognizes that matters of law involve matters of morals and ethics: "In representing a client, a lawyer shall exercise independent professional judgment and render candid advice. In rendering advice, a lawyer may refer not only to law but to other considerations such as moral, economic, social and political factors, that may be relevant to the client's situation."[4] The rules note that legal ethics stem from conflict between "lawyer's responsibilities to clients, to the legal system and to the lawyer's own interest in remaining an upright person while earning a satisfactory living."[5] Rules are only the start, of course. Beyond the high-profile failures of ethics, too little research has attempted to meet the continuing need for empirical evidence about how ethical principles are viewed and enacted in practice.

At the level of generality where ethical and policy debates occur, the expectations of the legal role and the asserted norms of behavior revolve around deceivingly clear public/private poles. On one-half of this divide, an account of lawyers as public servants, sometimes called the "purposivist" and "regulatory" models of lawyering, holds that lawyers are well placed to bring client behavior in line with the central goals of law. Though such statements may serve only as the "ceremonial rhetoric" of the American bar,[6] practitioners and scholars take seriously the opportunity to advance the cause of justice through the deliberate use of counseling discretion.[7] As an instrument of society, lawyer-counselors can minimize the antisocial impulses of clients and direct them to a vision of the common good.[8] In economic terms, lawyers create value in society when they guide clients in this way, because they help reduce the negative externalities laws were intended to address. The public-oriented approach, as applied in fields with expert agencies, requires a supply of norms to use as leverage against the economic impulses of attorneys representing companies. A potential source may be the professional ideology of the field such as environmentalism or industrial health. Akin to this, one legal scholar has argued that a "public service model" of environmental counseling might involve "declining to inform" clients about statutory and regulatory interpretations that run contrary to the attorneys' understanding of the law's public purpose, or advising clients to comply with the letter of the law even if regulatory agencies are unable to inspect and enforce it. Others firmly challenge these tactics as implausible, noting that any lawyers who so thoroughly adopt the agency's interests would lose most business and possibly face malpractice charges.[9] Public-oriented understandings of lawyers' work run head-long into norms with significant capital, particularly the somewhat clichéed expectation that lawyers represent clients "zealously within the bounds of the law."[10]

In opposition to public-spirited lawyering is the norm that the lawyer as "hired gun" accommodates as far as possible a client's wishes, usually motivated purely by economic interest. The significance of "hired gun" attorneys lies in being translators and conduits for corporations, not counselors. They do not exert special or extraordinary effort to ensure that clients' decisions are rational, virtuous, or principled. After accepting clients, any qualms about their course or the means necessary are irrelevant as long as both goals and strategies remain within arguable interpretations of the law.[11] All lawyers need to provide is, as Oliver Wendell Holmes wrote, mere "prophecies of what the courts will do in fact, and nothing more pretentious . . ."[12] In the most adversarial statements of this pole, lawyers who become involved in litigation provide zealous, morality-free advice and advocacy. Hired gun lawyering is value-free but not valueless. Rather than supplant clients' values with their own privileged perspectives, lawyers may face expectations to adopt and promote client values and objectives in the legal marketplace.[13]

Scholars have sometimes made cautious concessions to the influence of legal counseling on corporate compliance.[14] Though examples may be found at the poles and in the space between, it is difficult to capture the varieties of legal practice found both across and within fields of law.[15] Zealous advocacy does not demand valueless lawyering any more than the public servant role demands capitulation to the government. Attorneys have a range of options to suggest to clients: what the letter of the law requires, what will be sustainable in court, or what is the proverbial "right thing to do" above and beyond the statute or rule. Even Holmes's "bad man" wants to avoid the fines and jail time, so at a minimum we would expect lawyers to guide clients to bare compliance. In particular circumstances, lawyers may be able to finesse apparent conflicts. The crux of the empirical inquiry, then, involves whether, when, and why attorneys will negotiate the competing norms and expectations of work, seeking compromises and results that maximize (or at least increase) the public weal without injuring the client's interests. We should not assume that at the heart of the ethical debate are ethics. Instead, compliance counseling is embedded in routines and practices negotiated within a complex world of interests and norms.

ATTORNEYS AND OSHA COUNSELING

As shown in chapter 2, next to enforcement defense, regulatory counseling consumes the largest portion of the OSHA bar's time – 33.4 percent. The proportion of time devoted to counseling certainly varies across types of practice and perhaps with the era. Jerome Carlin found that "conferring with clients" was the highest-ranked activity for 80 percent of the senior partners in large Wall Street law firms.[16] No evidence suggests that a majority, or even a sizable percentage, of companies use attorneys as a primary source of advice. Interviewed attorneys recognized that, as valuable as they perceived their own services, the need for health and safety consultations is often regarded as a nonessential item. OSHA compliance can take a back-burner among the leading legal issues of the day, not to mention competitive pressures. "Firms make assessments of how much they're going to spend on prophylactic work based upon the extent of the liability they're facing and the extent of exposure," said one interviewee as he explained his clients' costs and benefits. Among his potential clients,

> everybody wants a sexual harassment policy, everybody wants an employment-at-will policy, and pretty much everyone wants an employee handbook. People are now really focused on noncompetition, confidentiality, and trade secret agreements. Is everybody really focused on OSHA? No . . . OSHA's really not at the top of your list, if you have limited resources, to spend a lot on a safety and health plan.

A cost–benefit model would predict variation in OSHA compliance across industries, and attention to occupational safety and health does vary across industries. This attorney's clients in semi-conductor manufacturing produced few substantial hazards. Another attorney who represented manufacturers of high explosives was at the opposite end of the spectrum. His clients were accustomed to "a level of detail and safety precautions [that are] probably of a higher order than in any other industry." Discrete industries can even develop cultures of safety, as an attorney who had represented electric utility companies found. "Their working techniques are very different than a chemical refinery," he concluded, "because of the experience they have dealing with high voltage – which is the best regulator of all." Simply put, some industries are more enlightened than others.

Ignorance and sophistication among clients

What is the need for counseling in companies regulated by OSHA? The precept "ignorance of the law is no defense" warns citizens that law enforcers often do not need to establish transgressors' intent or state of mind when punishing deviance. Even when ignorant of the law, citizens coincidentally fall within the realm of legality when other forces – such as technological necessity, efficiency, or common sense – dictate the same behavior, as with electrical workers trying to avoid electro-cution. Administrative regulations may also codify currently accepted practices, but the obscurity, complexity, and volume of modern regula-tions hamper even well-intentioned efforts to unearth, much less abide by, the spirit and letter of the law. Companies and individuals wish-ing to identify, understand, and comply with regulations therefore often appeal to professional advisors.

Though libertarian critics of regulation may attack all government intervention, perhaps a more common dynamic of rhetoric and prac-tice is found in the distinction between the spirit of regulation and its instruments or mechanics. An employer likely will remember and understand that they should, for example, put guards on machines or monitor for airborne contaminants. They may disagree, however, on the stringency of a regulation or the incidents of regulation, such as certification requirements, formalized training programs, written pro-cedures, and recordkeeping, which are more easily overlooked, misun-derstood, ignored, or despised. "All those types of procedures, forms, and programs," create gaps in compliance, a management attorney observed.

> A lot of my practice is actually developing, implementing, and estab-
> lishing the programs that they're required to have that they would not
> have otherwise when an inspector shows up. I've been doing some of
> that today: a package of training that has been conducted as a result
> of my going in, doing an audit, and telling them what they needed
> to do. A half-dozen programs have been set up in this one company
> [for] emergency response, evacuation plans, lockout/tagout, confined
> spaces, and respiratory protection. The company was doing things on
> all of these, but they weren't doing things in the way the regulations
> required.

The call to counsel, then, may not be a crucial marker in predicting the absolute level of compliance with regulations – at question may be the form or style that lawyers can supply.

Client needs for information topped these attorneys' descriptions of their involvement in regulatory counseling. As shown in table 6.1, the most common problem – and at 89.2 percent of surveyed attorneys, a nearly ubiquitous concern – is the client's demand for help in under-standing and interpreting regulations as applied to particular situations. Similarly important is clients' need for updates about new rules and reg-ulations. OSHA attorneys least frequently found themselves involved

TABLE 6.1: Most common counseling issues encountered by OSHA counsel (attorneys selected up to three)

	%
Client needs help understanding/interpreting regulations	89.2
Client needs an update about new rules and regulations	60.8
Compliance not technically feasible for client	30.7
Compliance not economically feasible for client	29.2
OSHA issues involved in labor relations/bargaining	17.0
Client needs due diligence performed for a transaction	12.3
OSHA regulations conflict with another law/regulation	11.3

Source: 1998 Survey of OSHA Bar (N = 212).

in situations where OSHA regulations conflicted with other laws or regulations, and where clients needed "due diligence" assessments of risks before companies could finalize financial transactions. These data suggest that the primary role of regulatory counselors is channeling information to clients about the requirements of government regulation. One attorney spoke plainly: "I think my role is staying ahead of the curve, knowing what things are about to come out [from OSHA], and figuring out policies and procedures so that things don't blow up."

We would expect that the capacity of lawyers to fill this need depends on their familiarity and experience with OSHA regulations. That is, counseling should be another area where attorneys can claim that "expertise" has some distinct advantage. Indeed, wider attorney involvement in compliance-related activities correlates strongly with attorney identification as an OSHA specialist (.427, sig. <.001) and with the percentage of their practice devoted to OSHA work (.586, sig. <.001).[17] That is, compliance work and enforcement defense are distinct practices – a wider number of attorneys can be drawn into the latter.

Broadly stated, the core of attorneys' counseling activities involves a comparison between "the law" and a specific factual situation – only outside the watchful eye of the agency. Regulatory counseling, then, might be seen as enforcement through other means, but lawyers do not aim single-mindedly to bridge the gap between generalities and specifics. In the private setting of compliance practice, the understandings of the law are constructed through the negotiation of perspectives between lawyers and clients. Their work can involve helping clients avoid doing what might be impossible (in perception or reality), and attorneys frequently reported that clients commonly confronted regulations that were perceived as technologically or economically infeasible. Combining the data in table 6.1, 44.8 percent of surveyed attorneys mentioned at least one of these issues. The creative tension between complying with and avoiding law permeates counseling activities in an inevitable duality.[18] The strain permeated one description of counseling work by a management attorney who sees

> a lot of questions coming in from clients about whether or not they are complying with a particular standard. A lot of times they want options – they want to know what are the different things that they can do and what are the different things they can't do. And usually there's something they don't want to do, so we have to deal with those types of issues, too.

The sentiment is understandable, if not noble. Few taxpayers, if any, try to maximize the amount paid to the government, and even fewer would seek out tax advisors who operated with this goal. The empirical problem lies in better understanding when and how lawyers supplement their learned repositories of information with norms and behaviors that produce gaps in consensus.

It seems highly likely that the level of attorney-assisted, regulatory *avoidance* may vary across fields of regulation, depending in part on types of activity being regulated and the level and type of enforcement activity. Given the low probability of a programmed OSHA inspection (absent an accident or complaint to trigger an inspection), companies are more likely to passively neglect compliance rather than aggressively seek out new strategies for avoiding the letter of the law. To some extent, then, hiring attorneys as counselors is an affirmative step *per se*, and it means that attorneys often preach to the converted.

All interviewees were asked where they felt most and least influential in their work. The question invited and received a fair amount of braggadocio but also gleaned impressive self-disclosure. Attorneys believe (and want to believe) that clients heed their advice, but they cannot ascertain why clients do so. Is the advice independently persuasive? This question may have been among those most affected by selection bias to the extent that many interviewees came from the elite firms serving elite clients. Nevertheless, three attorneys all drove at the financial roots of their influence:

> You're influential whenever what you're saying is taken into account and usually it is acted upon. You're least influential when you have a client that wants the advice and wants to understand what his options are but in the end . . . is going to make the decision for whatever particular reasons are driving it. If you have a client who's going to do whatever he wants to do even though he's paying for advice, I guess in the end you're not very influential. But I think most of the time we are influential because that's why we're hired.

> Within the companies, I think we're very influential. I don't know any company that pays us as much as they do to tell them what to do that ignores our advice. They just don't do it. I don't know whether that's because of what we charge them and the perception of value or what, but I hope it's because what we tell them is well argued, well written, and makes sense.

> We can cut through all the red tape . . . and get a result for our client in the shortest amount of time. That's a good result. We can do it because we know the players. We know the people in Washington, we know the people in the regions, they know us, and we don't have to spend a lot of time doing a dance . . . That's where we're at our best. We're at our worst, I think, when we're dealing with some of our smaller clients. We see they need to do certain things and they simply can't afford it. There's nothing that I can say, short of giving them money, that's going to change that. That's where we're not at our best. We tend to deal, at least in this practice, in very large companies.

These responses are tinged with the argument that expertise carried a price that made it valuable and hence difficult to acquire. Clients were both willing and able to seek their counsel. Many companies without health and safety advisors were either unwilling or unable to afford compliance assistance. Depending on the structure of a regulatory system, companies' use of counsel thus may be a predictor, if not a cause, of proactive corporate compliance.

To explain variances in business response to regulation, these attorneys commonly asserted that the companies seeking OSHA counseling were the "sophisticated" and "more enlightened companies." Typical was one management attorney's lament that the attorneys' message was not always enthusiastically received:

In the absence of [an enforcement action], the client has to be sophisticated enough, educated enough, and prudent enough to know that, "alright, the government is not pestering me now, but down the road they may be if I don't do this, so it's worth my time and dollar to [have you] help us out before we're in trouble," – which is a message that gets mixed results in this competitive era.

"Client sophistication" serves as lawyerly shorthand for management's ability to analyze short-term expenditures versus long-term liabilities – i.e., their willingness to afford priority and trust to lawyers. A leading component of sophistication is the difference between large and small companies. Economies of scale affect the likelihood of experiencing serious injuries or fatalities as a "routine" product of work. Some of the largest companies have a 100 percent chance of being inspected; the smallest, as low as 0.002 percent chance.[19] Also considering their greater financial resources and labor union activity, large firms are more likely to hire professional safety and health managers. In one management attorney's experience, larger companies found it easier to absorb new regulations into their organizations; while they may sharply oppose proposed regulations, they ultimately were better positioned for compliance. As a general rule, he said, "big companies have big staffs . . . So they're spending the money on it and they can afford to have people who understand and work to implement it, whereas the little guy wants to know, 'do I have to do this?' or 'do I have to do that?' And mostly they don't want to do any of it."

Interviewees never equated sophistication with altruism or even implied a higher-level morality in corporate ethics. The term truncates, rather, the web of economic and social factors that induce some companies to incorporate safety and health concerns into internal policy- and decisionmaking. The differences between large and small firms profoundly affect corporations' orientation to the regulatory environment. The development of large business organizations aggregated the potential harm to society and concomitantly intensified the social reaction to corporate misbehavior, as Union Carbide discovered in India and Exxon found out in Alaska.[20] Added scale exposed corporations to regulatory sanctions and greater social pressures, from labor relations to corporate reputations.[21] Corporate size may distance decisionmakers emotionally from workplace safety and health, but those corporate bureaucracies increase the regularity and precision of large companies' behavior. Interestingly, legal commentators have suggested that growing sophistication in corporate use of legal services has diminished their lawyers' capacity to serve as independent, critical advisors.[22]

Both the status of "sophisticated" companies and the importance of company size match important findings from Fiona Haines's study of Australian occupational health and safety compliance.[23] Haines found that economic forces and the tools of enforcement explained only some of industry compliance; highly important was her distinction between "virtuous" and "blinkered" companies. Virtuous companies actively sought to incorporate regulatory requirements into their organizations, which can sometimes lead governmental action in terms of commitment to safety. The culture of virtuous (or sophisticated) companies reinforces, rather than opposes, external pressures for the protection of workers' lives. The reports of American management attorneys mirror closely Haines's evidence of active compliance. She found that virtuous companies had a mature safety bureaucracy with safety personnel who had direct access to those in power.[24] Additionally, there was an emphasis on written procedures, safety committees with both workers and management, and a supportive organization. As others have identified, professionals involved in making regulations an integral part of organizations must have "clout," which is composed of numerous conditions at many levels – personal, organizational, and even external to the organization.[25] The ability of lawyers to persuade corporate decisionmakers about the importance of compliance with regulation, and the desire of lawyers even to try, depends upon factors such as attorneys' attitudes and economic pressures, their status within the corporate hierarchy, the receptivity of the clients, and the whole resources provided by legal texts, penalty structures, and other variables in the environment. Small companies may be more susceptible to punitive enforcement policies, but the cultural disposition to active compliance can be found more often among large companies. In the least, attorneys' involvement can signal the type of structure and culture that makes companies responsive to regulation. Perhaps, even, attorneys alter the structural and cultural arrangements within their clients' affairs, ultimately affecting the reception of the law in corporate boardrooms and managers' offices.

Prophets of the law

Regulatory agencies, OSHA included, often provide formal and informal mechanisms for communicating to regulated companies how they will enforce administrative rules and regulations. By providing detailed and specific information outside regular enforcement activities, administrative agencies allow well-intentioned firms additional opportunities to satisfy the government before imposing sanctions on every deviation from the rules. But the government's compliance assistance concedes a larger reality: gaps in corporate knowledge regarding applicable regulations are not entirely the companies' fault. The challenge of regulatory counseling again recalls one of the most enduring themes of modern administrative law: agencies need regulatory flexibility – even vagueness – so that rules can apply to all circumstances, yet regulated entities need precision to know how to comply.[26] At stake for regulatory schemes is due process versus efficiency.

The OSH Act's primary tool for tailoring compliance to context is the authority to issue temporary and permanent variances.[27] Employers can receive temporary (one-year) relief from newly promulgated standards by demonstrating their inability to comply by the effective date and the existence of an "effective program" for bringing the workplace up to code as soon as possible. To win permanent variances under Section 7(d), employers must demonstrate that their practices, conditions, and operations are as safe and healthful as those prescribed by established standards. Filing for variances does not exclude OSHA from issuing citations while applications await approval. Since companies filing for variances send the agency notice of noncompliance, there is a strong incentive to apply only when OSHA has already become aware of a problem. The low approval rate – less than 10 percent of the 2,380 applications received through mid-2001 – further discourages variance applications.[28]

In its history, OSHA has offered about 1,000 letters of "clarification," which avoid variances' cumbersome procedures, and which require, for example, announcements in the *Federal Register*. Clarification letters extend the agency's definitive explanations about the applicability of standards in specific situations, and they generally receive equal weight to variances with OSHA's regional offices. Unlike more formal compliance directives, interpretive letters typically focus on highly specialized issues of compliance. From the perspective of management attorneys, variances and interpretive letters are useful resources but unreliable, because the agency retains complete flexibility. Variances and compliance letters apply only to the employer for whom they were issued, and the Review Commission has conceded that they do not bind OSHA's interpretation in other cases.[29] At the same time, they can "lock in" unfavorable interpretations. One management attorney gets

TABLE 6.2: Most common means of compliance
assistance by OSHA attorneys in the past twelve months

	%
Provided informal compliance advice to your client	79.8
Reviewed or audited clients' procedures or programs	58.3
Developed procedures or programs for your client	52.0
Sought informal compliance advice from OSHA	50.2
Hired health and safety consultants to do the inspection	44.8
Inspected clients' facility for overall compliance	24.7
Sought formal compliance advice from OSHA	12.6
Sought a variance from an established standard	9.0

Source: 1998 Survey of OSHA Bar (N = 232).

official interpretations from OSHA "in a lot of situations . . . [where]
you have a pretty good idea of what the interpretation is supposed to be
and it really serves everybody's interest to have it clearly articulated
and written down somewhere." Still, he cautioned, "there are other
situations where you're not going to get" compliance letters.

> The lawyers' adage is don't ask a question you don't know the answer
> to, and that applies in spades in regulatory law because if you write a
> question and get the wrong answer it takes years and many, many more
> dollars to try to fix the situation . . . Because enforcement is such a
> low probability event, in those situations you're probably better off not
> asking the question at all and relying on your own judgment and your
> own intuition.

It is easier, he thought, to argue the merits of a particular compliance
method in an enforcement action than to overturn the presumption
given to a letter of interpretation.

The various incentives and burdens limit the use of formal compliance advice. Table 6.2 reports the frequency of various tools used by
attorneys. Fewer than one-fifth (19.7 percent) of surveyed attorneys had
sought either a variance or a formal interpretive letter in the past year.[30]
At the other end of the spectrum, four-fifths of surveyed attorneys (and
86.8 percent of OSHA specialists) had rendered informal compliance
advice to their clients in the past year.

The vital cleavage concerns whether attorneys informally consulted
with OSHA regarding their clients' compliance problems. OSHA specialists sought out informal advice from the agency more frequently

than nonspecialists did (60.3 percent to 28.6 percent).[31] The relative frequency of hands-on compliance counseling by attorneys suggests a high level of comfort dealing with OSHA standards, particularly regarding procedures and programs that involve compliance "on paper" as opposed to the factory floor.

Through the years, OSHA has used a number of means to provide technical compliance advice. The most significant barrier to on-site consultation has been the policy by federal OSHA requiring the issuance of citations for every observed violation. Compliance assistance has been channeled through states instead, either via state plans or through contracts and direct grants supporting consultants in states otherwise covered by the federal enforcement program. Employers taking advantage of state consultative services remain subject to future inspections, though information gathered from on-site consultative visits remains separate from enforcement activities. OSHA publicizes consultation services, but its assurances are not enough to convince some employers of the agency's good intentions. Again, the contrast between large and small clients was sharp. A leading management attorney reported that his clients typically had "no problem whatsoever with going to OSHA and saying 'look, we have a situation; hypothetically, what would you do in this situation?'" A trade association representative for many small and medium-sized employers by contrast, found herself "spending a lot of time on the phone with our members who have questions about OSHA but don't want to call them directly."

> For our members, OSHA is still very much a watchdog, but we're trying to do a lot to change that. [Members] still feel very threatened, they don't like to call them directly, and they don't like to label themselves, so I act as an in-between between them and the government.

Although the growth of voluntary compliance schemes begun during the Reagan administration, and Republican-sponsored legislative reforms designed to enhance agency compliance programs have helped to ease company fears, the perception remains in the private sector that OSHA strongly prefers the stick to the carrot. In one dispute, a number of leading attorneys publicly recounted their clients' perception that failure to join a "cooperative" compliance program would result in the "white glove" treatment from local OSHA area offices.[32]

199

In lieu of formal options, the OSHA bar has sought to enhance its credentials as teachers and prophets: a combination of practical health and safety knowledge plus the knowledge of what OSHA, the solicitors, and the Review Commission are likely to do. Instead of sending their clients to the agency, attorneys can interpose themselves between the two, becoming the voice for the agency. Two lawyers described the types of issues that they need to communicate to their clients:

> We're always very careful to say "here are the possibilities," and we're also very careful to say, "well listen, this is what the law allows you to do, but we'll tell you right now, you're probably going to get a citation because OSHA doesn't necessarily agree with this interpretation." And even if there's a case out there [supporting this interpretation] the compliance officers probably haven't seen it, so you always have to tell people, "we think you're right in doing this this way, but we can never tell you that there's not going to be a whole lot of controversy or conflict in proving that you're right." So a lot of times there's a safe way to do it, there's the legal way to do it – which turns out is going to take a lot of time to prove that it's the legal way – and there's the pseudo-legal and easy way to do it.

> Our emphasis is on avoiding situations with people that end up in court, whether that be an enforcement action from an OSHA compliance officer or a lawsuit or something like that . . . So most of what we do, I'd say by far the majority, is communications to clients about what the standards say, how OSHA is interpreting them, how do you get into compliance, and what are the defensible legal positions that you can take regarding ambiguous or uncertain language – and there are lots of them.

Counseling issues radiate in shades of gray rather than bright lines, and attorneys and clients naturally exhibit different threshold points for risks. When lawyers find relative certainty in a situation – both the clarity of the rule *per se* and whether the employer is non-compliant – the advice is that of a teacher, direct and simple. Clients often want to take advantage of any regulatory uncertainty, however, and attorneys may help to generate it even in areas of seeming clarity. The rule is not enough, because the starting point for attorneys' analysis is the "bad man's" understanding – what the agency will do in fact. Their risk assessments supplant the agency's interpretations, become the foundation of compliance, and contribute to the meaning of the law in practice. More significant uncertainty can enhance the lawyer's role. Even while criticizing vague regulations, one lawyer felt that:

from an attorney's standpoint, more often than not I don't look at [vagueness] as being a real problem because it gives us some options in terms of interpreting the compliance requirements . . . More often than not we like to have a little flexibility in being able to say, "well, here are your options, here's what you probably should be doing, here's what other people have done, and here's the way the agency has interpreted it in the past."

In short, regulatory vagueness allows space for legal creativity.

The role of ethics in such circumstances is constrained. One management attorney interviewed indicated that he tried to have a "constructive role on the ultimate decision" made by a client by laying out all considerations that might bear on the decision, including those not "purely" legal; ethical judgments remained the client's. Survey data appear to confirm findings made by other scholars that only a small segment of the bar has ever refused a client or a case on ethical grounds.[33] Just 6.8 percent of surveyed attorneys had ever refused to take on a new client (or a case from an existing one) because of a company's lack of commitment to safety and health.[34] By contrast, one-third (32.6 percent) had refused a new case for reasons other than a conflict of interest, the most common of which was "inability to pay," closely followed by "disagreement as to style or strategy."

Even within non-adversarial settings such as counseling, the norm of zealous advocacy in pursuit of client self-interest informs the perspective of the management bar. In a dialogue sketched by a prominent management attorney, serving public interest can be advanced by serving the best interest of clients.

It's a strange role to be in, but very often we're the messenger bringing the news to the client that, "no, whether innocently or otherwise, you can't continue to do things this way," or "you're going to have to start doing things this way." If your question is, "how can I avoid liability?" it's simple: avoid accidents. You don't need me if people don't get hurt. Next, get in compliance. That's how you avoid having to talk to me. "Well, what does it mean to get in compliance?" Well, let's see what you're doing. Do you have the requisite elements of a program, do you have this, do you have that? Some of the work we do is preventive. We do compliance audits, the purpose of which is to make sure our clients are in compliance so as to avoid liability and also to be protecting people.

Attorneys of many stripes asserted a similar view: clients are well served when they do what is right, not just what is legally acceptable. An in-house counsel for a trade association echoed the thought that although many member companies would say "we don't want an ergonomics standard, we don't want a safety and health program standard," she reminded them, "OK, guys, there are reasons we haven't done some of this stuff in the past, but we need to look at it." The reason for encouraging compliance was simple: when member companies improve their ergonomics programs, workers' compensation premiums sharply decline. Being able to serve the public interest and client interests – at least in attorneys' minds – prevents role conflict and cognitive dissonance. "I like doing preventive stuff, even though I enjoy litigation," one practitioner declared, "because you really feel like you're accomplishing protection at the same time you're serving your client. You're doing good things."[35] Survey results suggest that, nearly universally, attorneys will claim this attitude as an expectation of their role: 95.4 percent of attorneys agreed with the statement that "I advise my clients that proactive compliance with OSHA standards makes good business sense."[36]

The importance of being a prophet of regulatory agencies animates the otherwise routine professional differences between management OSHA lawyers and private, safety-and-health consultants. Consultants far outnumber attorneys.[37] The work of lawyers and safety-and-health consultants frequently overlaps. As documented in table 6.2, attorneys often complete audits, develop procedures, or even perform full compliance inspections; but 44.8 percent also reported having referred some issues to health and safety consultants. Lawyers may recognize the expertise of other professionals but also defend their own. Some interviewees argued that nonlawyer consultants were either "practicing law without a license" or doing their clients a disservice when they attempted to play the prophet. One leading attorney pointedly emphasized his enforcement experience as the source of his counseling expertise.

> You can have a consultant come in and do a health and safety audit and try to bring your facility into compliance with the letter of the standards. And how will that consultant do it? By reading those standards and trying to match your performance to those standards. That's fine, as long as the standards are not open to much debate as to what they mean. If they are open to much debate about what they mean, that consultant could be missing the mark because what the consultant doesn't have is a sense of what will really fly with OSHA and what won't fly with OSHA . . . It's possible that for certain standards [compliance officers] will actually

let you get away with more than the standard might imply, and for some standards they won't let you get away with anywhere near what you'd think you can get away with based upon the standard. And there's no way of knowing that unless you've been in enforcement.

Counseling roles may be influenced by ideologies of professional ethics but are more immediately grounded by experience, here provided by the OSHA bar's crossover from enforcement to counseling. Having witnessed the law in action, counsel can help clients weave a zealous course through the maze of regulations, perhaps by directing them to do the proverbial "right thing" but also by offering prophecies.

Counseling for inspection preparedness

Enforcement experience shapes counseling activities in another way. As discussed in chapter 5, many pitfalls of enforcement actions can be defused or prevented if companies anticipate and prepare for them.[38] The ability to provide this type of advice, attorneys argue, further distinguishes OSHA attorneys from nonlawyer safety-and-health professionals. The pitfalls are both procedural and personal, so advice meant to change employers' readiness deepens the legal profession's perceived role as personal *counselors*.

For some lawyers, interviews revealed, inspection preparedness dominates their counseling practice. Understanding "ideal" responses to accidents, emergencies, and investigations allows some attorneys to expand the market for their services. Having developed basic handbooks, guidelines, and training for middle managers in one company, these lawyers realized they could easily provide the same materials to others with no upstart costs. Inspection procedures and policies may include information such as who to notify in the company, the bounds of inspector authority, employee rights during inspections, and what not to say to inspectors, employees, or the media. In the market to provide compliance lawyering, attorneys who, for one reason or another, have not developed substantive expertise appear to emphasize preparedness counseling. For some with diversified practices, occasional involvement in enforcement matters gives them a better grounding in the process than industrial health and safety. One attorney reported that since his large-company clientele had substantial safety and health personnel in-house, his services were limited to inspection issues. Some attorneys with a client base of small companies found it difficult to sell inspection preparedness at all. Because they receive fewer inspections to serve as warnings, attorneys argued that this mixed blessing meant that managers "unsophisticated" about OSHA risks sometimes let inspection preparation fall victim to short-term costs.

To tap this market of work, lawyers urge comparison between the cost of readiness and the cost of full, by-the-book compliance. A common corporate axiom of "burdensome" regulation is that, if OSHA had the enforcement resources, the agency would find at least one violation in every workplace. Now, the agency has neither the will nor the resources to test that claim, but if provoked, compliance officers can uncover minor violations in individual inspections that even well-intentioned employers could not root out. One attorney's preparedness training includes instructions on *how* to say things so that relatively routine inspections stay routine; these lessons complement his work to standardize employers' written materials with compliance officers' expectations. The objective, he thought, was to place the precise language of Review Commission decisions into employer programs. "You're going to be putting those key words or key phrases in to make it more acceptable when the OSHA inspector comes in," he said.

> Most inspections turn on fairly mundane kinds of things such as process safety management or hazcom [hazard communications]. It's just book-keeping. You want to make sure you have all the right things in place. It may not protect you if something has actually gone wrong, but it probably will keep people from looking at you too hard. If they see all the magic words and phrases there, you're probably not going to get into as much trouble.

After an accident – where there's blood on the floor – companies probably cannot avoid scrutiny, but they can use counsel's advice to excise the emotional triggers that could provoke spiraling conflict in other cases. The particular context of regulation and the norms within the agency's staff generate a form that lawyers can match. Thus, lawyers drawing on their knowledge of the inspectorate fill the gaps between full, literal compliance and what the government will in fact demand of companies.

In the most creative strategies, compliance work can be parlayed into an attempt to prevent inspection. Some attorneys want their work to be a flag of trust to the agency, and this involves an element of marketing. Consider the following strategic response to head OSHA off at the pass when the agency begins an "emphasis" program for certain hazards or industries on its enforcement agenda. One company attorney, heavily involved in compliance consulting, explained his approach to reduce chances that his client would become the "example" case. Working with the company and, if possible, employee groups, he encourages them to develop corporate programs on the issues being emphasized by OSHA. After the company implements the programs, he launches a public relations campaign:

> You then may take that program and say to the regional [agency] folks, "here's what we're doing in Maine, we want you to be aware of this. We think it's a good program and this is what we've learned out of the program already." And through some education the [agency] folks in Maine would say, "why would I want to inspect these guys when nobody else that we know of is doing this? We might as well spend our time in an environment where there's likely greater risk to workers."

In effect, it is hoped, the company and the agency will trade voluntary compliance for less regulatory oversight, with the lawyer communicating the company's intentions.

Unrevealed by this attorney's account, of course, is whether the programs are as effective as those that the agency might have imposed, a legitimate concern for any self-regulatory or cooperative arrangement. Also unknown is the strategy's actual success rate in "diverting" regulatory bodies. Plain, however, is the potential for attorneys, in their zealous preparedness, to use compliance as justification for inspection avoidance. The OSHA bar splits on cooperative and aggressive strategies in enforcement, but most members agree on avoiding uncontrolled conflict. The "most effective" contribution of pre-enforcement consulting, as one lawyer asserted, is "smoothing the relationships, making sure that when the agency and the companies clash or do come into contact with each other that that relationship is handled properly."

Measures of success
Deprived of a scorecard for wins, losses, and settlements, regulatory counseling might be thought a frustrating enterprise. While some measures of corporate success exist, such as workdays lost, injury and illness rates, and workers' compensation expenses, attorneys do not always witness the results of efforts. From a public policy perspective, too, there are few ways to weigh the impact of lawyers on regulatory compliance. Attorneys' roles, companies' interests, and the law's objectives potentially overlap, but the question remains: do the perceived roles and conduct of attorneys further or frustrate the goal of corporate compliance?

One reason why it may be impossible to disentangle the influence of lawyers is that, as many interviewees noted, clients' cultural disposition toward OSHA compliance predicts the lawyers' involvement. Where OSHA standards have codified workplace "common sense," a lawyer may do little more than animate the company's latent desire to comply. For other companies, practitioners have little role available to offer other than "hired gun" advocacy. Asked to appraise his effectiveness, one attorney replied that he was

> ineffective with clients who don't want to hear it, and some folks just don't want to hear it. It's called the "I don't wanna" defense – "I don't wanna." You can only give your advice. You can't run the company, you can't make the choices, and that happens sometimes. You run into people who aren't going to change the way they do business. It doesn't happen often, but it happens.

Whenever clients respond in this way, attorneys have little choice but to become the client's advocate, get creative, or quit.

Lawyerly persuasion, whenever determinative, may stem from the client's trust that attorneys are ideologically "on their side." Trust is as much a matter of culture as of cognition, and cultural mediation is necessary for gulfs as wide as the employers–OSHA divide. Identification with clients' political interests should not be interpreted as a lack of autonomy, then, but as a keystone of regulatory mediation. Sometimes the obstacle is less the message than how the listener hears it. Lawyers may bring a different voice to the table. One OSHA practitioner boasted that it made all the difference. In the course of his work, he said,

> I used to kid with my old friends at OSHA all the time that I do a lot more good for health and safety than they do because at least when I tell my client to do something they do it. And it's true. A client will call us in because I have years of experience in this field and they'll say "can you look at this program, tell us what you think needs to be changed, what needs to be done, should we change the discipline system or something else?" And generally, if I tell them to do something and I give them good reasons why it should be done, it will be done. There's no fighting.

This lawyer's unspoken premise is that both he and the government had identical goals for the client – compliance. Companies may be closer to OSHA's fundamental goals than they realize; attorneys help build cultural bridges to close the gap.

Attorneys also must supply the "good reasons" to achieve this apparently "self-regulated" compliance. The presence of government and third parties in the networks of health and safety issues provides the reasons. Labor relations contribute significantly to this dynamic. An interviewee widely regarded for his cooperative style of lawyering draws on unions in both cooperative compliance work and active enforcement actions, encouraging union officials to become involved. His advice when counseling is:

> at a minimum, be in compliance; where you can, show you're doing better. And the test is our judgment plus what do your employees say. If you're organized, what does your union say? If a company comes to OSHA and they want a particular position taken on a rule, if a company goes in and the union's there with them, OSHA's going to listen a lot quicker.

Union assistance in particular cases affirms to OSHA that management has closed the cultural chasm. Recurring interaction among companies, organized labor, and agency officials thus sustains a tripartite regulatory scheme, within which attorneys can push clients toward a unity of the law's goals and the client's interests.[39]

Caveats necessarily apply to this mediating, moderating role. For one, most businesses and especially small companies are likely to make compliance choices without the assistance of counsel. Indeed, a leading union attorney assessed the state of OSHA regulation by calling for greater involvement by management OSHA lawyers in compliance activities.

> The more I hear that people are being represented the better it is, because in the long run, regulation *qua* regulation isn't going to do it. It's going to have to be voluntary compliance, and you don't get voluntary compliance unless you get an educated and informed client base. So from totally selfish reasons what I want to see happen is more and more employers turn to lawyers for legitimate assistance. Not to fight everything, but to educate them, inform them, work with them in the venture of trying to see what it takes to come into compliance.
> Q: And you've seen private lawyers play an important role there with their clients?
> A: Oh, absolutely. Absolutely no doubt about that. My job is to do everything I can to help persuade my counterpart lawyer to turn to his client and say, "if we don't do that, these other characters are going to launch this initiative or that initiative and in the long run we'd

> be much better served by not turning this into a donnybrook and work our way through the problem." That's the most satisfying thing in the world. When you think in part a solution has been generated by the fact that your [management] counterparts are *using you*, so to speak, as part of the leverage in dealing with their respective clients to solve a problem, that's good.

This union lawyer's unequivocal conclusion provides a hopeful window for compliance counseling, a space in which lawyers respond to client interests with leverage toward compliance rather than simply finding and facilitating "creative" compliance.[40]

Beyond the potential for regulatory lawyers to aid compliance, survey evidence points to the limits of the OSHA bar's collective aspiration to any role wider than that of prophet: 62.3 percent frequently or always recommended factoring in the likelihood of the client being inspected when counseling clients about compliance.[41] What the agency will do concerns attorneys as much as what clients are commanded to do. When the government, unions, and lawyers are absent, companies face compliance decisions alone. What then becomes of the law's aspirations? A leading management practitioner concluded: "Long term, it's very hard to say. Short term I think it works because I can see it work. I'll check up on it. But long term, a year later, are they still doing what I think they should be? Don't know. Don't know."

CONCLUSION

Aspirations within the OSHA bar, even if only partially fulfilled in practice, suggest that third parties within regulatory networks – situated between the regulators and regulated companies – can help negotiate and overcome contentious political and scientific battles. Given the reality of general rules and finite enforcement, the minimum one would expect in regulatory arenas would be the prophets who predict agency behavior. By predicting the state of the law-in-practice but washing hands of client decisions based on that information, lawyers avoid conflicts with clients over visions of what compliance should be. Some attorneys may regard the role as the maximum obligation. An axiom for lobbyists is that legislators depend on reliable information; so do regulated entities, and a regulatory bar may define its ambitions purely in those terms. Other attorneys appear called to more: reconciling client interests with the public good. The stands that lawyers take behind closed doors will remain subjects of speculation for outside observers, but interview data point to some scope for accommodation between public and private interests, orchestrated by attorneys. Interviewees supplied a wide range of reasons for this goal, from clients' long-term interests to the personalities involved; and union lawyers and OSHA officials can confirm the potential behaviors, if not the motivations.

There must be skepticism about the extent to which the process of counseling and the involvement of lawyers bears any relationship to regulatory outcomes. The process itself is complex. Ideology, culture, attorney–client relationships, cost–benefit analyses, regulatory structures, regulatory clarity, and other forces factor into the equation. The role of attorneys in OSHA law may be conditioned by factors as yet beyond identification that explain the empirical roles of lawyers there. But it is at least clear from the process that lawyers must be situated within the daily practice of the OSHA bureaucracy, and in those practices the logic and illogic of behavior are constructed. Beyond cost and benefit, safety and health is the product of a complex interaction of parties whose fates are linked within the realm, and in the shadows, of the administrative process.

CHAPTER SEVEN

CONCLUSION

The administrative process and administrative law are vital to contemporary societies. Though individual issues often belong among the most arcane matters of public policy and implementation, there is little question of the importance to those who are the targets or beneficiaries of regulation. Beyond occupational safety and health, a complete itemization of the regulatory ambitions of the modern state – from securities markets to airplane safety to species protection to immigration control – draws appreciative gasps from even informed audiences. The realm is so large and rich that academicians will be guaranteed years of future employment simply providing a window into how these systems "work" in practice across policy areas, across countries, and over time.

Administrative governments, as systems of legal and political foundation, also raise enduring and critical issues of general interest. The process of governing discrete instances of human behavior through the application of general principles – nearly a fundamental definition of "law" itself – cannot escape an inherent strain between ambition and fruition. The failings of language, the inevitability of competing interests, and the unpredictability of circumstances, to name just a few impediments, breed disagreements over how legal principles or rules should apply in particular instances. To this must be added the unresolvable controversy about what principles *should* govern a particular case. These realistic assessments are not unique to administrative law or even contemporary society, yet the scope and ambitions of the modern administrative state expose more acutely the difficulties of creating and enforcing rules of general applicability. The numerous veins of scholarly research that converge on administrative rulemaking, enforcement, and counseling are critical proof of gaps in the effectiveness and legitimacy of administrative regulation.

Law has a seemingly curious place in administrative systems, both in the United States and in places where evolving discussions of accountability are putting legal control on the agenda. Contemporary discussions begin from the recognition that the authority of the state is constrained, as formal hierarchies are diluted by interdependence with private interests.[1] Simply put, "law is more marginal . . . than lawyers might assume."[2] Yet, "the law" is attractive in public discussions as a mechanism of control. Any perceived tension here dissolves on closer scrutiny. Whereas "law" once might have meant the authority to command and control through specific but limited delegations of power, we now understand law as a tool that can be wielded by public agencies and private-sector regulated entities alike. The interdependence, continuing relationships and strategic interactions of public–private regulatory encounters are all consistent with a situation in which the legal setting of administrative regulation gives bargaining chips to both public and private actors. American regulatory politics, absent an absolute power, is an incessant negotiation over competing claims, for which assertions about what the law *is* and *should be* have particular currency. Lawyers prove important in those discussions, helping to frame and articulate the ambitions of clients through stages that are legislative and judicial in varying degrees. This chapter concludes this study by returning to the themes introduced in chapter 1, particularly the roles of lawyers in the American administrative process and the significance of their practices for regulatory systems more generally.

LAWYERS AS INTEREST REPRESENTATIVES

In the social sciences, a scholar's hope is usually to find a theoretical explanation of simplicity and elegance for the data at hand. Sometimes, however, it is equally important to be reminded of, and even to embrace, the complexity of the politics of the administrative process in the trenches. We can understand administrative settings only by accounting for the remarkable array of influences on regulators, regulated entities and intermediaries. Complexity appears to be the norm for regulatory politics within policy areas. Across areas, complexity is unavoidable.

Legal practices pulsate at the heart of OSHA's administrative process. With the landscape of possibilities suggested by formal law, incentives propelled by numerous factors, and added layers of perception, belief, and cultures reverberating through it all, lawyers have had a particularly noteworthy place. But unlike the larger-than-life persona of Clark Clifford, the identities of these individuals as lawyers are not essential to the story. At one level, even their status as lawyers can be bracketed to one side. Most public–private negotiation and settlement in rulemaking and enforcement enacts the more universal clash of interests across a negotiating table. Negotiations occur in this context whether lawyers or nonlawyers lead the bargaining. What is essential is that interest representatives are commonly missing from accounts of regulatory processes. This gap leaves an opportunity cost: the opportunity to see how individuals with continuing involvement in the life of public–private discussions are shaped by numerous forces, yet also transform it through their individual actions. We can find in interest representatives, then, a link between the enduring qualities of regulatory interaction and the behavior of interests who may be irregular or infrequent participants in a policy network.

The roles that lawyers may play as interest representatives, the selection and potency of strategies, and the relative power exercised in public–private regulatory encounters are shaped by a wide palate of conditions and uncertainties. As derived from the interactions in OSHA's realm, table 7.1 brings together a range of influences that emerge from these struggles. In the richness of life, the politics of regulation can become slave to individual personalities at work, or any of a host of other **individual factors**. For example, a "mission-minded" agency like OSHA has been populated by individuals with a commitment to worker safety and health, and corporate decisionmakers can be no less locked into ideological commitments against regulation. **Situational factors** produce many of the case-by-case variations that occur within this setting. A common thread when speaking with regulatory lawyers is to find the constraints on their behavior that derive from their understanding about what the "facts" require. Facts can be socially constructed, but behavior makes them real: a "clear" interpretation of a law presses on someone. Not all situational factors are constructed in this way – the "feasibility" of compliance is in part an expression of interests, but one subject to outer limits set by science. Even more broadly, **environmental factors** frame and constrain interactions. In the background of any interaction or struggle are social, political, and economic conditions

TABLE 7.1: Partial typology of influences in OSHA regulatory interactions

	Individual	Situational	Environmental
Client	• repeat-player • ideological commitments	• facts of case or situation • economic cost–benefits	• competitive pressures • norms and social expectations in client's industry
Attorney	• specialization • socialization, e.g., legal education, government experience	• reputation with government officials • strength of relationships with government and client	• economic pressures • professional liability and ethical codes
Government	• professional orientation • working relationship within government • capacity for discretion	• political controls from legislative or executive branches • level of judicial oversight	• resource limitations • institutional culture • diffuse effect of political controls
Common	• personality	• prior law (statutory, precedents, norms) • institutional processes	• shared cost of breakdown in relationships

that set the stage for the art of the possible. These forces influence decisionmakers on all sides, including private interests, the government, and attorneys who may be between them. Some conditions are shared. These factors come into play selectively and interact with one another, making for highly multivariate problems.

Many of the factors described in table 7.1 provide the resources and liabilities that establish strategic positions. Included here are the effects of having repeated interactions over the content or application of regulations. With repeat play in administrative politics, case-by-case influences on behavior give way to more enduring elements, such as the reputations that individuals may seek to maintain or, as I will argue below, the law that is created and revised interstitially. Thus, the law appears here as background, but a network with a notion of "law" or "rules" is not inherently stagnant when the rules are a focus of inter-action. Lawyers, with a professional concern for the process of regula-tion, are among those who most clearly play for the rules, seeking to set precedents and standards, both formal and informal.

The highly situational and tangled web of factors in regulatory encounters – table 7.1 is only a partial, suggestive itemization of these factors – produces a wide range of roles that can be filled by interme-diaries. OSHA lawyers assert for themselves many different roles, per-ceived or real. Taking a rather bi-polar, grease/friction approach, one attorney interviewee, for example, argued that the intra-governmental differences made a significant difference.

> I see my role as a two-headed monster, one as a facilitator in the early-going, and when I run into what I decide is an unreasonable position taken by the other side, then I become an advocate or someone who is going to be obstructive to that process, making it difficult to resolve rather than easy. Particularly with the Solicitor's Office, sometimes you sort of team up, so I think you're wearing two hats and it really depends on who you're dealing with . . . You really are a two-headed monster, I guess.

Interviewees from trade associations, unions, and the government reg-istered assertions about lawyers, as well, and the available evidence supports some of these. The labels we would attach to roles are lin-guistic creations to evoke an empirical condition. Depending on one's reading and categorization of those behaviors in context, upwards of a dozen roles might be asserted. Only a few need be mentioned before it becomes clear that regulatory lawyering encompasses a wide range of activities. As summarized in table 7.2, the work of OSHA lawyers crystallizes into at least five roles – dynamic, overlapping, and interactive – that are sometimes conscious and chosen strategically, or sometimes are the functional outcomes of situations.

Advocate The popular image of attorneys is as gladiators who champion competing claims before neutral adjudicators. American administrative systems employ a surfeit of adversarial processes, despite efforts to promote "informal" and negotiated decisionmaking. Work-place safety and health, a battleground for labor and business interests, enhances the opportunities for advocacy. In rulemaking, unions and employers have often challenged OSHA standards, leading to extensive

TABLE 7.2: Roles of lawyers as interest representatives

Role	Description
Advocate	Traditional advocacy in formal settings, through either written or oral communication
Shepherd	Guide through administrative processes
Educator	Informs client of norms in regulatory interactions; promotes compliance, cooperation, or resistance to norms
Diplomat	Go-between or representative in negotiations
Power-broker	Strategist for the situation; ability to leverage client's resources and advantages vis-à-vis other parties

post-rulemaking litigation in courts of appeal. The National Association of Manufacturers' challenge to the lockout/tagout rule was a classic instance of attorneys advancing legal claims in an attempt to strike down regulations. Enforcing standards, moreover, can provoke litigation before administrative law judges and the Occupational Safety and Health Review Commission prior to judicial review. As in other legal contexts, zealous advocacy is both a perceived responsibility and a tactic that may induce settlement.

Shepherd Legal representatives, like good shepherds, guard client interests from known and unknown dangers. Handholding is the starting point for inexperienced clients, and the role is influenced by the understanding of "sophistication" that lawyers bring to their client relationships. Lawyers may attempt to orient clients to a regulation scheme and shape their attitudes about the crossroads ahead. Professional training pushes lawyers to think of processes holistically, considering how client behavior can affect later strategic positions. For instance, patrolling the record in "notice and comment" rulemaking may be the epitome of a legal role permeating into the administrative process. OSHA counsel also claim a role after a workplace accident or an inspection, because they believe their emotional detachment prevents client missteps. Shepherding clients, for most lawyers, thus extends beyond merely "legal" questions into the range that attorneys and clients negotiate for their relationship.

Educator Learning and adaptation form essential elements of administrative governance, especially depending on the level of uncertainty or complexity contained within a body of regulation. Expertise as a category is found across national systems of regulation; legal expertise is less common. So, it is an interesting facet of the American system that has lawyers claiming particular expertise, though they compete with company staffs and other professionals to provide that expertise. In particular, OSHA lawyers believe that their legal perspective and experience allow them to be effective educators. This role is multi-faceted. At a minimum, lawyers explain to clients how the government interprets and enforces regulations, as well as the risks and alternative options, before deferring to client judgments. Some attorneys may encourage and guide executives to comply with robust regulatory interpretations by emphasizing the clients' long-term interests in developing good relationships with the agency and unions. Even further, norms can be communicated through attorney advice, or may assist client efforts to avoid compliance by creatively interpreting regulations. The stories of counsel add up to a strong motif: representing clients is laden with potential for educating others – clients, adversaries, regulators, scientists, and themselves – about the formal and informal rules of the administrative system.

Diplomat   For most attorneys, successful representation in regulatory law entails helping clients balance many interests. Client concerns about public and union relations, ideological aims, competitiveness, and bottom-line profits all figure in regulatory disputes. As go-betweens in rulemaking, enforcement, and counseling, attorneys may play many roles. They are negotiators, helping clients obtain the most favorable outcome possible by satisfying the needs of other parties. In some cases, attorneys have led rulemaking negotiations in which all parties have bargained over new rules. They seek out the forum that offers greatest potential for victory or settlement, such as working with the Solicitor's Office. Accommodating private and public interests with a form of diplomacy thus becomes an intrinsic by-product of attorneys' work.

Power-broker   Bureaucracies are subject to external control by both Congress and executive officials, and political appointees may not share the professional ideology of the staff, so private interests may try to sway decisionmakers through the exercise of political power. As recent research has suggested, lawyers alone seldom have enough clout or skill to alter an agency's goals substantially. Still, an undercurrent of politics may pull lawyers to mobilize or suppress political actors for narrow objectives. Management OSHA counsel have appealed to the OMB, a potent resource during Republican administrations, to delay or excise regulations. The final settlement of the formaldehyde rulemaking controversy suggests that attorneys had enough influence to dampen the OMB's objections after initially summoning its assistance. Just as some

OSHA practitioners may galvanize political power, so others may repel or avoid it. Recognizing their limited influence, some attorneys disavow a strategy of sending clients to members of Congress to bring pressure in OSHA enforcement cases.

These roles do not map squarely across notions, introduced in chapter 1, of attorneys as grease and friction in regulatory systems. Regulatory practices in complex settings both transcend and unite those accounts by providing the ad hoc, creative representation that works to advance client interests through whatever style necessary. Policy science could not hope to design "frictionless" administrative systems, in which discretionary judgments would not inspire any efforts to advance or hinder regulation, except by obliterating the interests that drive interaction in a public sphere. The practices of lawyers, as interest representatives, fit into that landscape through a spectrum of roles responsive to the interdependent, continuing and strategic regulatory relationships. The distribution or frequency of lawyer behaviors is an unresolved question. The administrative process for governing occupational safety and health in the United States unquestionably puts particular emphasis on adversarial, quasi-judicial proceedings; nevertheless, a range of roles assists the process of translating interests into the logic of the system. Future study moving across policy areas and national boundaries will be able to expose more fully the influences that drive the range of roles in practice.

MAKING POLITICS, MAKING LAW

The flexible roles of lawyers in regulatory politics are a necessary condition of practice, driven at the individual level by the commitments to clients and the need to reduce pervasive uncertainty. Lawyers adapt during the pursuit of enduring goals, both for the client and for themselves. Beyond individual interactions, however, if lawyers do not sit at the core of regulatory policymaking, and if they appear episodically and with variable roles, what can we say that lawyers *do* within specialized areas of policymaking, such as occupational safety and health? Attorneys do more than simply transmit signals and messages as a kind of regulatory courier. In at least some examples, attorneys have been afforded broader roles. At other times, whatever the role for attorneys, the unquestionably legal tenor and character of interactions dominate the proceedings. An important answer to this question is that attorneys make clear to us how the dynamic and fluid world of contemporary regulatory politics has some forms of stability at its core. As the hierarchy of the administrative state breaks down to a seemingly open and even unaccountable mass of public and private interests, attorneys, as interest representatives, help clients find order in law and law-like norms. "The law," broadly considered, remains an important element of regulation, even as the authority of the state has been questioned. Public–private interaction draws life from the power of law in its many guises, and it is worth considering further how the production of formal and informal law can help us understand regulatory politics.

Certainly, a notion of law, usually meaning the "hard law" of formal decrees and binding rules, has always been background for the traditional accounts of administration offered by lawyers and even many social scientists. Law is sometimes conceived of as a fixed boundary that either establishes a process for regulatory encounters or places substantive limits on the state (sometimes enforceable by courts). Approached in this way, the formal law relied upon by hierarchical models of administration commonly becomes a foil for the emergence of informal norms, private sector self-regulation and non-state influence on regulatory outcomes. Having cast aside the bogeyman of formal law, social scientists have been slow to probe too deeply into the logic of law or to integrate accounts of legal actors into their theories of regulation, due perhaps to the complexity of legal issues or the belief (not discouraged by the legal profession itself) that law is only a 'technical' translation of regulatory policymaking.[3] For their part, many legal scholars work largely within a discourse that presumes the centrality of law and only occasionally bring empirical research to bear on these questions. Some scholars have sought the Archimedean point between legal and social scientific perspectives on regulation, though empirical research to date has scarcely followed that lead.[4]

Law is background, to be sure, figuring prominently in OSHA policymaking at all levels. Regulation expressed through law can take on multiple layers of significance in the struggle to ensure compliance and accountability by private actors.[5] Most immediately, whether by setting the structure of rulemaking or guiding the conduct of inspections, law establishes processes through which the agency develops and implements its agenda for regulation. To members of the OSHA bar, law is a real presence guiding behavior, even if it is subject to debate. Management attorneys can use it as a check on the agency, or union lawyers can use it to spur agency action. Industries facing compliance questions look to it for the minimum standards imposed. The existence of the term "feasible" in the OSH Act introduces a constraint on agency action, just as other terms give the agency a "general duty" to protect workers. Ultimately, substantive outcomes reflect the basic suppositions set as the formal parameters of agency action, either as granted by statute or, particularly in the US, as elaborated by courts.

The episodes recounted in this book, and the practices described by attorneys and their opposing parties, make clear that "the law" is not as simple and fixed as words in a book. For one, the practices of OSHA attorneys and their roles within the regulatory arena make clear the informal dimensions of law and its meanings. At the micro-level, what "the law" is – or is perceived to mean – is crucial to how interest representatives (lawyers and non-lawyers alike) engage the agency and one another. In practice, lawyers and nonlawyers give meanings to these words and are affected by their understandings of the same. The shadow of the law produced by vague words and uncertain futures further carves out paths of behavior. In the case of compliance, the effective meaning of law is little more than the understandings that flow through corporate discussions and courses of action. Creativity and discretion are not infinite; the language and logic of law limits public and private actors. Lawyers furnish meanings that cut a path between the public and private interests. Law will not always be able to evaluate corporate performance, since for many companies compliance officers rarely have cause to visit. So, the legal opinion of the attorney can be central to what we say the "law" is in practice. The settlement of much enforcement and rulemaking litigation provides another informal process by which the law takes its meaning. Outside of a process clearly defined by statute, public and private parties – or even just private parties – come together to create a version of the law that only sometimes is formalized into law "on the books." Attorneys in the American regulatory state have the power to give effect to the law and shape the meaning of law through their influence with both private parties and the state.

A second observation about administrative lawmaking flows from the work of lawyers recounted here. Regulatory interactions are not discrete events. In the United States, a central focus of regulatory systems is the creation and articulation of law. What marks out the work of regulatory lawyers as representatives is the degree to which their work aims, sometimes deliberately and sometimes coincidentally, at both immediate results and the gradual reworking of the institutions in which they and their clients find themselves. Elite representatives (not necessarily exclusive to lawyers) bring to regulatory interactions an eye for recurring struggle, and they articulate to clients a conception of administration that draws from and gives value to repeated play. Regulatory politics in turn reflects a capacity for institutional change through the accumulation of legal struggles. In a world in which the creation of law is an explicit goal of some participants (especially elite participants), actions are contributions to a larger, more enduring structure of rules and norms. The goals sought by attorneys for their clients become a body of law in action that acts as a repository and transmitter to future interactions. That is, the behavior of public and private actors not only is conditioned by legal considerations, but is directed at making "law" out of interest preferences. In repeated regulatory encounters, as iterations of a political game, each result affects in some way the calculations of parties who will meet again.[6] Each encounter matters when weight is accorded to formal precedents and, as is more universally the case, informal norms. Standard-setting by a public body or in concert with private power aims toward the creation of governing rules, and implementation involves negotiation premised on the need to articulate the rules in specific cases.[7] Because OSHA regulates in a domain where claims of law and right matter a great deal – to private parties, to judges, and to OSHA itself – who "wins" is measured with both immediate results and the rule, decision, norm, or understanding gained as a result. Regulating through law produces a politics that is directed at multiple timeframes. Strategic frameworks and reputations are among the evolving systems that open and close future possibilities, and these in turn shape the nature of future interaction. A form of reflexivity is present in networks, then, and this reflexivity is demonstrated by OSHA's regulatory policymaking from Washington to the field.

It is in light of this observation that attacks on the role of lawyers in American regulation simultaneously hit at the fundamental problem of private power in public lawmaking. Lawyers do not only inject grease or friction in a procedural sense, a view which would limit lawyers to the cogs of the administrative state. Lawyers in their many roles make law while contesting it, and they supply it through their capacity for creativity. The creation of rules is the stage of the process most commonly recognized as a site for the influence of private actors, but the process of challenging these rules, as well as finding and exposing legal gaps in enforcement, involves intentionality by parties. In US administrative politics, the view that administrative policymaking is an act of lawmaking – governed in the fullest sense by statutes and judges – makes law the medium for interaction and a malleable set of abstractions where political choices are hammered out. The values of private parties are not simply injected into public policy, and the state retains an important role in setting the context for negotiation, interaction, and struggle. Any system can evolve, potentially in directions that can see a regulator further and further marginalized as advantages are pressed into the structure that feeds future advantages.

Similar concerns could be raised with any class of individuals who act for private interests, such as compliance professionals or corporate officials, since in the age of governance a key question is to understand how the values of the state permeate into those of private parties.[8] Yet, while other groups look outside the law for their inspiration – as, for example, technical experts might look to their socialization to environmentalism – lawyers sit substantively and symbolically closer to the public sphere. In the wake of Enron and similar financial collapses, we are particularly cognizant that professionals as counselors share in the accountability for regulatory failures. Networks generally need co-ordination, strategizing and intermediation,[9] and lawyers may represent the specialization of those functions in the US context, but working through law and lawyers brings something distinctive to regulatory politics. At the individual level, "law" is a force on behavior, and more structurally, the drive to make law out of politics – naturally driven by lawyers – makes "relevant" certain ideas, language, strategies, and skills.

Some scholars have probed these directions. Perhaps the most sustained body of such research paralleling this concerns international and transnational networks.[10] Transnational affairs are usually only cousins of the regulatory policymaking that is the focus here, yet the presence of law in these accounts is striking because in the transnational realm very often the raw "stuff" of the law is absent. This parallel is instructive because, over and above the research in a domestic context that shows law and politics reflexively informing one another,[11] varieties of informal law, "soft law," and norms can be seen to play a role even when the "state" is non-existent. From what has been written about the absence of essentially state-led hierarchy and control in modern regulation, one might have doubted the existence of the state. Order exists, albeit through a widened definition of law, through these public–private negotiations of regulation. Law is an enactment of existing relationships and structures, which can evolve or endure in its setting. Numerous other theoretical formulations contribute to the general order: law structures and engenders attitudes; law embodies cultural and technological assumptions undergirding decisionmaking; law creates perceptions by actors about who possesses legitimate authority, thus helping to structure informal relationships; and further, the absence of formal law in some contexts can create space for the emergence of its replacements.

These possibilities might be thought to be in tension. Like the reassembled shards of a shattered stained glass window, it may be difficult to find order in it, but it may still impress. Law is a versatile tool. It can fill gaps and shape reality. It shapes and is shaped. It gives order and is subject to change. Law has the allure of certainty, the temptation of authority, and the genius of flexibility. Indeed, much of the world now may be asking to what extent notions of law and legal actors should be at the center of its administrative process as a vehicle for accountability. Regulation grounded in law has its risks and rewards. OSHA traveled a risky path, and the OSHA bar collectively realized many of the rewards, arriving at a place of influence in the politics of the administrative process.

RESEARCH METHODS

Researching lawyers' behavior presents substantial hurdles. Foremost is the attorney–client privilege, which prevents attorneys from discussing specific information about professional relationships with clients. Individual attorneys construe the privilege differently, preventing systematic collection of data. While scholars have been able to secure wider access in mainstream areas of the law, such as divorce proceedings, the heightened sensitivities of elite attorneys and their corporate clients present nearly insurmountable challenges.[1] A second hurdle is that lawyers' accounts of their work can be tinged with self-serving defensiveness. This problem, perhaps a reaction to the popular bias that lawyering requires an ability to defend the indefensible and advocate half-truths, is compounded by lawyers' strong professional identity. In regulatory processes, parties tend to overstate the importance of their formal and net contributions to decisionmaking while denying (or refusing to acknowledge) their informal influences on decisionmakers. Some components of the "lawyers as friction" critique, such as *ex parte* communications, usually are intended to evade detection, and their full contribution to the process (if any) will never be appreciated. In order to surmount these obstacles, I actively employed multiple sources of data for the same set of questions. While methodological pluralism does not guarantee that the evidence is free of errors, it decreases the likelihood that the systematic biases of one approach will escape notice.

INTERVIEW DATA

Interviews with attorneys and other leading participants in the OSHA process provided the primary source of information about attorneys' roles in regulatory law. The majority of interviews were conducted in Washington, DC, during a three-month period in the summer of 1997. Additional and follow-up interviews were conducted in the succeeding year, frequently by phone. The Department of Labor, numerous labor unions, and most trade associations are headquartered in Washington, of course, and a substantial number of OSHA attorneys locate their practices there. While the OSHA bar in Washington is in some important respects atypical, it also displays the diversity of any major metropolitan area.

The Washington-based attorneys served as an entry point into the OSHA policy system. Because occupational safety and health is a relatively narrow field, random selection was unnecessary. Instead, I tried to reach the entire universe. Letters were sent to all Washington-based attorneys, both management and union, listed in the membership directory of the American Bar Association's Occupational Safety and Health Law Committee and the encyclopedic *Martindale-Hubbell Law Directory*. Interviewees were invited to recommend other individuals for my research among government attorneys, OSHA staff, and trade association officials, as well as unlisted attorneys active in safety and health issues. These suggestions proved useful. While some trade association staff have "safety and health" titles, the names suggested reflected diverse organizational treatment of OSHA issues. The names of governmental interviewees suggested to me formed a narrow, stable cadre of OSHA officials who typically had served a decade or more in government. I also selected a stratified sample of union "directors of safety and health."

Eighty-eight letters yielded sixty-two (70.5 percent) semi-structured interviews, twelve of which (19.4 percent) were conducted by telephone. Fifty-four of the sixty-two interviews (87.1 percent) were tape-recorded, yielding over 900 pages of transcripts. Interviews ranged in length from thirty minutes to three hours, with an average of one hour.

Questions were open-ended and necessarily tailored to respondents' specialization. Still, approximately ten questions were asked of nearly all respondents. A majority of interviewees (75.8 percent) were attorneys; nearly half (46.8 percent) were representatives for

TABLE A1.1: Primary background of interviewees about
OSHA regulation

Management	
Private-practice attorneys	24
Trade association and company in-house attorneys	5
Union	
Private-practice, public interest, and union in-house attorneys	8
Nonattorney union representatives	6
Government: current or former OSHA, OSHRC, or DOL officials	
Attorneys	10
Nonattorneys	9

management. Many interviewees spoke from varied experiences, but
table A1.1 delineates their primary perspectives.

WRITTEN SURVEY DATA

OSHA rulemaking activity occurs mostly within the confines of Washington and its more-limited community. OSHA enforcement takes
place on-site throughout the country. Interviews with Washington-
based practitioners reflected diverse practices by type of issue (e.g.,
construction or manufacturing), client size, and the size of their practices. Nevertheless, a written survey of all private practice, management
OSHA attorneys was required to describe the contours of the bar as a
whole and to confirm the interview data. A written survey also presented an opportunity to collect data regarding some new hypotheses
generated, but not answered, by the interviews. The survey, reproduced
in appendix 2, was designed with three objectives: to obtain descriptive
information about the OSHA bar as a whole, including demographics;
to identify the dynamics of OSHA law practice, such as the frequency and types of involvement in OSHA matters; and to acquire
opinion data which could be analyzed against the other two types of
information.

Again considering the small size of the OSHA bar, I sought to survey
the entire universe of private practitioners who regularly represent
management clients in OSHA rulemaking or enforcement matters, or
who maintain an OSHA law practice, broadly construed. This goal
assumed an ability to identify those attorneys. "Regulatory bars," in
general, are united only by attorneys' shared attribute of having clients

whose interests are affected by the work of a federal agency. Unlike a state bar, attorneys do not require special memberships or designations in order to practice OSHA law. A database of attorneys was created through a combination of three sources: "management" attorneys listed in the directory of the ABA's OSH Law Committee; attorneys claiming safety and health as a practice area in the *Martindale-Hubbell Law Directory*; and all attorneys-of-record in cases reported in the most recent volume of the leading digest of OSHA case law.[2] In-house counsel were then excluded and all names were checked in *Martindale-Hubbell*'s online database for their current addresses.

Surveys and two reminder postcards were sent to the resulting 783 attorneys. Twenty-one surveys returned "undeliverable," leaving a sample size of 762 attorneys. Of these, 232 attorneys (30.4 percent) returned completed surveys, and another 28 (3.7 percent) either returned uncompleted surveys or contacted me to explain their non-participation, resulting in a net return rate of 34.1 percent.[3] This return rate, though modest, is acceptable in light of the survey's design. The sources used to define the "OSHA bar" and the target population are both under-inclusive and over-inclusive. The ABA and Martindale directories rely on self-selection. Attorneys and government officials interviewed concurred that the ABA's OSH Committee enjoys broad acceptance in the legal community and serves as an adequate surrogate for the "core" of the OSHA bar, but not all lawyers identify their areas of practice in their *Martindale-Hubbell* biographies. On the other hand, associates of law firms are sometimes encouraged to join the ABA or to list a practice area even if they maintain no independent client base. Also, some attorneys maintain listings in *Martindale-Hubbell* whether or not they have practiced in that area in recent years. Inclusion in a directory does not reflect an active OSHA law practice, only previous activity or interest in the field.

Representation in a reported case may be an even more transitory OSHA experience. Attorneys whose only interaction with OSHA was representation in one reported case would likely have found the survey questions, particularly the subjective assessment questions, difficult to answer or inapplicable. Indeed, attorneys who had been named in two, or all three, of the sources responded at an appreciably higher rate than those who had been identified through only one of the sources did.

Shown in table A1.2, these attorneys devoted a larger percentage of their practice to OSHA work and overwhelmingly identified themselves as "OSHA specialists." Only infrequently do researchers know

TABLE A1.2: Response rate by number of sources identifying the attorney, and comparative attributes of sub-samples

Number of sources	Surveys mailed	Response rate (%)	OSHA specialists (%)	Amount of OSHA work (% of attorneys' time)
1	697	32.4	59.7	14.0
2	75	46.7	91.4	33.7
3	11	54.5	100	52.1
All	783	34.1	65.5	18.1

the characteristics of those *not* responding. These data support the presumption that many attorneys opting not to participate were those with the least experience in the field.

ARCHIVAL RECORDS AND AGENCY DATA

Since by statute OSHA must collect and report numerous statistics regarding its activities, researchers have a rich collection of data available to them. OSHA's enforcement figures since 1973, including the number of inspections and citations, penalties, contest rates, industry subtotals, and regional and state subtotals, were provided to me by staff in OSHA's Office of Management Data Systems pursuant to the Freedom of Information Act, but omitting any formal letter or process for making the request.[4] OSHA also makes a significant amount of enforcement data available online. The OSH Review Commission similarly collects information regarding its activities for its reports to Congress. Those data, reported in chapter 5, were provided by the OSHRC Office of Public Information.[5]

The Freedom of Information Act (FOIA), passed in 1966–7 and subsequently amended, provides an opportunity for interested parties to review nearly all data, information, and documents relating to the workings of the government, with some exceptions such as privacy and information related to current law enforcement investigations. Two formal FOIA requests, each covering multiple subject areas, were made separately to OSHA and the Solicitor's Office of the Department of Labor in October 1997. Though I continued to make inquiries, including personal visits, until 2003, neither organization ever produced any documents or data in response to these requests, save a brief index to the documents available in OSHA's Docket Office. The process was veritably Kafka-esque, with numerous changes in personnel, reports of lost documents, and assertions that there were simply no documents, even in response to some very broadly worded requests. I did access limited agency documents that are available from the National Archives of the United States. Many of these documents belonged to the personal archives of past Secretaries of Labor or Assistant Secretaries of Labor for OSHA during 1970 to 1984.

More substantially, the OSHA Docket Office at the United States Department of Labor in Washington retains all documents and transcripts submitted to the public record for agency rulemakings. Since dockets constitute the formal record on which the agency must make its decision, these documents allow the researcher to reconstruct the issues and controversies of past rulemakings. Most of the records examined for this book are available on-site only, although OSHA is moving toward electronic retention and publication of rulemaking dockets. Some data reported in chapters 3 and 4 were collected from the docket collections of this office.

SURVEY INSTRUMENT

Your individual responses to this survey will be held confidential and all data will be reported only in the aggregate. The zip code label is for tracking purposes only.

I. DESCRIPTION OF PRACTICE

1. In which state is your practice primarily located?
2. Which of the following best describes your practice?
   ____ Solo practitioner
   ____ Small firm (2 to 20 attorneys)
   ____ Medium-size firm (21 to 99 attorneys)
   ____ Large firm (100+ attorneys)
   ____ Other (please specify where):
3. If you are in a law firm, what is your title?
   ____ Partner
   ____ Associate
   ____ Of counsel
   ____ Other (please specify):
4. Do you regard yourself as a specialist in OSHA law?
   ____ No
   ____ Yes
5. Do you regard yourself as a specialist in any other area(s) of the law? (check as many as appropriate)
   ____ No specialization/General practice

_____ Administrative law
_____ Admiralty & maritime
_____ Antitrust
_____ Appellate practice
_____ Banking & finance
_____ Bankruptcy
_____ Commercial litigation
_____ Construction law
_____ Corporate law (including contracts)
_____ Criminal defense
_____ Environmental law
_____ Government contracts
_____ Insurance/Personal injury defense
_____ Labor law – General
_____ Labor law – Employment discrimination
_____ Labor law – Labor relations
_____ Labor law – Other:
_____ Litigation – General
_____ Mine safety (MSHA)
_____ Municipal law
_____ Patent/Trademarks
_____ Personal injury plaintiff
_____ Probate, trusts & estate
_____ Real estate
_____ Securities
_____ Tax law
_____ Toxic torts
_____ Workers' compensation
_____ Other (please specify):

6. In your practice as a whole, approximately what percentage of your billable time is devoted to OSHA work?

_____%

7. In your OSHA work of the past five years, approximately how have you divided your time?
_____% OSHA enforcement defense
_____% Counseling clients regarding OSHA issues
_____% OSHA rulemaking
_____% OSHA policy issues
_____% Other (please specify):

8. In the past five years, in what forums have you engaged in your OSHA practice? (check all that apply)
_____ Federal OSHA – national office
_____ Federal OSHA – multiple regions
_____ Federal OSHA – one particular region only
_____ State OSHA – multiple state plans
_____ State OSHA – one particular state plan only
_____ OSHRC Administrative Law Judges
_____ State OSHA Review Board
_____ OSH Review Commission (DC)
_____ Federal Circuit Courts of Appeals

9. In the past five years, approximately what proportion of your OSHA clients fall into the following categories?
_____% Manufacturing
_____% Construction
_____% Maritime
_____% Other (please specify):

10. In the past five years, approximately what proportion of your OSHA clients fall into the following categories?
_____% Trade or industry association
_____% Large business (250+ employees)
_____% Medium-size business (100–249 employees)
_____% Small business (1–99 employees)
_____% Other (please specify):

11. Are you a member of the American Bar Association?
_____ No
_____ Yes

12. If you are also a member of the ABA's Committee on OSHA, in what year did you first join the Committee?

_____

13. Why have you maintained membership in ABA's Committee on OSHA? (check all that apply)
_____ Source of information from leading attorneys and/or OSHA leadership
_____ Professional obligation or responsibility
_____ To interact and socialize with other OSHA attorneys
_____ Source of new client and case referrals
_____ To build relationships across management–union lines
_____ Other (please explain):

II. BACKGROUND INFORMATION

1. What is your age? _____
2. Are you (circle one) male or female?
3. What is your race?
   _____ African American
   _____ American Indian
   _____ Asian, Pacific Islander
   _____ Caucasian
   _____ Hispanic
   _____ Other (please specify):
4. What is your religious preference?
   _____ Jewish
   _____ Protestant (please specify):
   _____ Roman Catholic
   _____ Other (please specify):
   _____ None
5. How would you identify your political party affiliation?
   _____ Democrat
   _____ Republican
   _____ Independent
   _____ Other (please specify):
6. Education:
   a. What law school did you attend?

   _____

   b. In what year did you graduate?

   _____

7. How many years have you been in private practice?

   _____

8. In which capacities have you worked in government? (check all that apply)
   _____ No public sector experience
   _____ OSHA, Federal (nonlawyer position)
   _____ DOL – Office of Solicitor for OSHA
   _____ Federal Government, other (please specify):
   _____ State OSHA (nonlawyer position)
   _____ State OSHA litigator
   _____ Other (please specify):

III. OSHA ENFORCEMENT AND COUNSELING EXPERIENCE

1. Over the last twelve months, how many OSHA enforcement cases have you handled?

2. While in private practice, have you handled (individually, or with others) any cases under OSHA Compliance Directive 2.80, the "Egregious Penalty Policy"?

   _____ No

   _____ Yes   If yes, how many cases? _____

3. What was source of your most recent OSHA case?

   _____ Previously represented the client in other matters

   _____ Referral by another client

   _____ Referral by another lawyer

   _____ Referral by a trade association or union

   _____ Selected because of professional reputation

   _____ Other (please specify):

4. Over the past five years, approximately, at what stage in the process have you first become involved in your cases?

   ____% Before OSHA began the inspection

   ____% While inspection was in progress

   ____% After inspection, but before notice of contest

   ____% After employer has contested the citation(s)

   ____% Other (please specify):

5. In the cases you have handled in the past five years, what have been the average initial penalties assessed by OSHA?

   _____ Less than $5,000

   _____ Between $5,000 and $10,000

   _____ Between $10,000 and $50,000

   _____ Between $50,000 and $100,000

   _____ Between $100,000 and $500,000

   _____ Over $500,000

6. In the past five years, approximately what proportion of your cases have been resolved at the following stages?

   ____% Reached pre-citation settlement

   ____% Reached settlement with OSHA (after citations were issued)

   ____% Reached settlement with solicitors/counsel

   ____% Resolved by ALJ or initial court decision

———% Resolved by full Review Commission or appeals court decision

———% Other (please specify):

7. Ranking the following seven items from 1, "most important" to 7, "least important," what issues have been the most important for clients when you have discussed their objectives and strategies in OSHA enforcement matters?

——— Minimizing total penalties

——— Avoiding possible criminal referral

——— Winning on the merits (being vindicated)

——— Modifying the time or costs of abatement

——— Minimizing legal expenses, burden on company

——— Preserving relationship with union or public

——— Avoiding secondary litigation, such as plaintiffs' suits

8. Which resources do you consult to keep abreast of developments in OSHA issues? (check all that apply)

——— BNA or CCH OSHA Reporters

——— "Inside OSHA"

——— Informal contacts with agency/DOL

——— Communication with other attorneys

——— ABA conferences

——— Other (please specify):

9. Have you ever refused to take on a new client or a case from an existing client, for reasons other than a conflict of interest?

——— No

——— Yes

a. If yes, which of the following reasons was most important?

——— Disagreement as to style or strategy

——— Disagreement as to the merits

——— Client not committed to health and safety

——— Inability to pay

——— Other (please explain):

10. In the past twelve months, which of the following services have you performed (outside the context of an active OSHA enforcement action)? (check all that apply)

——— Sought a variance from an established standard

——— Sought formal compliance advice from OSHA

——— Sought informal compliance advice from OSHA

——— Provided informal compliance advice to your client

_____ Reviewed or audited clients' procedures or programs

_____ Developed procedures or programs for your client

_____ Inspected clients' facility for overall compliance

_____ Hired health and safety consultants to do inspection

_____ Other (please specify):

11. What are the three *most common* OSHA consulting issues that you encounter with clients? (select up to three)

_____ OSHA regulations conflict with another law/regulation

_____ Client needs an update about new rules and regulations

_____ Client needs help understanding/interpreting regulations

_____ Compliance not technically feasible for client

_____ Compliance not economically feasible for client

_____ OSHA issues involved in labor relations/bargaining

_____ Client needs due diligence performed for a transaction

_____ Other (please specify):

IV. OSHA POLICY AND RULEMAKING EXPERIENCE

1. Have you ever participated in or advised a client about participating in a Federal OSHA rulemaking (i.e. other than filing a suit)?

_____ No

_____ Yes   If yes, in how many rulemakings have you participated?_____

a. Which of the following services have you provided? (check all that apply)

_____ Assisted client in deciding what position to take

_____ Advised client on process and strategy

_____ Wrote comment letter

_____ Reviewed comment letter written by client

_____ Prepared client's hearing testimony

_____ Observed hearing but did not participate

_____ Cross-examined witnesses at hearing

_____ Attended stakeholders' meetings

_____ Met with OSHA informally prior to rule proposal

_____ Met with OSHA after final rule was promulgated

_____ Other (please specify):

2. Have you ever participated in a suit in the US Court of Appeals challenging a Federal OSHA standard?

_____ No

_____ Yes   If yes, how many? _____

    a. When you and your client last contemplated a suit chal-
lenging an OSHA rule and developed a strategy for the
suit, what was the leading objective the suit was designed
to accomplish? (If you have participated in more than
one case, please refer to the latest case.)

_____ To overturn the rule

_____ To win concessions from OSHA in settlement

_____ To defend the rule from another suit

_____ To compel reconsideration by OSHA on remand

_____ To postpone the rule's implementation

_____ To shape how the rule would be interpreted

_____ Other (please explain):

3. Approximately what proportion of your OSHA rulemaking clients
fall into the following categories?

____% Trade or industry association

____% Large business (250+ employees)

____% Medium-size business (100–249 employees)

____% Small business (1–99 employees)

____% Other (please specify):

4. Have you ever counseled or represented clients regarding a state
OSHA rulemaking?

_____ No

_____ Yes   If yes, which state(s)?____

5. Have you ever contacted Congress (House or Senate) regarding an
OSHA issue on behalf of a client?

_____ No

_____ Yes

    a. For what issues have you contacted Congress? (check all
that apply)

_____ An OSHA reform proposal

_____ An appropriations rider blocking rulemaking

_____ An appropriations request in general

_____ A review of an OSHA rulemaking

_____ A review of an enforcement action

_____ General oversight hearings

_____ Other (please specify):

    b. What did the representation involve?

_____ Meeting with congressional staff

_____ Meeting with Congressperson
_____ Writing letter to Congressperson
_____ Drafting legislation
_____ Giving testimony to committee
_____ Assisting client testimony
_____ Other (please explain):

6. Have you ever contacted OMB/OIRA on behalf of a client in an OSHA rulemaking?
   _____ No
   _____ Yes

V. IMPORTANT ISSUES FOR OSHA PRACTITIONERS

For each of the following please use this scale:

1 strongly disagree
2 disagree
3 agree
4 strongly agree
0 don't know

_____ The General Duty Clause, while controversial, has not been a significant problem for my clients.

_____ OSHA practice often involves assisting clients' efforts to comply with OSHA regulations.

_____ The OSHA enforcement process provides ample opportunity to settle disputes to the satisfaction of all parties.

_____ I frequently deal with OSHA officials and solicitors whom I've encountered before with other clients.

_____ My clients are less likely to turn to outside counsel for their OSHA matters than for other issues.

_____ I advise my clients that pro-active compliance with OSHA standards makes good business sense.

_____ Most of my clients already commit sufficient personnel and resources to health and safety compliance.

_____ My reputation for advancing clients' safety and health gives clients an extra measure of "good faith" with OSHA.

_____ Companies interested in providing written comments to a rulemaking should participate through a trade association and should not participate individually.

_____ OSHA work is more personally rewarding than other work in my firm or my own practice.

_____ My OSHA practice mostly involves "one-shot" clients who then do not require further representation or counsel.

_____ OSHA work is less lucrative than most other work in my firm or my own practice.

_____ Clients usually know my style or approach to litigation when they hire me.

_____ I often find that new clients are reluctant to cooperate with OSHA compliance officers and administrators.

_____ Penalty increases in recent years have made my clients more attentive to workplace health and safety.

_____ My role as an attorney includes helping clients build good working relationships with OSHA.

_____ In my experience, Federal OSHA enforcement is more professional, skillful, and fair than state OSHA enforcement.

_____ My clients seek and usually accept my advice regarding choice of strategies in OSHA litigation.

_____ My reputation as a tough litigator has produced settlements on terms very favorable to my clients.

For the remaining questions, please use the following scale:

1 I never recommend it
2 I sometimes recommend it
3 I frequently recommend it
4 I always recommend it
0 don't know

When counseling clients outside the context of active OSHA investigations, should an attorney . . .

_____ Encourage clients to bring compliance issues to OSHA for assistance?

_____ Factor in the likelihood of the client being inspected in the future?

_____ Encourage clients to enter a cooperative compliance program (such as STAR, CCP, or MAINE 200)?

In the course of an OSHA investigation, should an attorney . . .

_____ Advise clients to refuse the warrantless entry of compliance officers?

_____ Perform a full audit of the worksite after an accident?

_____ Attend the on-site investigation and walkaround?

_____ Refuse a request for documents unless accompanied by a subpoena?

_____ Brief clients but limit direct attorney involvement to avoid antagonizing OSHA compliance officers?

After a citation has been issued against a client, should an attorney . . .

_____ Seek a review of the enforcement action with the national office?

_____ Seek the assistance of union representatives (in a unionized workplace)?

_____ Make broad discovery requests and begin extensive depositions of OSHA officials or staff?

_____ Focus on settling the matter with the Labor Department solicitors rather than with the OSHA officials?

_____ Propose a corporatewide settlement agreement?

Thank you for your participation in this research. I would be happy to send you a copy of results at your request, or you may review the results at http://www.cpinternet.com/~schmidt as they become available.

NOTES

1 Introduction

Portions of this book have appeared in other forms: "Pursuing Regulatory Relief: Strategic Participation and Litigation in US OSHA Rulemaking" by Patrick Schmidt first appeared in print in *Business and Politics* 4 (2002), 71–89, http://www.tandf.co.uk/journals and remains available in an online version with the Berkeley Electronic Press: vol. 4: No. 1, Article 3, http://www.bepress.com/bap/vol4/iss1/art3; Patrick Schmidt, "Law in the Age of Governance: Regulation, Networks and Lawyers," in Jacint Jordana and David Levi-Faur (eds.), *The Politics of Regulation* (Cheltenham, UK: Edward Elgar, 2004), ch. 12, pp. 296–319.

1. Douglas Frantz and David McKean, *Friends in High Places: The Rise and Fall of Clark Clifford* (Boston, MA: Little, Brown & Co., 1995), p. 108.
2. Denis J. Galligan, *Discretionary Powers: A Legal Study of Official Discretion* (New York, NY: Oxford University Press, 1986).
3. Recent contributions to the critical literature include Catherine Crier, *The Case Against Lawyers* (New York, NY: Broadway, 2002); Walter K. Olson, *The Rule of Lawyers: How the New Litigation Elite Threatens America's Rule of Law* (New York, NY: Truman Talley, 2003); Ralph Nader and Wesley J. Smith, *No Contest: Corporate Lawyers and the Perversion of Justice in America* (New York, NY: Random House, 1996); Sol Linowitz with Martin Mayer, *The Betrayed Profession: Lawyering at the End of the Twentieth Century* (Baltimore, MD: Johns Hopkins University Press, 1996); Anthony T. Kronman, *The Lost Lawyer: Failing Ideals in the Legal Profession* (Cambridge, MA: Belknap Press of Harvard University, 1993); and Mary Ann Glendon, *A Nation Under Lawyers: How the Crisis in the Legal Profession is Transforming American Society* (New York, NY: Farrar, Straus and Giroux, 1994). But see Lawrence M. Friedman, *Total Justice* (New York, NY: Russell Sage Foundation, 1985) (legal system has followed, not led, cultural forces).

4. Kenneth Hanf, "Introduction," in Hanf and Fritz W. Scharpf (eds.), *Interorganizational Policy Making: Limits to Coordination and Central Control* (London: Sage, 1978), p. 12.
5. Patrick Kenis and Volker Schneider, "Policy Networks and Policy Analysis: Scrutinizing a New Analytical Toolbox," in Bernd Marin and Renate Mayntz (eds.), *Policy Networks: Empirical Evidence and Theoretical Consideration* (Boulder, CO: Westview Press, 1991), pp. 34–5; Mike Marinetto, "Governing beyond the Centre: A Critique of the Anglo-Governance School," *Political Studies* 51 (2003), 592–608.
6. J. A. de Bruijn and A. B. Ringeling, "Normative Notes: Perspectives on Networks," in Walter J. M. Kickert, Erik-Hans Klijn, and Joop F. M. Koppenjan, *Managing Complex Networks: Strategies for the Public Sector* (London: Sage Publications, 1997), p. 154.
7. Hugh Heclo, "Issue Networks and the Executive Establishment: Government Growth in an Age of Improvement," in Anthony King (ed.), *The New American Political System* (Washington, DC: American Enterprise Institute, 1978); Thomas L. Gais, Mark A. Peterson, and Jack L. Walker, "Interest Groups, Iron Triangles and Representative Institutions in American National Government," *British Journal of Political Science* 14 (1984), 161–85.
8. Kickert, Klijn, and Koppenjan, *Managing Complex Networks*.
9. Frans Van Waarden, "Dimensions and Types of Policy Networks," *European Journal of Political Research* 21 (1992), 29–52, 37–8.
10. Erik-Hans Klijn and Geert R. Teisman, "Strategies and Games in Networks," in Kickert, Klijn, and Koppenjan, *Managing Complex Networks*, p. 104.
11. See Robert O. Keohane and Elinor Ostrom, "Introduction," in Keohane and Ostrom (eds.), *Local Commons and Global Interdependence: Heterogeneity and Cooperation in Two Domains* (London: Sage Publications, 1995).
12. Leigh Hancher and Michael Moran, "Organizing Regulatory Space," in Hancher and Moran (eds.), *Capitalism, Culture, and Regulation* (Oxford: Clarendon Press, 1989).
13. R. A. W. Rhodes, *The National World of Local Government* (London: Allen and Unwin, 1986).
14. Kathryn Sikkink, "Human Rights, Principle Issue-Networks, and Sovereignty in Latin America," *International Organization* 47 (1993), 411.
15. See, e.g. Christopher Ham, *Policy-making in the National Health Service: A Case Study of the Leeds Regional Hospital Board* (London: Macmillan Press, 1981); Anne-Marie Burley and Walter Mattli, "Europe before the Court: A Political Theory of Legal Integration," *International Organization* 47 (1993), 41–76.
16. Yves Dezalay, "The Forum Should Fit the Fuss: The Economics and Politics of Negotiated Justice," in Maureen Cain and Christine B. Harrington (eds.), *Lawyers in a Postmodern World: Translation and Transgression* (New York, NY: New York University Press, 1994); Doreen McBarnet, "Law and Capital: The Role of Legal Form and Legal Actors," *International Journal of the Sociology of Law* 12 (1984), 231.

17. For first outlining the broad contours of these perspectives, I am indebted to Stewart Macaulay, "Business Adaptation to Regulation: What Do We Know and What Do We Need to Know?" *Law and Policy* 15 (1993), 259.
18. See, e.g. David Schoenbrod, *Power Without Responsibility: How Congress Abuses the People Through Delegation* (New Haven, CT: Yale University Press, 1993). See also Mark Thatcher and Alec Stone Sweet (eds.), *The Politics of Delegation* (London: Frank Cass, 2003).
19. The idea of neutral implementation of general principles, long discarded in legislative politics, retains vitality in judicial politics. See Philip Bobbitt, "Is Law Politics?" *Stanford Law Review* 41 (1989), 1233.
20. Charles A. Horsky, *The Washington Lawyer* (Westport, CT: Greenwood Press, 1981 reprint, 1952). "Washington lawyers" includes all attorneys who represent the clients before the agencies and branches of the federal government, whether or not located in Washington, DC.
21. *Ibid.*, p. 117.
22. *Ibid.*, p. 131.
23. *Ibid.*, p. 126.
24. *Ibid.*, p. 10.
25. See Howard C. Westwood, "The Influence of Washington Lawyering," *George Washington Law Review* 38 (1970), 607.
26. Lee Loevinger, "A Washington Lawyer Tells What It's Like," *George Washington Law Review* 38 (1970), 531, 539.
27. Herbert M. Kritzer, *The Justice Broker: Lawyers and Ordinary Litigation* (New York, NY: Oxford University Press, 1990).
28. Mark C. Suchman and Mia L. Cahill, "The Hired Gun as Facilitator: Lawyers and the Suppression of Business Disputes in Silicon Valley," *Law and Social Inquiry* 21 (1996), 679.
29. See Frantz and McKean, *Friends in High Places*.
30. E. Donald Elliot, Jr., "The Dis-Integration of Administrative Law: A Comment on Shapiro," *Yale Law Journal* 92 (1983), 1523, 1536.
31. Marver Bernstein, *Regulating Business by Independent Commission* (Princeton, NJ: Princeton University Press, 1955); Anthony Downs, *Inside Bureaucracy* (Boston, MA: Little, Brown, and Co., 1967); Heclo, "Issue Networks."
32. Paul J. Quirk, *Industry Influence in Federal Regulatory Agencies* (Princeton, NJ: Princeton University Press, 1981), p. 4.
33. The popular literature on this subject is vast. See e.g., Joseph C. Goulden, *The Superlawyers: The Small and Powerful World of the Great Washington Law Firms* (New York, NY: Weybright and Talley, 1972); Mark J. Green, *The Other Government: The Unseen Power of Washington Lawyers* (New York, NY: Grossman Publishers, 1975); Ralph Nader and Mark Green (eds.), *Verdicts on Lawyers* (New York, NY: Cromwell, 1976); and more recently, Frantz and McKean, *Friends in High Places*.
34. Peter H. Irons, *The New Deal Lawyers* (Princeton, NJ: Princeton University Press, 1982), pp. 298–300; Kenneth Lipartito, "What Have Lawyers Done for American Business? The Case of Baker & Botts of Houston," *Business History Review* 64 (1990), 489; Ronen Shamir, *Managing Legal*

Uncertainty: Elite Lawyers in the New Deal (Durham, NC: Duke University Press, 1995).

35. Joseph A. Califano, Jr., "The Washington Lawyer: When to Say No," in Nader and Green, *Verdicts on Lawyers*, p. 189.

36. Harold J. Laski, *The American Democracy: A Commentary and An Interpretation* (New York, NY: Viking Press, 1948), p. 591.

37. Robert B. Reich, "Regulation by Confrontation or Negotiation?" *Harvard Business Review* 59 (May–June 1981), 82–93.

38. Gary C. Bryner, *Bureaucratic Discretion: Law and Policy in Federal Regulatory Agencies* (New York: Pergamon Press, 1987), p. 36.

39. Doreen McBarnet, "Legal Creativity: Law, Capital, and Legal Avoidance," in Cain and Harrington, *Lawyers in a Postmodern World*, p. 83.

40. Theodore Roosevelt, *Presidential Addresses and State Papers: May 10, 1905 to April 12, 1906* (1910) cited in Jerold S. Auerbach, *Unequal Justice: Lawyers and Social Change in Modern America* (New York, NY: Oxford University Press, 1976), p. 33.

41. Austin Sarat and William F. Felstiner, *Divorce Lawyers and Their Clients: Power and Meaning in the Legal Process* (New York, NY: Oxford University Press, 1995), pp. 18–19.

42. *Ibid.*, p. 21.

43. Maureen Cain, "The Symbol Traders," in Cain and Harrington, *Lawyers in a Postmodern World*, p. 36.

44. Stewart Macaulay, "Lawyers and Consumer Protection Laws," *Law and Society Review* 14 (1979), 115. For a review and critique of the functionalist orientation of much of the literature on lawyering in the administrative state, see Christine B. Harrington, "Outlining a Theory of Legal Practice," in Cain and Harrington, *Lawyers in a Postmodern World*, pp. 51–5.

45. Macaulay, "Lawyers and Consumer Protection Laws," 162.

46. *Ibid.*, 152.

47. A trio of books by one group of scholars has done the most to advance this line of research: James Eisenstein and Herbert Jacob, *Felony Justice: An Organizational Analysis of Criminal Courts* (Boston, MA: Little, Brown, and Co., 1977); Eisenstein, Roy B. Flemming, and Peter F. Nardulli, *The Contours of Justice: Communities and Their Courts* (Boston, MA: Little, Brown, and Co., 1988); and Flemming, Nardulli, and Eisenstein, *The Craft of Justice: Politics and Work in Criminal Court Communities* (Philadelphia, PA: University of Pennsylvania Press, 1992). Also, Kritzer, *The Justice Broker*.

48. David Knoke, *Political Networks: The Structural Perspective* (New York, NY: Cambridge University Press, 1990), pp. 144–5.

49. John P. Heinz, Edward O. Laumann, Robert L. Nelson, and Robert H. Salisbury, *The Hollow Core: Private Interests in National Policy Making* (Cambridge, MA: Harvard University Press, 1993).

50. Robert L. Nelson and John P. Heinz, with Edward O. Laumann and Robert H. Salisbury, "Lawyers and the Structure of Influence in Washington," *Law and Society Review* 22 (1988), 237.

51. Herbert M. Kritzer, "'Data, Data, Data, Drowning in Data': Crafting *The Hollow Core*," *Law and Social Inquiry* 21 (1996), 761.
52. Jos Huigen, *Information Supply and the Implementation of Policy: Playing with Ambiguity and Uncertainty in Policy Networks* (Delft: Eburon, 1994), p. 150.
53. The contours of this dimension are set out by Joseph V. Rees, *Reforming the Workplace: A Study of Self-Regulation in Occupational Safety* (Philadelphia, PA: University of Pennsylvania Press, 1986), p. 9.
54. Carl Gersuny, *Work Hazards and Industrial Conflict* (Hanover, NH: University Press of New England, 1981), p. 31.
55. Lawrence M. Friedman and Jack Ladinsky, "Social Change and the Law of Industrial Accidents," *Columbia Law Review* 67 (1967), 50–82.
56. Gersuny, *Work Hazards*, p. 104, citing Frank Lewis, "Employers' Liability," *Atlantic Monthly* 103 (January 1909), 60.
57. Charles Noble, *Liberalism at Work: The Rise and Fall of OSHA* (Philadelphia, PA: Temple University Press, 1986), p. 55.
58. Nicholas A. Ashford, *Crisis in the Workplace: Occupational Disease and Injury* (Cambridge, MA: MIT Press, 1976), p. 50.
59. See Carl A. Auerbach, Willard Hurst, Lloyd K. Garrison, and Samuel Mermin, *The Legal Process: An Introduction to Decision Making by Judicial, Legislative, Executive, and Administrative Agencies* (San Francisco, CA: Chandler Publishing Co., 1961), ch. 9.
60. Marc Allen Eisner, *Regulatory Politics in Transition* (Baltimore, MD: Johns Hopkins University Press, 1993), p. 121.
61. Some older regulatory agencies, notably the Food and Drug Administration and the Federal Trade Commission, fit within this understanding of "social regulatory" agencies.
62. See, e.g., Albert L. Nichols and Richard Zeckhauser, "Government Comes to the Workplace: An Assessment of OSHA," *Public Interest* 49 (1977), 39, 42, observing that "both politically and practically it has been a failure. It has generated fierce antagonism in the business community and is viewed by many as the quintessential government intrusion. And it has had virtually no noticeable impact on work-related injuries and illnesses."
63. Wayne B. Gray and John T. Scholz, "Does Regulatory Enforcement Work? A Panel Analysis of OSHA Enforcement," *Law and Society Review* 27 (1993), 177; John T. Scholz, "Cooperative Regulatory Enforcement and the Politics of Administrative Effectiveness," *American Political Science Review* 85 (1991), 115; Leon S. Robertson and J. Philip Keeve, "Worker Injuries: The Effects of Workers' Compensation and OSHA Inspections," *Journal of Health Politics, Policy & Law* 8 (1983), 581.
64. See, e.g., Steven Kelman, *Regulating America, Regulating Sweden: A Comparative Study of Occupational Safety and Health Policy* (Cambridge, MA: MIT Press, 1981); Keith Hawkins and Bridget M. Hutter, "The Response of Business to Social Regulation in England and Wales: An Enforcement Perspective," *Law and Policy* 15 (1993), 199; Richard Brown, "Theory and Practice of Regulatory Enforcement: Occupational Health and Safety Regulation in British Columbia," *Law and Policy* 16 (1994), 63; and Sylvia Gräbe, "Regulatory Agencies and Interest Groups in Occupational Health

and Safety in Great Britain and West Germany: A Perspective from West Germany," *Law and Policy* 13 (1991), 55.

65. Robert A. Kagan, *Adversarial Legalism: The American Way of Law* (Cambridge, MA: Harvard University Press, 2001), pp. 3, 181. See also Kagan and Lee Axelrad (eds.), *Regulatory Encounters: Multinational Corporations and American Adversarial Legalism* (Berkeley, CA: University of California Press, 2000).

66. Giandomenico Majone, *Evidence, Argument and Persuasion in the Policy Process* (New Haven, CT: Yale University Press, 1989), p. 2.

67. Bronwen Morgan, *Social Citizenship in the Shadow of Competition: The Bureaucratic Politics of Regulatory Justification* (Aldershot, UK: Ashgate Press, 2003).

68. Michael Moran, "Understanding the Regulatory State," *British Journal of Political Science* 32 (2002), 391.

69. See Tony Prosser, *Law and the Regulators* (Oxford, UK: Clarendon Press, 1997).

70. Stephen Wilks with Ian Bartle, "The Unanticipated Consequences of Creating Independent Competition Agencies," in Thatcher and Stone Sweet, *The Politics of Delegation*, p. 170.

71. The seminal work here is Giandomenico Majone, *Regulating Europe* (London, UK: Routledge, 1996).

72. Mark Thatcher and Alec Stone Sweet, "Theory and Practice of Delegation to Non-Majoritarian Institutions," in Thatcher and Stone Sweet, *The Politics of Delegation*, p. 12.

73. A. J. Harcourt and C. M. Radaelli, "Limits to EU Technocratic Regulation?" *European Journal of Political Research* 35 (1999), 107–22, 119.

74. R. Daniel Keleman, "The Rise of Adversarial Legalism in the European Union: Beyond Policy Learning and Regulatory Competition," in David Levi-Faur and Vigoda-Gadot Eran (eds.), *International Public Policy and Management: Policy Learning Beyond Regional, Cultural and Political Boundaries* (New York, NY: Marcel Dekker, 2004).

75. Keith Hawkins, *Law as Last Resort: Prosecution Decision-Making in a Regulatory Agency* (Oxford, UK: Oxford University Press, 2002), pp. 162–5.

76. Alfred C. Aman, Jr., "The Globalizing State: A Future-Oriented Perspective on the Public/Private Distinction, Federalism, and Democracy," *Vanderbilt Journal of Transnational Law* 31 (1998), 769–870, 773.

77. Martin Shapiro, "The Institutionalization of European Administrative Space," in Alec Stone Sweet, Wayne Sandholtz, and Neil Fligstein (eds.), *The Institutionalization of Europe* (Oxford, UK: Oxford University Press, 2001), pp. 94–112, 97.

78. Sonia Mazey and Jeremy Richardson, "Institutionalizing Promiscuity: Commission–Interest Group Relations in the European Union," in Stone Sweet, et al., *Institutionalization of Europe*, pp. 71–93, 72.

79. Damien Geradin and Nicolas Petit, "The Development of Agencies at EU and National Levels: Conceptual Analysis and Proposals for Reform," Harvard Jean Monnet Working Paper No. 01/04

(http://www.jeanmonnetprogram.org/papers/04/040101.html) (2004), pp. 35, 61.
80. Anne-Marie Slaughter, "The Accountability of Government Networks," *Indiana Journal of Global Legal Studies* 8 (2001), 347–67.
81. David Mullan and Antonella Ceddia, "The Impact on Public Law of Privatization, Deregulation, Outsourcing, and Downsizing: A Canadian Perspective," *Indiana Journal of Global Legal Studies* 10 (2003), 199–246, 200.
82. Martin Shapiro and Alec Stone Sweet, *On Law, Politics, and Judicialization* (Oxford, UK: Oxford University Press, 2002), p. 224.
83. See, as a recent example of this literature, the studies in numerous contexts in Marc Hertogh and Simon Halliday (eds.), *Judicial Review and Bureaucratic Impact: International and Interdisciplinary Perspectives* (Cambridge, UK: Cambridge University Press, 2004). Also, Carol Harlow, *Accountability in the European Union* (Oxford, UK: Oxford University Press, 2002), p. 165.
84. Shapiro, "Institutionalization of European Administrative Space," p. 98.

2 The contours of a regulatory bar
1. E.g., Curtis J. Milhaupt and Mark D. West, "Law's Dominion and the Market for Legal Elites in Japan," *Law and Policy in International Business* 34 (2003), 451–98; Susan D. Carle, "Elites, Ethics, and the Public Good: Race, Class, and Legal Ethics in the Early NAACP," *Law and History Review* 20 (2002), 97–146; John P. Heinz and Edward O. Laumann, "The Constituencies of Elite Urban Lawyers," *Law and Society Review* 31 (1997), 441–72; Ronen Shamir, *Managing Legal Uncertainty: Elite Lawyers in the New Deal* (Durham, NC: Duke University Press, 1995); David A. Bell, *Lawyers and Citizens: The Making of a Political Elite in Old Regime France* (New York, NY: Oxford University Press, 1994); Kevin T. McGuire, *The Supreme Court Bar: Legal Elites in the Washington Community* (Charlottesville, VA: University of Virginia Press, 1993); Robert Granfield, *Making Elite Lawyers: Visions of Law at Harvard and Beyond* (New York, NY: Routledge, 1992); James C. Foster, *The Ideology of Apolitical Politics: Elite Lawyers' Response to the Legitimation Crisis of American Capitalism, 1870–1920* (New York, NY: Garland, 1990); William E. Nelson, "Contract Litigation and the Elite Bar in New York City, 1960–1980," *Emory Law Journal* 39 (1990), 413–62; Michael J. Powell, *From Patrician to Professional Elite: The Transformation of the New York City Bar Association* (New York, NY: Russell Sage Foundation, 1988); William H. Simon, "Judicial Clerkships and Elite Professional Culture," *Journal of Legal Education* 36 (1986), 129–37; G. Edward White, "Felix Frankfurter, the Old Boy Network, and the New Deal: The Placement of Elite Lawyers in Public Service in the 1930s," *Arkansas Law Review* 39 (1986), 631–67; Howard A. Glickstein, "Law Schools: Where the Elite Meet to Teach," *Nova Law Journal* 10 (1986), 541–6.
2. I exclude government attorneys from this chapter, though I consider some of the problems facing government lawyers in chapters 3 and 5.

3. *Martindale-Hubbell Law Directory* (Summit, NJ: Martindale-Hubbell, 2004). This reflects about a 20 percent increase since 1997, when the survey reported here was conducted.

4. Figures provided to author by American Bar Association. In addition to a category of "other" (11 percent), the ABA's categorization includes neutral parties (no affiliation claimed) (7.6 percent) and plaintiffs' attorneys (1.2 percent). A major group of attorneys covered by "other" and "neutral" includes government attorneys.

5. Frank Dobbin and John R. Sutton, "The Strength of a Weak State: The Rights Revolution and the Rise of Human Resources Management Divisions," *American Journal of Sociology* 104 (1998), 441–76.

6. $N = 228$. These statistics are based on survey question I.7, "In your OSHA work of the past five years, approximately how have you divided your time?" In chapter 3, I report rulemaking activity by attorneys based on question IV.1, "Have you ever participated in or advised a client about participating in a Federal OSHA rulemaking?" The former question establishes the attorneys who have rulemaking activity as an active part of their practice. The latter includes those who may have advised clients about rulemaking without ultimately participating in it; it also is not time-bound. Approximately twice as many attorneys reported rulemaking activity when gauged by question IV.1 versus question I.7.

7. $N = 28$.

8. Distribution of work within OSHA practices was very similar between specialist and nonspecialist respondents, with enforcement work virtually identical (61.6 percent versus 61.5 percent, respectively). Only rulemaking (3.2 percent versus 1.5 percent) and policy work (1.9 percent versus 0.9 percent) differed.

9. The bar's growth over the past twenty-five years has attended a rise in penalties. In Fiscal Year 1979, the average final penalty assigned following federal inspections was $279. By the mid-1990s (FY 1996), 24,024 federal inspections resulted in final penalties of $66,833,691, an average of $2,782 per inspection, though in FY 2002 the average penalty slumped to $1,942 over 37,493 federal inspections. See US Department of Labor, *Twenty Years of OSHA Federal Enforcement Data: A Review and Explanation of the Major Trends* (Washington, DC: January 1993); and "OSHA Facts," http://www.osha.gov/as/opa/oshafacts.html.

10. Of the 302 ALJ and Review Commission decisions handed down between January 18, 1995 and September 24, 1997, and reported in BNA OSHA, volume 17, sixty cases (19.87 percent) involved *pro se* litigants. In three cases the representative of record was general counsel for the company.

11. See, e.g., John P. Heinz and Edward O. Laumann, *Chicago Lawyers: The Social Structure of the Bar* (New York, NY: Russell Sage Foundation, 1982); Erwin O. Smigel, *The Wall Street Lawyer* (Bloomington, IL: Indiana University Press, 1964); Emily P. Dodge, "Evolution of a City Law Office," *Wisconsin Law Review* 40 (1956), 35–56.

12. Marc Galanter and Thomas Palay, *Tournament of Lawyers: The Transformation of the Big Law Firm* (Chicago, IL: University of Chicago Press, 1991), p. 47.

13. Barbara A. Curren and Clara N. Carson, *The Lawyer Statistical Report: The US Legal Profession in the 1990s* (Chicago, IL: American Bar Foundation, 1994), p. 236.

14. Charles A. Horsky, *The Washington Lawyer* (Westport, CT: Greenwood Press, 1981 reprint, originally published 1952), p. 8.

15. OSHA lawyers deserve the "Washington lawyer" moniker even when appearing before a *state* OSHA enforcer, because the minimum standards are set at the federal level and OSHA oversight lends a federal imprimatur to the state enforcement.

16. Curren and Carson, *Lawyer Statistical Report*, p. 237.

17. The high number of Ohio lawyers in the target population does not appear to be biased by inclusion of infrequent or inactive OSHA attorneys. Ohio lawyers constituted an even larger proportion (14.2 percent) of the 232 survey responses, and the Buckeye bar devotes a nearly identical percentage of its time to OSHA law (18.1 percent vs. 18.0 percent for the remainder of the nation).

18. Richard L. Abel, *American Lawyers* (New York, NY: Oxford University Press, 1989), p. 85.

19. *Ibid.*, p. 91.

20. Robert L. Nelson, "The Futures of American Lawyers: A Demographic Profile of a Changing Profession in a Changing Society," *Case Western Reserve Law Review* 44 (1994), 345–406, 377.

21. Cynthia Fuchs Epstein, et al., "Glass Ceilings and Open Doors: Women's Advancement in the Legal Profession," *Fordham Law Review* 64 (1995), 291.

22. John Gibeaut, "Marking a Decade of Struggle," *ABA Journal* 83 (October 1997), 100. Among all corporate law firms, blacks hold an even lower percentage of partnerships: just over 1 percent. See David B. Williams and G. Mitu Gulati, "Why Are There So Few Black Lawyers in Corporate Law Firms? An Institutional Analysis," *California Law Review* 84 (1996), 493–625, 506, citing Ann Davis, "Big Jump in Minority Associates, But . . ." *National Law Journal* (April 29, 1996), 1.

23. Nelson, "The Futures of American Lawyers," 378.

24. These data do not suggest that *no* African-American or Asian-American lawyers practice OSHA law. Interviewees could point to isolated individuals fitting these backgrounds, though the mere act of identifying them emphasized how rare they are in this bar.

25. Indeed, women surveyed averaged 40.1 years old (N = 35) and men averaged 46.3 years (N = 195).

26. See Heinz and Laumann, *Chicago Lawyers*, pp. 446–7, appendix B, table B.5.

27. Sources: US Bureau of the Census, *Statistical Abstracts of the United States* (Washington, DC, 1997) (for national bar sex data and all national population data); American Bar Association Commission on

Opportunities for Minorities in the Profession, *Miles to Go: Progress of Minorities in the Legal Profession* (Chicago, IL: ABA, http://www.abanet.org/minorities/home.html, 1998) (for national bar race data); Carl A. Auerbach, "Legal Education and Its Discontents," *Journal of Legal Education* 34 (1984), 73–6 (for national bar religion data); Donald D. Landon, *Country Lawyers: The Impact of Context on Professional Practice* (Westport, CT: Praeger, 1990) (for rural bar data); McGuire, *The Supreme Court Bar*, pp. 35, 43 (for Supreme Court bar data).

28. Heinz and Laumann, "The Constituencies of Elite Urban Lawyers," 460.
29. *Statistical Abstract* reports "white" persons and treats "Hispanic" persons as an overlapping category. Subtracting "Hispanic" from "white" derives the "Caucasian" percent.
30. Heinz and Laumann, The Constituencies of Elite Urban Lawyers, 461.
31. McGuire, *The Supreme Court Bar*, p. 45.
32. Harold W. Stanley and Richard G. Niemi, *Vital Statistics on American Politics, 1997–1998* (Washington, DC: Congressional Quarterly, 1997), p. 111.
33. "LawPoll," *American Bar Association Journal*, 1983, cited in McGuire, *The Supreme Court Bar*, p. 45.
34. See Granfield, *Making Elite Lawyers*, passim.
35. See Susan Daicoff, "Lawyer, Know Thyself: A Review of Empirical Research on Attorney Attributes Bearing on Professionalism," *American University Law Review* 46 (1997), 1337.
36. McGuire, *The Supreme Court Bar*, p. 39; *The Official Guide to US Law Schools 1998–99* (Newtown, PA: Law School Admission Services, 1998)
37. *Gourman Report: Rating of Graduate and Professional Programs in American and International Universities* (Los Angeles, CA: National Education Standards, 1994). The methodologies of all ranking schemes are subject to considerable attack, though many criticisms derive from the rankings' misuse or from disagreements regarding specific schools' placements. In the broad contours, the schemes substantially agree regarding, for example, the nation's top ten schools, even if their precise order is in doubt. Following McGuire, I have modified the labels, changing "very strong" to "distinguished," "acceptable plus" to "average," and "adequate" to "below average."

3 Administrative rulemaking

1. See John P. Heinz, Edward O. Laumann, Robert L. Nelson, and Robert H. Salisbury, *The Hollow Core: Private Interests in National Policy Making* (Cambridge, MA: Harvard University Press, 1993). Heinz, et al. studied four policy domains, including labor policy, of which OSHA is a subset.
2. Robert W. Hamilton, "The Role of Nongovernmental Standards in the Development of Mandatory Federal Standards Affecting Safety or Health," *Texas Law Review* 56 (1978), 1329–1484, 1388–9.
3. Benjamin W. Mintz, *OSHA: History, Law, and Policy* (Washington, DC: Bureau of National Affairs, 1984), p. 29.

4. Though some parties have questioned the propriety of *ex parte* communications with OMB and private parties, courts have applied a strict bar on this practice only for formal or adjudicatory agency actions such as decisions about licensing.
5. The circuit courts of appeal are split on the precise definition of "substantial evidence" in the OSHA context, with the Fifth and Eleventh Circuits adopting a "harder look" standard and the DC Circuit a more deferential standard. Any real difference in meaning between the tests is less pronounced than the attitude of the reviewing court toward regulation in general.
6. 29 U.S.C. 651 et seq. (1970) (P.L. 91–596), at §6(b)(5).
7. N = 40. NPRMs gathered more attention on average (168.6 per NPRM, N = 24), though with strongly similar proportions of commenter types (business, union, government, etc.).
8. Mancur Olson, *The Logic of Collective Action: Public Goods and the Theory of Groups* (Cambridge, MA: Harvard University Press, 1971), p. 143.
9. Neil J. Mitchell, *The Conspicuous Corporation: Business, Public Policy and Representative Democracy* (Ann Arbor, MI: University of Michigan Press, 1997).
10. Olson, *The Logic of Collective Action*, p. 143.
11. Business interest groups blossomed in the 1970s, as reactions to the new regulatory environment, economic pressures, and appreciation of the advantages of cooperation. David Plotke, "The Political Mobilization of Business," in Mark P. Petracca (ed.), *The Politics of Interests: Interest Groups Transformed* (Boulder, CO: Westview Press, 1992), p. 190.
12. While there has been a general trend toward increasing in-house staffs, individual trade associations experience cycles of expansion and contraction. Some interviewees suggested that a handful of trade associations are "run by" law firms, with attorneys having created the trade association as a "front" for clients. These claims comport with the anecdotal evidence of law firms running trade associations as virtual "wholly owned subsidiaries," reported by Heinz, et al., *The Hollow Core*, p. 382.
13. Important nuances deserve mention. Union officials may informally communicate and consult with labor counsel without assuming a formal lawyer–client relationship. Also, attorney involvement may increase when OSHA has initiated a rulemaking in response to either a court order or a remand from a previous rulemaking attempt. Attorneys who assisted in the litigation are well positioned to provide further counsel, since all parties must interpret the court's remand order and work toward changes which will satisfy the reviewing court.
14. Interest groups generally use consultants to monitor rulemaking irregularly. In one study, 43.8 percent of interest groups reported having only one use of a consultant per year or less; 23.4 percent used consultants for monitoring "a couple of times per year"; and 14.1 percent reported monthly and 10.9 percent reported weekly use. Cornelius M. Kerwin, *Rulemaking: How Government Agencies Write Law and Make Policy*, 3rd edn (Washington, DC: Congressional Quarterly, 2003), p. 187, table 5–6.

15. Stakeholder efforts include use of the advisory committees provided in the OSH Act.
16. Administrative law practice introduces some variants but does not fundamentally change the problem. See Jamie G. Heller, "Legal Counseling in the Administrative State: How to Let the Client Decide," *Yale Law Journal* 103 (1994), 2503–30.
17. Robert L. Nelson and David M. Trubek, "Arenas of Professionalism: The Professional Ideologies of Lawyers in Context," in Nelson, Trubek, and Rayman L. Solomon (eds.), *Lawyers' Ideals/Lawyers' Practices: Transformations in the American Legal Profession* (Ithaca, NY: Cornell University Press, 1992).
18. Management OSHA representation is not a "cause" and tends to attract attorneys for other reasons, including "serendipity" and "I needed a job." While some interviewees laid bare their sympathies for the views of industry vis-à-vis labor unions, one can hypothesize that conflicts between lawyers and clients would be more common among management attorneys that were attracted to the practice of law by more personal reasons such as anticipated income or social status.
19. Heinz, et al., *The Hollow Core*, pp. 188–9.
20. Gabriel Kolko, *The Triumph of Conservatism: A Reinterpretation of American History 1900–1916* (New York, NY: Free Press of Glencoe, 1963).
21. OSHA had proposed a more stringent rule under the Carter administration but withdrew it in March 1981. The 1983 rule was challenged by the United Steelworkers of America, and on remand OSHA expanded the scope of the rule in 1987. Several industry groups then filed suit to contest these revisions. OSHA initiated a second wave of rulemaking in 1988 to review a number of issues and promulgated a modified rule in 1994.
22. Client sophistication controls the contribution that an attorney makes. One study of lawyer–client interaction in a legal services program for the poor concluded that the attorneys exercised "considerable" control. Carl J. Hosticka, "We Don't Care About What Happened, We Only Care About What Is Going To Happen: Lawyer–Client Negotiations of Reality," *Social Problems* 26 (1979), 599–610, 609.
23. On the social psychological dimensions of the "lock-in" of agency thinking, see Stephanie Stern, "Cognitive Consistency: Theory Maintenance and Administrative Rulemaking," *University of Pittsburgh Law Review* 63 (2002), 589–644.
24. Notably, Sidney A. Shapiro and Thomas O. McGarity, "Reorienting OSHA: Regulatory Alternatives and Legislative Reform," *Yale Journal on Regulation* 6 (1989), 1–63, and John M. Mendlehoff, *The Dilemma of Toxic Substance Regulation: How Overregulation Causes Underregulation at OSHA* (Cambridge, MA: MIT Press, 1988).
25. *Industrial Union Department, AFL-CIO v. American Petroleum Institute*, 448 U.S. 607 (1980) and *American Textile Manufacturers' Institute v. Donovan*, 452 U.S. 490 (1981), respectively. On the *Benzene* case, see Noga Morag-Levine, *Chasing the Wind: Regulating Air Pollution in the Common Law State* (Princeton, NJ: Princeton University Press, 2003), pp. 32–8.

26. Much of the early law particularly concerned the meaning of §6(b)(5) governing toxic chemical and health risks. Some related issues for safety standards were resolved more recently. See *International Union, UAW* v. *OSHA*, 37 F.3d 665 (D.C. Cir. 1994), discussed in chapter 4. Of course, some issues remain unresolved, but the consensus of interviewees and legal texts is that the important issues are "settled." Victoria L. Bor and Ilise Levy Feitshans (eds.), *Occupational Safety and Health Law: 1995 Cumulative Supplement* (Washington, DC: Bureau of National Affairs, 1995), chs. 19 and 20.

27. *Color Pigments Manufacturers Association* v. *OSHA*, 16 F.3d 1157 at 1160 (11th Cir. 1994), quoting *Universal Camera Corp.* v. *NLRB*, 340 U.S. 474 at 477 (1951) and *Asbestos Information Association* v. *OSHA*, 727 F.2d 415 (5th Cir. 1984).

28. *AFL-CIO* v. *Marshall*, 617 F.2d 636 (D.C. Cir. 1979) at 649.

29. *Synthetic Organic Chemical Manufacturers Association* v. *OSHA*, 503 F.2d 1155 (3rd Cir. 1974) (setting aside laboratory provisions of ethyleneimine standard); *American Iron & Steel Institute* v. *OSHA*, 577 F.2d 825 (3rd Cir. 1978) (setting aside coke oven emissions standard as applied to construction workers).

30. Janet A. Gilboy, "Regulatory and Administrative Agency Behavior: Accomodation, Amplification, and Assimilation," *Law and Policy* 17 (1995), 3–22. See also Thomas O. McGarity, "Some Thoughts on 'Deossifying' the Rulemaking Process," *Duke Law Journal* 41 (1993), 1385–1462, 1400.

31. See Cary Coglianese, "Challenging the Rules: Litigation and Bargaining in the Administrative State," Ph.D. thesis, University of Michigan (1994), p. 168.

32. Kerwin, *Rulemaking*, p. 202, table 5–7.

33. A participant can also incorporate by reference the entire record of a different rulemaking into the one at hand. The evidence previously presented is then available on court review. This move is sometimes taken when OSHA begins a rulemaking for a specific industry, such as construction or shipyard employment, after completing a "general industry" standard for the identical hazard.

34. But one person suggested that member companies sending comments may do so because of a disagreement with the trade association, which hinders efforts to create an unambiguous record.

35. See Richard B. Stewart, "The Reformation of American Administrative Law," *Harvard Law Review* 88 (1975), 1669–1813.

36. Memorandum to Daniel P. Boyd, "Subject: Strategies for Assessing Feasibility," dated August, 1975, *General Records Relating to OSHA Organization, Mission, and Functions, 1971–1981*, Box #7, file ADM 11–1 "Nat'l (Reorganizations)," National Archives of the United States, p. 10.

37. Donald L. Horowitz, *The Jurocracy: Government Lawyers, Agency Programs, and Judicial Decisions* (Lexington, MA: Lexington Books, 1977), p. 113.

38. Others before me have used the length of the *Federal Register*, which over the long term has increased considerably, as an indicator

of numerous trends in government. Most often critics have used the number of pages as a proxy for growth in the regulatory bureaucracy. E.g.,
Wendy L. Gramm, Testimony before the United States House Committee on Government Reform on H.R. 2432, the Paperwork and Regulatory Improvements Act of 2003, July 22, 2003, available at http://www.
mercatus.org/article.php/363.html (last accessed, March 23, 2004); also,
Clyde Wayne Crews, Jr., "Ten Thousand Commandments: An Annual
Snapshot of the Federal Regulatory State" (Washington, DC: Cato Institute, 2003: available at http://www.cato.org/tech/pubs/10kc_2002.pdf, last
accessed, March 23, 2004). Used in this way, the *Federal Register* provides a
poor indicator; the reach and impact of the regulatory bureaucracy depends
deeply on the substance of the rules that is not captured in such a snapshot. Here, I regard pages as what they are: statements defending rules.
While the length of rulemaking preambles likely is influenced over time
by factors such as the contentiousness of issues and an agency's decision
to opt for shorter, easier rules over more challenging ones, the core reason
for variations in the length of *Federal Register* documents is the amount of
"defending" that agencies view necessary. For a discussion of measures of
regulatory "accretion," including using *Federal Register* pages, see J. B. Ruhl
and James Salzman, "Mozart and the Red Queen: The Problem of Regulatory Accretion in the Administrative State," *Georgetown Law Journal* 91
(2003), 757–850, 771–2.
39. *Dry Color Manufacturers' Association v. Department of Labor*, 486 F.2d 98
(3d Cir. 1973) and *Associated Industries of NY State v. Department of Labor*,
487 F.2d 342 (2d Cir. 1973).
40. The late 1980s and early 2000s show declines in the median length as
the average length peaked. Both are attributable to the impact of gargan-
tuan rulemaking efforts by OSHA: the 651-page effort in 1999 to update
OSHA's Permissible Exposure Limits, and the 2000 publication of a 609-
page Ergonomics rule. With resources diverted to these projects, most
other health rules were relatively modest, reflected in the lower medians
with higher means.
41. See Mintz, OSHA: History, Law, and Policy, p. 95.
42. R. Shep Melnick, *Regulation and the Courts: The Case of the Clean Air Act*
(Washington, DC: Brookings Institution, 1983); David O'Brien, "Administrative Discretion, Judicial Review, and Regulatory Politics," in Douglas
H. Shumavon and H. Kenneth Hibbeln (eds.), *Administrative Discretion
and Public Policy Implementation* (New York, NY: Praeger, 1986).
43. OSHA had already reopened the record twice in 1992 for further
comments.
44. Two letters were written on behalf of the PRMA as a whole.
45. Exhibit #115–17. Letter from Harold Markey, PRMA to OSHA Docket
Officer, April 22, 1994. Docket #H–071A, OSHA Docket Office.
46. Mintz, OSHA: History, Law, and Policy, p. 251. On regulatory overinclu-
siveness generally, see Eugene Bardach and Robert A. Kagan, *Going by
the Book: The Problem of Regulatory Unreasonableness* (Philadelphia, PA:
Temple University Press, 1982).

47. Richard J. Pierce, Jr., "Judicial Review of Agency Actions in a Period of Diminishing Agency Resources," *Administrative Law Review* 49 (1997), 61–94; Sidney A. Shapiro, "Substantive Reform, Judicial Review, and Agency Resources: OSHA as a Case Study," *Administrative Law Review* 49 (1997), 645–70; Paul Verkuil, "Rulemaking Ossification – A Modest Proposal," *Administrative Law Review* 47 (1995), 453–9; Thomas O. McGarity, "Some Thoughts on 'Deossifying' the Rulemaking Process," *Duke Law Journal* 41 (1992), 1385–1462; Stephen Breyer, "Judicial Review of Questions of Law and Policy," *Administrative Law Review* 38 (1987), 363–98; Jerry Mashaw and David Harfst, "Regulation and Legal Culture: The Case of Motor Vehicle Safety," *Yale Journal on Regulation* 4 (1987), 257–316.
48. See Sheila Jasanoff, "Science and the Limits of Administrative Rulemaking: Lessons from the OSHA Cancer Policy," *Osgoode Hall Law Journal* 20 (1982), 536–61.
49. Since a "participant" typically is an organization, one person may make the presentation while another team-member, such as an attorney, may ask questions.
50. I am assuming here the "adversarial" cross-examination by participants other than OSHA. Participants also use "friendly" cross-examination, more akin to "direct" examination in a trial, in order to make explicit the assumptions or conclusions of a person's testimony. Questions by OSHA's standard-writers or lawyers are designed to get further evidence on particular points, or to clarify others' objections to the rule.
51. See, e.g., Steven Kelman, *Regulating America, Regulating Sweden: A Comparative Study of Occupational Safety and Health Policy* (Cambridge, MA: MIT Press, 1981), p. 26.
52. Ironically, the complaint flows in the opposite direction during the implementation of the rule. Management attorneys report frustration by workers in the field who must answer "stupid" questions from compliance officers who have little or no training in the specifics of a plant or industry. Both complaints highlight the tension between general rules and specific applications.
53. Maureen Cain, "The Symbol Traders," in Cain and Christine B. Harrington (eds.), *Lawyers in Postmodern World: Translation and Transgression* (New York, NY: New York University Press, 1994), pp. 15–48.

4 Rulemaking litigation
1. See, generally, Glen O. Robinson, *American Bureaucracy: Public Choice and Public Law* (Ann Arbor, MI: University of Michigan Press, 1991); David Schoenbrod, *Power Without Responsibility: How Congress Abuses the People Through Delegation* (New Haven, CT: Yale University Press, 1993); Cornelius M. Kerwin, *Rulemaking: How Government Agencies Write Law and Make Policy*, 2nd edn (Washington, DC: CQ Press, 1999).
2. R. Shep Melnick, *Regulation and the Courts: The Case of the Clean Air Act* (Washington, DC: Brookings Institution, 1983); Jerry L. Mashaw and David L. Harfst, "Regulation and Legal Culture: The Case of Motor Vehicle Safety," *Yale Journal on Regulation* 4 (1987), 257–316; Richard

J. Pierce, Jr., "The Unintended Effects of Judicial Review of Agency Rules: How Federal Courts Have Contributed to the Electricity Crisis of the 1990s," *Administrative Law Review* 43 (1991), 7–29; Thomas O. McGarity, "Some Thoughts on 'Deossifying' the Rulemaking Process," *Duke Law Journal* 41 (1992), 1385–1462; Stephen Breyer, *Breaking the Vicious Circle: Toward Effective Risk Regulation* (Cambridge, MA: Harvard University Press, 1993); Richard J. Pierce, Jr., "Judicial Review of Agency Actions in a Period of Diminishing Agency Resources," *Administrative Law Review* 49 (1997), 61–94.

3. Steven Kelman, *Regulating America, Regulating Sweden: A Comparative Study of Occupational Safety and Health Policy* (Cambridge, MA: MIT Press, 1981); Charles Noble, *Liberalism at Work: The Rise and Fall of OSHA* (Philadelphia, PA: Temple University Press, 1986); John M. Mendlehoff, *The Dilemma of Toxic Substance Regulation: How Overregulation Causes Underregulation at OSHA* (Cambridge, MA: MIT Press, 1988); Thomas O. McGarity and Sidney A. Shapiro, *Workers At Risk: The Failed Promise of the Occupational Safety and Health Administration* (Westport, CT: Praeger Press, 1993).

4. Select contributions and work reviewing this literature include: Jody Freeman, "Collaborative Governance," *UCLA Law Review* 45 (1997), 1–98; Cary Coglianese, "Is Consensus an Appropriate Basis for Regulatory Policy?" in Eric Orts and Kurt Deketelaere (eds.), *Environmental Contracts: Comparative Approaches to Regulatory Innovation in the United States and Europe* (Boston, MA: Kluwer Law International, 2001); Philip J. Harter, "In Search of Goldilocks: Democracy, Participation, and Government," *Penn State Environmental Law Review* 10 (2002), 113–34. Not all proposals aiming at these values are entirely consistent; e.g., deliberation does not necessarily require consensus in order to be effective.

5. Sidney A. Shapiro, "Substantive Reform, Judicial Review, and Agency Resources: OSHA as a Case Study," *Administrative Law Review* 49 (1997), 645–70.

6. See, e.g., the Mine Safety and Health Act of 1977, 30 U.S.C. §811(d), and the Clean Air Act, 42 U.S.C. §7607(d)(7)(b).

7. But see *Fire Equipment Manufacturers' Association v. Marshall*, 679 F.2d 679 (7th Cir. 1982).

8. 29 U.S.C. 655 §6(f). A sixty-day window is common within regulatory statutes. See, e.g., the Consumer Product Safety Commission, 15 U.S.C. §2060; the Mine Safety and Health Administration, 30 U.S.C. §811; the Clean Air Act, 42 U.S.C. §7607; and the Toxic Substance Control Act, 15 U.S.C. §2618.

9. Richard B. Stewart, "The Reformation of American Administrative Law," *Harvard Law Review* 88 (1975), 1669–1813, 1723.

10. Jerry L. Mashaw, "Improving the Environment of Agency Rulemaking: An Essay on Management, Games, and Accountability," *Law and Contemporary Problems* 57 (1994), 185–257, 231.

11. For example, a "specification" standard for the prevention of hearing loss could specify that all manufacturing equipment be fitted with approved

noise-reducing dampers. A "performance" version could require that worker exposure does not exceed 85 decibels for more than eight hours. If, on inspection, noise was above approved levels, employers could meet the standard by adopting engineering controls *or* by providing ear protection to workers, so long as the latter was adequate in that environment.

12. E.g., Robert C. Gombar, Arthur G. Sapper, and Melissa A. Bailey, "Sweeping Changes in Store with OSHA's Safety Program Standard," *Occupational Hazards* 59 (May 1997), 25.

13. Cary Coglianese, "Challenging the Rules: Litigation and Bargaining in the Administrative State," Ph.D. thesis, University of Michigan (1994), p. 136.

14. A pair of factors frustrates efforts to collect litigation data for OSHA. Unlike the EPA, the Solicitor's Office does not maintain a docket book of petitions filed against the agency, owing to the relatively small docket it oversees. Second, OSHA's authorizing legislation allows suits in any circuit, not just the DC Circuit.

15. See Herbert M. Kritzer, "Adjudication to Settlement: Shading in the Gray," *Judicature* 70 (1986), 161–5.

16. Mashaw, "Improving the Environment of Agency Rulemaking," 203.

17. Susan M. Olson, *Clients and Lawyers: Securing the Rights of Disabled Persons* (Westport, CT: Greenwood Press, 1984).

18. The distinction between these two types is drawn by Michael E. Abramowitz, "Bureaucrats and Lawyers: Myths and Realities," *Bureaucrat* 2 (1973), 257–8.

19. McGarity and Shapiro, *Workers At Risk*, p. 193.

20. Donald L. Horowitz, *The Jurocracy: Government Lawyers, Agency Programs, and Judicial Decisions* (Lexington, MA: Lexington Books, 1977), p. 75.

21. Mashaw, "Improving the Environment of Agency Rulemaking," 216.

22. Richard B. Stewart, "The Discontents of Legalism: Interest Group Relations in Administrative Regulation," *Wisconsin Law Review* (1985), 655–86, 673.

23. Coglianese, "Challenging the Rules," pp. 146–9.

24. See David R. Cherrington, "The Race to the Courthouse: Conflicting Views Toward the Judicial Review of OSHA Standards," *Brigham Young University Law Review* (1994), 95–128. Scholars have confirmed differences in the political ideology between federal circuits. See Martha Anne Humphries and Donald F. Songer, "Law and Politics in Judicial Oversight of Administrative Agencies," *Journal of Politics* 61 (1999), 207–20; Deborah J. Barrow and Thomas G. Walker, *A Court Divided: The Fifth Circuit Court of Appeals and the Politics of Judicial Reform* (New Haven, CT: Yale University Press, 1988); J. Woodford Howard, Jr., *Courts of Appeals in the Federal Judicial System: A Study of the Second, Fifth, and District of Columbia Circuits* (Princeton, NJ: Princeton University Press, 1981).

25. 28 U.S.C. §2112(a) (amended by Public Law 100–236, signed January 8, 1988).

26. "Affidavit for Lead Industries Association," in Benjamin W. Mintz, *OSHA: History, Law, and Policy* (Washington, DC: Bureau of National Affairs, 1984), pp. 218–19.
27. *United Steelworkers v. Marshall*, 592 F.2d 693 (3d Cir. 1979).
28. Regardless of the number of petitioners in a given region, each circuit with petitions receives one entry into a drum. Rule 24, "Random Selection," Rules of Procedure of the Judicial Panel on Multidistrict Litigation, added June 14, 1988.
29. *Asbestos Information Association v. Reich*, 117 F.3d 891 (5th Cir. 1997).
30. Sidney A. Shapiro and Thomas O. McGarity, "Not So Paradoxical: The Rationale for Technology-Based Regulation," *Duke Law Journal* (1991), 729–38, 738.
31. *AFL-CIO v. OSHA*, 965 F.2d 962, 983–4 (11th Cir. 1992).
32. "The Control of Hazardous Energy Sources (Lockout/Tagout): Proposed Rule," *Federal Register* 53 (April 29, 1988), 15496–528, 15515.
33. *Ibid.*, 15496.
34. *Ibid.*, 15519, emphasis supplied.
35. OSHA routinely gives exemptions to construction and maritime employment, which are covered by similar but separate sets of standards, and agricultural employment, which also received a categorical exemption in the lockout/tagout rulemaking.
36. One distinction OSHA recognized lay between the operation and maintenance of utilities, for which unique rules applied, and construction-related safety occurring on utilities' property, to be covered by safety standards for construction practices generally.
37. "Electrical Standards for Construction: Final Rule," *Federal Register* 51 (July 11, 1986), 25294–335.
38. Letter from John A. Pendergrass, OSHA, October 3, 1986, cited in *Edison Electric Institute v. OSHA*, 849 F.2d 611, 623 (D.C. Cir. 1988). OSHA further denied that utilities must show the unfeasibility of locks before using a tagging system.
39. *Edison Electric Institute v. OSHA*, 849 F.2d 611, 624 (D.C. Cir. 1988).
40. Letter from Stephen Yohay to Docket Officer, June 28, 1988, Exhibit #2-33, Docket #S-012A, OSHA Docket Office, Washington, DC.
41. Transcript, "Proposed Rule on Control of Hazardous Energy Sources: Informal Public Hearing," Volume I, Docket #S-012A, OSHA Docket Office, Washington, DC (September 22, 1988), p. 120.
42. Transcript, "Proposed Rule on Control of Hazardous Energy Sources: Informal Public Hearing," Volume I, Docket #S-012A, OSHA Docket Office, Washington, DC (September 23, 1988), p. 5.
43. "Electric Power Generation, Transmission, and Distribution: Electrical Protective Equipment: Final Rule," *Federal Register* 59 (January 31, 1994), 4320–476.
44. Nevertheless, the subsequent rulemaking for the electrical utilities "vertical standard" brought a union challenge to industry claims that tagout systems were safe. In its final rule, OSHA relied heavily on the general industry standard and adopted a virtually identical preference of lockout over

NOTES TO PAGES 117–23

tagout. Some provisions differed from the general industry standard and OSHA recognized that utilities' tagging systems generally provide protection equivalent to lockout systems, but the agency determined that utilities were not "so unique" that they require a completely different rule. Petitioning OSHA to stay the effective date of the new standard, the EEI attacked OSHA's conclusions as "infeasible," "indefensible," and "unacceptable." See Exhibit #L-73, Letter from Stephen C. Yohay, McDermott Will & Emery, to Thomas Shepich, Directorate of Safety Standards, Docket #S-015, OSHA Docket Office, Washington, DC (March 4, 1994).

45. Letter from C. T. Sawyer, American Petroleum Institute to Docket Officer, Exhibit #2-36, Docket #S-012A, OSHA Docket Office, Washington, DC (June 28, 1988).

46. Confidential interview by author.

47. Letter from C. T. Sawyer, American Petroleum Institute, to Docket Officer, Exhibit #57, Docket #S-012A, OSHA Docket Office, Washington, DC (December 23, 1988).

48. Letter from Dr. Geraldine V. Cox, Chemical Manufacturers' Association, to Docket Office, Exhibit #56, Docket #S-012A, OSHA Docket Office, Washington, DC (December 23, 1988).

49. "Control of Hazardous Energy Sources (Lockout/Tagout); Machinery, Equipment Maintenance: Final Rule," *Federal Register* 54 (September 1, 1989), 36644–90, 36690.

50. "Corrections and Technical Amendments to the Final Rule on Control of Hazardous Energy Sources (Lockout/Tagout)," *Federal Register* 55 (September 20, 1990), 38677–88, 38684, emphasis added. Under a work permit system, employees could "sign in and out" for locks that were needed for extended periods, rather than removing and replacing individual locks at the end of each shift.

51. *American Textile Manufacturers' Institute, Inc. v. Donovan*, 452 U.S. 490 (1981) (the "*Cotton Dust*" case).

52. Final Brief of Petitioner, National Association of Manufacturers, *International Union, UAW v. OSHA* (D.C. Cir. 1991, No. 89–1559 and consolidated cases), pp. 12–14.

53. Brief for Petitioner, International Union, UAW, and Intervenor, Oil, Chemical & Atomic Workers' Union; in *UAW v. OSHA*, pp. 20–2.

54. Brief for the Secretary of Labor, in *UAW v. OSHA*, p. 15.

55. *Industrial Union Department, AFL-CIO v. American Petroleum Institute*, 448 U.S. 607 (1980).

56. *International Union, UAW v. OSHA*, 938 F.2d 1310 (D.C. Cir. 1991), 1317.

57. The court recognized that "cost–benefit" analysis is a disputed concept. Quoting from Benjamin Franklin, the panel demanded only a "moral or prudential algebra" systematically weighing pros and cons. *UAW v. OSHA*, p. 1321.

58. The court also remanded substantive issues that hinged on the standard to be met, such as the cost–benefits of lockout over tagout and the relative risks posed by different industries.

59. *International Union, UAW v. OSHA*, 976 F.2d 749, 751 (D.C. Cir. 1992).

60. "Control of Hazardous Energy Sources (Lockout/Tagout): Final Rule; Supplemental Statement of Reasons", *Federal Register* 58 (March 30, 1993), 16612–23.
61. *International Union, UAW* v. *OSHA*, 37 F.3d 665 (D.C. Cir. 1994), 669.
62. "Notice of Public Meeting on Review of the Control of Hazardous Energy Sources (Lockout/Tagout) Standard (29 CFR 1910.147)," *Federal Register* 62 (May 29, 1997), 29089–90.
63. "The Control of Hazardous Energy (Lockout/Tagout): Notice of the Availability of a Lookback Review Pursuant to the Regulatory Flexibility Act and Executive Order 12866," *Federal Register* 65 (June 20, 2000), 38302–4.
64. Neil J. Mitchell, *The Conspicuous Corporation: Business, Public Policy and Representative Democracy* (Ann Arbor, MI: University of Michigan Press, 1997).
65. Mike H. Ryan, *Corporate Strategy, Public Policy, and the Fortune 500: How America's Major Corporations Influence Government* (Oxford: Basil Blackwell, 1987), p. 200.
66. On the dynamics of repeated interaction in rulemaking litigation, see Cary Coglianese, "Litigating within Relationships: Disputes and Disturbance in the Regulatory Process," *Law and Society Review* 30 (1996), 735–65.
67. Stephen R. M. Wilks and Maurice Wright, "Conclusion: Comparing Government–Industrial Relations: States, Sectors, and Networks," in Wilks and Wright (eds.), *Comparative Government–Industry Relations: Western Europe, the United States, and Japan* (Oxford: Clarendon Press, 1987), p. 286.
68. Due in part to barriers to accessing the work of lawyers as interest representatives in regulatory politics, inferences at the microlevel must be drawn from broadly anecdotal accounts of the process. See Joseph C. Goulden, *The Superlawyers: The Small and Powerful World of the Great Washington Law Firms* (New York, NY: Weybright and Talley, 1972); Douglas Frantz and David McKean, *Friends in High Places: The Rise and Fall of Clark Clifford* (Boston, MA: Little, Brown, & Co., 1995). The limited scholarly attention to the subject urges caution but has concentrated on the structure of lawyers' relationships at the expense of the political inputs and implications of this work. Kathleen Kemp, "Lawyers, Politics and Economic Regulation," *Social Science Quarterly* 64 (1986), 267–82; Robert L. Nelson and John P. Heinz, with Edward O. Laumann and Robert H. Salisbury, "Lawyers and the Structure of Influence in Washington," *Law and Society Review* 22 (1988), 237–300; John P. Heinz, Edward O. Laumann, Robert L. Nelson, and Robert H. Salisbury, *The Hollow Core: Private Interests in National Policy Making* (Cambridge, MA: Harvard University Press, 1993).
69. Jeffrey M. Gaba, "Informal Rulemaking by Settlement Agreement," *Georgetown Law Journal* 73 (1985), 1241–82. More generally, settlement for the creation of rules of general applicability is criticized on these grounds. Owen M. Fiss, "Against Settlement," *Yale Law Journal* 93 (1984), 1073–90; David Luban, "Settlements and the Erosion of the Public Realm," *Georgetown Law Journal* 83 (1995), 2619–62.

70. Philip J. Harter, "Negotiating Regulations: A Cure for Malaise," *Georgetown Law Journal* 71 (1982), 1–118.
71. See Cary Coglianese, "Assessing Consensus: The Promise and Performance of Negotiated Rulemaking," *Duke Law Journal* 46 (1997), 1255–1349, 1257, 1262.
72. Laura I. Langbein and Cornelius M. Kerwin, "Regulatory Negotiation versus Conventional Rule Making: Claims, Counterclaims, and Empirical Evidence," *Journal of Public Administration Research and Theory* 10 (2000), 599–632; Jody Freeman and Laura I. Langbein, "Regulatory Negotiation and the Legitimacy Benefit," *New York University Environmental Law Journal* 9 (2000), 60–151.
73. Department of Labor, "Framework for the use of Negotiated Rulemaking in the Department of Labor," http://www.dol.gov/asp/programs/negreg/nrbprta.htm (last accessed: 6 April 2004). This recommendation flows directly from the Negotiated Rulemaking Act of 1990, 5 U.S.C. §§581–90 (Supp. III, 1991) at §565(b) (1994).
74. Daniel J. Fiorino, "Regulatory Negotiation as a Policy Process," *Public Administration Review* 48 (1988), 764–72, 770–1.
75. Coglianese, "Assessing Consensus," 1277.
76. The rule did not escape challenge. See *Steel Joist Institute* v. *OSHA*, 287 F.3d 1165 (D.C. Cir. 2002).
77. *Ibid.*, 1308.
78. See, e.g., Joseph A. Dear, Assistant Secretary for Occupational Safety and Health, Statement before the House Judiciary Subcommittee on Commercial and Administrative Law, June 27, 1996 (available from OSHA Office of Public Affairs).
79. Philip J. Harter, "Fear of Commitment: An Affliction of Adolescents," *Duke Law Journal* 46 (1997), 1389–1429, 1419.
80. John B. Moran, Bill Kojola, and James Melius, "Asphalt Paving Exposure Controls: A Model for the Future?" *Applied Occupational and Environmental Hygiene* 12 (1997), 407–9, 408.
81. The availability of ventilation systems lowered the uncertainty and economic impact of the agreement. A number of OSHA rulemakings, including lead and cotton dust, have been intended as "technology forcing" regulations, meaning that only a portion of the industry would be able to reach the new standards, depending on their ability to afford new and emerging technologies.
82. Coglianese, "Assessing Consensus," 1329.
83. Elizabeth Fisher and Patrick Schmidt, "Seeing the 'Blind Spots' in Administrative Law: Theory, Practice, and Rulemaking Settlements in the United States," *Common Law World Review* 30 (2001), 348–72; Jim Rossi, "Bargaining in the Shadow of Administrative Procedure: The Public Interest in Rulemaking Settlement," *Duke Law Journal* 51 (2001), 1015–58.
84. See Nicholas A. Ashford, C. William Ryan, and Charles C. Caldart, "A Hard Look at Federal Regulation of Formaldehyde: A Departure from Reasoned Decisionmaking," *Harvard Environmental Law Review* 7 (1983), 297–370, 348.

85. See "OMB Disapproves Formaldehyde Standard Labeling and MSDS Requirements," *Employment Safety and Health Guide* (March 15, 1988) ¶ 9590 at p. 10,701, summarizing a February 2, 1988 letter from the OMB to the Labor Department's Assistant Secretary for Administration and Management. At the same time, the OMB and OSHA were locked in a dispute over provisions of the "generic" hazard communication standard. That dispute ultimately reached the US Supreme Court. *Dole v. United Steelworkers of America*, 494 U.S. 26 (1990).
86. *International Union, UAW v. Pendergrass*, 878 F.2d 389, 395 (D.C. Cir. 1989).
87. See "Oversight of the Occupational Safety and Health Administration," Hearings before the Senate Committee on Labor and Human Resources, April 18–20, 1988, pp. 468–9.
88. Eleven participants sat on behalf of OSHA and the Department of Labor, four of whom were attorneys from the Solicitor's Office. Four of the ten industry and union representatives were counsel.
89. Summary of comments made by Alan McMillan, Deputy Assistant Secretary, OSHA in Exhibit #300. "Memorandum for Formaldehyde Docket" from Cynthia L. Attwood, Associate Solicitor for Occupational Safety and Health, July 10, 1990. Docket #H-225D, OSHA Docket Office.
90. One attorney representing Public Citizen and one representing the National Particleboard Association were in attendance, along with three attorneys from the Solicitor's Office. See Exhibit #300. "Memorandum for Formaldehyde Docket," from Barbara Werthmann, Counsel for Appellate Litigation, OSH Division, July 10, 1990. Docket #H-225D, OSHA Docket Office.
91. *Ibid.*
92. Exhibit #301-4. Letter from James B. MacRae, Jr., Office of Information and Regulatory Affairs, to Jennifer Dorn, US Department of Labor, November 28, 1990. Docket #H-225D, OSHA Docket Office.
93. Exhibit #301-3. Letter from Gerard F. Scannell, Assistant Secretary for Occupational Safety and Health, to James B. MacRae, Jr., April 26, 1991. Docket #H-225D, OSHA Docket Office.
94. Exhibit #301-2. Letter from James B. MacRae, Jr., Office of Information and Regulatory Affairs, to Gerald [sic] Scannell, Assistant Secretary for Occupational Safety and Health, June 11, 1991. Docket #H-225D, OSHA Docket Office.
95. One late comment contained a copy of a fax the employer received from a major law firm, revealing the attorneys' role as instigator. The fax, titled "Client Alert Memorandum," notified the client about the terms of the proposed rule and the shortened comment period. The fax highlighted how the new rule would impact formaldehyde users and made no mention of the labor–management origins of the proposal. Exhibit #L304-1. Facsimile letter from King & Spalding, Washington, DC, July 22, 1991. Docket #H-225D, OSHA Docket Office.

5   Enforcement

1. E.g., Fiona Haines, *Corporate Regulation: Beyond "Punish or Persuade"* (Oxford: Clarendon Press, 1997); Sally S. Simpson, *Corporate Crime, Law, and Social Control* (New York, NY: Cambridge University Press, 2002); Neil Gunningham, Robert A. Kagan, and Dorothy Thornton, *Shades of Green: Business, Regulation, and Environment* (Stanford, CA: Stanford University Press, 2003).

2. Michael McCann, *Rights at Work: Pay Equity Reform and the Politics of Legal Mobilization* (Chicago, IL: University of Chicago Press, 1989); John Brigham, *The Constitution of Interests: Beyond the Politics of Rights* (New York, NY: New York University Press, 1996), p. 26.

3. Keith Hawkins, *Law as Last Resort: Prosecution Decision-Making in a Regulatory Agency* (Oxford: Oxford University Press, 2002), pp. 433–5.

4. Julia Black, "Regulatory Conversations," *Journal of Law and Society* 29 (2002), 163–96; Michael P. Vanderbergh, "Beyond Elegance: A Testable Typology of Social Norms in Corporate Environmental Compliance," *Stanford Environmental Law Journal* 22 (2003), 55–144, 78.

5. Johan A. de Bruijn and Ernst F. ten Heuvelhof, "Policy Networks and Governance," in David L. Weimer (ed.), *Institutional Design* (Boston, MA: Kluwer Academic Publishers, 1995), p. 163.

6. James Eisenstein and Herbert Jacob, *Felony Justice: An Organizational Analysis of Criminal Courts* (Boston, MA: Little, Brown, and Co., 1977), p. 23.

7. William H. Clune, III, "A Political Model of Implementation and Implications of the Model for Public Policy, Research, and the Changing Roles of Law and Lawyers," *Iowa Law Review* 69 (1983), 47–125, 55.

8. A component of the OSH Act not crucial here is the involvement of states in enforcement. Any state may assume responsibility for occupational safety and health by submitting a plan to OSHA that provides for a state agency with health and safety standards that are "at least as effective" as federal OSHA standards. In practice, most "state plan states" simply adopt national standards, although states sometimes raise the federal floor or address a hazard not regulated by OSHA. Twenty-one states have claimed full jurisdiction for occupational safety and health, and three other state plans (New York, New Jersey, and Connecticut) cover only public sector employees.

9. *Marshall v. Barlow's, Inc.*, 436 U.S. 307 (1978).

10. Basil J. Whiting, "OSHA's Enforcement Policy," *Labor Law Journal* 31 (1980), 259–82, 259. Despite the clear legislative history behind first-instance citation policy, OSHA has developed some exceptions and limited cooperative programs. Sidney A. Shapiro and Randy S. Rabinowitz, "Punishment Versus Cooperation in Regulatory Enforcement," *Administrative Law Review* 49 (1997), 703–37.

11. US Department of Labor, "OSHA Inspections," pamphlet (2002, revised), pp. 3–4.

12. General Accounting Office, "Occupational Safety and Health: Penalties for Violations Are Well Below Maximum Allowable Penalties," April 6, 1992, p. 6.

13. The Justice Department and OSHA struggled bitterly over the boundaries of their respective litigation authority, until reaching a settlement in 1975. Donald L. Horowitz, *The Jurocracy: Government Lawyers, Agency Programs, and Judicial Decisions* (Lexington, MA: Lexington Books, 1977), pp. 109–14.

14. See Edwin Bowers, "OSHA's Legal Professional," *Job Safety & Health Quarterly* 3 (Fall 1991), 21.

15. Don J. Lofgren, *Dangerous Premises: An Insider's View of OSHA Enforcement* (Ithaca, NY: ILR Press, 1989), pp. 221–5.

16. Such conferences have resulted in regional workload-sharing agreements and formation of an Enforcement Litigation Strategy Committee. "Memo from Joseph A. Dear, Assistant Secretary and Thomas A. Williamson, Jr., Solicitor of Labor, regarding Enforcement Litigation Strategy," March 24, 1995, published in *Occupational Safety and Health Reporter* 24 (April 5, 1995), 2218.

17. See Michael Herz, "The Attorney Particular: Governmental Role of the Agency General Counsel," in Cornell W. Clayton (ed.), *Government Lawyers: The Federal Legal Bureaucracy and Presidential Politics* (Lawrence, KS: University Press of Kansas, 1995), p. 143.

18. Daniel J. Gifford, "Federal Administrative Law Judges: The Relevance of Past Choices to Future Directions," *Administrative Law Review* 49 (1997), 1–60, 7.

19. See Stephen A. Bokat and Horace A. Thompson, III (eds.), *Occupational Safety and Health Law* (Washington, DC: Bureau of National Affairs, 1988), pp. 442–7.

20. E-Z Trials are used for cases involving one or more of the following: less than $10,000 proposed penalties, no "willful" citations, relatively simple issues of law or fact, hearings expected to require less than two days, and a small employer. Occupational Safety and Health Review Commission, *Guide to Review Commission Procedures* (November 1997), 22.

21. Any commissioner may then direct a case for review, though in rare circumstances a commissioner will direct a case for review *absent* a petition. See *Secretary of Labor* v. *Oscar Renda Contracting, Inc.*, 17 OSHC 1883 (1997).

22. One widely accepted explanation is that during the passage of the Act, one Congressman insisted nonlawyers be permitted so that he might eventually be eligible to sit on the Commission.

23. *Martin, Secretary of Labor* v. *OSHRC* (the "*CF&I Steel*" case) 499 U.S. 144 (1991).

24. George Robert Johnson, Jr., "The Split-Enforcement Model: Some Conclusions From the OSHA and MSHA Experiences," *Administrative Law Review* 39 (1987), 315–51.

25. See Terry Moe, "The Politics of Bureaucratic Structure," in John E. Chubb and Paul E. Peterson (eds.), *Can the Government Govern?* (Washington, DC: The Brookings Institution, 1989).

26. Kenneth A. Kovach and Nancy Greer Hamilton, "Labor's Efforts Sustain Workplace Safety," *Labor Studies Journal* 22 (1997), 57. There have been

some noteworthy defeats, as well, such as the 2001 repeal of OSHA's rule governing ergonomics.

27. Approximately 5 percent of OSHA's compliance officers investigate "11(c)" cases of discharged employees and discrimination against employee complainants.

28. *Secretary of Labor* v. *Boise Cascade Corp.*, 14 OSHC 1993 (Review Commission, 1991).

29. Rejecting union claims to a wider veto, the Supreme Court held that the Secretary of Labor's role as enforcer carries "the authority to withdraw a citation and enter into settlement discussions with the employer." *Cuyahoga Valley Railway* v. *United Transportation Union*, 474 U.S. 3 (1985).

30. Charles Noble, *Liberalism at Work: The Rise and Fall of OSHA* (Philadelphia, PA: Temple University Press, 1986), pp. 129–31.

31. David Weil, "Building Safety: The Role of Construction Unions in the Enforcement of OSHA," *Journal of Labor Research* 13 (1992), 121–32. Unionized construction sites receive more frequent and intense inspections, and union participation during the inspection results in more violations and shorter abatement periods.

32. Cited in Thomas E. Quigley, "Employee Involvement in the OSHA Settlement Process," *Detroit College of Law Review* (1990), 579–97, 593.

33. See, e.g., Barry R. Weingast and Mark J. Moran, "Bureaucratic Discretion or Congressional Control: Regulatory Policymaking by the Federal Trade Commission," *Journal of Political Economy* 91 (1984), 765–800; Terry M. Moe, "Control and Feedback in Economic Regulation: The Case of the NLRB," *American Political Science Review* 79 (1985), 1094–1116, 1094; B. Dan Wood, "Principles, Bureaucrats, and Responsiveness in Clean Air Enforcement," *American Political Science Review* 82 (1988), 213–34; B. Dan Wood and James B. Anderson, "The Politics of US Antitrust Regulation," *American Journal of Political Science* 37 (1993), 1–39. But see Jeff Worsham, Marc Allen Eisner, and Evan J. Ringquist, "Assessing the Assumptions: A Critical Analysis of Agency Theory," *Administration & Society* 28 (1997), 419–42.

34. Communications in *Records of the Occupational Safety and Health Administration*, Office of the Assistant Secretary for Occupational Safety and Health, Correspondence, 1981, Box 7, file "Inspection/Investigation/ Complaints," National Archives of the United States, College Park, Maryland.

35. *Hern Iron Works, Inc.* v. *Donovan*, 670 F.2d 838 (9th Cir. 1982).

36. Among the major disasters which have provoked oversight hearings are: a series of six grain elevator explosions in December 1977 and January 1978, killing sixty-two people; the 1978 collapse of a cooling tower at Willow Island, West Virginia which resulted in over fifty fatalities; a 1983 fire and explosion at a Newark, New Jersey Texaco tank facility; the 1985 explosion at Aerlex Corporation's fireworks factory in Oklahoma; and the 1985 release of hazardous chemicals at Union Carbide's Institute, West Virginia facility, just one year after Union Carbide's infamous disaster at Bhopal, India.

37. Both dimensions have remained relatively consistent over time, except that during the 1970s, manufacturing companies received the plurality of inspections. See United States Department of Labor, *Twenty Years of OSHA Federal Enforcement Data: A Review and Explanation of the Major Trends* (January 1993).
38. The nature of construction sites inflates the construction firm data. A single worksite can involve multiple subcontractors. When a compliance officer visits, each subcontractor evaluated is recorded as an independent inspection. OSHA's penalty structure, which awards penalty deductions for smaller employers, helps to explain the discrepancy in penalties.
39. The "size of firm" data has been recalculated to exclude trade association advocacy (4.9 percent) and the negligible "other" (0.3 percent).
40. Fiscal year 1997 ran from October 1996 through September 1997. A wide array of current year data is available from the OSHA Statistics and Data web page: http://www.osha.gov/oshstats/. Historical data on OSHA inspections is available from the agency by Freedom of Information Act (FOIA) request.
41. Many attorneys have had clients break the norm by contacting them before the onset of an OSHA investigation.
42. Between 1990 and 1996, an average of 1,202 investigations per year followed accidents and accounted for 3.1 percent of all inspections (source: OSHA internally generated statistical reports acquired by Freedom of Information Act request).
43. The importance of accidents for safety inspectors in the United Kingdom suggests a general socio-psychological tendency among safety inspectors. See Bridget M. Hutter and Sally Lloyd-Bostock, "The Power of Accidents: The Social and Psychological Impact of Accidents and the Enforcement of Safety Regulations," *British Journal of Criminology* 30 (1990), 409–22.
44. Robert C. Gombar, Arthur G. Sapper, and Melissa A. Bailey, "Sweeping Changes in Store with OSHA's Safety Program Standard," *Occupational Hazards* 59 (May 1997), 25.
45. Hawkins, *Law as Last Resort*, p. 334.
46. David Barstow and Lowell Bergman, "Deaths on the Job, Slaps on the Wrist," *New York Times,* January 10, 2003, p. A15.
47. 1998 Survey of OSHA Bar (N = 204).
48. The overlapping roles of educator and advocate strain the applicability of the "teacher" label. But see Kimberlee K. Kovach, "The Lawyer as Teacher: The Role of Education in Lawyering," *Clinical Law Review* 4 (1998), 359–90.
49. Gunningham, et al., *Shades of Green*, p. 133.
50. OSHA conducted the survey of 740 general industry companies as part of the Clinton administration's National Performance Review. "Most Employers, Workers Satisfied with OSHA Inspections, Survey Discovers," *Occupational Safety and Health Reporter* 24 (January 25, 1995), 1723.
51. The response of this attorney, a former Labor Department official and a partner in a very large firm, supported a conclusion that the large corporate clients are the least prone to naiveté. "I won't discuss that with you," he

said, "as it would reflect both on my practice and my clients. Let's put it this way: I charge them a very high hourly rate and they expect to see a meaningful result in the case based on what it is."

52. Marc Galanter, "Why the 'Haves' Come Out Ahead: Speculations on the Limits of Legal Change," *Law and Society Review* 9 (1974), 95–160.
53. Robert B. Reich, quoted in US Department of Labor News Release 96–286, Office of Public Affairs (July 12, 1996), p. 1.
54. "DeCoster Got Caught In Net After Enforcers Changed Their Approach," *Maine Sunday Telegraph*, July 8, 1996, pp. 1A, 12A.
55. Eugene Bardach and Robert A. Kagan, *Going by the Book: The Problem of Regulatory Unreasonableness* (Philadelphia, PA: Temple University Press, 1982); John Braithwaite, *To Punish or Persuade: Enforcement of Coal Mine Safety* (Albany, NY: State University of New York Press, 1985); John T. Scholz, "Cooperative Regulatory Enforcement and the Politics of Administrative Effectiveness," *American Political Science Review* 85 (1991), 115–36; Ian Ayres and John Braithwaite, *Responsive Regulation: Transcending the Deregulation Debate* (New York, NY: Oxford University Press, 1992).
56. Robert A. Kagan, *Adversarial Legalism: The American Way of Law* (Cambridge, MA: Harvard University Press, 2001), p. 206.
57. N = 211 and 147 respectively. Specialist versus nonspecialist significance: $\chi^2 = 32.3, p < .001, df = 3$. Among OSHA specialists, over a third (37.4 percent) "strongly" agreed.
58. Survey Question V.30: After a citation has been issued against a client, should an attorney make broad discovery requests and begin extensive depositions of OSHA officials or staff? (N = 196).
59. W. Scott Railton, *OSHA Compliance Handbook* (Rockford, MD: Government Institutes, Inc., 1992), p. 207.
60. "Firms That Deny OSHA Entry Draw Higher Fines, Cited For More Alleged Violations, Study Shows," *Occupational Safety and Health Reporter* 23 (February 23, 1994), 1275.
61. Letter from survey respondent #164, June 4, 1998.
62. N = 219.
63. This interpretation receives specific support from John P. Heinz, Edward O. Laumann, Robert L. Nelson, and Robert H. Salisbury, *The Hollow Core: Private Interests in National Policy Making* (Cambridge, MA: Harvard University Press, 1993).
64. Between 1991 and 1996, ALJs issued an average of 182.5 decisions after hearings and 3,069.5 without hearings – i.e., settled cases only requiring judicial approval – with a combined post-contest settlement rate of 94.1 percent. For the 90 percent estimate, see "OSHA Admits to Ad Hoc Settlement Policy. Scant Oversight," *Inside OSHA* (April 7, 1997), 3, quoting Ray Donnelly, OSHA director for general industry compliance assistance; Mark A. Rothstein, "OSHA After Ten Years: A Review and Some Proposed Reforms," *Vanderbilt Law Review* 34 (1980), 71–139, 116; and "Special Report: OSHA Settlement Agreements," *BNA OSHA* 27 (July 23, 1997), 244.

65. Litigation has since partially undermined the availability of per-employee penalties. *Reich v. Arcadian Corporation*, 110 F.3d 1192 (5th Cir. 1997).
66. *Secretary of Labor v. Ho*, OSHRC No. 98-1645, 98-1646 (OSHRC, Sept. 29, 2003). OSHA has appealed this decision.
67. "Hudson Foods Has 'Long History' of Safety, Health Violations, OSHA Says," *Washington Post*, August 23, 1997, p. A11.
68. Barstow and Bergman, "Deaths on the Job," p. A15.
69. BNA OSHA, "Special Report", 245, quoting former Solicitor of Labor George Salem, an attorney with the law firm of Akin, Gump, Strauss, Hauer & Feld.
70. Five respondents, writing in the margins, faulted the survey for excluding the "characterization of the citation" as an independent choice, since the issue often arises in attorney–client discussions. Characterizations undoubtedly serve as an *apparent* focus for negotiations and litigation with OSHA, but characterizations interact with many factors described in this section: "willful" citations carry higher penalties, provide strong evidence of negligence in secondary litigation, provide unions with firm evidence of management recalcitrance, and insult company officials who disclaim having *willfully* caused employees harm. Thus, the survey did not offer characterization as an option.
71. Bivariate correlation = 0.030, significance = .630, N = 192.
72. In a fully proportional system, the perceived impact of penalties would remain constant.
73. Pre-citation settlements, discussed below, uniquely combine agency and solicitor decisionmakers.
74. "OSHA Oversight: Worker Health and Safety at Union Carbide, Institute, WV, Facility," Hrg. before the Subcommittee on Health and Safety of the Committee on Education and Labor, US House of Representatives, 99th Congress, October 2, 1985, p. 36.
75. Labor unions have strongly objected to OSHA and Congress about exclusion from pre-citation settlement. See "Oversight of the Occupational Safety and Health Administration," Hrgs. before the Committee on Labor and Human Resources, US Senate, 100th Congress, April 18–20, 1988, p. 714
76. "Special Report," 247.
77. Three of the government officials integrally involved in the creation of the policy later moved to private law firms. Two have won recognition for bringing clients to pre-citation settlements. The third joined the firm representing Union Carbide and helped another client develop a legal strategy attacking the Egregious Penalty Policy.
78. Hawkins, *Law as Last Resort*.
79. See "Muffed Mission: Labor Secretary's Bid to Push Plant Safety Runs Into Skepticism," *Wall Street Journal*, August 19, 1994, p. A1; *Secretary of Labor v. Dayton Tire*, 16 OSHC 1961, 1961 (1994).
80. Robert B. Reich, *Locked in the Cabinet* (New York: Vintage paperback edition, 1998), p. 166.
81. See Weil, "Building Safety."

82. N = 177.
83. Some management counsel seem keenly aware of how their representation might shape OSHA law, and some undoubtedly hope that, while seeking relief for their clients, their efforts may mold precedent to their political ideology. It is difficult to gauge, however, whether management attorneys regard enforcement advocacy as "cause" lawyering in even the mildest sense.
84. N = 226.

6 Regulatory counseling

1. In the area of occupational safety and health, see Andrew Hopkins, "Social Values in Occupational Safety Law," *Legal Studies Forum* 13 (1989), 135–50; K. Carson and Richard Johnstone, "The Dupes of Hazard: Occupational Health and Safety and the Victorian Sanctions Debate," *Australian and New Zealand Journal of Sociology* 26 (1990), 126–41; see also John C. Coffee, Jr., "'No Soul to Damn: No Body to Kick': An Unscandalized Inquiry into the Problem of Corporate Punishment," *Michigan Law Review* 79 (1981), 386–459, 407–9; Susan P. Shapiro, *Wayward Capitalists: Target of the Securities and Exchange Commission* (New Haven, CT: Yale University Press, 1984).
2. Christopher D. Stone, *Where the Law Ends: The Social Control of Corporate Behavior* (New York, NY: Harper and Row, 1975); Eugene Bardach and Robert A. Kagan, *Going by the Book: The Problem of Regulatory Unreasonableness* (Philadelphia, PA: Temple University Press, 1982); John Braithwaite, "Enforced Self-Regulation: A New Strategy for Corporate Crime Control," *Michigan Law Review* 80 (1982), 1466–1507; Braithwaite, *To Punish or Persuade: Enforcement of Coal Mine Safety* (Albany, NY: State University of New York Press, 1985); Ian Ayres and John Braithwaite, *Responsive Regulation: Transcending the Deregulation Debate* (New York, NY: Oxford University Press, 1992).
3. A recitation of this literature is beyond the scope of this book.
4. American Bar Association, House of Delegates, *Model Rules of Professional Conduct* (Chicago, IL: ABA Center for Professional Responsibility, 1994 edn), Rule 2.1.
5. *Ibid.*, preamble.
6. Robert W. Gordon, "The Independence of Lawyers," *Boston University Law Review* 68 (1988), 1–83, 24.
7. William H. Simon, "Ethical Discretion in Lawyering," *Harvard Law Review* 101 (1988), 1083–1145.
8. William H. Simon, "The Ideology of Advocacy: Procedural Justice and Professional Ethics," *Wisconsin Law Review* (1978), 29–144. Simon's proposal does not assign loyalty to the state but to lawyers' understanding of justice.
9. David Dana, "Environmental Lawyers and the Public Service Model of Lawyering," *Oregon Law Review* 74 (1995), 57–83; George H. Brown, "Environmental Lawyers and the Public Interest: A Response to David Dana," *Oregon Law Review* 74 (1995), 85–98, 89; and Ted Schneyer, "Fuzzy

Models of the Corporate Lawyer as Environmental Compliance Counselor," *Oregon Law Review* 74 (1995), 99–119.

10. American Bar Association, *Model Code of Professional Responsibility* (1981), Canon 7, EC 7–1.

11. Joseph Allegretti, "Have Briefcase Will Travel: An Essay on the Lawyer as Hired Gun," *Creighton Law Review* 24 (1990–1), 747–80, 749.

12. Oliver Wendell Holmes, "The Path of the Law," *Harvard Law Review* 10 (1897), 457–78.

13. Richard L. Abel, *American Lawyers* (New York, NY: Oxford University Press, 1989), pp. 239–48.

14. See passing remarks by Robert A. Kagan and Robert Eli Rosen, "On the Social Significance of Large Law Firm Practice," *Stanford Law Review* 37 (1985), 399–443, 414.

15. Margaret Ann Wilkinson, Peter Mercer, and Terra Strong, "Mentor, Mercenary or Melding: An Empirical Inquiry into the Role of the Lawyer," *Loyola University of Chicago Law Journal* 28 (1996), 373–418.

16. Jerome E. Carlin, *Lawyers' Ethics: A Survey of the New York City Bar* (New York, NY: Russell Sage Foundation, 1966).

17. N = 221 and 219, respectively. Involvement in compliance-related activities was represented by a summary scale of the responses reported in table 6.2. The scale ranged from zero to eight, with a mean of 3.31 and a standard deviation of 2.11.

18. Doreen McBarnet, "Legal Creativity: Law, Capital, and Legal Avoidance," in Maureen Cain and Christine B. Harrington (eds.), *Lawyers in a Postmodern World: Translation and Transgression* (New York, NY: New York University Press, 1994), pp. 73–84; Doreen McBarnet and Christopher Whelan, *Creative Accounting and the Cross-eyed Javelin Thrower* (Chichester: J. Wiley, 1999).

19. Charles Brown, James Hamilton, and James Medoff, *Employers Large and Small* (Cambridge, MA: Harvard University Press, 1990), pp. 84–5.

20. Dawn-Marie Driscoll, W. Michael Hoffman, and Joseph E. Murphy, "Business Ethics and Compliance: What Management is Doing and Why," *Business and Society Review* 99 (1998), 35–51, 38–9.

21. Richard J. Pierce, Jr., "Small is Not Beautiful: The Case Against Special Regulatory Treatment of Small Firms," *Administrative Law Review* 50 (1998), 537–78, 564–6.

22. Ronald J. Gilson, "The Devolution of the Legal Profession: A Demand Side Perspective," *Maryland Law Review* 49 (1990), 869–916, 900–1.

23. Fiona Haines, *Corporate Regulation: Beyond "Punish or Persuade"* (Oxford: Clarendon Press, 1997).

24. *Ibid.*, p. 164.

25. Christine Parker, *The Open Corporation: Effective Self-regulation and Democracy* (Cambridge, UK: Cambridge University Press, 2002), p. 183.

26. Tension exists beyond administrative regulation as well. See, e.g., the related area of the Federal Sentencing Guidelines for Corporations. Note, "Growing the Carrot: Encouraging Effective Corporate Compliance," *Harvard Law Review* 109 (1996), 1783–1800, 1791.

27. The Act also provides for variances in aid of research or national defense, both rarely issued.
28. Most requests for variance do not receive a grant/deny decision, but rather clarification is given by OSHA compliance staff. Randy S. Rabinowitz, *Occupational Safety and Health Law*, 2nd edn (Washington, DC: Bureau of National Affairs, 2002), p. 538.
29. See dicta in *Secretary of Labor* v. *Bethlehem Steel Corp.*, 9 OSHC 2177, 2182 (1981).
30. Further examination revealed a statistically significant difference between specialist and non-specialist OSHA practitioners ($\chi^2 = 10.47$, significance $<.01$, df $= 3$, N $= 221$) but even then only about one-quarter (25.8 percent) of OSHA specialists had sought either type of formal compliance action.
31. $\chi^2 = 19.22$, significance $< .001$, df $= 3$, N $= 221$.
32. "Compliance Program Draws Criticism, Advice. Inspections as Sanctions Raise Attorneys' Ire," *Occupational Safety and Health Reporter* 27 (March 18, 1998), 1486–7, 1487.
33. Robert L. Nelson and John P. Heinz, with Edward O. Laumann and Robert H. Salisbury, "Lawyers and the Structure of Influence in Washington," *Law and Society Review* 22 (1988), 237–300, 287.
34. N $= 221$.
35. A number of other attorneys agreed that they personally enjoyed litigation but recognized it usually did not serve their clients' best interests. One interviewee, not among the top tier of enforcement defense counsel, came to the same perspective on preventative work from the opposite starting point: "My personal predilection is, I must admit, that I don't like the litigation aspect, the antagonistic aspect of practicing law, very much. That's just sort of my personal take on things. So I consider my more useful function to be showing clients what they have to do to comply."
36. N $= 216$. Of all attorneys 42.7 percent "strongly" agreed.
37. Among various professional groups, the American Society of Safety Engineers alone claims 2,000 consultants among its 33,000 members, and the American Industrial Hygiene Association has over 12,000 members. Like the legal profession, safety and health professionals split between private practice and in-house for companies.
38. See also Ian D. Meklinsky, "What To Do When the OSHA Inspector Knocks (Part I)," *The Practical Lawyer* 43 (March 1997), 63, 65, stating that "the employer who has prepared for the possibility of an OSHA inspection will find the inspection far less disruptive than the employer who has never given an inspection any thought or who believes 'it will never happen here.'"
39. See also Haines, *Corporate Regulation*, p. 225, on the influence of tripartite regulatory arrangements in workplace safety and health.
40. This tension can be observed in other legal fields, such as securities regulation. Patrick Schmidt, "Let's (Not) Kill All the Lawyers: Corporate Regulatory Compliance and Attorneys' Divided Roles," *Business and Society Review* 105 (2000), 269–87.

41. N = 196. Of the remainder, 29.5 percent sometimes recommend it and 8.2 percent never do so.

7 Conclusion

1. Of cross-national interest, see Gary Marks, Fritz W. Scharpf, Philippe C. Schmitter, and Wolfgang Streeck, *Governance in the European Union* (London: Sage, 1996); Susan Strange, *The Retreat of the State: The Diffusion of Power in the World Economy* (Cambridge, UK: Cambridge University Press, 1996); Jon Pierre and B. Guy Peters, *Governance, Politics and the State* (Basingstoke, UK: Palgrave Macmillan, 2000); Julia Black, "Decentring Regulation: Understanding the Role of Regulation and Self-Regulation in a 'Post-Regulatory' World," *Current Legal Problems* 54 (2001), 103–46; Colin Scott, "Analysing Regulatory Space: Fragmented Resources and Institutional Design," *Public Law* (Summer 2001), 329–53.
2. Scott, "Analyzing Regulatory Space," 334.
3. As one exception, see Clare Hall, Colin Scott, and Christopher Hood, *Telecommunications Regulation: Culture, Chaos and Interdependence Inside the Regulatory Process* (London: Routledge, 2000).
4. Gunther Teubner, *Law as an Autopoietic System* (Oxford, UK: Blackwell, 1993); Julia Black, "Proceduralizing Regulation: Part I," *Oxford Journal of Legal Studies* 20 (2000), 597–614; Black, "Proceduralizing Regulation: Part II," *Oxford Journal of Legal Studies* 21 (2001), 33–58.
5. Christine Parker, *The Open Corporation: Effective Self-regulation and Democracy* (Cambridge, UK: Cambridge University Press, 2002), pp. 295–9.
6. Erik-Hans Klijn and Geert R. Teisman, "Strategies and Games in Networks," in Walter J. M. Kickert, Erik-Hans Klijn, and Joop F. M. Koppenjan (eds.), *Managing Complex Networks: Strategies for the Public Sector* (London: Sage Publications, 1997).
7. Jody Freeman, "The Private Role in Public Governance," *New York University Law Review* 75 (2000), 543–675, 548.
8. See, e.g., Parker, *The Open Corporation*.
9. See Jeremy Boissevain, *Friends of Friends: Networks, Manipulators and Coalitions* (Oxford: Basil Blackwell, 1974).
10. For example: Annelise Riles, *The Network Inside Out* (Ann Arbor, MI: University of Michigan Press, 2000); Richard P. Appelbaum, William L. F. Felstiner, and Volkmar Gessner (eds.), *Rules and Networks: The Legal Culture of Global Business Transactions* (Oxford, UK and Portland, OR: Hart Publishing, 2001); Anne-Marie Slaughter, "The Accountability of Government Networks," *Indiana Journal of Global Legal Studies* 8 (2001), 347–67.
11. Such as: Leigh Hancher and Michael Moran (eds.), *Capitalism, Culture, and Regulation* (Oxford, UK: Clarendon Press, 1989); Hall, Scott, and Hood, *Telecommunications Regulation*; Bruce G. Carruthers and Terence C. Halliday, *Rescuing Business: The Making of Corporate Bankruptcy Law in England and the United States* (Oxford, UK: Clarendon Press, 1998).

Appendix 1   Research methods

1. But see John A. Flood, "Anatomy of Lawyering: An Ethnography of a Corporate Law Firm," Ph.D. thesis, Northwestern University (1987) (in which the researcher joined a law firm as part-time associate in order for the firm to avoid breaches of confidentiality).

2. *The Martindale-Hubbell Law Directory* allows attorneys to indicate their areas of practice. With the online searchable directory (http://www.martindale.com/locator), I drew names from six categories: OSHA, Occupational Safety, Occupational Health, Employee Health and Safety, Workplace Safety, and Worker Health and Safety. Volume 17 of the *Occupational Safety and Health Reporter* (Washington, DC: Bureau of National Affairs) covers cases decided between December 1994 and September 1997. The majority of court decisions in the *BNA OSHA Reporter* series emanate from the OSH Review Commission's administrative law judges, and the full Review Commission, with additional coverage given to state OSHA review boards and federal and state appeals courts.

3. Attorneys explaining their nonparticipation in the study most frequently mentioned that they were not in private practice (including many who are now in-house counsel for companies) or no longer practiced OSHA law.

4. Portions of the data I received have been published previously. See Frederic B. Siskind, *Twenty Years of OSHA Federal Enforcement Data: A Review and Explanation of the Major Trends* (Washington, DC: US Department of Labor, Office of the Assistant Secretary for Policy, 1993).

5. Personal Correspondence from Linda A. Whitsett, Public Relations Specialist/FOIA Officer, August 22, 1997.

BIBLIOGRAPHY

Abel, Richard L., *American Lawyers* (New York, NY: Oxford University Press, 1989)

Abramowitz, Michael E., "Bureaucrats and Lawyers: Myths and Realities," *Bureaucrat* 2 (1973), 257–8

Allegretti, Joseph, "Have Briefcase Will Travel: An Essay on the Lawyer as Hired Gun," *Creighton Law Review* 24 (1990–1), 747–80

Aman, Jr., Alfred C., "The Globalizing State: A Future-Oriented Perspective on the Public/Private Distinction, Federalism, and Democracy," *Vanderbilt Journal of Transnational Law* 31 (1998), 769–870

American Bar Association, *Model Code of Professional Responsibility* (1981)

American Bar Association, House of Delegates, *Model Rules of Professional Conduct* (Chicago, IL: ABA Center for Professional Responsibility, 1994 edn)

American Bar Association Commission on Opportunities for Minorities in the Profession, *Miles to Go: Progress of Minorities in the Legal Profession* (Chicago, IL: ABA, http://www.abanet.org/minorities/home.html, 1998)

Appelbaum, Richard P., William L. F. Felstiner, and Volkmar Gessner (eds.), *Rules and Networks: The Legal Culture of Global Business Transactions* (Oxford and Portland, OR: Hart Publishing, 2001)

Ashford, Nicholas A., *Crisis in the Workplace: Occupational Disease and Injury* (Cambridge, MA: MIT Press, 1976)

Ashford, Nicholas A., C. William Ryan, and Charles C. Caldart, "A Hard Look at Federal Regulation of Formaldehyde: A Departure from Reasoned Decisionmaking," *Harvard Environmental Law Review* 7 (1983), 297–370

Auerbach, Carl A., "Legal Education and Its Discontents," *Journal of Legal Education* 34 (1984), 73–6

Auerbach, Carl A., Willard Hurst, Lloyd K. Garrison, and Samuel Mermin, *The Legal Process: An Introduction to Decision Making by Judicial, Legislative, Executive, and Administrative Agencies* (San Francisco, CA: Chandler Publishing Co., 1961)

Auerbach, Jerold S., *Unequal Justice: Lawyers and Social Change in Modern America* (New York NY: Oxford University Press, 1976)

Ayres, Ian and John Braithwaite, *Responsive Regulation: Transcending the Deregulation Debate* (New York, NY: Oxford University Press, 1992)

Bardach, Eugene and Robert A. Kagan, *Going by the Book: The Problem of Regulatory Unreasonableness* (Philadelphia, PA: Temple University Press, 1982)

Barrow, Deborah J. and Thomas G. Walker, *A Court Divided: The Fifth Circuit Court of Appeals and the Politics of Judicial Reform* (New Haven, CT: Yale University Press, 1988)

Bell, David A., *Lawyers and Citizens: The Making of a Political Elite in Old Regime France* (New York, NY: Oxford University Press, 1994)

Bernstein, Marver, *Regulating Business by Independent Commission* (Princeton, NJ: Princeton University Press, 1955)

Black, Julia, "Decentring Regulation: Understanding the Role of Regulation and Self-Regulation in a 'Post-Regulatory' World," *Current Legal Problems* 54 (2001), 103–46

"New Institutionalism and Naturalism in Socio-Legal Analysis: Institutionalist Approaches to Regulatory Decision Making," *Law and Policy* 19 (1997), 51–93

"Proceduralizing Regulation: Part I," *Oxford Journal of Legal Studies* 20 (2000), 597–614

"Proceduralizing Regulation: Part II," *Oxford Journal of Legal Studies* 21 (2001), 33–58

"Regulatory Conversations," *Journal of Law and Society* 29 (2002), 163–96

Bobbitt, Philip, "Is Law Politics?" *Stanford Law Review* 41 (1989), 1233–1312

Boissevain, Jeremy, *Friends of Friends: Networks, Manipulators and Coalitions* (Oxford: Basil Blackwell, 1974)

Bokat, Stephen A. and Horace A. Thompson, III (eds.), *Occupational Safety and Health Law* (Washington, DC: Bureau of National Affairs, 1988)

Bor, Victoria L. and Ilise Levy Feitshans (eds.), *Occupational Safety and Health Law: 1995 Cumulative Supplement* (Washington, DC: Bureau of National Affairs, 1995)

Bowers, Edwin, "OSHA's Legal Professional," *Job Safety & Health Quarterly* 3 (Fall 1991), 21

Braithwaite, John, "Enforced Self-Regulation: A New Strategy for Corporate Crime Control," *Michigan Law Review* 80 (1982), 1466–1507

To Punish or Persuade: Enforcement of Coal Mine Safety (Albany, NY: State University of New York Press, 1985)

Breyer, Stephen, *Breaking the Vicious Circle: Toward Effective Risk Regulation* (Cambridge, MA: Harvard University Press, 1993)
  "Judicial Review of Questions of Law and Policy," *Administrative Law Review* 38 (1987), 363–98

Brigham, John, *The Constitution of Interests: Beyond the Politics of Rights* (New York, NY: New York University Press, 1996)

Brown, Charles, James Hamilton, and James Medoff, *Employers Large and Small* (Cambridge, MA: Harvard University Press, 1990)

Brown, George H., "Environmental Lawyers and the Public Interest: A Response to David Dana," *Oregon Law Review* 74 (1995), 85–98

Brown, Richard, "Theory and Practice of Regulatory Enforcement: Occupational Health and Safety Regulation in British Columbia," *Law and Policy* 16 (1994), 63–91

Bryner, Gary C., *Bureaucratic Discretion: Law and Policy in Federal Regulatory Agencies* (New York: Pergamon Press, 1987)

Burley, Anne-Marie and Walter Mattli, "Europe before the Court: A Political Theory of Legal Integration," *International Organization* 47 (1993), 41–76

Cain, Maureen, "The Symbol Traders," in Maureen Cain and Christine B. Harrington (eds.), *Lawyers in a Postmodern World: Translation and Transgression* (New York, NY: New York University Press, 1994), 15–48

Cain, Maureen and Christine B. Harrington (eds.), *Lawyers in a Postmodern World: Translation and Transgression* (New York, NY: New York University Press, 1994)

Carle, Susan D., "Elites, Ethics, and the Public Good: Race, Class, and Legal Ethics in the Early NAACP," *Law and History Review* 20 (2002), 97–146

Carlin, Jerome E., *Lawyers' Ethics: A Survey of the New York City Bar* (New York, NY: Russell Sage Foundation, 1966)

Carruthers, Bruce G. and Terence C. Halliday, *Rescuing Business: The Making of Corporate Bankruptcy Law in England and the United States* (Oxford, UK: Clarendon Press, 1998)

Carson, K. and Richard Johnstone, "The Dupes of Hazard: Occupational Health and Safety and the Victorian Sanctions Debate," *Australian and New Zealand Journal of Sociology* 26 (1990), 126–41

Cherrington, David R., "The Race to the Courthouse: Conflicting Views Toward the Judicial Review of OSHA Standards," *Brigham Young University Law Review* (1994), 95–128

Chubb, John E. and Paul E. Peterson (eds.), *Can the Government Govern?* (Washington, DC: The Brookings Institution, 1989)

Clayton, Cornell W. (ed.), *Government Lawyers: The Federal Legal Bureaucracy and Presidential Politics* (Lawrence, KS: University Press of Kansas, 1995)

Clune, III, William H., "A Political Model of Implementation and Implications of the Model for Public Policy, Research, and the Changing Roles of Law and Lawyers," *Iowa Law Review* 69 (1983), 47–125

Coffee, Jr., John C., "'No Soul to Damn: No Body to Kick': An Unscandalized Inquiry into the Problem of Corporate Punishment," *Michigan Law Review* 79 (1981), 386–459

Coglianese, Cary, "Assessing Consensus: The Promise and Performance of Negotiated Rulemaking," *Duke Law Journal* 46 (1997), 1255–1349

"Challenging the Rules: Litigation and Bargaining in the Administrative State," Ph.D. thesis, University of Michigan (1994)

"Litigating within Relationships: Disputes and Disturbance in the Regulatory Process," *Law and Society Review* 30 (1996), 735–65

Conley, John M. and William M. O'Barr, *Just Words: Law, Language, and Power* (Chicago, IL: University of Chicago Press, 1998)

Crews, Jr., Clyde Wayne, "Ten Thousand Commandments: An Annual Snapshot of the Federal Regulatory State" (Washington, DC: Cato Institute, 2003: available at http://www.cato.org/tech/pubs/10kc_2002.pdf)

Crier, Catherine, *The Case Against Lawyers* (New York, NY: Broadway, 2002)

Curren, Barbara A. and Clara N. Carson, *The Lawyer Statistical Report: The US Legal Profession in the 1990s* (Chicago, IL: American Bar Foundation, 1994)

Daicoff, Susan, "Lawyer, Know Thyself: A Review of Empirical Research on Attorney Attributes Bearing on Professionalism," *American University Law Review* 46 (1997), 1337–1427

Daintith, Terence C., "A Regulatory Space Agency?" *Oxford Journal of Legal Studies* 9 (1989), 534–56

Dana, David, "Environmental Lawyers and the Public Service Model of Lawyering," *Oregon Law Review* 74 (1995), 57–83

Davis, Ann, "Big Jump in Minority Associates, But . . ." *National Law Journal* (April 29, 1996), 1

de Bruijn, Johan A. and Ernst F. ten Heuvelhof, "Policy Networks and Governance," in David L. Weimer (ed.), *Institutional Design* (Boston, MA: Kluwer Academic Publishers, 1995)

Dezalay, Yves, "The Forum Should Fit the Fuss: The Economics and Politics of Negotiated Justice," in Maureen Cain and Christine B. Harrington (eds.), *Lawyers in a Postmodern World: Translation and Transgression* (New York, NY: New York University Press, 1994), 155–82

Dobbin, Frank and John R. Sutton, "The Strength of a Weak State: The Rights Revolution and the Rise of Human Resources Management Divisions," *American Journal of Sociology* 104 (1998), 441–76

Dodge, Emily P., "Evolution of a City Law Office," *Wisconsin Law Review* 40 (1956), 35–56

Downs, Anthony, *Inside Bureaucracy* (Boston, MA: Little, Brown, 1967)

Driscoll, Dawn-Marie, W. Michael Hoffman, and Joseph E. Murphy, "Business Ethics and Compliance: What Management is Doing and Why," *Business and Society Review* 99 (1998), 35–51

Eisenstein, James, Roy B. Flemming, and Peter F. Nardulli, *The Contours of Justice: Communities and Their Courts* (Boston, MA: Little, Brown, and Co., 1988)

Eisenstein, James and Herbert Jacob, *Felony Justice: An Organizational Analysis of Criminal Courts* (Boston, MA: Little, Brown, and Co., 1977)

Eisner, Marc Allen, *Regulatory Politics in Transition* (Baltimore, MD: Johns Hopkins University Press, 1993)

Elliot, Jr., E. Donald, "The Dis-Integration of Administrative Law: A Comment on Shapiro," *Yale Law Journal* 92 (1983), 1523–36

Epstein, Cynthia Fuchs, et al., "Glass Ceilings and Open Doors: Women's Advancement in the Legal Profession," *Fordham Law Review* 64 (1995), 291

Fiorino, Daniel J., "Regulatory Negotiation as a Policy Process," *Public Administration Review* 48 (1988), 764–72

Fisher, Elizabeth and Patrick Schmidt, "Seeing the 'Blind Spots' in Administrative Law: Theory, Practice, and Rulemaking Settlements in the United States," *Common Law World Review* 30 (2001), 348–72

Fiss, Owen M., "Against Settlement," *Yale Law Journal* 93 (1984), 1073–90

Flemming, Roy B., Poter F. Nardulli, and James Eisenstein, *The Craft of Justice: Politics and Work in Criminal Court Communities* (Philadelphia, PA: University of Pennsylvania Press, 1992)

Flood, John A., "Anatomy of Lawyering: An Ethnography of a Corporate Law Firm," Ph.D thesis, Northwestern University (1987)

Foster, James C., *The Ideology of Apolitical Politics: Elite Lawyers' Response to the Legitimation Crisis of American Capitalism, 1870–1920* (New York, NY: Garland, 1990)

Frantz, Douglas and David McKean, *Friends in High Places: The Rise and Fall of Clark Clifford* (Boston, MA: Little, Brown, & Co., 1995)

Freeman, Jody, "Collaborative Governance," *UCLA Law Review* 45 (1997), 1–98

"The Private Role in Public Governance," *New York University Law Review* 75 (2000), 543–675

Freeman, Jody and Laura I. Langbein, "Regulatory Negotiation and the Legitimacy Benefit," *New York University Environmental Law Journal* 9 (2000), 60–151

Friedman, Lawrence M., *Total Justice* (New York, NY: Russell Sage Foundation, 1985)

Friedman, Lawrence M. and Jack Ladinsky, "Social Change and the Law of Industrial Accidents," *Columbia Law Review* 67 (1967), 50–82

Gaba, Jeffrey M., "Informal Rulemaking by Settlement Agreement," *Georgetown Law Journal* 73 (1985), 1241–82

277

Gais, Thomas L., Mark A. Peterson and Jack L. Walker, "Interest Groups, Iron Triangles and Representative Institutions in American National Government," *British Journal of Political Science* 14 (1984), 161–85

Galanter, Marc, "Why the 'Haves' Come Out Ahead: Speculations on the Limits of Legal Change," *Law and Society Review* 9 (1974), 95–160

Galanter, Marc and Thomas Palay, *Tournament of Lawyers: The Transformation of the Big Law Firm* (Chicago, IL: University of Chicago Press, 1991)

Galligan, Denis, "Authoritarianism in Government and Administration: The Promise of Administrative Justice," *Current Legal Problems* 54 (2001), 79–102

   Discretionary Powers: A Legal Study of Official Discretion (New York, NY: Oxford University Press, 1986)

Geradin, Damien and Nicolas Petit, "The Development of Agencies at EU and National Levels: Conceptual Analysis and Proposals for Reform," Harvard Jean Monnet Working Paper No. 01/04 (http://www.jeanmonnetprogram.org/papers/04/040101.html) (2004)

Gersuny, Carl, *Work Hazards and Industrial Conflict* (Hanover, NH: University Press of New England, 1981)

Gibeaut, John, "Marking a Decade of Struggle," *ABA Journal* 83 (October 1997), 100

Gifford, Daniel J., "Federal Administrative Law Judges: The Relevance of Past Choices to Future Directions," *Administrative Law Review* 49 (1997), 1–60

Gilboy, Janet A., "Regulatory and Administrative Agency Behavior: Accommodation, Amplification, and Assimilation," *Law and Policy* 17 (1995), 3–22

Gilson, Ronald J., "The Devolution of the Legal Profession: A Demand Side Perspective," *Maryland Law Review* 49 (1990), 869–916

Glendon, Mary Ann, *A Nation Under Lawyers: How the Crisis in the Legal Profession is Transforming American Society* (New York, NY: Farrar, Straus and Giroux, 1994)

Glickstein, Howard A., "Law Schools: Where the Elite Meet to Teach," *Nova Law Journal* 10 (1986), 541–6

Gombar, Robert C., Arthur G. Sapper, and Melissa A. Bailey, "Sweeping Changes in Store with OSHA's Safety Program Standard," *Occupational Hazards* 59 (May 1997), 25

Gordon, Robert W., "The Independence of Lawyers," *Boston University Law Review* 68 (1988), 1–83

Goulden, Joseph C., *The Superlawyers: The Small and Powerful World of the Great Washington Law Firms* (New York, NY: Weybright and Talley, 1972)

Gourman Report: Rating of Graduate and Professional Programs in American and International Universities (Los Angeles, CA: National Education Standards, 1994)

Gräbe, Sylvia, "Regulatory Agencies and Interest Groups in Occupational Health and Safety in Great Britain and West Germany: A Perspective from West Germany," *Law and Policy* 13 (1991), 55–72

Gramm, Wendy L., Testimony before the United States House Committee on Government Reform on H.R. 2432, the Paperwork and Regulatory Improvements Act of 2003, July 22, 2003 (available at http://www.mercatus.org/article.php/363.html)

Granfield, Robert, *Making Elite Lawyers: Visions of Law at Harvard and Beyond* (New York, NY: Routledge, 1992)

Gray, Wayne B. and John T. Scholz, "Does Regulatory Enforcement Work? A Panel Analysis of OSHA Enforcement," *Law and Society Review* 27 (1993), 177–213

Green, Mark J., *The Other Government: The Unseen Power of Washington Lawyers* (New York, NY: Grossman Publishers, 1975)

Gunningham, Neil, Robert A. Kagan, and Dorothy Thornton, *Shades of Green: Business, Regulation, and Environment* (Stanford, CA: Stanford University Press, 2003)

Haines, Fiona, *Corporate Regulation: Beyond "Punish or Persuade"* (Oxford: Clarendon Press, 1997)

Hall, Clare, Colin Scott, and Christopher Hood, *Telecommunications Regulation: Culture, Chaos and Interdependence Inside the Regulatory Process* (London: Routledge, 2000)

Ham, Christopher, *Policy-making in the National Health Service: A Case Study of the Leeds Regional Hospital Board* (London: Macmillan Press, 1981)

Hamilton, Robert W., "The Role of Nongovernmental Standards in the Development of Mandatory Federal Standards Affecting Safety or Health," *Texas Law Review* 56 (1978), 1329–1484

Hancher, Leigh, *Regulating for Competition: Government, Law, and the Pharmaceutical Industry in the United Kingdom and France* (Oxford: Clarendon Press, 1990)

Hancher, Leigh and Michael Moran (eds.), *Capitalism, Culture, and Regulation* (Oxford, UK: Clarendon Press, 1989)

Hanf, Kenneth and Fritz W. Scharpf (eds.), *Interorganizational Policy Making: Limits to Coordination and Central Control* (London: Sage, 1978)

Harcourt, A. J. and C. M. Radaelli, "Limits to EU Technocratic Regulation?" *European Journal of Political Research* 35 (1999), 107–22

Harlow, Carol, *Accountability in the European Union* (Oxford, UK: Oxford University Press, 2002)

Harrington, Christine B., "Outlining a Theory of Legal Practice," in Maureen Cain and Christine B. Harrington (eds.), *Lawyers in a Postmodern World: Translation and Transgression* (New York, NY: New York University Press, 1994), 49–69

Harter, Philip J., "Fear of Commitment: An Affliction of Adolescents," *Duke Law Journal* 46 (1997), 1389–1429

"In Search of Goldilocks: Democracy, Participation, and Government," *Penn State Environmental Law Review* 10 (2002), 113–34

"Negotiating Regulations: A Cure for Malaise," *Georgetown Law Journal* 71 (1982), 1–118

Hawkins, Keith, *Law as Last Resort: Prosecution Decision-Making in a Regulatory Agency* (Oxford: Oxford University Press, 2002)

Hawkins, Keith and Bridget M. Hutter, "The Response of Business to Social Regulation in England and Wales: An Enforcement Perspective," *Law and Policy* 15 (1993), 199–217

Heinz, John P. and Edward O. Laumann, *Chicago Lawyers: The Social Structure of the Bar* (New York, NY: Russell Sage Foundation, 1982)

"The Constituencies of Elite Urban Lawyers," *Law and Society Review* 31 (1997), 441–72

Heinz, John P., Edward O. Laumann, Robert L. Nelson, and Robert H. Salisbury, *The Hollow Core: Private Interests in National Policy Making* (Cambridge, MA: Harvard University Press, 1993)

Heller, Jamie G., "Legal Counseling in the Administrative State: How to Let the Client Decide," *Yale Law Journal* 103 (1994), 2503–30

Hertogh, Marc and Simon Halliday (eds.), *Judicial Review and Bureaucratic Impact: International and Interdisciplinary Perspectives* (Cambridge, UK: Cambridge University Press, 2004)

Holmes, Oliver Wendell, "The Path of the Law," *Harvard Law Review* 10 (1897), 457–78

Hopkins, Andrew, "Social Values in Occupational Safety Law," *Legal Studies Forum* 13 (1989), 135–50

Horowitz, Donald L., *The Jurocracy: Government Lawyers, Agency Programs, and Judicial Decisions* (Lexington, MA: Lexington Books, 1977)

Horsky, Charles A., *The Washington Lawyer* (Westport, CT: Greenwood Press, 1981 reprint, originally published 1952)

Hosticka, Carl J., "We Don't Care About What Happened, We Only Care About What Is Going To Happen: Lawyer–Client Negotiations of Reality," *Social Problems* 26 (1979), 599–610

Howard, Jr., J. Woodford, *Courts of Appeals in the Federal Judicial System: A Study of the Second, Fifth, and District of Columbia Circuits* (Princeton, NJ: Princeton University Press, 1981)

Huigen, Jos, *Information Supply and the Implementation of Policy: Playing with Ambiguity and Uncertainty in Policy Networks* (Delft: Eburon, 1994)

Humphries, Martha Anne and Donald F. Songer, "Law and Politics in Judicial Oversight of Administrative Agencies," *Journal of Politics* 61 (1999), 207–20

Hutter, Bridget M. and Sally Lloyd-Bostock, "The Power of Accidents: The Social and Psychological Impact of Accidents and the Enforcement of Safety Regulations," *British Journal of Criminology* 30 (1990), 409–22

Irons, Peter H., *The New Deal Lawyers* (Princeton, NJ: Princeton University Press, 1982)

Jasanoff, Sheila, "Science and the Limits of Administrative Rule-making: Lessons from the OSHA Cancer Policy," *Osgoode Hall Law Journal* 20 (1982), 536–61

Johnson, Jr., George Robert, "The Split-Enforcement Model: Some Conclusions From the OSHA and MSHA Experiences," *Administrative Law Review* 39 (1987), 315–51

Jordana, Jacint and David Levi-Faur (eds.), *The Politics of Regulation: Institutions and Regulatory Reforms for the Age of Governance* (Cheltenham, UK: Edward Elgar, 2004)

Kagan, Robert A., *Adversarial Legalism: The American Way of Law* (Cambridge, MA: Harvard University Press, 2001)

"Introduction: Comparing National Styles of Regulation in Japan and the United States," *Law and Policy* 22 (2000), 225–44

Kagan, Robert A. and Lee Axelrad (eds.), *Regulatory Encounters: Multinational Corporations and American Adversarial Legalism* (Berkeley, CA: University of California Press, 2000)

Kagan, Robert A. and Robert Eli Rosen, "On the Social Significance of Large Law Firm Practice," *Stanford Law Review* 37 (1985), 399–443

Keleman, R. Daniel, "The Rise of Adversarial Legalism in the European Union: Beyond Policy Learning and Regulatory Competition," in David Levi-Faur and Vigoda-Gadot Eran (eds.), *International Public Policy and Management: Policy Learning Beyond Regional, Cultural and Political Boundaries* (New York, NY: Marcel Dekker, 2004)

Kelman, Steven, *Regulating America, Regulating Sweden: A Comparative Study of Occupational Safety and Health Policy* (Cambridge, MA: MIT Press, 1981)

Kemp, Kathleen, "Lawyers, Politics and Economic Regulation," *Social Science Quarterly* 64 (1986), 267–82

Keohane, Robert O. and Elinor Ostrom, "Introduction," in Keohane and Ostrom (eds.), *Local Commons and Global Interdependence: Heterogeneity and Cooperation in Two Domains* (London: Sage Publications, 1995)

Kerwin, Cornelius M., *Rulemaking: How Government Agencies Write Law and Make Policy* 3rd edn (Washington, DC: CQ Press, 2003)

Kickert, Walter J. M., Erik-Hans Klijn, and Joop F. M. Koppenjan (eds.), *Managing Complex Networks: Strategies for the Public Sector* (London: Sage Publications, 1997)

King, Anthony (ed.), *The New American Political System* (Washington, DC: American Enterprise Institute, 1978)

Klijn, Erik-Hans, "Analyzing and Managing Policy Processes in Complex Networks: A Theoretical Examination of the Concept Policy Network and Its Problems," *Administration & Society* 28 (1996), 90–119

Knoke, David, *Political Networks: The Structural Perspective* (New York, NY: Cambridge University Press, 1990)

Kolko, Gabriel, *The Triumph of Conservatism: A Reinterpretation of American History 1900–1916* (New York, NY: Free Press of Glencoe, 1963)

Kovach, Kenneth A. and Nancy Greer Hamilton, "Labor's Efforts Sustain Workplace Safety," *Labor Studies Journal* 22 (1997), 57

Kovach, Kimberlee K., "The Lawyer as Teacher: The Role of Education in Lawyering," *Clinical Law Review* 4 (1998), 359–90

Kritzer, Herbert M., "Adjudication to Settlement: Shading in the Gray," *Judicature* 70 (1986), 161–5

"'Data, Data, Data, Drowning in Data': Crafting *The Hollow Core*," *Law and Social Inquiry* 21 (1996), 761–804

The Justice Broker: Lawyers and Ordinary Litigation (New York, NY: Oxford University Press, 1990)

Kronman, Anthony T., *The Lost Lawyer: Failing Ideals in the Legal Profession* (Cambridge, MA: Belknap Press of Harvard University, 1993)

Landon, Donald D., *Country Lawyers: The Impact of Context on Professional Practice* (Westport, CT: Praeger, 1990)

Langbein, Laura I. and Cornelius M. Kerwin, "Regulatory Negotiation versus Conventional Rule Making: Claims, Counterclaims, and Empirical Evidence," *Journal of Public Administration Research and Theory* 10 (2000), 599–632

Laski, Harold J., *The American Democracy: A Commentary and An Interpretation* (New York, NY: Viking Press, 1948)

Lewis, Frank, "Employers' Liability," *Atlantic Monthly* 103 (January 1909), 60

Linowitz, Sol with Martin Mayer, *The Betrayed Profession: Lawyering at the End of the Twentieth Century* (Baltimore, MD: Johns Hopkins University Press, 1996)

Lipartito, Kenneth, "What Have Lawyers Done for American Business? The Case of Baker & Botts of Houston," *Business History Review* 64 (1990), 489–526

Loevinger, Lee, "A Washington Lawyer Tells What It's Like," *George Washington Law Review* 38 (1970), 531–45

Lofgren, Don J., *Dangerous Premises: An Insider's View of OSHA Enforcement* (Ithaca, NY: ILR Press, 1989)

Luban, David, "Settlements and the Erosion of the Public Realm," *Georgetown Law Journal* 83 (1995), 2619–62

Macaulay, Stewart, "Business Adaptation to Regulation: What Do We Know and What Do We Need to Know?" *Law and Policy* 15 (1993), 259–70

"Lawyers and Consumer Protection Laws," *Law and Society Review* 14 (1979), 115–71

"Non-Contractual Relations in Business: A Preliminary Study," *American Sociological Review* 28 (1963), 55–69

Majone, Giandomenico, *Evidence, Argument and Persuasion in the Policy Process* (New Haven, CT: Yale University Press, 1989)

Regulating Europe (London, UK: Routledge, 1996)

Marin, Bernd and Renate Mayntz (eds.), *Policy Networks: Empirical Evidence and Theoretical Consideration* (Boulder, CO: Westview Press, 1991)

Marinetto, Mike, "Governing beyond the Centre: A Critique of the Anglo-Governance School," *Political Studies* 51 (2003), 592–608

Marks, Gary, Fritz W. Scharpf, Philippe C. Schmitter, and Wolfgang Streeck, *Governance in the European Union* (London: Sage, 1996)

Martindale-Hubbell Law Directory (Summit, NJ: Martindale-Hubbell, 2004)

Mashaw, Jerry L., "Improving the Environment of Agency Rulemaking: An Essay on Management, Games, and Accountability," *Law and Contemporary Problems* 57 (1994), 185–257

Mashaw, Jerry L. and David L. Harfst, "Regulation and Legal Culture: The Case of Motor Vehicle Safety," *Yale Journal on Regulation* 4 (1987), 257–316

McBarnet, Doreen, "Law and Capital: The Role of Legal Form and Legal Actors," *International Journal of the Sociology of Law* 12 (1984), 231–8

"Legal Creativity: Law, Capital, and Legal Avoidance," in Maureen Cain and Christine B. Harrington (eds.), *Lawyers in a Postmodern World: Translation and Transgression* (New York, NY: New York University Press, 1994), 73–84

McBarnet, Doreen, and Christopher Whelan, *Creative Accounting and the Cross-eyed Javelin Thrower* (Chichester: J. Wiley, 1999)

McCann, Michael, *Rights at Work: Pay Equity Reform and the Politics of Legal Mobilization* (Chicago, IL: University of Chicago Press, 1989)

McGarity, Thomas O., "Some Thoughts on 'Deossifying' the Rulemaking Process," *Duke Law Journal* 41 (1993), 1385–1462

McGarity, Thomas O. and Sidney A. Shapiro, *Workers At Risk: The Failed Promise of the Occupational Safety and Health Administration* (Westport, CT: Praeger Press, 1993)

McGuire, Kevin T., *The Supreme Court Bar: Legal Elites in the Washington Community* (Charlottesville, VA: University of Virginia Press, 1993)

Meklinsky, Ian D., "What To Do When the OSHA Inspector Knocks (Part I)," *The Practical Lawyer* 43 (March 1997), 63

Melnick, R. Shep, *Regulation and the Courts: The Case of the Clean Air Act* (Washington, DC: Brookings Institution, 1983)

Mendlehoff, John M., *The Dilemma of Toxic Substance Regulation: How Over-regulation Causes Underregulation at OSHA* (Cambridge, MA: MIT Press, 1988)

Milhaupt, Curtis J. and Geoffrey P. Miller, "Regulatory Failure and the Collapse of Japan's Home Mortgage Lending Industry: A Legal and Economic Analysis," *Law and Policy* 22 (2000), 245–90

Milhaupt, Curtis J. and Mark D. West, "Law's Dominion and the Market for Legal Elites in Japan," *Law and Policy in International Business* 34 (2003), 451–98

Mintz, Benjamin W., *OSHA: History, Law, and Policy* (Washington, DC: Bureau of National Affairs, 1984)

Mitchell, Neil J., *The Conspicuous Corporation: Business, Public Policy and Representative Democracy* (Ann Arbor, MI: University of Michigan Press, 1997)

Moe, Terry M., "Control and Feedback in Economic Regulation: The Case of the NLRB," *American Political Science Review* 79 (1985), 1094–1116

Morag-Levine, Noga, *Chasing the Wind: Regulating Air Pollution in the Common Law State* (Princeton, NJ: Princeton University Press, 2003)

Moran, John B., Bill Kojola, and James Melius, "Asphalt Paving Exposure Controls: A Model for the Future?" *Applied Occupational and Environmental Hygiene* 12 (1997), 407–9

Moran, Michael, "Understanding the Regulatory State," *British Journal of Political Science* 32 (2002), 391–413

Morgan, Bronwen, *Social Citizenship in the Shadow of Competition: The Bureaucratic Politics of Regulatory Justification* (Aldershot, UK: Ashgate Press, 2003)

Mullan, David and Antonella Ceddia, "The Impact on Public Law of Privatization, Deregulation, Outsourcing, and Downsizing: A Canadian Perspective," *Indiana Journal of Global Legal Studies* 10 (2003), 199–246

Nader, Ralph and Mark Green (eds.), *Verdicts on Lawyers* (New York, NY: Cromwell, 1976)

Nader, Ralph and Wesley J. Smith, *No Contest: Corporate Lawyers and the Perversion of Justice in America* (New York, NY: Random House, 1996)

Nelson, Robert L., "The Futures of American Lawyers: A Demographic Profile of a Changing Profession in a Changing Society," *Case Western Reserve Law Review* 44 (1994), 345–406

Nelson, Robert L. and John P. Heinz, with Edward O. Laumann and Robert H. Salisbury, "Lawyers and the Structure of Influence in Washington," *Law and Society Review* 22 (1988), 237–300

Nelson, Robert L. and David M. Trubek, "Arenas of Professionalism: The Professional Ideologies of Lawyers in Context," in Nelson, Trubek, and

Rayman L. Solomon (eds.), *Lawyers' Ideals/Lawyers' Practices: Transformations in the American Legal Profession* (Ithaca, NY: Cornell University Press, 1992)

Nelson, William E., "Contract Litigation and the Elite Bar in New York City, 1960–1980," *Emory Law Journal* 39 (1990), 413–62

Nichols, Albert L. and Richard Zeckhauser, "Government Comes to the Workplace: An Assessment of OSHA," *Public Interest* 49 (1977), 39–69

Noble, Charles, *Liberalism at Work: The Rise and Fall of OSHA* (Philadelphia, PA: Temple University Press, 1986)

Note, "Growing the Carrot: Encouraging Effective Corporate Compliance," *Harvard Law Review* 109 (1996), 1783–1800

O'Brien, David, "Administrative Discretion, Judicial Review, and Regulatory Politics," in Douglas H. Shumavon and H. Kenneth Hibbeln (eds.), *Administrative Discretion and Public Policy Implementation* (New York, NY: Praeger, 1986)

The Official Guide to US Law Schools 1998–99 (Newtown, PA: Law School Admission Services, 1998)

Olson, Mancur, *The Logic of Collective Action: Public Goods and the Theory of Groups* (Cambridge, MA: Harvard University Press, 1971)

Olson, Susan M., *Clients and Lawyers: Securing the Rights of Disabled Persons* (Westport, CT: Greenwood Press, 1984)

Olson, Walter K., *The Rule of Lawyers: How the New Litigation Elite Threatens America's Rule of Law* (New York, NY: Truman Talley, 2003)

Orts, Eric and Kurt Deketelaere (eds.), *Environmental Contracts: Comparative Approaches to Regulatory Innovation in the United States and Europe* (Boston, MA: Kluwer Law International, 2001)

Parker, Christine, *The Open Corporation: Effective Self-regulation and Democracy* (Cambridge, UK: Cambridge University Press, 2002)

Pierce, Jr., Richard J., "Judicial Review of Agency Actions in a Period of Diminishing Agency Resources," *Administrative Law Review* 49 (1997), 61–94

"Small is Not Beautiful: The Case Against Special Regulatory Treatment of Small Firms," *Administrative Law Review* 50 (1998), 537–78

"The Unintended Effects of Judicial Review of Agency Rules: How Federal Courts Have Contributed to the Electricity Crisis of the 1990s," *Administrative Law Review* 43 (1991), 7–29

Pierre, Jon and B. Guy Peters, *Governance, Politics and the State* (Basingstoke, UK: Palgrave Macmillan, 2000)

Plotke, David, "The Political Mobilization of Business," in Mark P. Petracca (ed.), *The Politics of Interests: Interest Groups Transformed* (Boulder, CO: Westview Press, 1992)

Powell, Michael J., *From Patrician to Professional Elite: The Transformation of the New York City Bar Association* (New York, NY: Russell Sage Foundation, 1988)

Prosser, Tony, *Law and the Regulators* (Oxford, UK: Clarendon Press, 1997)

Quigley, Thomas E., "Employee Involvement in the OSHA Settlement Process," *Detroit College of Law Review* (1990), 579–97

Quirk, Paul J., *Industry Influence in Federal Regulatory Agencies* (Princeton, NJ: Princeton University Press, 1981)

Rabinowitz, Randy S., *Occupational Safety and Health Law*, 2nd edn (Washington, DC: Bureau of National Affairs, 2002)

Railton, W. Scott, *OSHA Compliance Handbook* (Rockford, MD: Government Institutes, Inc., 1992)

Rees, Joseph V., *Reforming the Workplace: A Study of Self-Regulation in Occupational Safety* (Philadelphia, PA: University of Pennsylvania Press, 1986)

Reich, Robert B., *Locked in the Cabinet* (New York: Vintage, 1998)
  "Regulation by Confrontation or Negotiation?" *Harvard Business Review* 59 (May–June 1981), 82–93

Rhodes, R. A. W., *The National World of Local Government* (London: Allen and Unwin, 1986)

Riles, Annelise, *The Network Inside Out* (Ann Arbor, MI: University of Michigan Press, 2000)

Robertson, Leon S. and J. Philip Keeve, "Worker Injuries: The Effects of Workers' Compensation and OSHA Inspections," *Journal of Health Politics, Policy & Law* 8 (1983), 581–97

Robinson, Glen O., *American Bureaucracy: Public Choice and Public Law* (Ann Arbor, MI: University of Michigan Press, 1991)

Rossi, Jim, "Bargaining in the Shadow of Administrative Procedure: The Public Interest in Rulemaking Settlement," *Duke Law Journal* 51 (2001), 1015–58

Rothstein, Mark A., "OSHA After Ten Years: A Review and Some Proposed Reforms," *Vanderbilt Law Review* 34 (1980), 71–139

Ruhl, J. B. and James Salzman, "Mozart and the Red Queen: The Problem of Regulatory Accretion in the Administrative State," *Georgetown Law Journal* 91 (2003), 757–850

Ryan, Mike H., *Corporate Strategy, Public Policy, and the Fortune 500: How America's Major Corporations Infl uence Government* (Oxford: Basil Blackwell, 1987)

Sarat, Austin and William F. Felstiner, *Divorce Lawyers and Their Clients: Power and Meaning in the Legal Process* (New York, NY: Oxford University Press, 1995)

Schmidt, Patrick, "Let's (Not) Kill All the Lawyers: Corporate Regulatory Compliance and Attorneys' Divided Roles," *Business and Society Review* 105 (2000), 269–87

"Pursuing Regulatory Relief: Strategic Participation and Litigation in US OSHA Rulemaking," *Business and Politics* 4 (2002), 71–89

Schneyer, Ted, "Fuzzy Models of the Corporate Lawyer as Environmental Compliance Counselor," *Oregon Law Review* 74 (1995), 99–119

Schoenbrod, David, *Power Without Responsibility: How Congress Abuses the People Through Delegation* (New Haven, CT: Yale University Press, 1993)

Scholz, John T., "Cooperative Regulatory Enforcement and the Politics of Administrative Effectiveness," *American Political Science Review* 85 (1991), 115–36

Scholz, John T. and Wayne B. Gray, "Can Government Facilitate Cooperation? An Informational Model of OSHA Enforcement," *American Journal of Political Science* 41 (1997), 693–717

Scott, Colin, "Analysing Regulatory Space: Fragmented Resources and Institutional Design," *Public Law* (Summer 2001), 329–53

Shamir, Ronen, *Managing Legal Uncertainty: Elite Lawyers in the New Deal* (Durham, NC: Duke University Press, 1995)

Shapiro, Martin and Alec Stone Sweet, *On Law, Politics, and Judicialization* (Oxford, UK: Oxford University Press, 2002)

Shapiro, Sidney A., "Substantive Reform, Judicial Review, and Agency Resources: OSHA as a Case Study," *Administrative Law Review* 49 (1997), 645–70

Shapiro, Sidney A. and Thomas O. McGarity, "Not So Paradoxical: The Rationale for Technology-Based Regulation," *Duke Law Journal* (1991), 729–38

"Reorienting OSHA: Regulatory Alternatives and Legislative Reform," *Yale Journal on Regulation* 6 (1989), 1–63

Shapiro, Sidney A. and Randy S. Rabinowitz, "Punishment Versus Cooperation in Regulatory Enforcement," *Administrative Law Review* 49 (1997), 703–37

Shapiro, Susan P., *Wayward Capitalists: Target of the Securities and Exchange Commission* (New Haven, CT: Yale University Press, 1984)

Sikkink, Kathryn, "Human Rights, Principle Issue-Networks, and Sovereignty in Latin America," *International Organization* 47 (1993), 411–41

Simon, William H., "Ethical Discretion in Lawyering," *Harvard Law Review* 101 (1988), 1083–1145

"The Ideology of Advocacy: Procedural Justice and Professional Ethics," *Wisconsin Law Review* (1978), 29–144

"Judicial Clerkships and Elite Professional Culture," *Journal of Legal Education* 36 (1986), 129–37

Simpson, Sally S., *Corporate Crime, Law, and Social Control* (New York, NY: Cambridge University Press, 2002)

Slaughter, Anne-Marie, "The Accountability of Government Networks," *Indiana Journal of Global Legal Studies* 8 (2001), 347–67

Smigel, Erwin O., *The Wall Street Lawyer* (Bloomington, IL: Indiana University Press, 1964)

Stanley, Harold W. and Richard G. Niemi, *Vital Statistics on American Politics, 1997–1998* (Washington, DC: Congressional Quarterly, 1997)

Stern, Stephanie, "Cognitive Consistency: Theory Maintenance and Administrative Rulemaking," *University of Pittsburgh Law Review* 63 (2002), 589–644

Stewart, Richard B., "The Discontents of Legalism: Interest Group Relations in Administrative Regulation," *Wisconsin Law Review* (1985), 655–86

"The Reformation of American Administrative Law," *Harvard Law Review* 88 (1975), 1669–1813

Stone, Christopher D., *Where the Law Ends: The Social Control of Corporate Behavior* (New York, NY: Harper and Row, 1975)

Stone Sweet, Alec, Wayne Sandholtz, and Neil Fligstein (eds.), *The Institutionalization of Europe* (Oxford, UK: Oxford University Press, 2001)

Strange, Susan, *The Retreat of the State: The Diffusion of Power in the World Economy* (Cambridge, UK: Cambridge University Press, 1996)

Suchman, Mark C. and Mia L. Cahill, "The Hired Gun as Facilitator: Lawyers and the Suppression of Business Disputes in Silicon Valley," *Law and Social Inquiry* 21 (1996), 679–712

Teubner, Gunther, *Law as an Autopoietic System* (Oxford, UK: Blackwell, 1993)

Thatcher, Mark and Alec Stone Sweet (eds.), *The Politics of Delegation* (London, UK: Frank Cass, 2003)

US Bureau of the Census, *Statistical Abstracts of the United States* (Washington, DC, 1997

US Department of Labor, "Framework for the use of Negotiated Rulemaking in the Department of Labor" (http://www.dol.gov/asp/programs/negreg/nrbprta.htm)

"OSHA Inspections", pamphlet (2002, revised)

Twenty Years of OSHA Federal Enforcement Data: A Review and Explanation of the Major Trends (Washington, DC: January 1993)

Van Waarden, Frans, "Dimensions and Types of Policy Networks," *European Journal of Political Research* 21 (1992), 29–52

Vanderbergh, Michael P., "Beyond Elegance: A Testable Typology of Social Norms in Corporate Environmental Compliance," *Stanford Environmental Law Journal* 22 (2003), 55–144

Verkuil, Paul, "Rulemaking Ossification – A Modest Proposal," *Administrative Law Review* 47 (1995), 453–9

Weil, David, "Building Safety: The Role of Construction Unions in the Enforcement of OSHA," *Journal of Labor Research* 13 (1992), 121–32

Weingast, Barry R. and Mark J. Moran, "Bureaucratic Discretion or Congressional Control: Regulatory Policymaking by the Federal Trade Commission," *Journal of Political Economy* 91 (1984), 765–800

Westwood, Howard C., "The Influence of Washington Lawyering," *George Washington Law Review* 38 (1970), 607–18

White, G. Edward, "Felix Frankfurter, the Old Boy Network, and the New Deal: The Placement of Elite Lawyers in Public Service in the 1930s," *Arkansas Law Review* 39 (1986), 631–67

Whiting, Basil J., "OSHA's Enforcement Policy," *Labor Law Journal* 31 (1980), 259–82

Wilkinson, Margaret Ann, Peter Mercer and Terra Strong, "Mentor, Mercenary or Melding: An Empirical Inquiry into the Role of the Lawyer," *Loyola University of Chicago Law Journal* 28 (1996), 373–418

Wilks, Stephen R. M. and Maurice Wright (eds.), *Comparative Government–Industry Relations: Western Europe, the United States, and Japan* (Oxford: Clarendon Press, 1987)

Williams, David B. and G. Mitu Gulati, "Why Are There So Few Black Lawyers in Corporate Law Firms? An Institutional Analysis," *California Law Review* 84 (1996), 493–625

Wood, B. Dan, "Principles, Bureaucrats, and Responsiveness in Clean Air Enforcement," *American Political Science Review* 82 (1988), 213–34

Wood, B. Dan and James B. Anderson, "The Politics of US Antitrust Regulation," *American Journal of Political Science* 37 (1993), 1–39

Worsham, Jeff, Marc Allen Eisner, and Evan J. Ringquist, "Assessing the Assumptions: A Critical Analysis of Agency Theory," *Administration & Society* 28 (1997), 419–42

Federal Register documents

"Control of Hazardous Energy Sources (Lockout/Tagout): Final Rule. Supplemental Statement of Reasons," *Federal Register* 58 (March 30, 1993), 16612–23

"Control of Hazardous Energy Sources (Lockout/Tagout); Machinery, Equipment Maintenance: Final Rule," *Federal Register* 54 (September 1, 1989), 36644–90

"The Control of Hazardous Energy (Lockout/Tagout): Notice of the Availability of a Lookback Review Pursuant to the Regulatory Flexibility Act and Executive Order 12866," *Federal Register* 65 (June 20, 2000), 38302–4

"The Control of Hazardous Energy Sources (Lockout/Tagout): Proposed Rule," *Federal Register* 53 (April 29, 1988), 15496–528

"Corrections and Technical Amendments to the Final Rule on Control of Hazardous Energy Sources (Lockout/Tagout)," *Federal Register* 55 (September 20, 1990), 38677–88

"Electric Power Generation, Transmission, and Distribution: Electrical Protective Equipment: Final Rule," *Federal Register* 59 (January 31, 1994), 4320–476

"Electrical Standards for Construction: Final Rule," *Federal Register* 51 (July 11, 1986), 25294–335

"Notice of Public Meeting on Review of the Control of Hazardous Energy Sources (Lockout/Tagout) Standard (29 CFR 1910.147)," *Federal Register* 62 (May 29, 1997), 29089–90

Newspapers and Industry Reporters

Barstow, David and Lowell Bergman, "Deaths on the Job, Slaps on the Wrist," *New York Times*, January 10, 2003, p. A15

"Compliance Program Draws Criticism, Advice. Inspections as Sanctions Raise Attorneys' Ire," *Occupational Safety and Health Reporter* 27 (March 18, 1998), 1486–7

"DeCoster Got Caught In Net After Enforcers Changed Their Approach," *Maine Sunday Telegraph*, July 8, 1996, pp. 1A, 12A

"Firms That Deny OSHA Entry Draw Higher Fines, Cited For More Alleged Violations, Study Shows," *Occupational Safety and Health Reporter* 23 (February 23, 1994), 1275

General Accounting Office, "Occupational Safety and Health: Penalties for Violations Are Well Below Maximum Allowable Penalties," April 6, 1992, p. 6

"Hudson Foods Has 'Long History' of Safety, Health Violations, OSHA Says," *Washington Post*, August 23, 1997, p. A11

"Memo from Joseph A. Dear, Assistant Secretary and Thomas A. Williamson, Jr., Solicitor of Labor, regarding Enforcement Litigation Strategy," March 24, 1995, published in *Occupational Safety and Health Reporter* 24 (April 5, 1995), 2218

"Most Employers, Workers Satisfied with OSHA Inspections, Survey Discovers," *Occupational Safety and Health Reporter* 24 (January 25, 1995), 1723

"Muffed Mission: Labor Secretary's Bid to Push Plant Safety Runs Into Skepticism," *Wall Street Journal*, August 19, 1994, p. A1

Occupational Safety and Health Review Commission, *Guide to Review Commission Procedures* (November 1997)

"OSHA Admits to Ad Hoc Settlement Policy. Scant Oversight," *Inside OSHA* (April 7, 1997), 3

"Special Report: OSHA Settlement Agreements," *BNA OSHA* 27 (July 23, 1997), 244

INDEX

interdependence of public and private
  actors 4, 5, 17, 55, 124, 185, 211, 217,
  218
interest groups 102, 135
International Brotherhood of Electrical
  Workers 116
International Union of Operating Engineers
  128

judicial review 26, 27, 75, 79, 93, 94, 96
  hybrid 73
  multi-party nature of 106
  standard of 58

Kritzer, Herbert 10

Labor, Department of 103, 124, 140–2, 146,
  178
labor–management conflict 18, 19, 21, 95,
  106, 107, 135, 180, 185
labor relations 30, 39, 158, 195, 207
Laborers' Health and Safety Fund 128
Laborers' International Union of North
  America 128
Laski, Harold 11
Laumann, Edward 15–17, 45, 47, 71
law 7–17, 196–203, 218, 221
  administrative 35, 41, 89, 126, 136, 210,
    218, 219
  creation of 137, 138, 217–22
  environmental 35, 39
  gap between practical and book 10, 138,
    153
  hard and soft 218, 221
  implementation of 9, 137, 220
  labor 39
  OSHA 126, 209
  place in administrative systems 211
law firms, size of 42, 43
lawyers
  behavior of 2, 108
  and their clients 59–67, 71, 76, 107–12,
    172, 190–6
  duties of 187
  expertise 10, 52, 71, 112, 152, 192, 194
  government 51, 104, 105
  industry 76, 79, 134
  influence of 1, 11, 23, 166, 169, 189,
    193–4, 206
  management 30, 35, 77, 149, 179, 201,
    216, 218; and rulemaking 77, 93, 122
  norms, professional 187–9
  professional autonomy 71, 75
  roles??: as advocates 9, 214–15; as
    communicators 24, 152; as educators
    153–4, 174, 200, 207, 215–16; in
    enforcement 38, 138, 146, 148, 149,

151, 153, 155, 158, 172, 192; as friction
  in the system 11–12, 185, 214, 217, 220;
  as grease in the system 8–10, 214, 217,
  220; as "hired guns" 188–9, 206;
  multiple 13, 212, 214–17; in regulation
  3, 4–17, 188, 211; as representing
  interests 211–17, 219; in rulemaking
  70–6, 104, 126–34, 135
  significance of 23, 94, 97
  styles of operation 159–66, 183, 185
  tactical preferences of 161, 162
  union 31, 93
  Washington lawyers 9–10, 34–5, 54, 59
Lead Industries Association 108
legal advice, political ramifications of 103–4
litigation 27, 38, 78, 100
  secondary 150, 171–2
litigation, rulemaking 58, 76–80, 96–113
Lockout/Tagout rule 97, 111, 112–26, 129,
  215
  criteria for application of 113, 123
  group lockout 114, 118, 119, 120

Macaulay, Stewart 14
management 75, 95, 99, 118
Martindale-Hubbell Law Directory 31
Mashaw, Jerry 100
McBarnet, Doreen 12
McGuire, Kevin 47, 49, 50
medical removal protection 132, 133,
  134
methylene chloride, standard for 83–6,
  134
methylenedianiline (MDA) 127
Mintz, Benjamin 83
Multidistrict Legislation, Judicial Panel on
  109–10

Nader, Ralph 34
National Asphalt Pavement
  Association 128
National Association of Manufacturers
  (NAM) 64, 121–4, 125, 135, 215
National Electric Code 114
National Electrical Safety Code (NESC) 114
National Institute for Occupational Safety
  and Health (NIOSH) 18, 60, 128
National Particle Board Association 133
negotiation 127, 132, 133, 135, 179, 189,
  193, 216, 220
  incentives for 177, 181
  limitations of 127
Nelson, Robert 15–17, 71
networks 4, 5, 6, 15, 166, 220, 221
  policy 23, 54, 125, 131
  regulatory 5, 17, 208
norms, professional 187–9